THE NAKED CITY ™

Marlowe & Company

First Marlowe & Company edition, 1996

Published by
Marlowe & Company
632 Broadway, Seventh Floor
New York, Ny 10012

Manufactured in the United States of America

ISBN: 1-56924-828-1

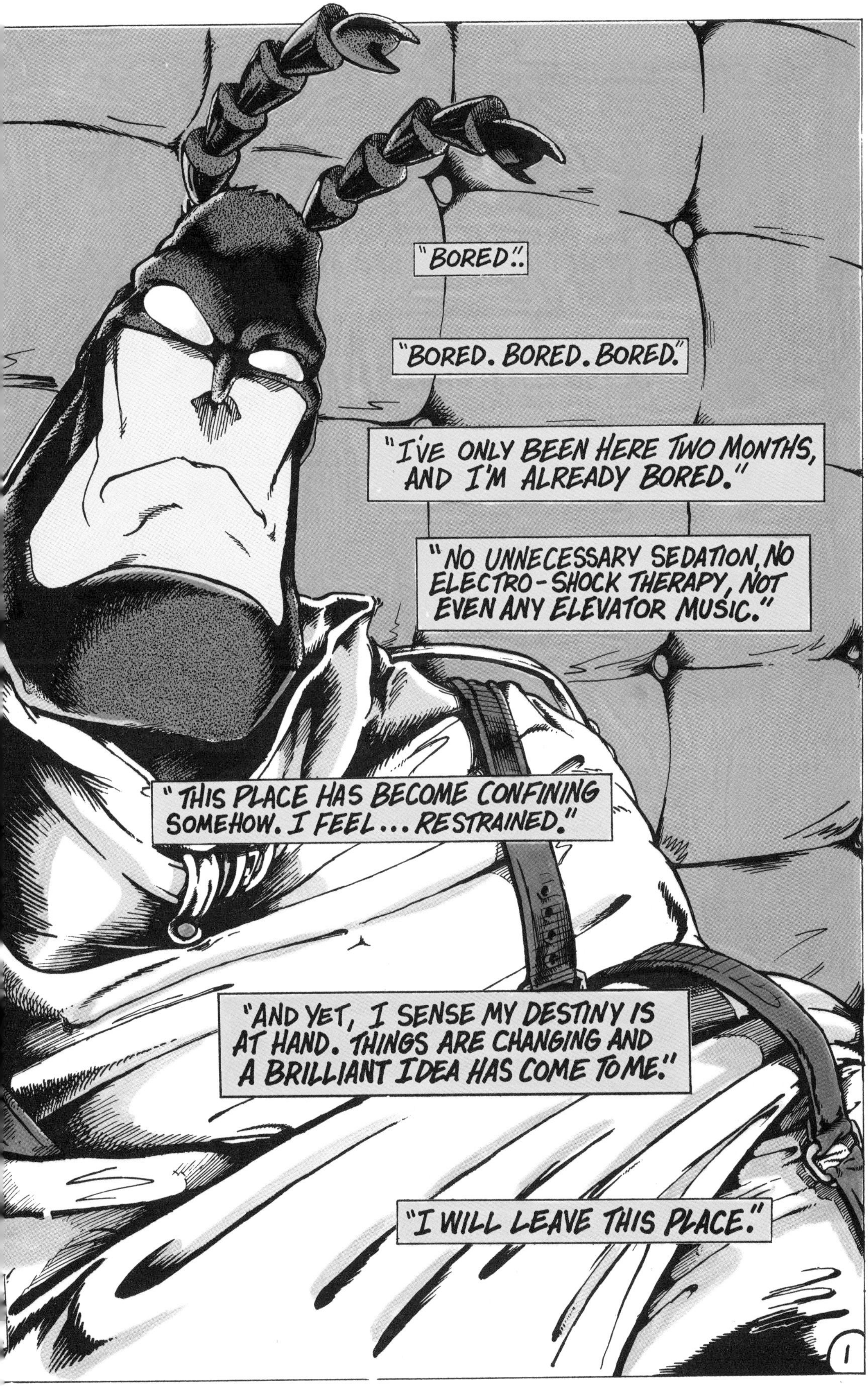
"BORED."
"BORED. BORED. BORED."
"I'VE ONLY BEEN HERE TWO MONTHS, AND I'M ALREADY BORED."
"NO UNNECESSARY SEDATION, NO ELECTRO-SHOCK THERAPY, NOT EVEN ANY ELEVATOR MUSIC."
"THIS PLACE HAS BECOME CONFINING SOMEHOW. I FEEL... RESTRAINED."
"AND YET, I SENSE MY DESTINY IS AT HAND. THINGS ARE CHANGING AND A BRILLIANT IDEA HAS COME TO ME."
"I WILL LEAVE THIS PLACE."
1

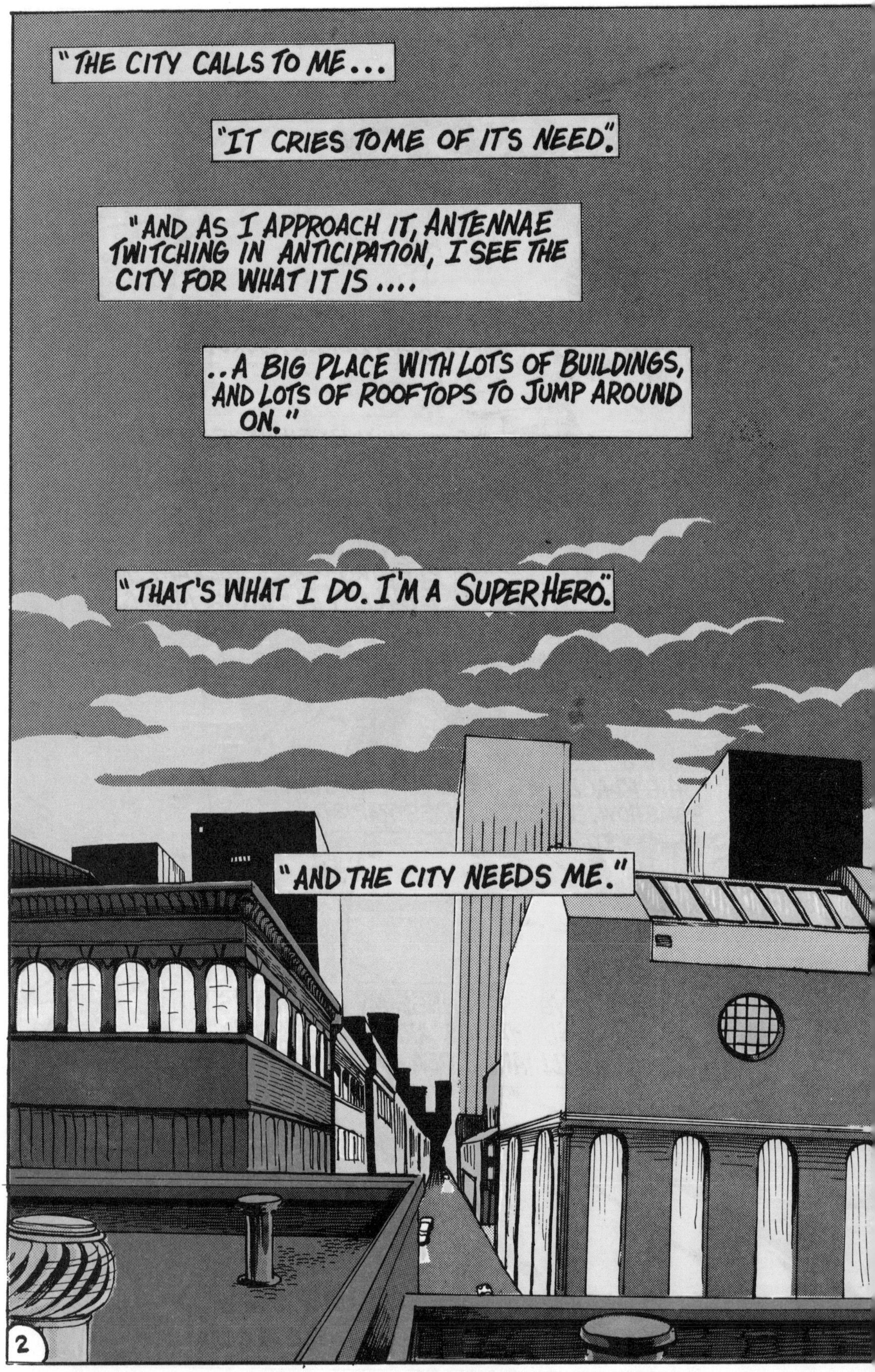
"THE CITY CALLS TO ME...
"IT CRIES TO ME OF ITS NEED".
"AND AS I APPROACH IT, ANTENNAE TWITCHING IN ANTICIPATION, I SEE THE CITY FOR WHAT IT IS....
..A BIG PLACE WITH LOTS OF BUILDINGS, AND LOTS OF ROOFTOPS TO JUMP AROUND ON."
"THAT'S WHAT I DO. I'M A SUPERHERO".
"AND THE CITY NEEDS ME."

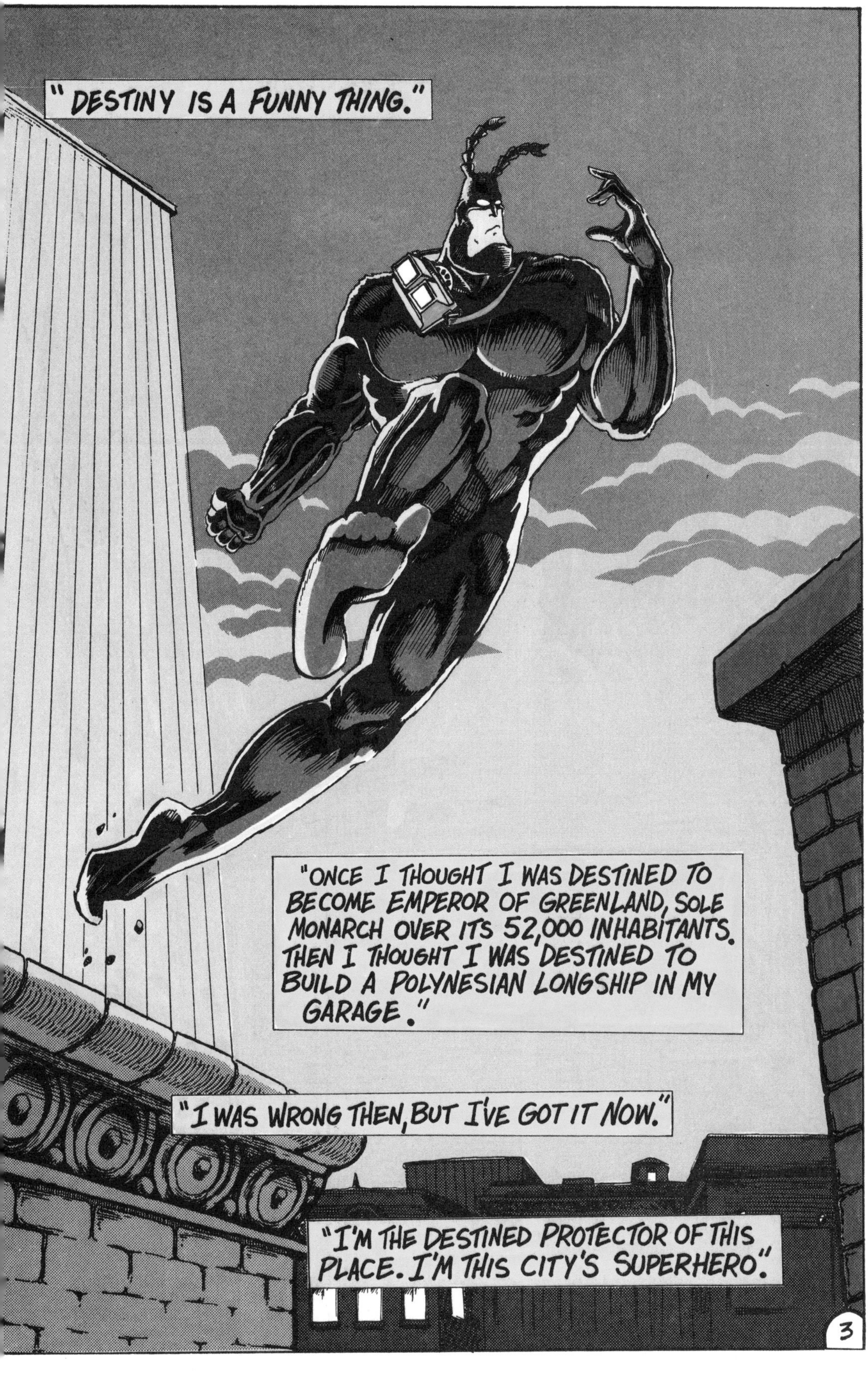
"DESTINY IS A FUNNY THING."
"ONCE I THOUGHT I WAS DESTINED TO BECOME EMPEROR OF GREENLAND, SOLE MONARCH OVER ITS 52,000 INHABITANTS. THEN I THOUGHT I WAS DESTINED TO BUILD A POLYNESIAN LONGSHIP IN MY GARAGE."
"I WAS WRONG THEN, BUT I'VE GOT IT NOW."
"I'M THE DESTINED PROTECTOR OF THIS PLACE. I'M THIS CITY'S SUPERHERO."
3

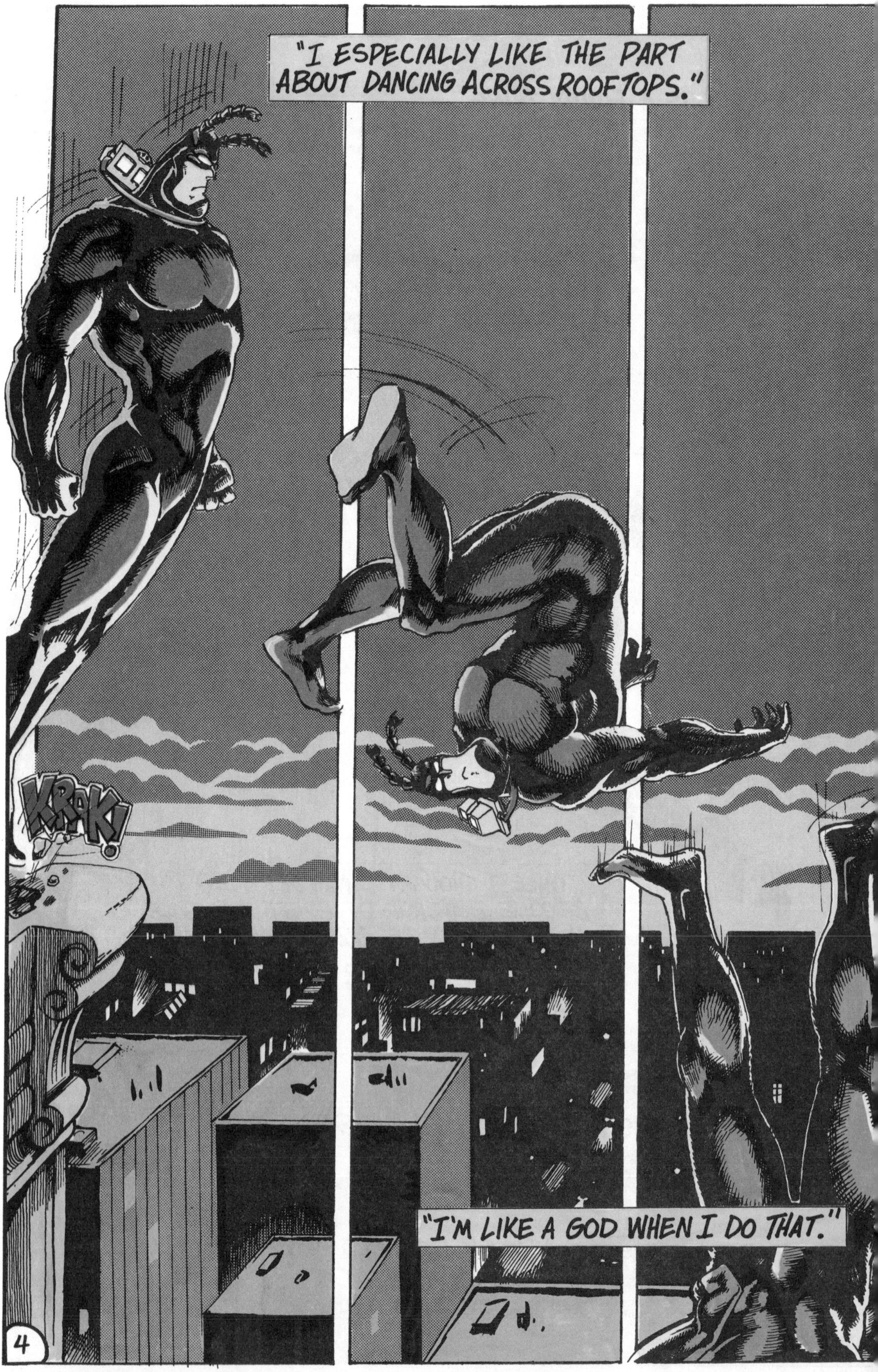
"I ESPECIALLY LIKE THE PART ABOUT DANCING ACROSS ROOFTOPS."
KRAK!
"I'M LIKE A GOD WHEN I DO THAT."
4

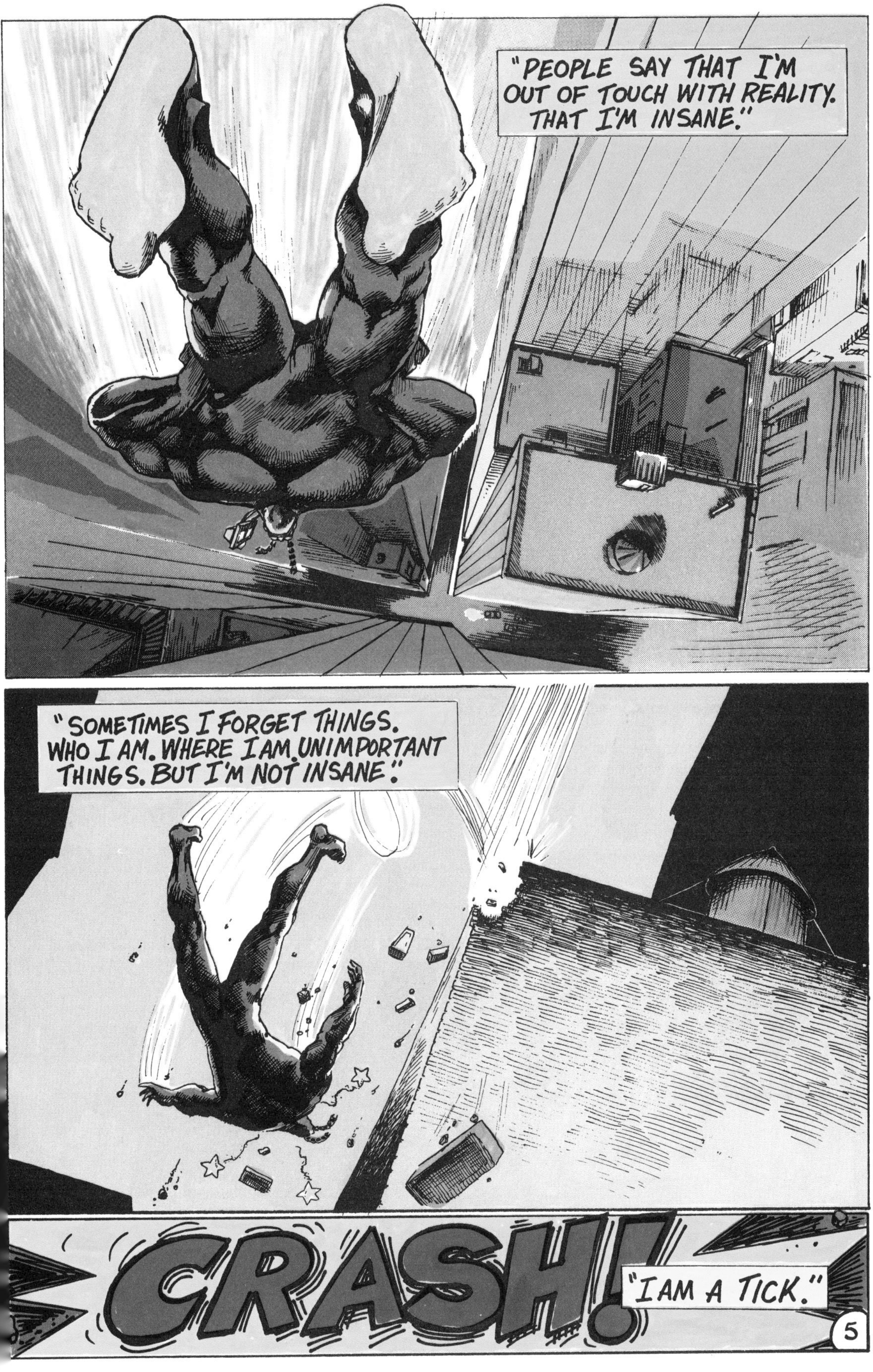
"PEOPLE SAY THAT I'M OUT OF TOUCH WITH REALITY. THAT I'M INSANE."
"SOMETIMES I FORGET THINGS. WHO I AM. WHERE I AM. UNIMPORTANT THINGS. BUT I'M NOT INSANE."
CRASH!
"I AM A TICK."

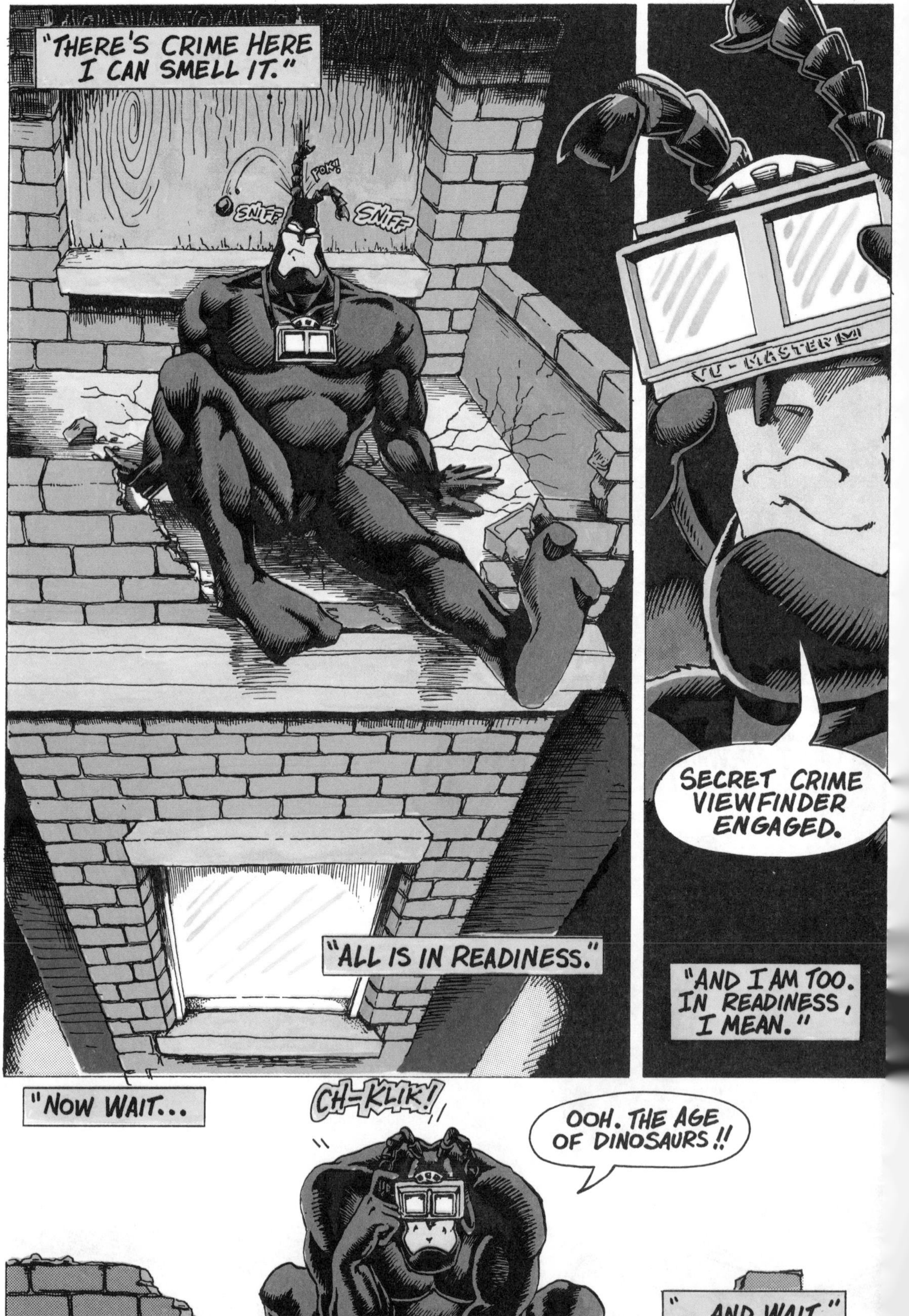
"THERE'S CRIME HERE I CAN SMELL IT."
POK!
SNIFF
SNIFF
"ALL IS IN READINESS."
VU-MASTER
SECRET CRIME VIEWFINDER ENGAGED.
"AND I AM TOO. IN READINESS, I MEAN."
"NOW WAIT...
CH-KLIK!
OOH. THE AGE OF DINOSAURS!!
"... AND WAIT."

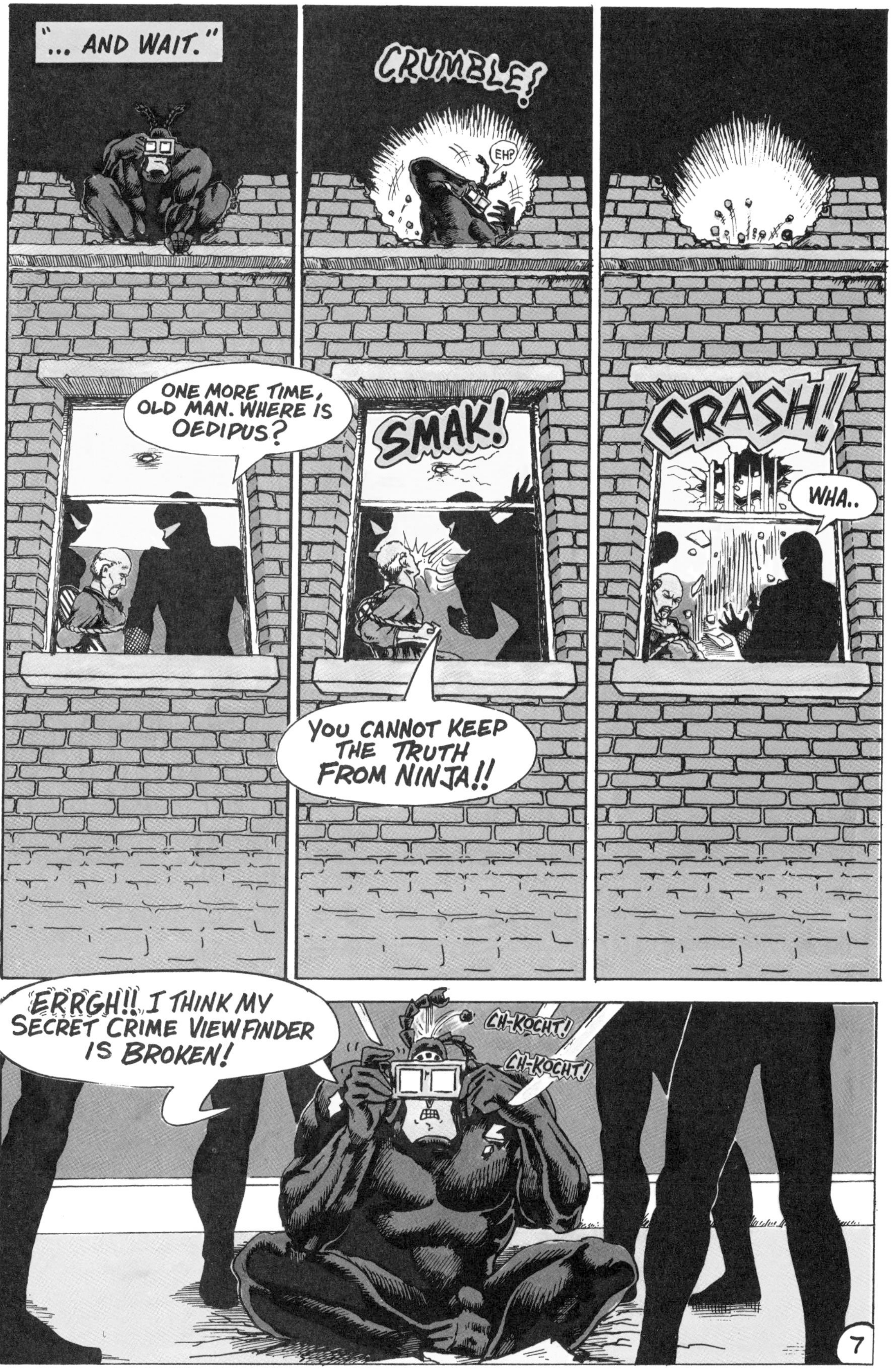
"... AND WAIT."
ONE MORE TIME, OLD MAN. WHERE IS OEDIPUS?
CRUMBLE!
EH?
SMAK!
YOU CANNOT KEEP THE TRUTH FROM NINJA!!
CRASH!
WHA..
ERRGH!! I THINK MY SECRET CRIME VIEWFINDER IS BROKEN!
CH-KOCHT!
CH-KOCHT!

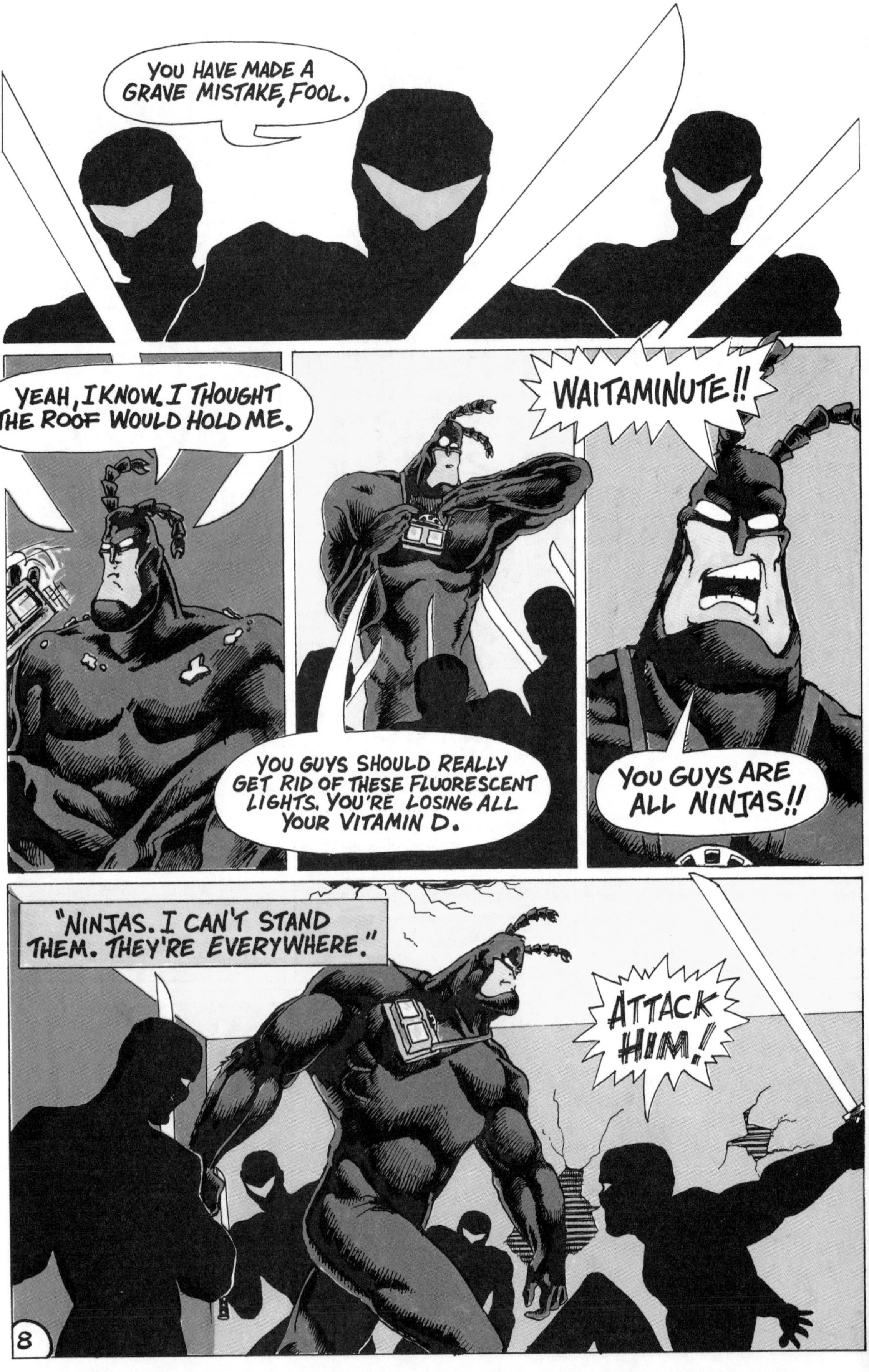
YOU HAVE MADE A GRAVE MISTAKE, FOOL.
YEAH, I KNOW. I THOUGHT THE ROOF WOULD HOLD ME.
YOU GUYS SHOULD REALLY GET RID OF THESE FLUORESCENT LIGHTS. YOU'RE LOSING ALL YOUR VITAMIN D.
WAITAMINUTE!!
YOU GUYS ARE ALL NINJAS!!
"NINJAS. I CAN'T STAND THEM. THEY'RE EVERYWHERE."
ATTACK HIM!

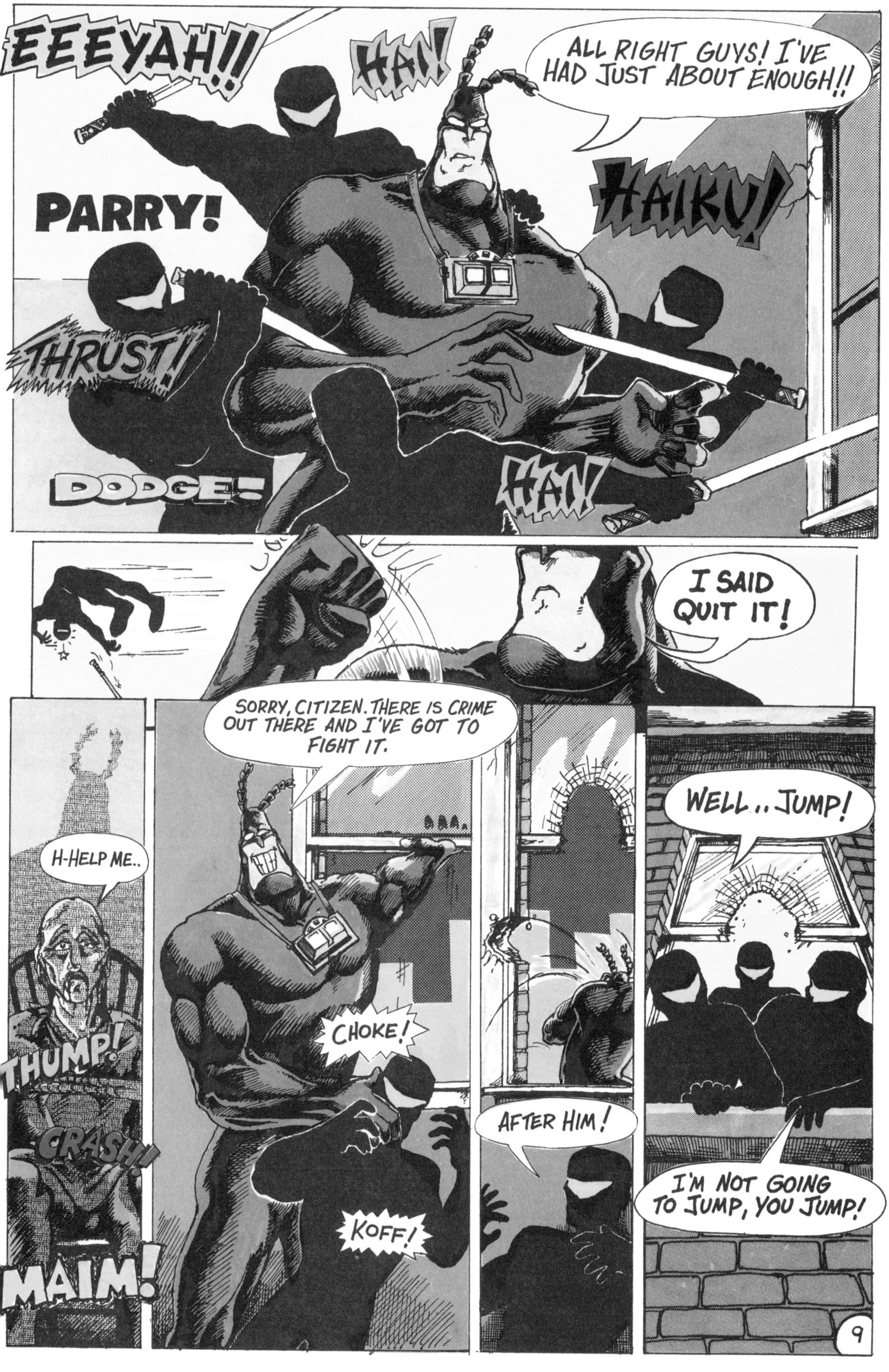
EEEYAH!!
HAN!
ALL RIGHT GUYS! I'VE HAD JUST ABOUT ENOUGH!!
PARRY!
HAIKU!
THRUST!
DODGE!
HAN!
I SAID QUIT IT!
H-HELP ME..
THUMP!
CRASH!
MAIM!
SORRY, CITIZEN. THERE IS CRIME OUT THERE AND I'VE GOT TO FIGHT IT.
CHOKE!
KOFF!
AFTER HIM!
WELL.. JUMP!
I'M NOT GOING TO JUMP, YOU JUMP!

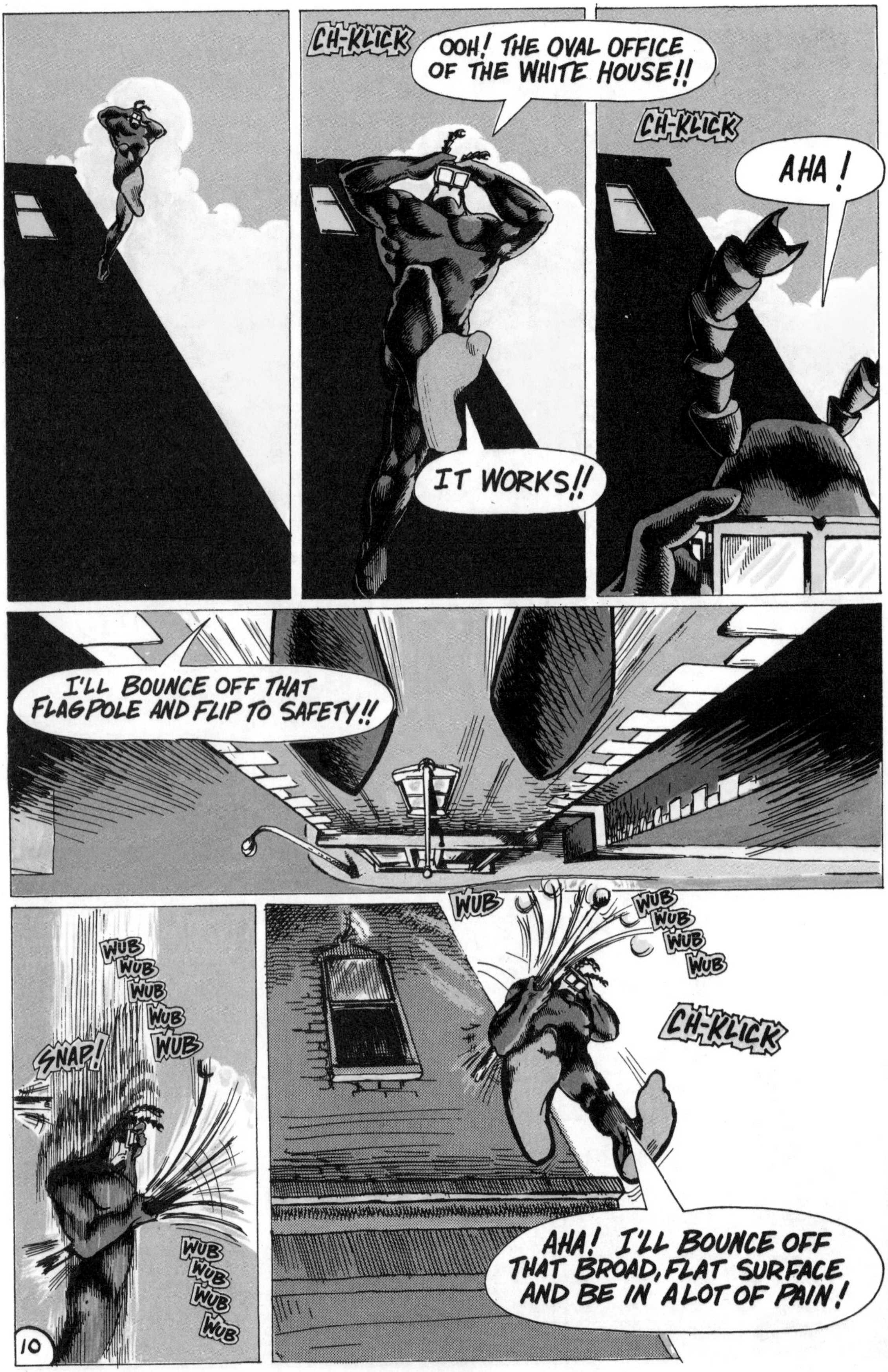
CH-KLICK
OOH! THE OVAL OFFICE OF THE WHITE HOUSE!!
IT WORKS!!
CH-KLICK
AHA!
I'LL BOUNCE OFF THAT FLAGPOLE AND FLIP TO SAFETY!!
WUB WUB WUB WUB WUB
SNAP!
WUB WUB WUB WUB
WUB
WUB WUB WUB WUB
CH-KLICK
AHA! I'LL BOUNCE OFF THAT BROAD, FLAT SURFACE AND BE IN ALOT OF PAIN!

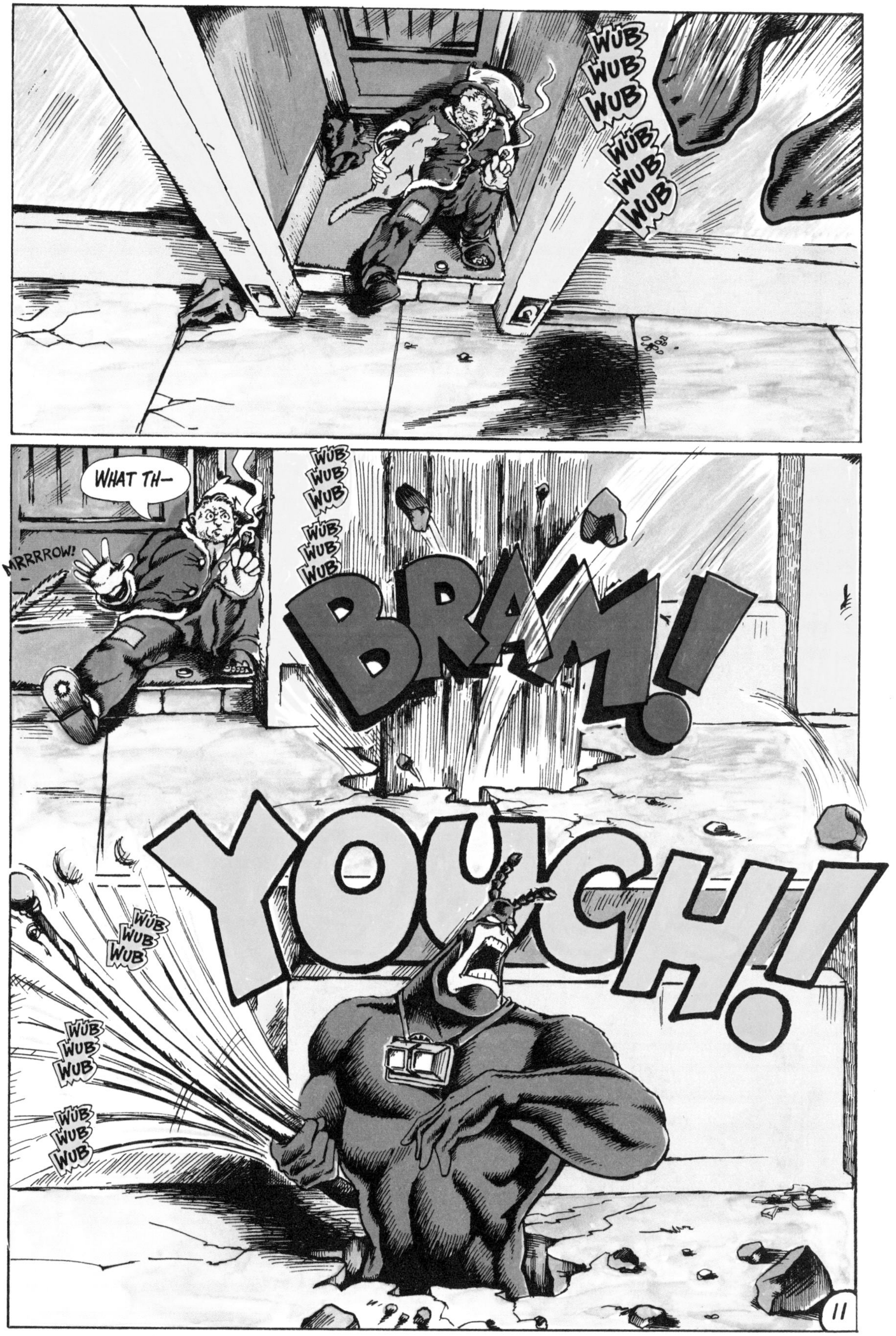
WUB WUB WUB
WUB WUB WUB
WHAT TH–
MRRRROW!
WUB WUB WUB
WUB WUB WUB
BRAM!
YOUCH!
WUB WUB WUB
WUB WUB WUB
WUB WUB WUB

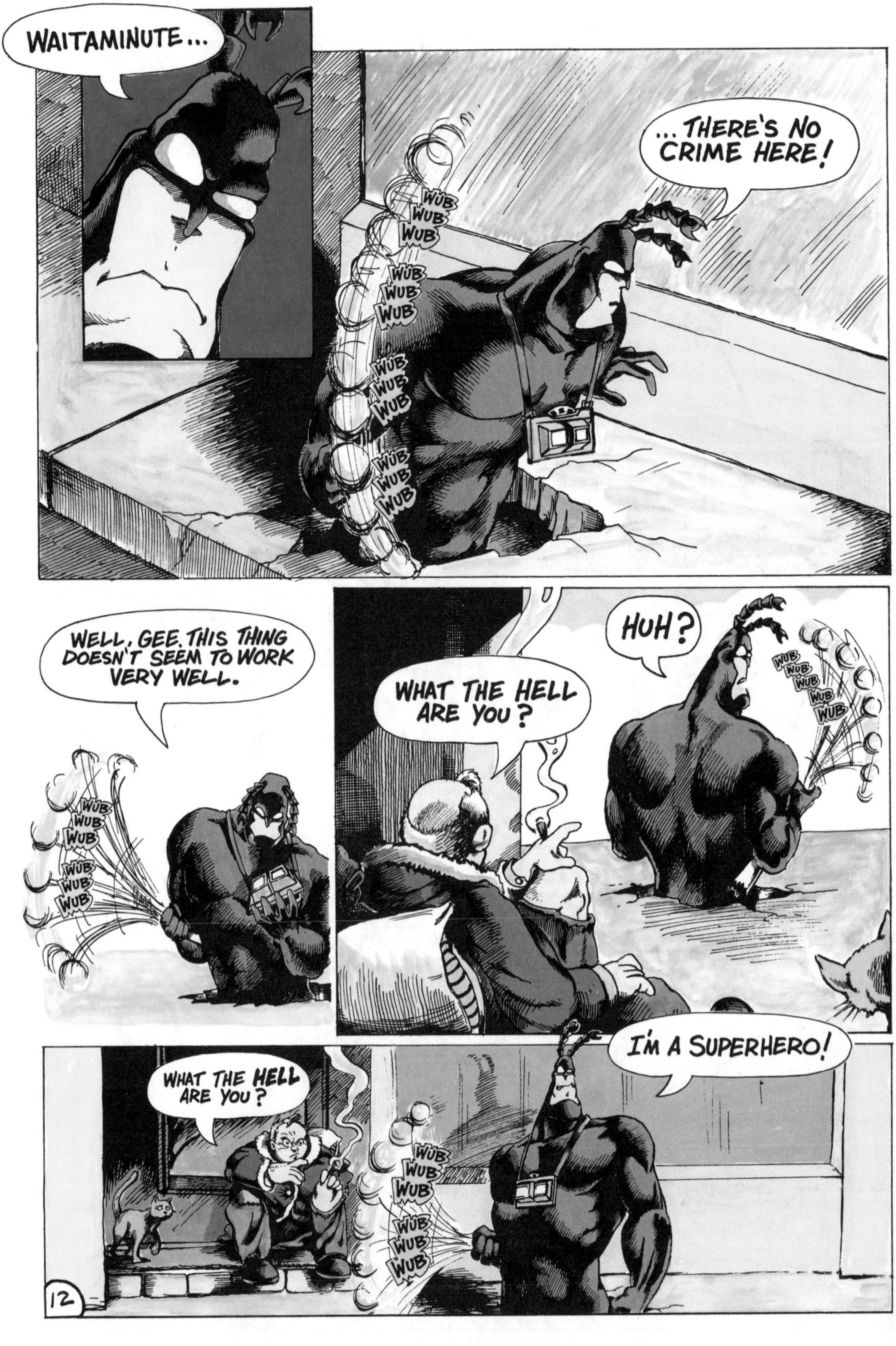
WAITAMINUTE...
WUB WUB WUB
WUB WUB WUB
WUB WUB WUB
WUB WUB WUB
...THERE'S NO CRIME HERE!
WELL, GEE. THIS THING DOESN'T SEEM TO WORK VERY WELL.
WUB WUB WUB
WUB WUB WUB
WHAT THE HELL ARE YOU?
HUH?
WUB WUB WUB WUB WUB
WHAT THE HELL ARE YOU?
WUB WUB WUB
WUB WUB WUB
I'M A SUPERHERO!
12

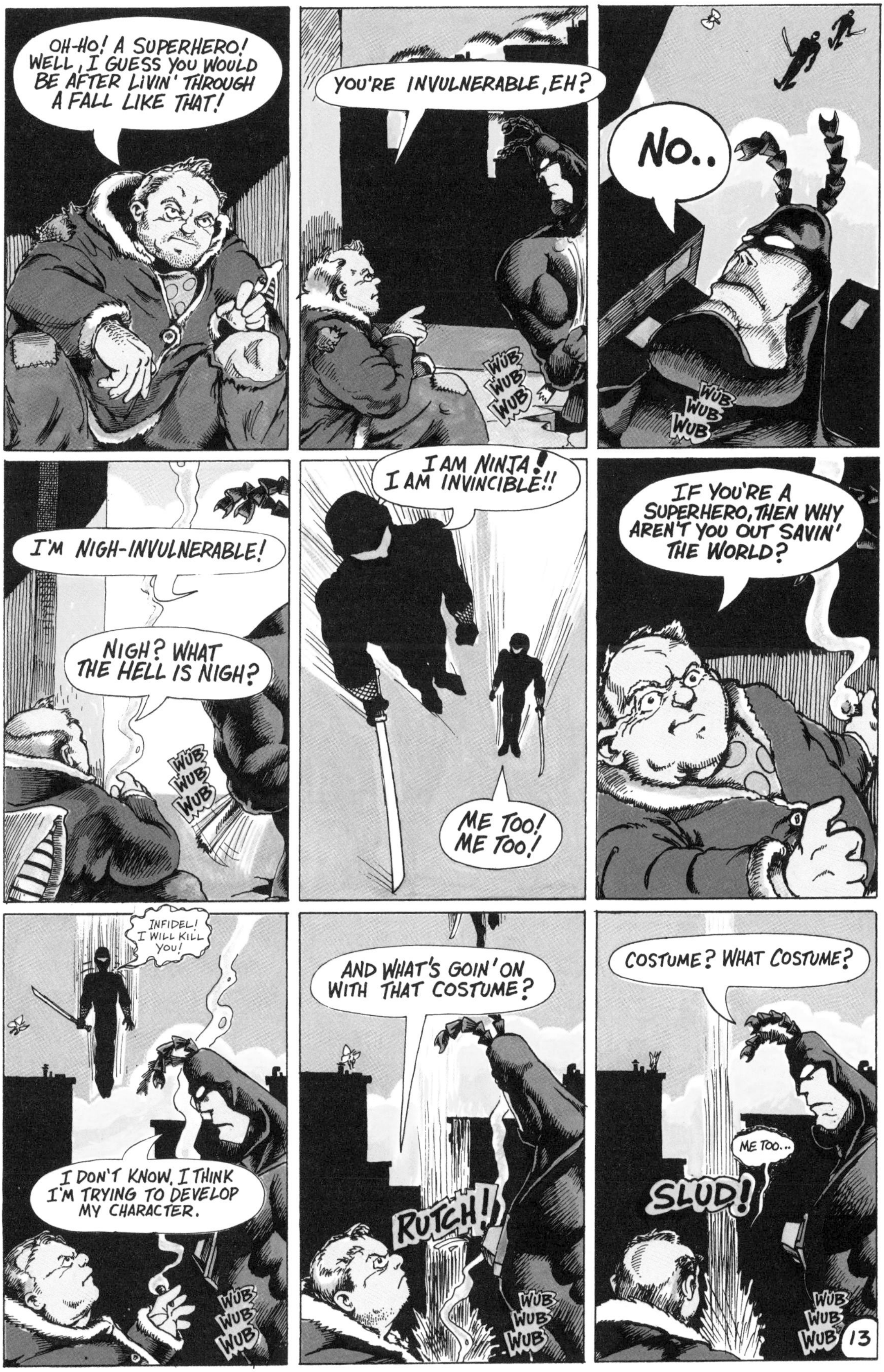
OH-HO! A SUPERHERO! WELL, I GUESS YOU WOULD BE AFTER LIVIN' THROUGH A FALL LIKE THAT!
YOU'RE INVULNERABLE, EH?
WUB WUB WUB
NO..
WUB WUB WUB
I'M NIGH-INVULNERABLE!
NIGH? WHAT THE HELL IS NIGH?
WUB WUB WUB
I AM NINJA! I AM INVINCIBLE!!
ME TOO! ME TOO!
IF YOU'RE A SUPERHERO, THEN WHY AREN'T YOU OUT SAVIN' THE WORLD?
INFIDEL! I WILL KILL YOU!
I DON'T KNOW. I THINK I'M TRYING TO DEVELOP MY CHARACTER.
WUB WUB WUB
AND WHAT'S GOIN' ON WITH THAT COSTUME?
RUTCH!
WUB WUB WUB
COSTUME? WHAT COSTUME?
ME TOO...
SLUD!
WUB WUB WUB

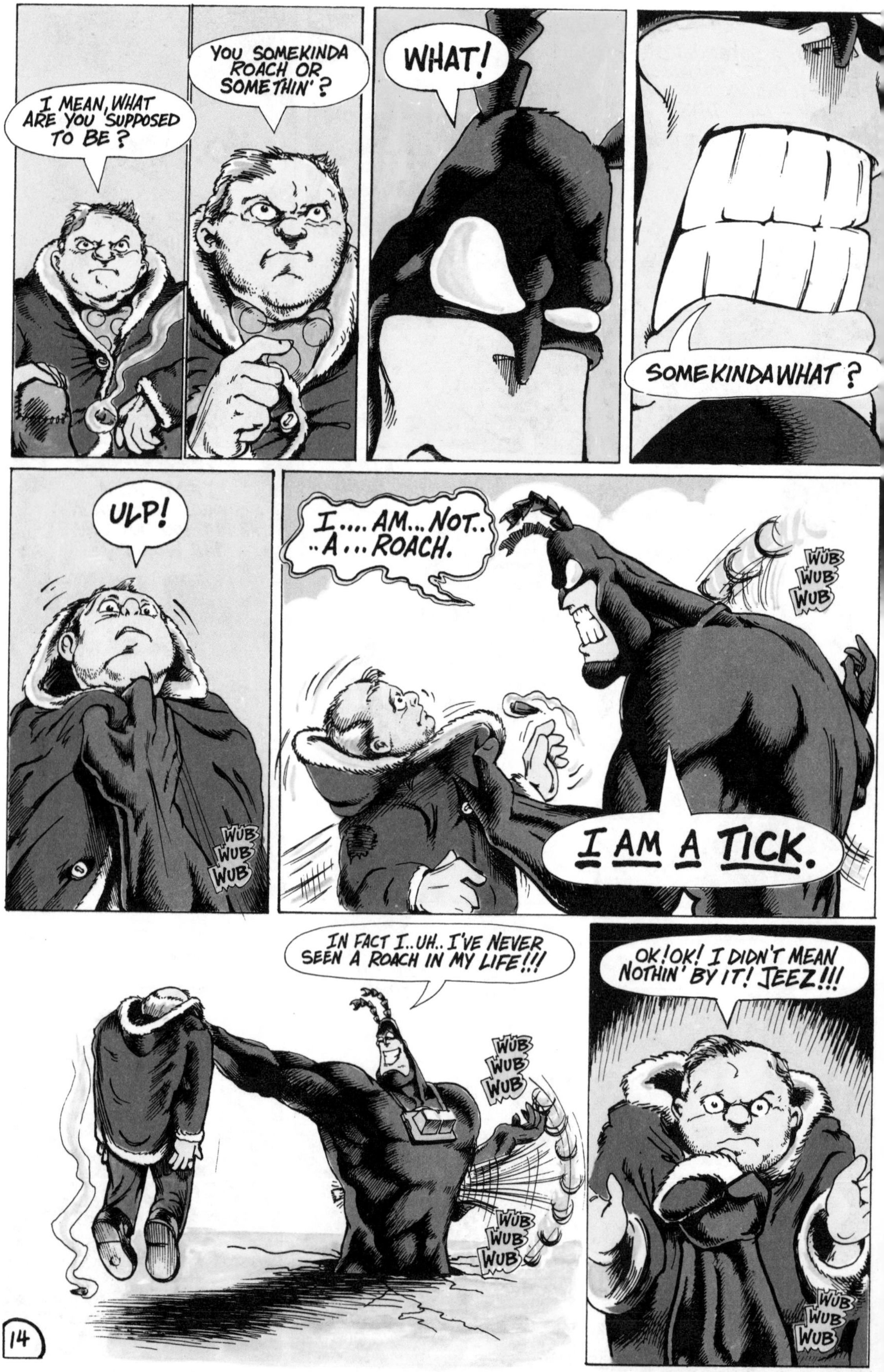
I MEAN, WHAT ARE YOU 'SUPPOSED TO BE?
YOU SOMEKINDA ROACH OR SOMETHIN'?
WHAT!
SOMEKINDAWHAT?
ULP!
I.... AM... NOT.. ..A... ROACH.
WUB WUB WUB
WUB WUB WUB
I AM A TICK.
IN FACT I..UH.. I'VE NEVER SEEN A ROACH IN MY LIFE!!!
WUB WUB WUB
WUB WUB WUB
OK! OK! I DIDN'T MEAN NOTHIN' BY IT! JEEZ!!!
WUB WUB WUB

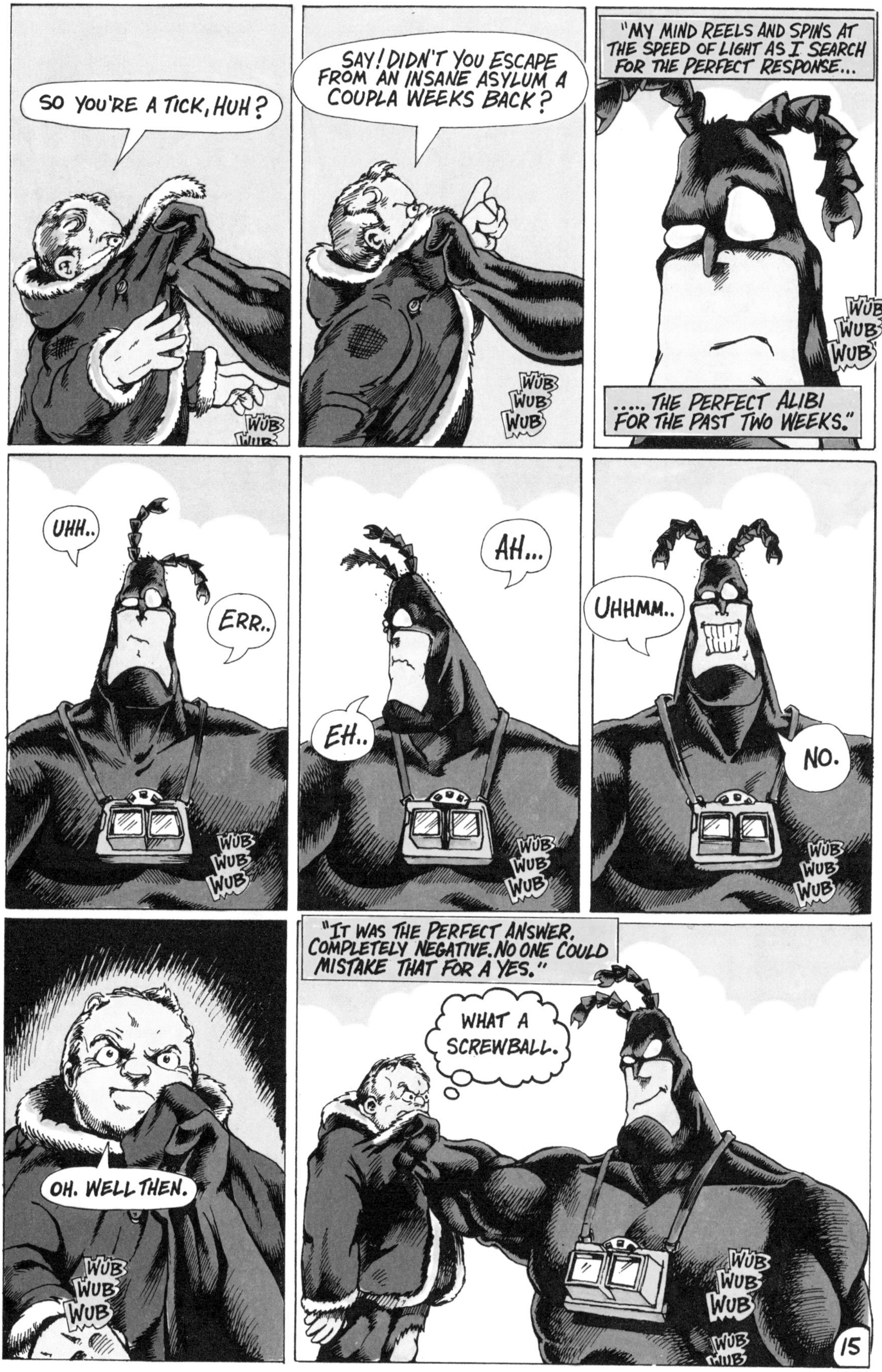
SO YOU'RE A TICK, HUH?
WUB
SAY! DIDN'T YOU ESCAPE FROM AN INSANE ASYLUM A COUPLA WEEKS BACK?
WUB WUB WUB
"MY MIND REELS AND SPINS AT THE SPEED OF LIGHT AS I SEARCH FOR THE PERFECT RESPONSE...
WUB WUB WUB
..... THE PERFECT ALIBI FOR THE PAST TWO WEEKS."
UHH..
ERR..
WUB WUB WUB
AH...
EH..
WUB WUB WUB
UHHMM..
NO.
WUB WUB WUB
OH. WELL THEN.
WUB WUB WUB
"IT WAS THE PERFECT ANSWER. COMPLETELY NEGATIVE. NO ONE COULD MISTAKE THAT FOR A YES."
WHAT A SCREWBALL.
WUB WUB WUB
WUB

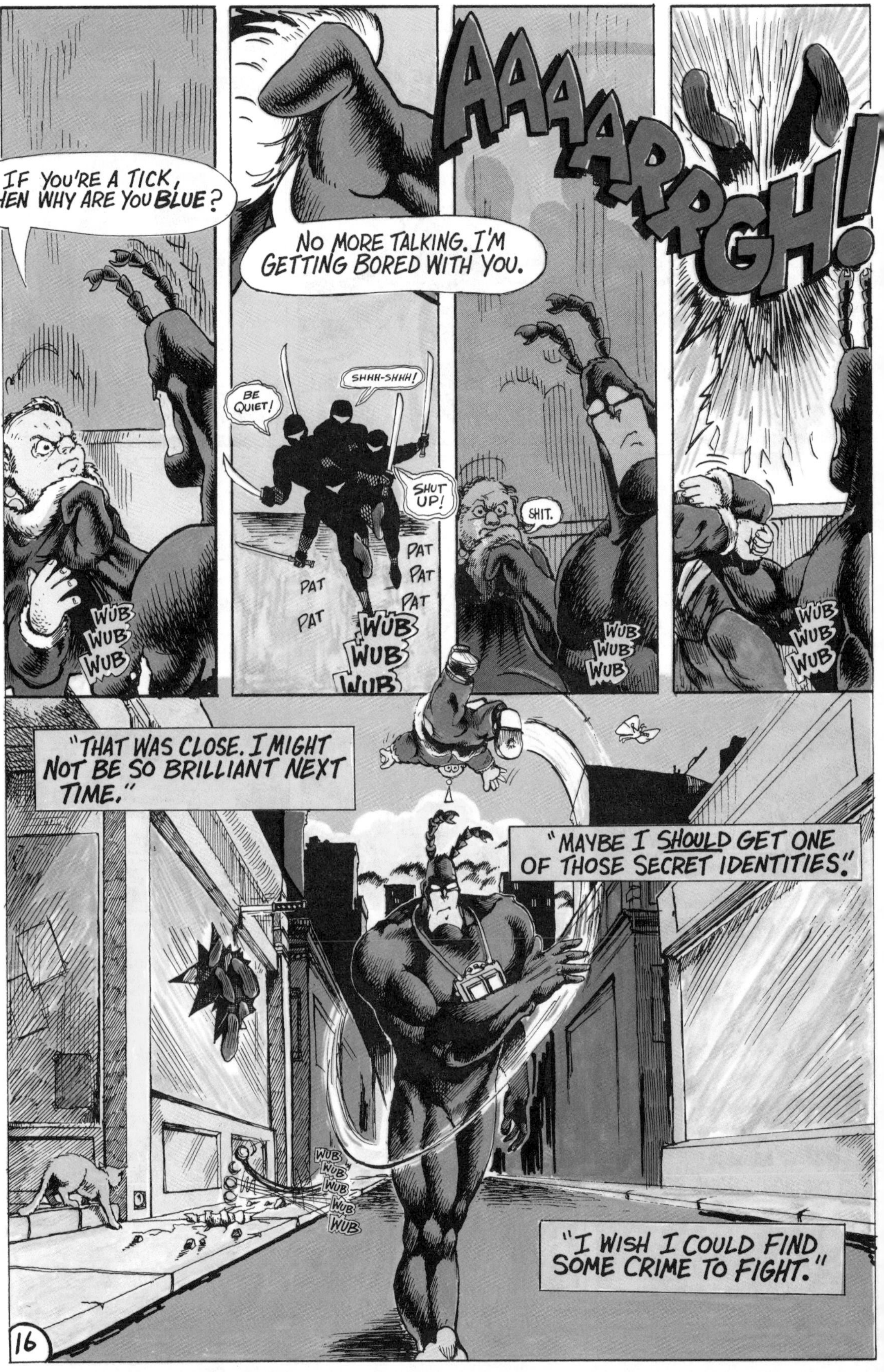
IF YOU'RE A TICK, THEN WHY ARE YOU BLUE?
WUB WUB WUB
NO MORE TALKING. I'M GETTING BORED WITH YOU.
BE QUIET!
SHHH-SHHH!
SHUT UP!
PAT PAT PAT PAT PAT PAT
WUB WUB WUB
AAAAARRGH!
SHIT.
WUB WUB WUB
WUB WUB WUB
"THAT WAS CLOSE. I MIGHT NOT BE SO BRILLIANT NEXT TIME."
"MAYBE I SHOULD GET ONE OF THOSE SECRET IDENTITIES."
WUB WUB WUB WUB WUB
"I WISH I COULD FIND SOME CRIME TO FIGHT."

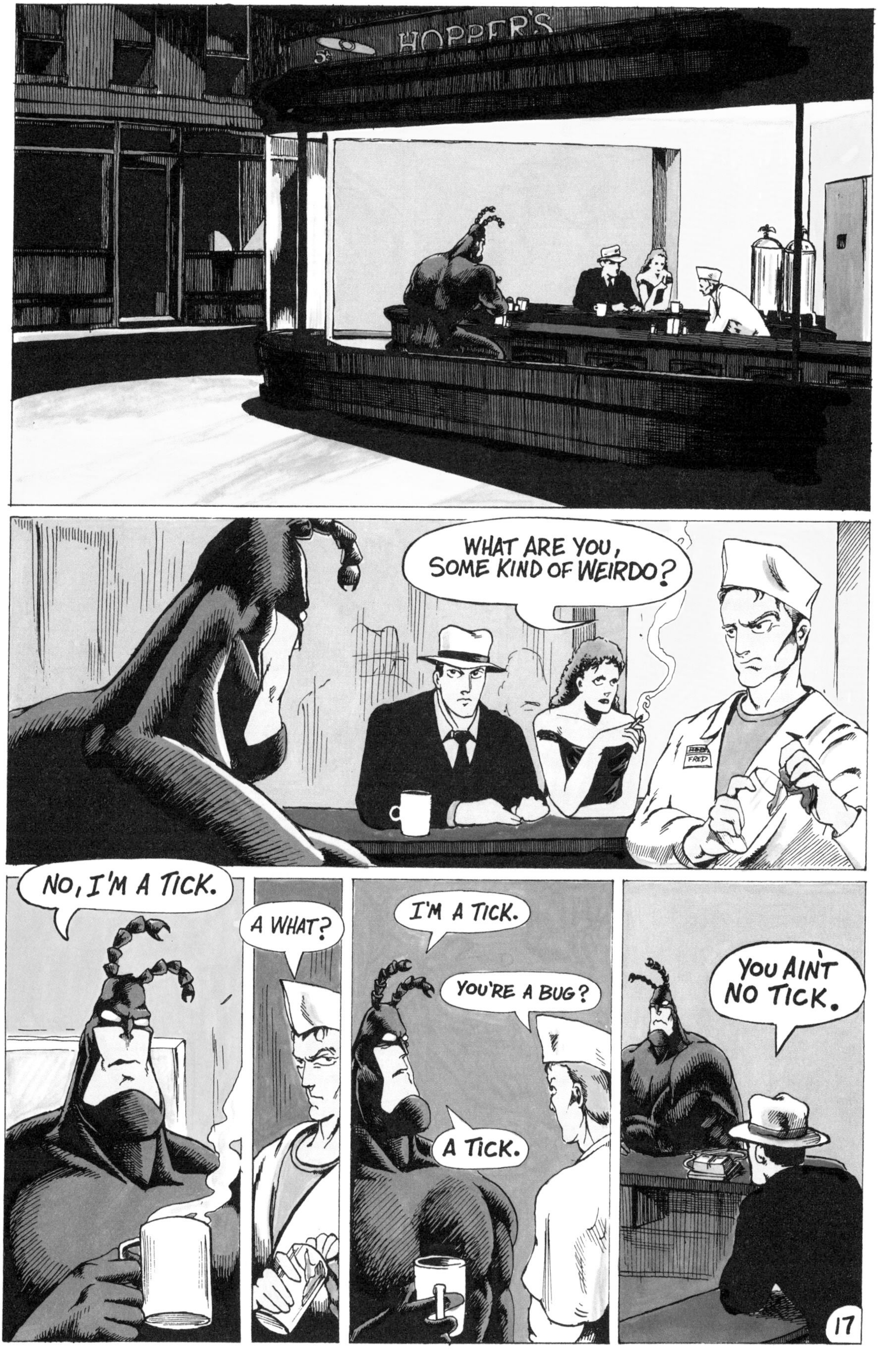
HOPPER'S
5¢
WHAT ARE YOU, SOME KIND OF WEIRDO?
FRED
NO, I'M A TICK.
A WHAT?
I'M A TICK.
YOU'RE A BUG?
A TICK.
YOU AIN'T NO TICK.

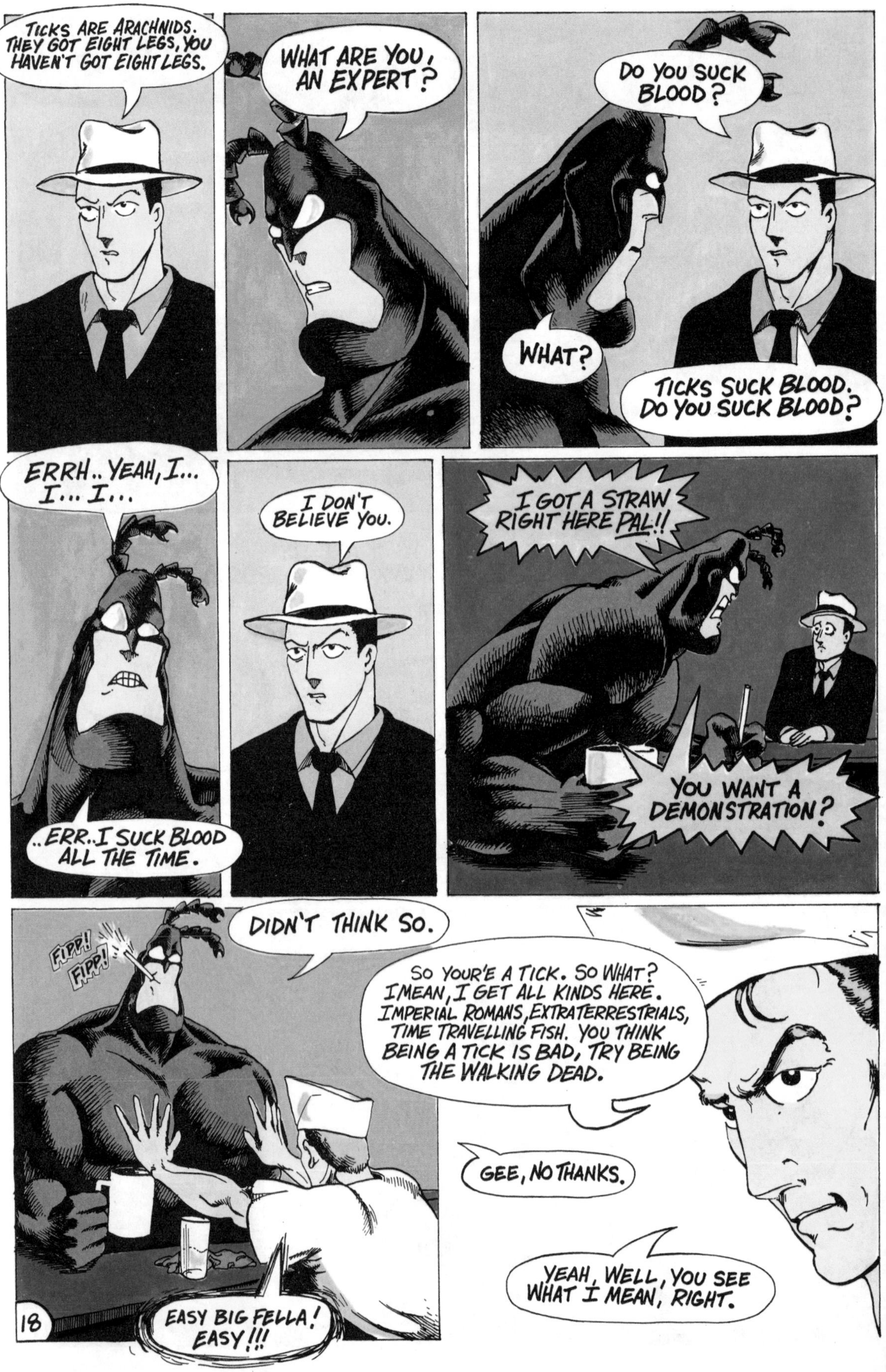
TICKS ARE ARACHNIDS. THEY GOT EIGHT LEGS, YOU HAVEN'T GOT EIGHT LEGS.
WHAT ARE YOU, AN EXPERT?
DO YOU SUCK BLOOD?
WHAT?
TICKS SUCK BLOOD. DO YOU SUCK BLOOD?
ERRH.. YEAH, I... I... I...
..ERR..I SUCK BLOOD ALL THE TIME.
I DON'T BELIEVE YOU.
I GOT A STRAW RIGHT HERE PAL!!
YOU WANT A DEMONSTRATION?
FIPP! FIPP!
DIDN'T THINK SO.
EASY BIG FELLA! EASY!!!
SO YOUR'E A TICK. SO WHAT? I MEAN, I GET ALL KINDS HERE. IMPERIAL ROMANS, EXTRATERRESTRIALS, TIME TRAVELLING FISH. YOU THINK BEING A TICK IS BAD, TRY BEING THE WALKING DEAD.
GEE, NO THANKS.
YEAH, WELL, YOU SEE WHAT I MEAN, RIGHT.
18

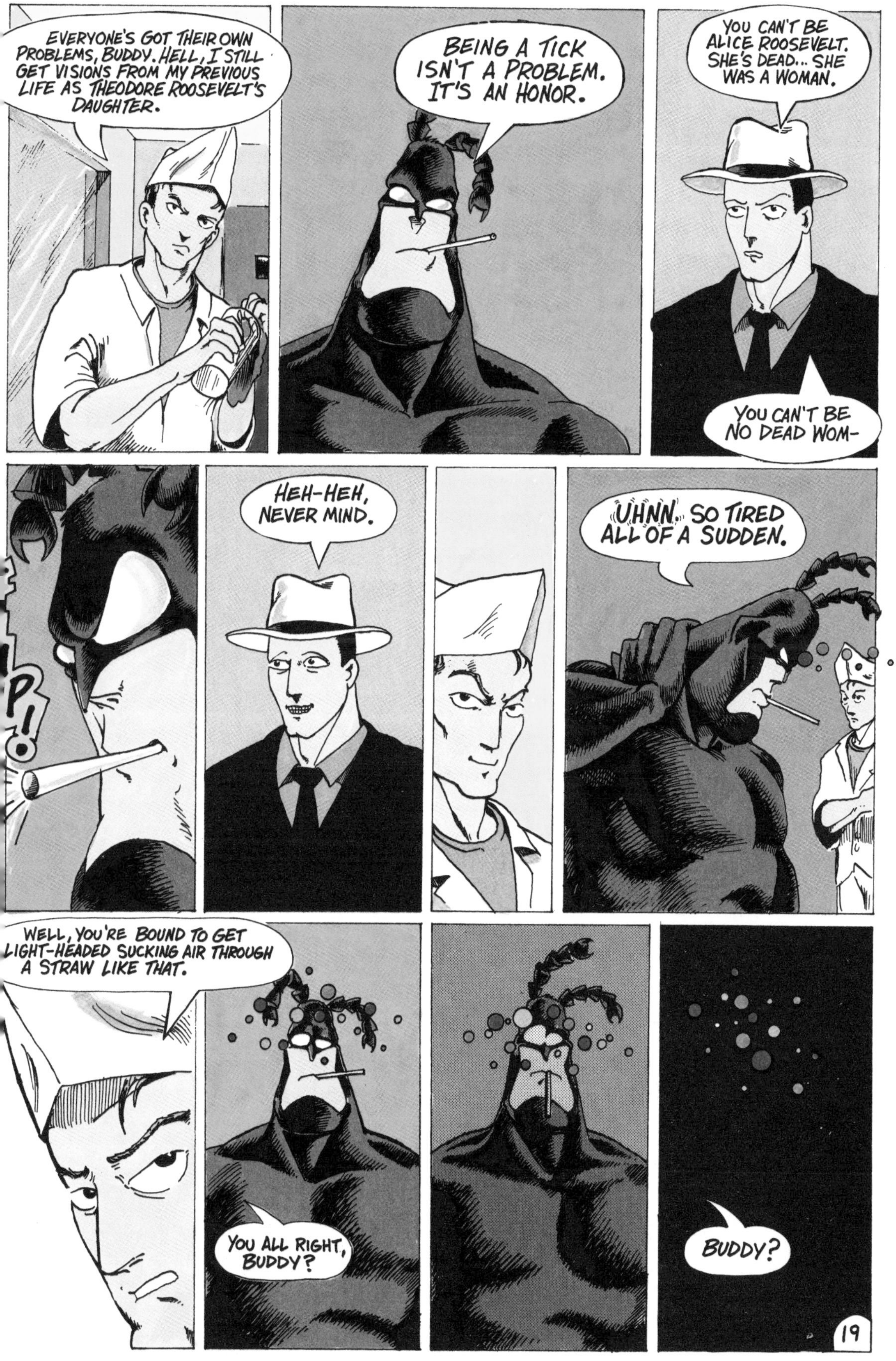
EVERYONE'S GOT THEIR OWN PROBLEMS, BUDDY. HELL, I STILL GET VISIONS FROM MY PREVIOUS LIFE AS THEODORE ROOSEVELT'S DAUGHTER.
BEING A TICK ISN'T A PROBLEM. IT'S AN HONOR.
YOU CAN'T BE ALICE ROOSEVELT. SHE'S DEAD... SHE WAS A WOMAN.
YOU CAN'T BE NO DEAD WOM-
HEH-HEH, NEVER MIND.
UHNN. SO TIRED ALL OF A SUDDEN.
WELL, YOU'RE BOUND TO GET LIGHT-HEADED SUCKING AIR THROUGH A STRAW LIKE THAT.
YOU ALL RIGHT, BUDDY?
BUDDY?

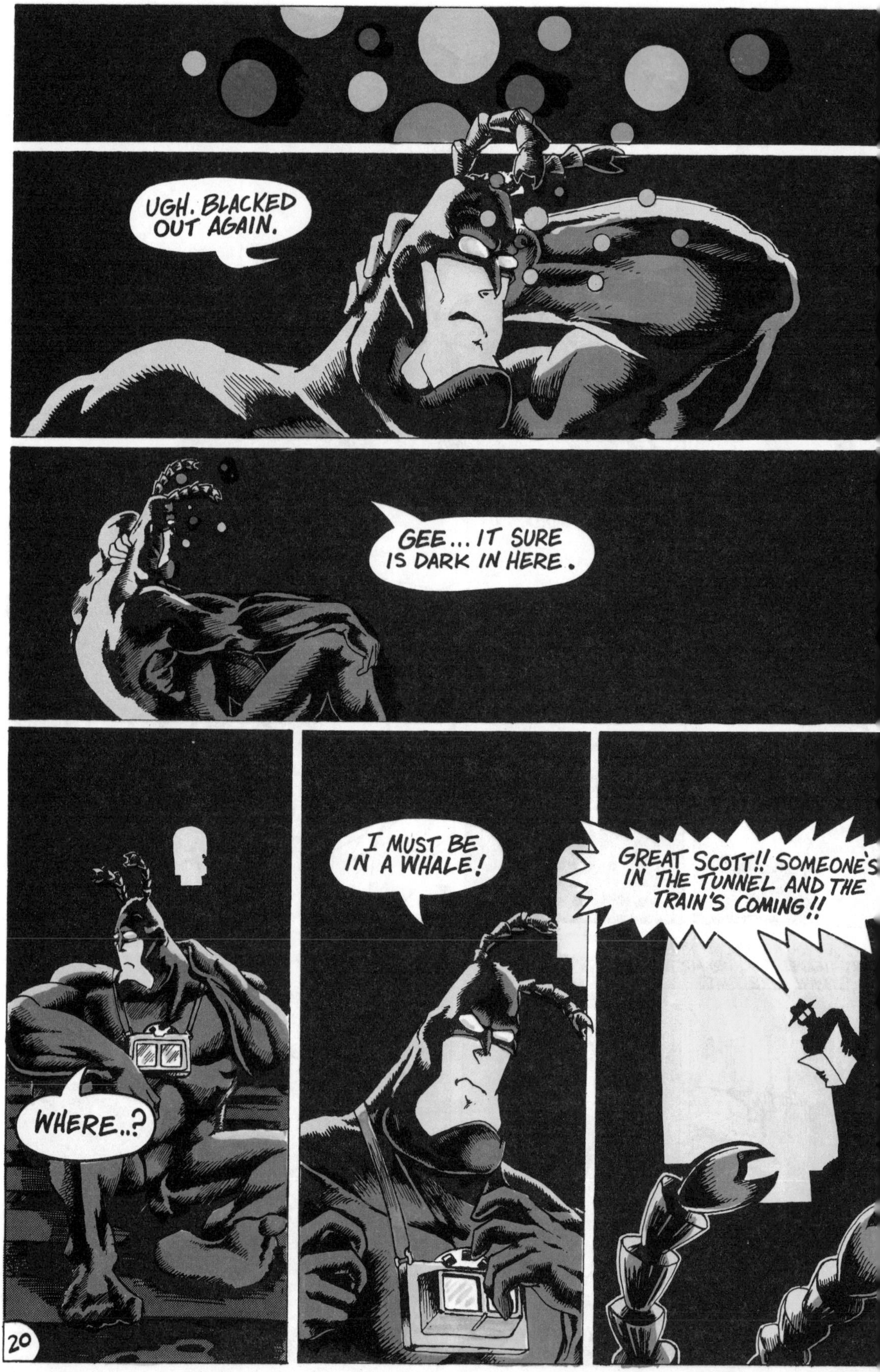

UGH. BLACKED OUT AGAIN.
GEE... IT SURE IS DARK IN HERE.
WHERE..?
I MUST BE IN A WHALE!
GREAT SCOTT!! SOMEONE'S IN THE TUNNEL AND THE TRAIN'S COMING!!

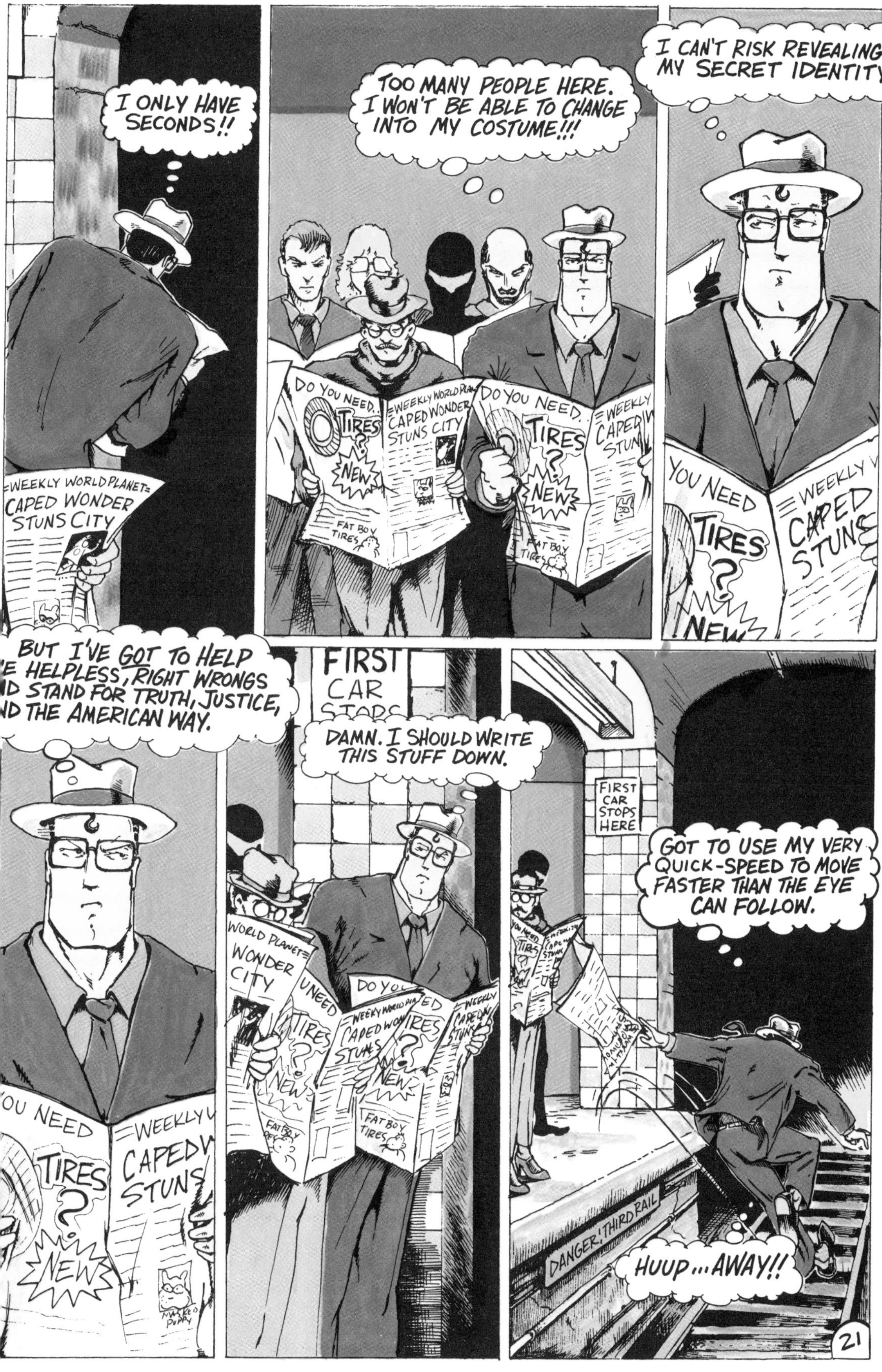

I ONLY HAVE SECONDS!!
WEEKLY WORLD PLANET
CAPED WONDER STUNS CITY
TOO MANY PEOPLE HERE. I WON'T BE ABLE TO CHANGE INTO MY COSTUME!!!
DO YOU NEED... TIRES? NEW
CAPED WONDER STUNS CITY
FAT BOY TIRES
I CAN'T RISK REVEALING MY SECRET IDENTITY.
BUT I'VE GOT TO HELP
E HELPLESS, RIGHT WRONGS
D STAND FOR TRUTH, JUSTICE,
D THE AMERICAN WAY.
FIRST CAR
DAMN. I SHOULD WRITE THIS STUFF DOWN.
FIRST CAR STOPS HERE
GOT TO USE MY VERY QUICK-SPEED TO MOVE FASTER THAN THE EYE CAN FOLLOW.
DANGER! THIRD RAIL
HUUP... AWAY!!

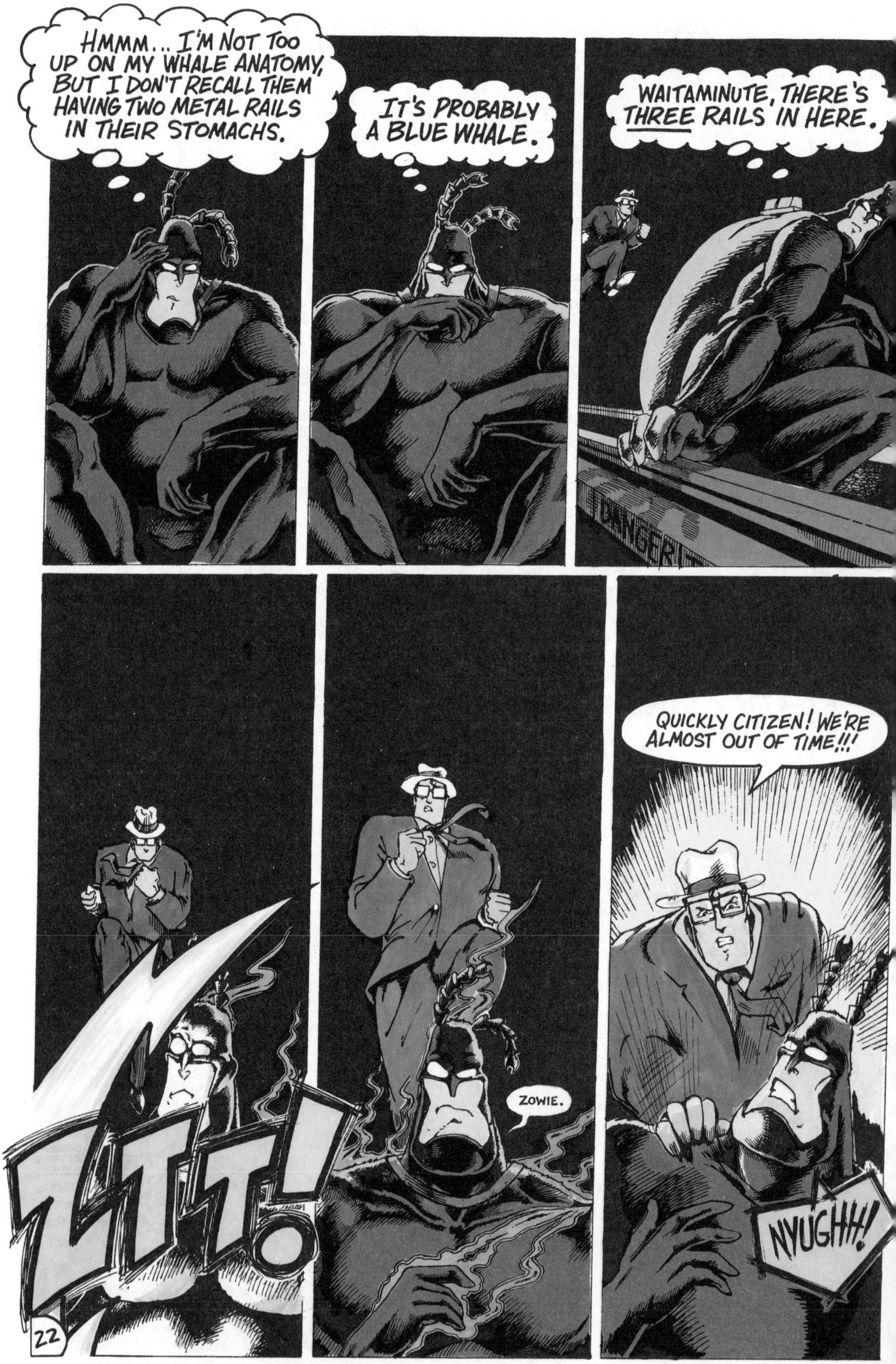
HMMM... I'M NOT TOO UP ON MY WHALE ANATOMY, BUT I DON'T RECALL THEM HAVING TWO METAL RAILS IN THEIR STOMACHS.
IT'S PROBABLY A BLUE WHALE.
WAITAMINUTE, THERE'S THREE RAILS IN HERE.
DANGER
ZTT!
ZOWIE.
QUICKLY CITIZEN! WE'RE ALMOST OUT OF TIME!!!
NYUGHH!

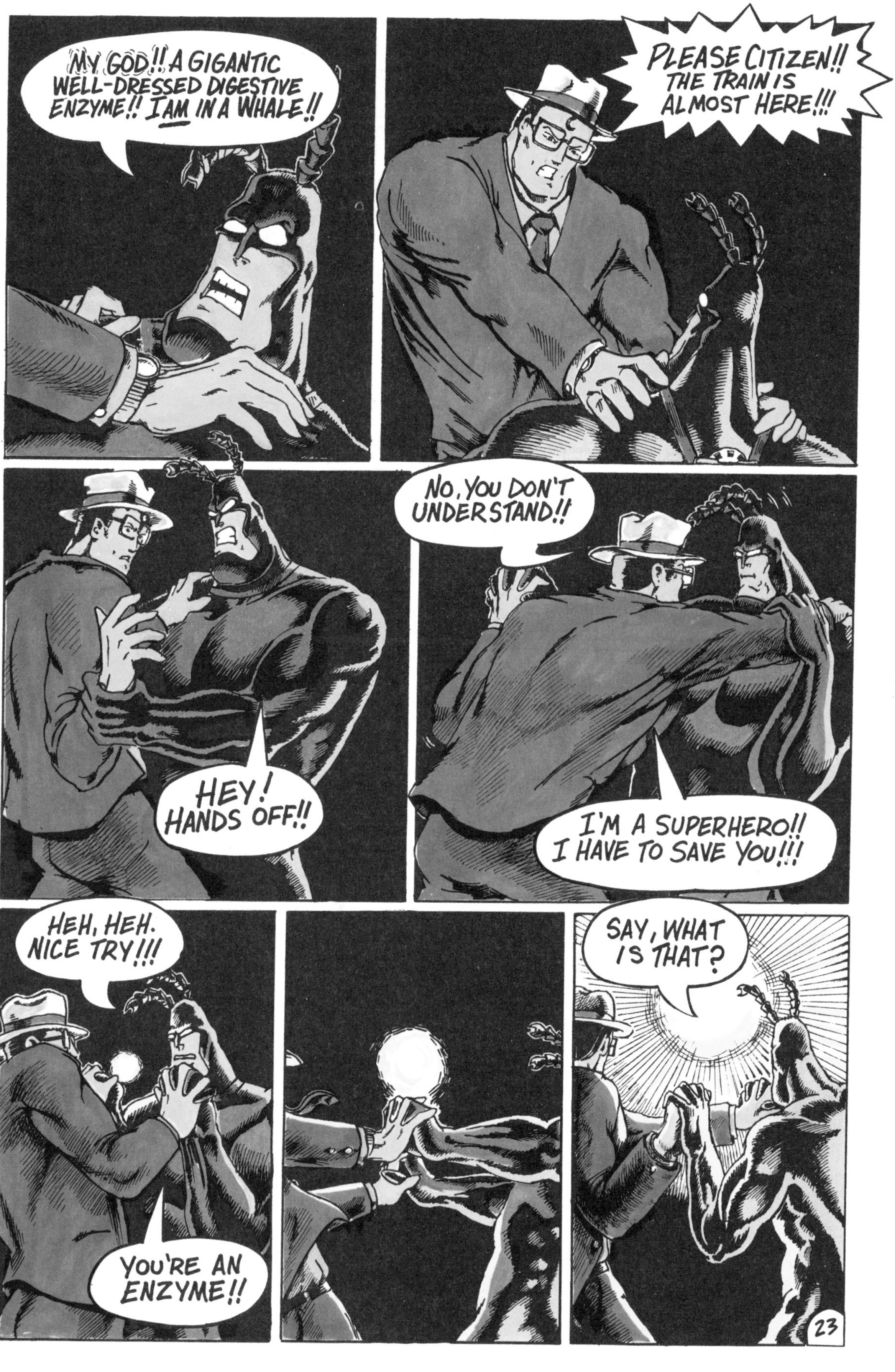
MY GOD!! A GIGANTIC WELL-DRESSED DIGESTIVE ENZYME!! I AM IN A WHALE!!
PLEASE CITIZEN!! THE TRAIN IS ALMOST HERE!!!
HEY! HANDS OFF!!
NO, YOU DON'T UNDERSTAND!!
I'M A SUPERHERO!! I HAVE TO SAVE YOU!!!
HEH, HEH. NICE TRY!!!
YOU'RE AN ENZYME!!
SAY, WHAT IS THAT?
23

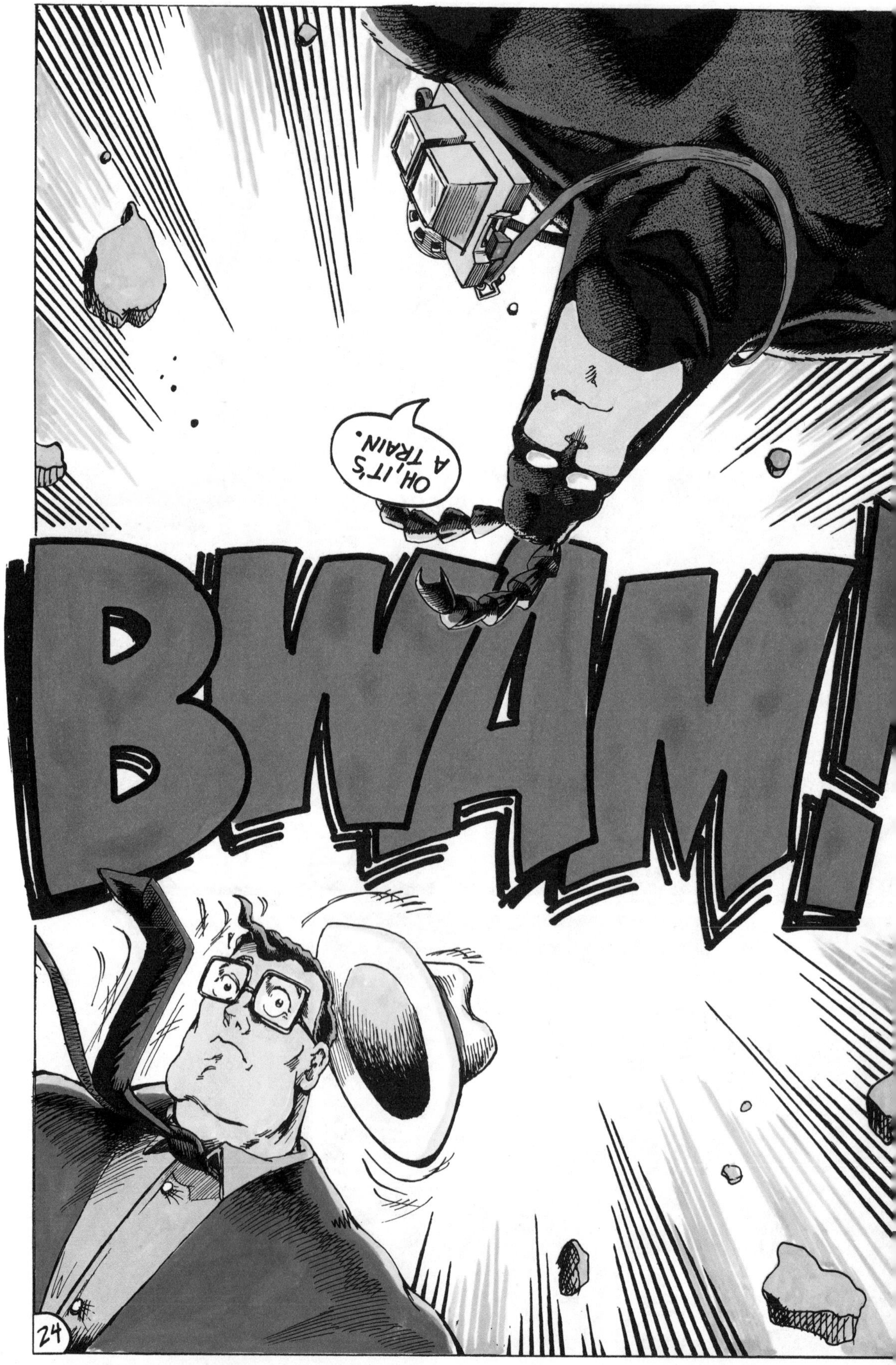
OH, IT'S A TRAIN.
BWAM!

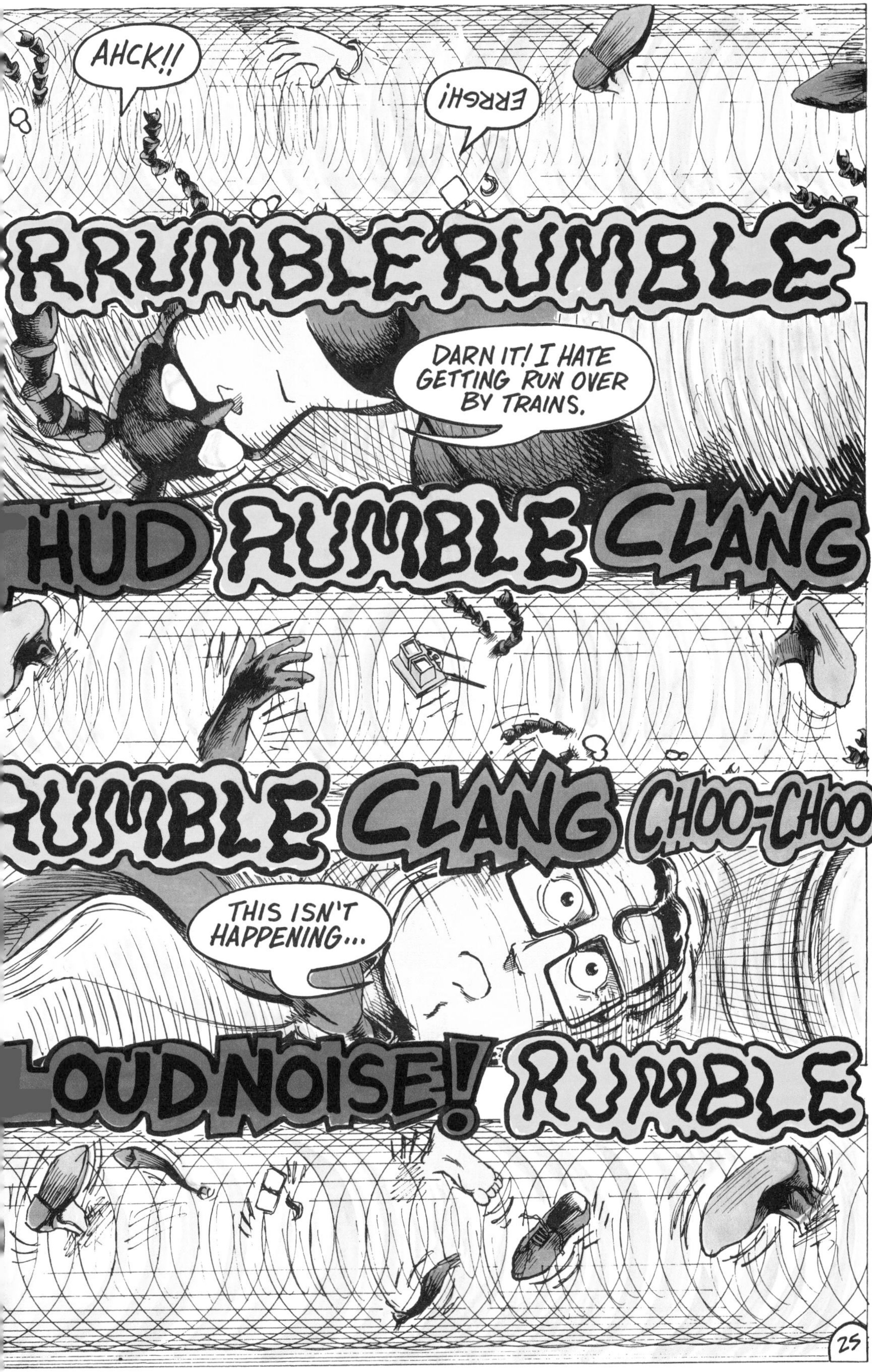
AHCK!!
ERRGH!
RRUMBLERUMBLE
DARN IT! I HATE GETTING RUN OVER BY TRAINS.
HUD RUMBLE CLANG
UMBLE CLANG CHOO-CHOO
THIS ISN'T HAPPENING...
OUDNOISE! RUMBLE

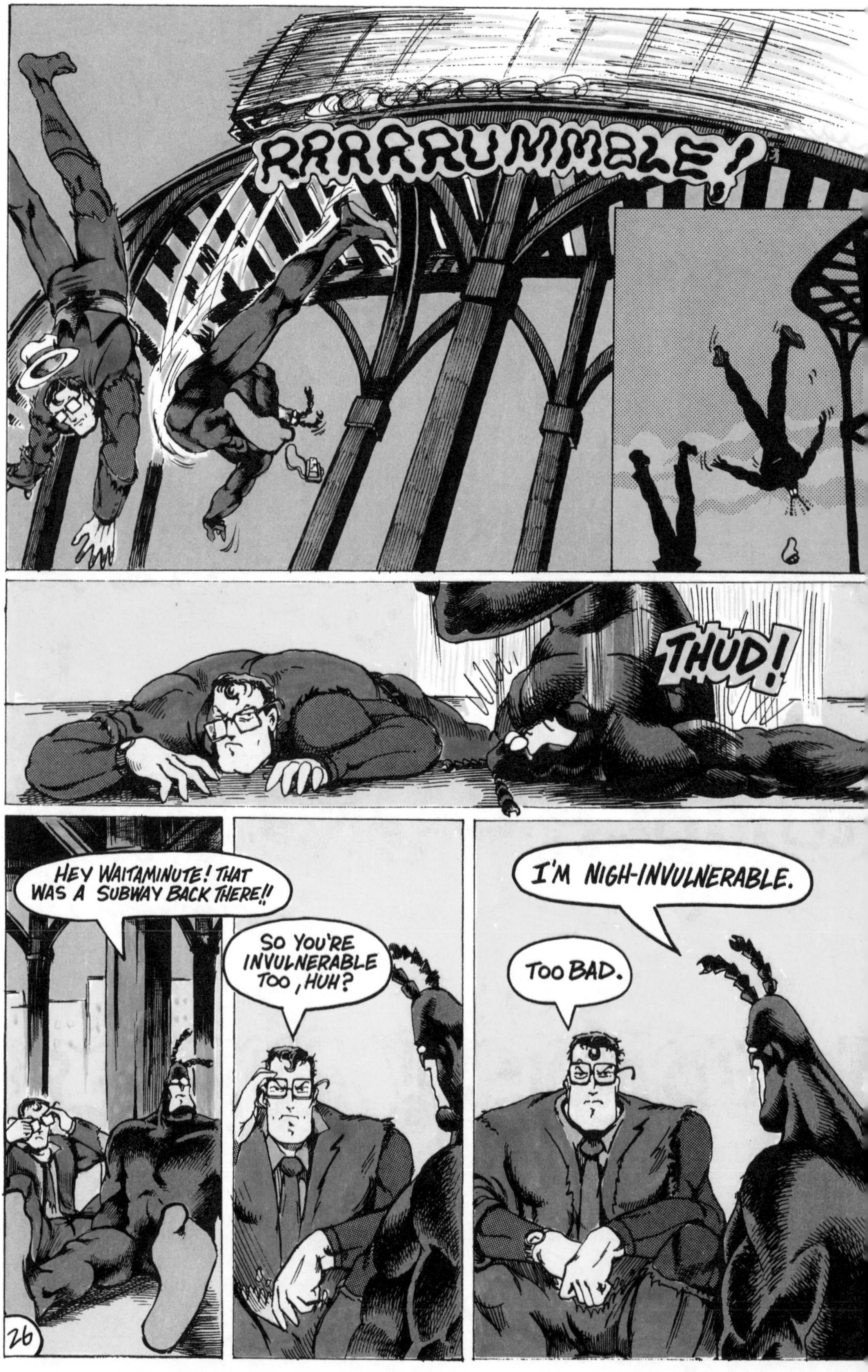
RRRRRUMMBLE!
THUD!
HEY WAITAMINUTE! THAT WAS A SUBWAY BACK THERE!!
SO YOU'RE INVULNERABLE TOO, HUH?
I'M NIGH-INVULNERABLE.
TOO BAD.

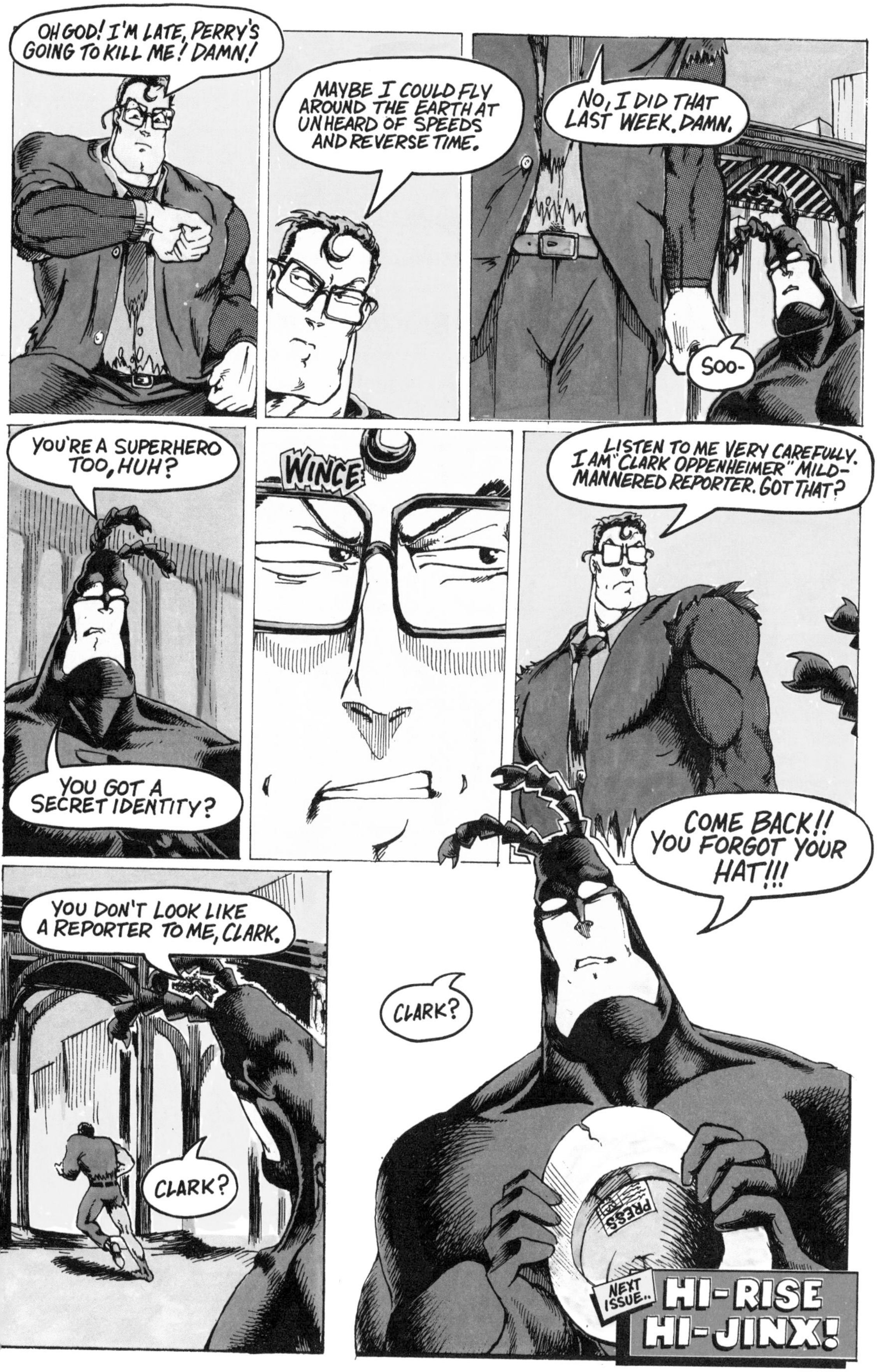
OH GOD! I'M LATE, PERRY'S GOING TO KILL ME! DAMN!
MAYBE I COULD FLY AROUND THE EARTH AT UNHEARD OF SPEEDS AND REVERSE TIME.
NO, I DID THAT LAST WEEK. DAMN.
SOO-
YOU'RE A SUPERHERO TOO, HUH?
YOU GOT A SECRET IDENTITY?
WINCE
LISTEN TO ME VERY CAREFULLY. I AM "CLARK OPPENHEIMER" MILD-MANNERED REPORTER. GOT THAT?
YOU DON'T LOOK LIKE A REPORTER TO ME, CLARK.
CLARK?
COME BACK!! YOU FORGOT YOUR HAT!!!
CLARK?
PRESS
NEXT ISSUE.. HI-RISE HI-JINX!

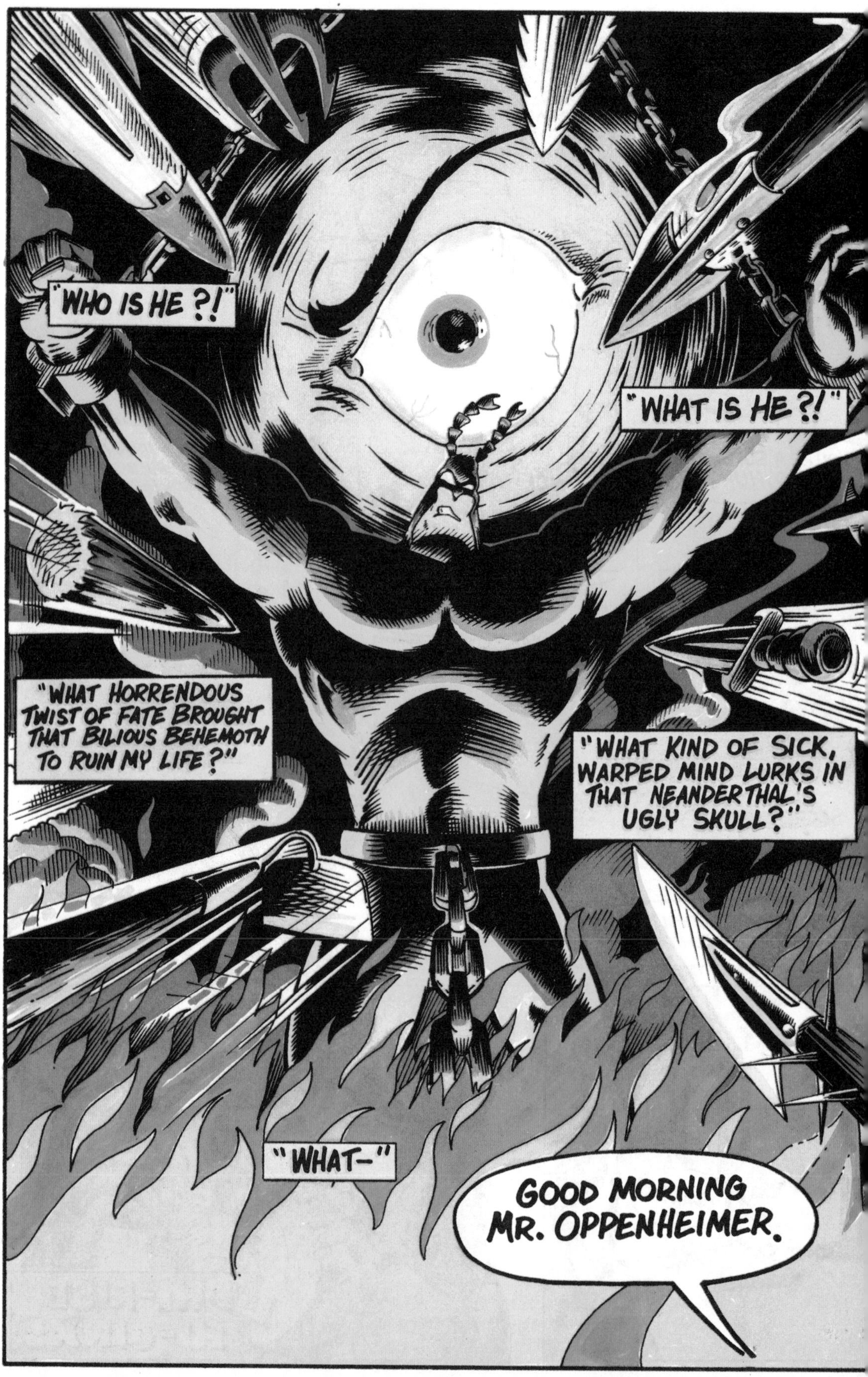
"WHO IS HE ?!"
"WHAT IS HE ?!"
"WHAT HORRENDOUS TWIST OF FATE BROUGHT THAT BILIOUS BEHEMOTH TO RUIN MY LIFE ?"
"WHAT KIND OF SICK, WARPED MIND LURKS IN THAT NEANDERTHAL'S UGLY SKULL?"
"WHAT-"
GOOD MORNING MR. OPPENHEIMER.

High Rise Hijinx

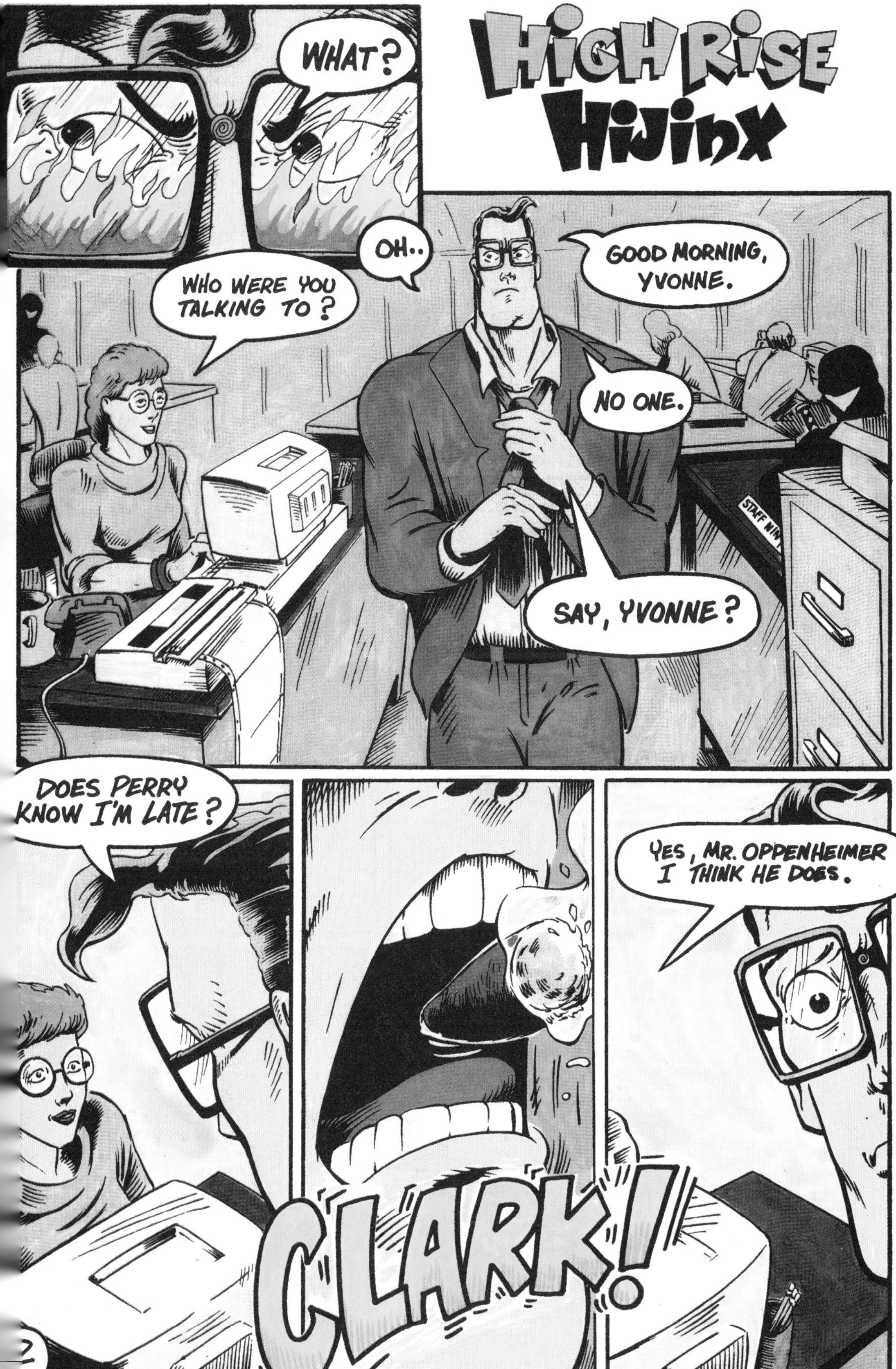
WHAT?
OH..
GOOD MORNING, YVONNE.
WHO WERE YOU TALKING TO?
NO ONE.
STAFF
SAY, YVONNE?
DOES PERRY KNOW I'M LATE?
YES, MR. OPPENHEIMER I THINK HE DOES.
CLARK!

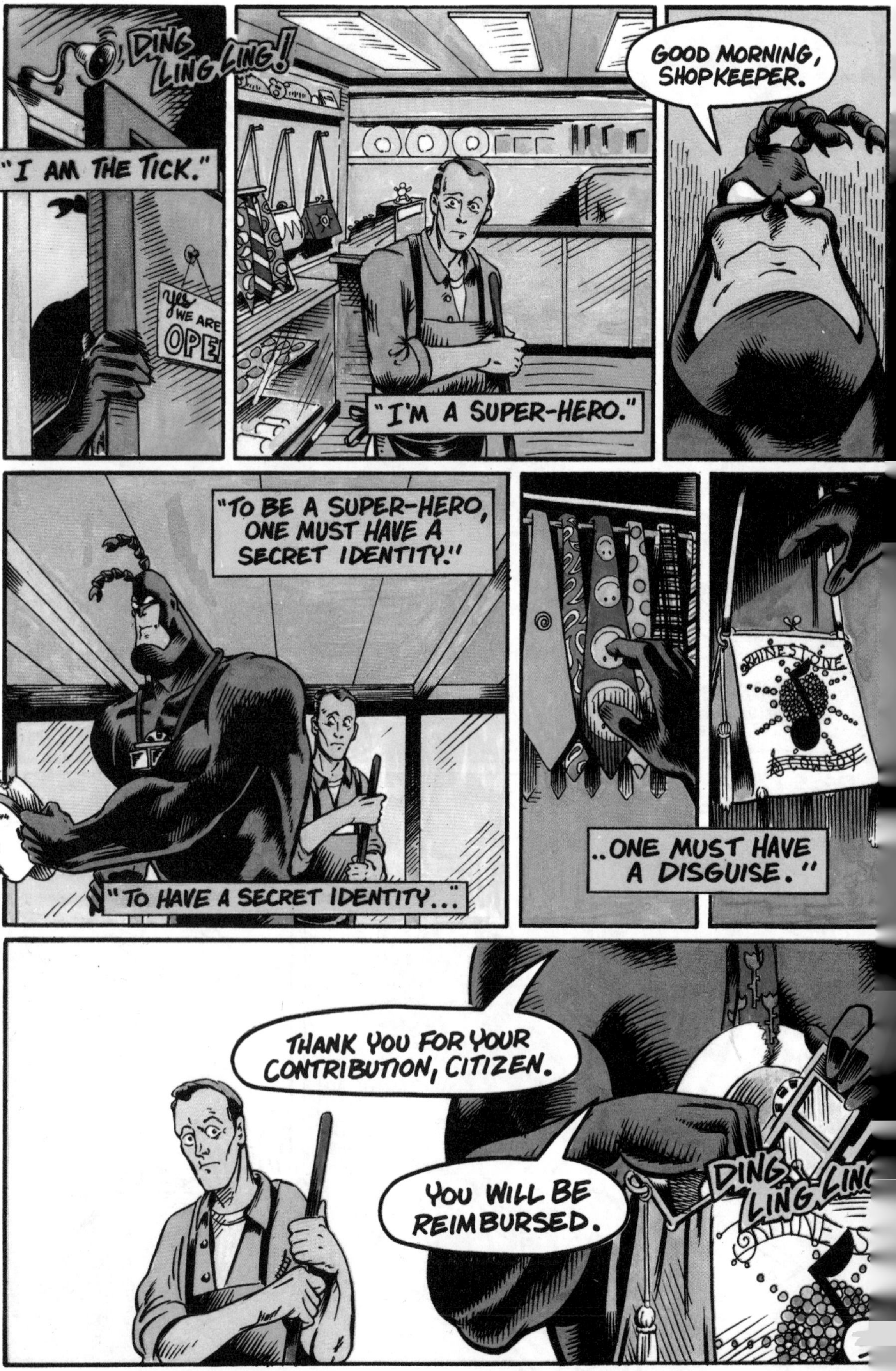

DING LING LING!
"I AM THE TICK."
yes WE ARE OPEN
"I'M A SUPER-HERO."
GOOD MORNING, SHOPKEEPER.
"TO BE A SUPER-HERO, ONE MUST HAVE A SECRET IDENTITY."
"TO HAVE A SECRET IDENTITY..."
..ONE MUST HAVE A DISGUISE."
RHINESTONE COWBOY
THANK YOU FOR YOUR CONTRIBUTION, CITIZEN.
YOU WILL BE REIMBURSED.
DING LING LING

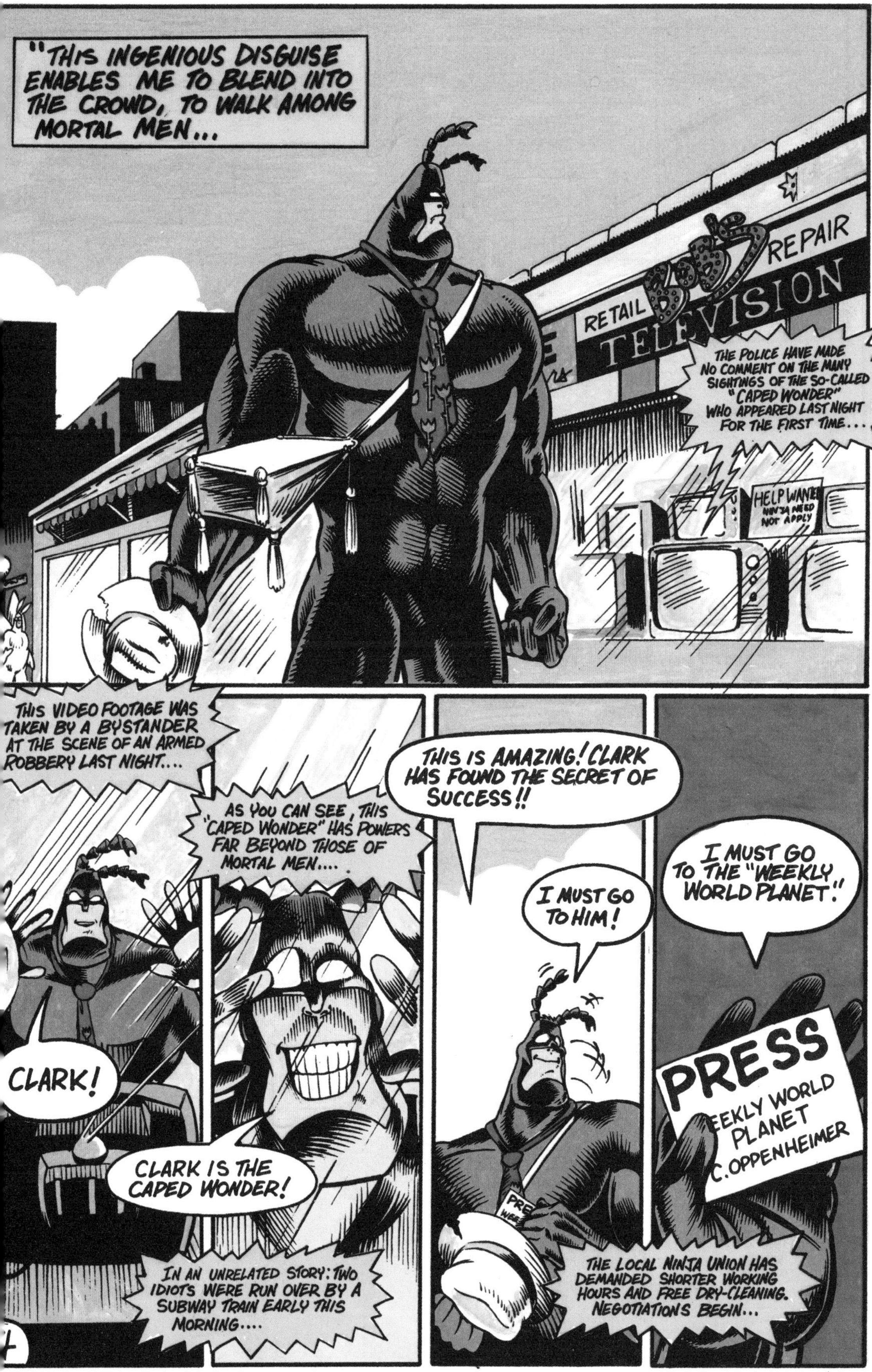
"THIS INGENIOUS DISGUISE ENABLES ME TO BLEND INTO THE CROWD, TO WALK AMONG MORTAL MEN...
BOB'S REPAIR
RETAIL
TELEVISION
THE POLICE HAVE MADE NO COMMENT ON THE MANY SIGHTINGS OF THE SO-CALLED "CAPED WONDER" WHO APPEARED LAST NIGHT FOR THE FIRST TIME...
HELP WANTED NINJA NEED NOT APPLY
THIS VIDEO FOOTAGE WAS TAKEN BY A BYSTANDER AT THE SCENE OF AN ARMED ROBBERY LAST NIGHT....
AS YOU CAN SEE, THIS "CAPED WONDER" HAS POWERS FAR BEYOND THOSE OF MORTAL MEN....
CLARK!
CLARK IS THE CAPED WONDER!
IN AN UNRELATED STORY: TWO IDIOTS WERE RUN OVER BY A SUBWAY TRAIN EARLY THIS MORNING....
THIS IS AMAZING! CLARK HAS FOUND THE SECRET OF SUCCESS!!
I MUST GO TO HIM!
I MUST GO TO THE "WEEKLY WORLD PLANET."
PRESS
EEKLY WORLD PLANET
C. OPPENHEIMER
THE LOCAL NINJA UNION HAS DEMANDED SHORTER WORKING HOURS AND FREE DRY-CLEANING. NEGOTIATIONS BEGIN...

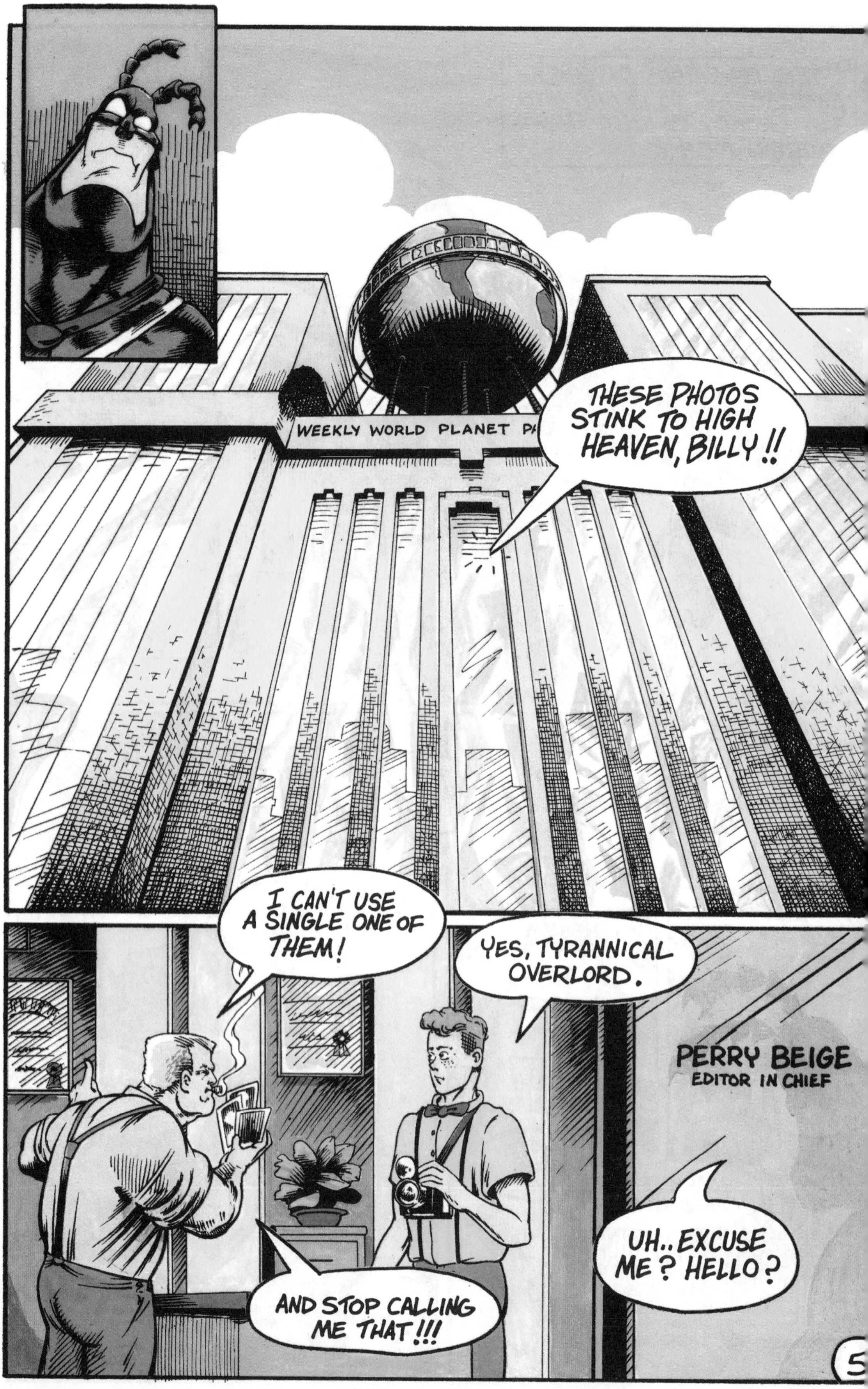

WEEKLY WORLD PLANET PA
THESE PHOTOS STINK TO HIGH HEAVEN, BILLY!!
I CAN'T USE A SINGLE ONE OF THEM!
YES, TYRANNICAL OVERLORD.
PERRY BEIGE
EDITOR IN CHIEF
AND STOP CALLING ME THAT!!!
UH.. EXCUSE ME? HELLO?

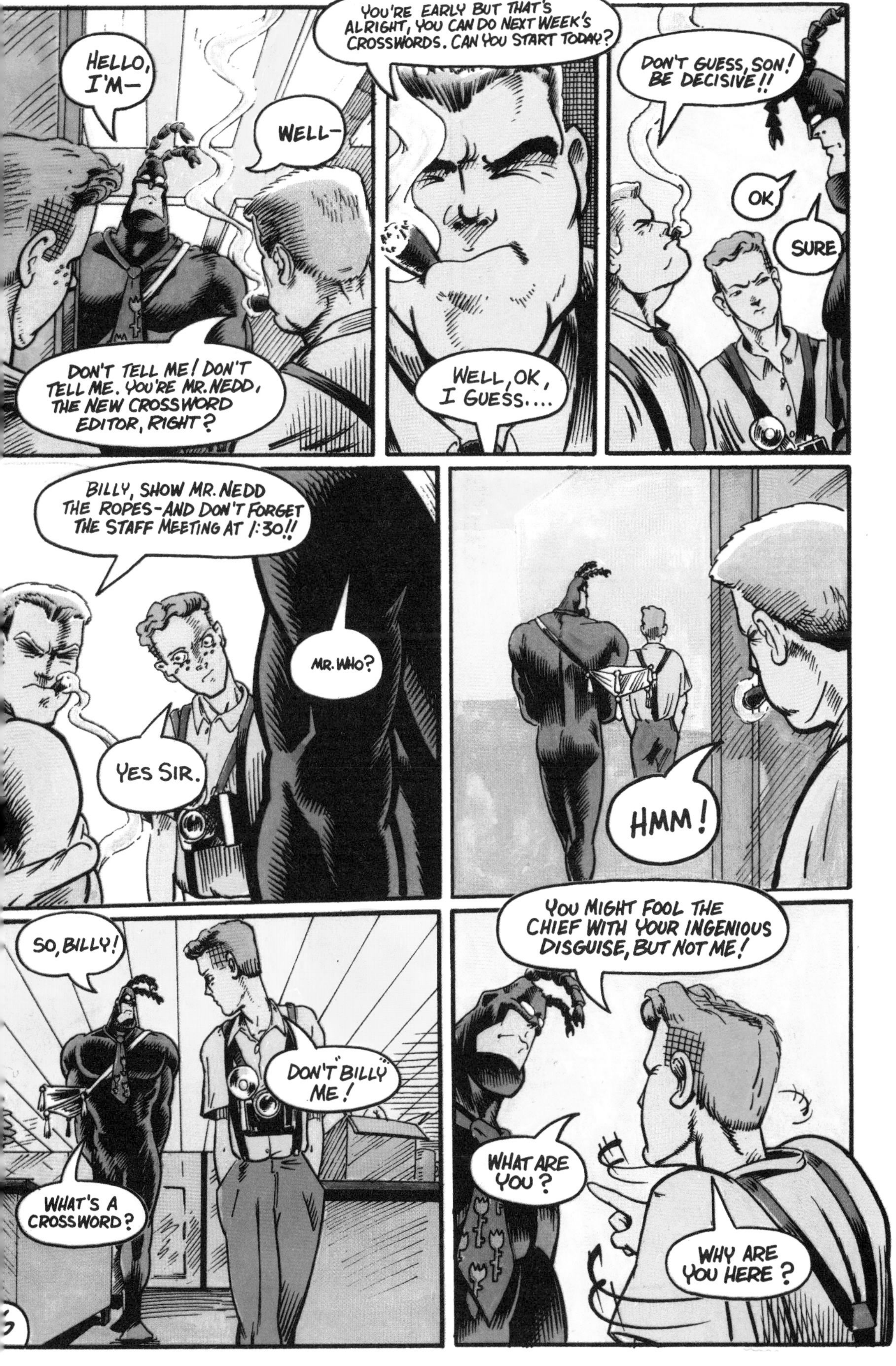
HELLO, I'M—
WELL—
DON'T TELL ME! DON'T TELL ME. YOU'RE MR. NEDD, THE NEW CROSSWORD EDITOR, RIGHT?
YOU'RE EARLY BUT THAT'S ALRIGHT, YOU CAN DO NEXT WEEK'S CROSSWORDS. CAN YOU START TODAY?
WELL, OK, I GUESS....
DON'T GUESS, SON! BE DECISIVE!!
OK
SURE
BILLY, SHOW MR. NEDD THE ROPES-AND DON'T FORGET THE STAFF MEETING AT 1:30!!
YES SIR.
MR. WHO?
HMM!
SO, BILLY!
DON'T "BILLY" ME!
WHAT'S A CROSSWORD?
YOU MIGHT FOOL THE CHIEF WITH YOUR INGENIOUS DISGUISE, BUT NOT ME!
WHAT ARE YOU?
WHY ARE YOU HERE?

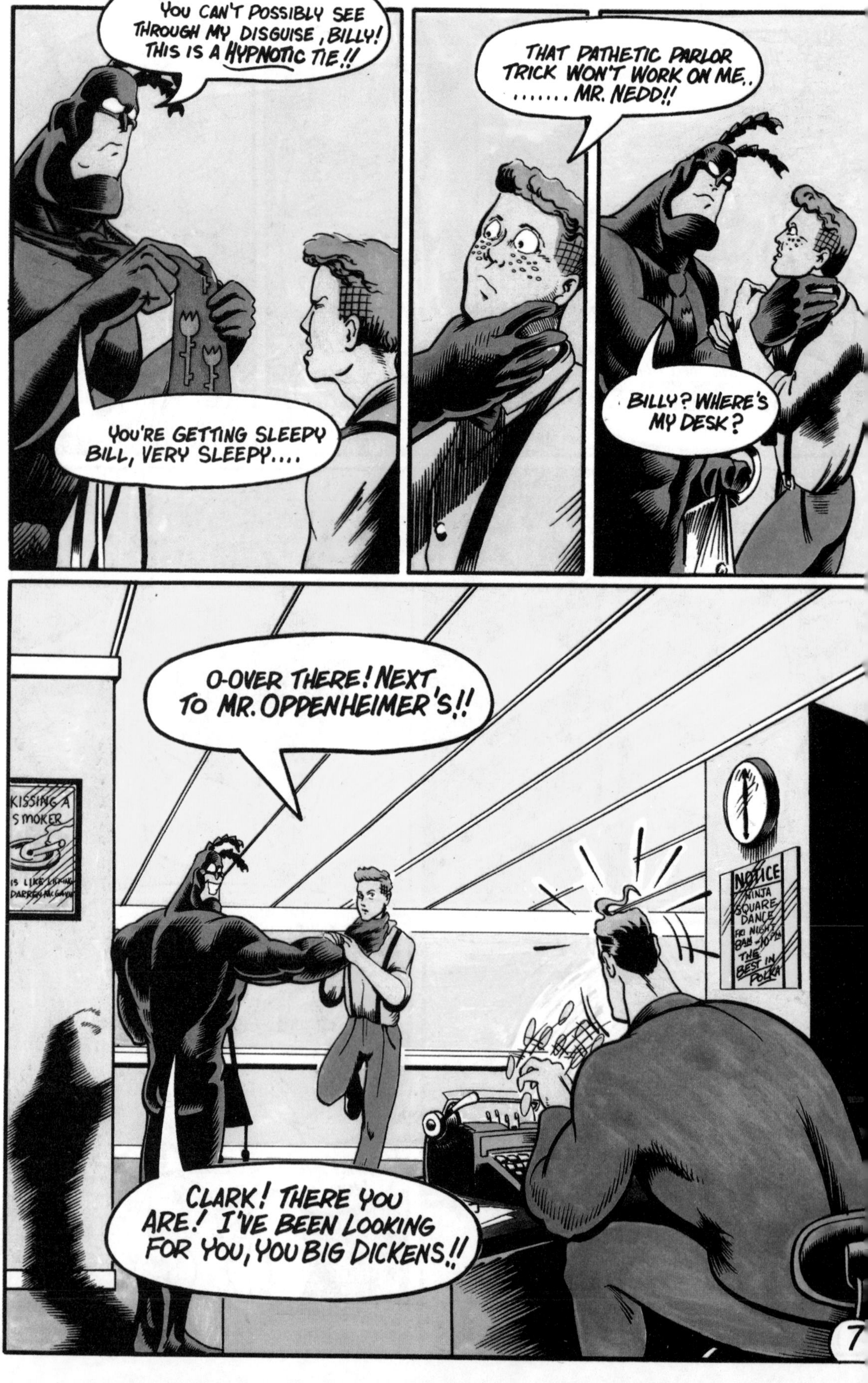
YOU CAN'T POSSIBLY SEE THROUGH MY DISGUISE, BILLY! THIS IS A HYPNOTIC TIE!!
YOU'RE GETTING SLEEPY BILL, VERY SLEEPY....
THAT PATHETIC PARLOR TRICK WON'T WORK ON ME.. ....MR. NEDD!!
BILLY? WHERE'S MY DESK?
O-OVER THERE! NEXT TO MR. OPPENHEIMER'S!!
KISSING A SMOKER
NOTICE
NINJA SQUARE DANCE
THE BEST IN POLKA
CLARK! THERE YOU ARE! I'VE BEEN LOOKING FOR YOU, YOU BIG DICKENS!!

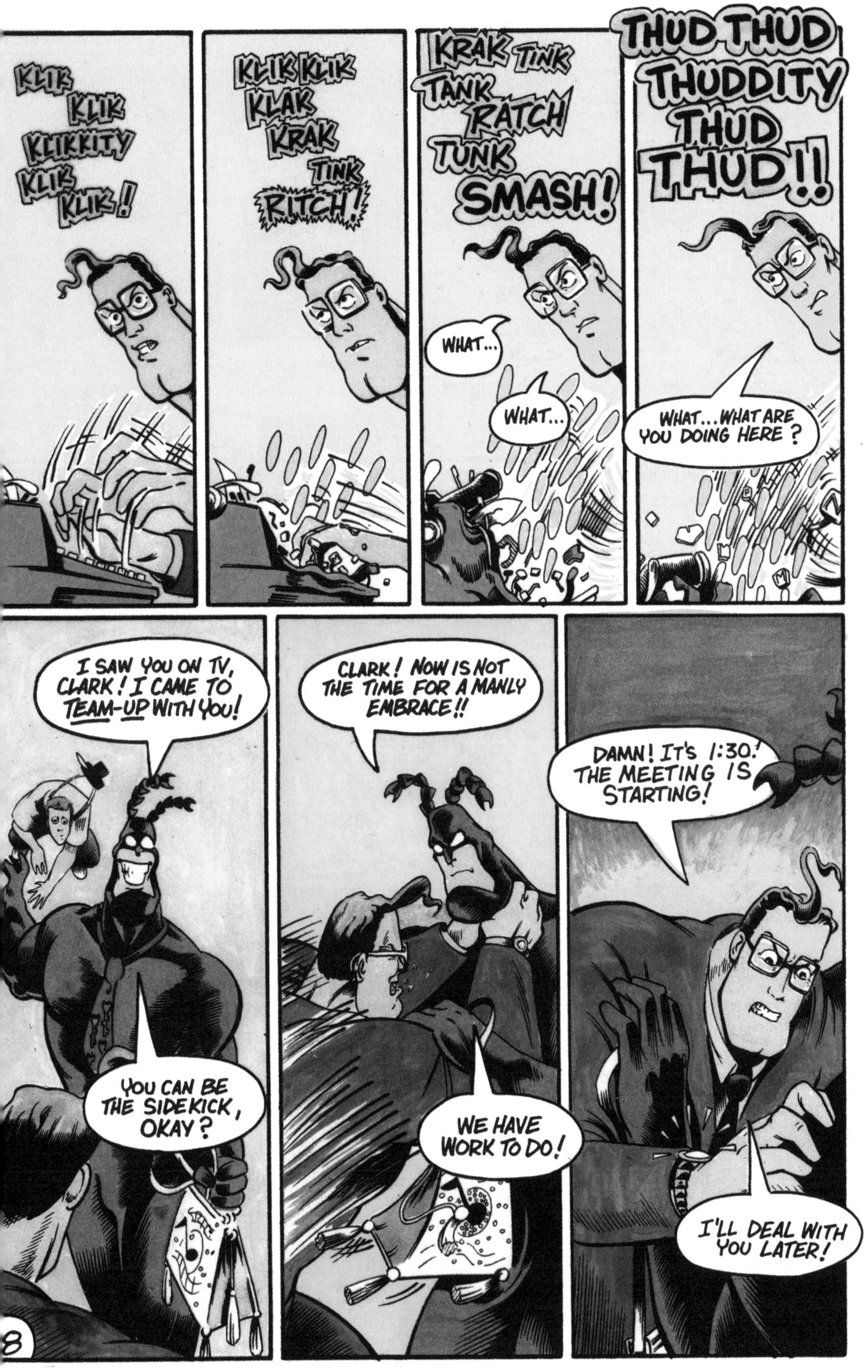
KLIK KLIK KLIKKITY KLIK KLIK!
KLIK KLIK KLAK KRAK TINK RITCH!
KRAK TINK TANK RATCH TUNK SMASH!
WHAT...
WHAT...
THUD THUD THUDDITY THUD THUD!!
WHAT... WHAT ARE YOU DOING HERE?
I SAW YOU ON TV, CLARK! I CAME TO TEAM-UP WITH YOU!
YOU CAN BE THE SIDEKICK, OKAY?
CLARK! NOW IS NOT THE TIME FOR A MANLY EMBRACE!!
WE HAVE WORK TO DO!
DAMN! IT'S 1:30! THE MEETING IS STARTING!
I'LL DEAL WITH YOU LATER!

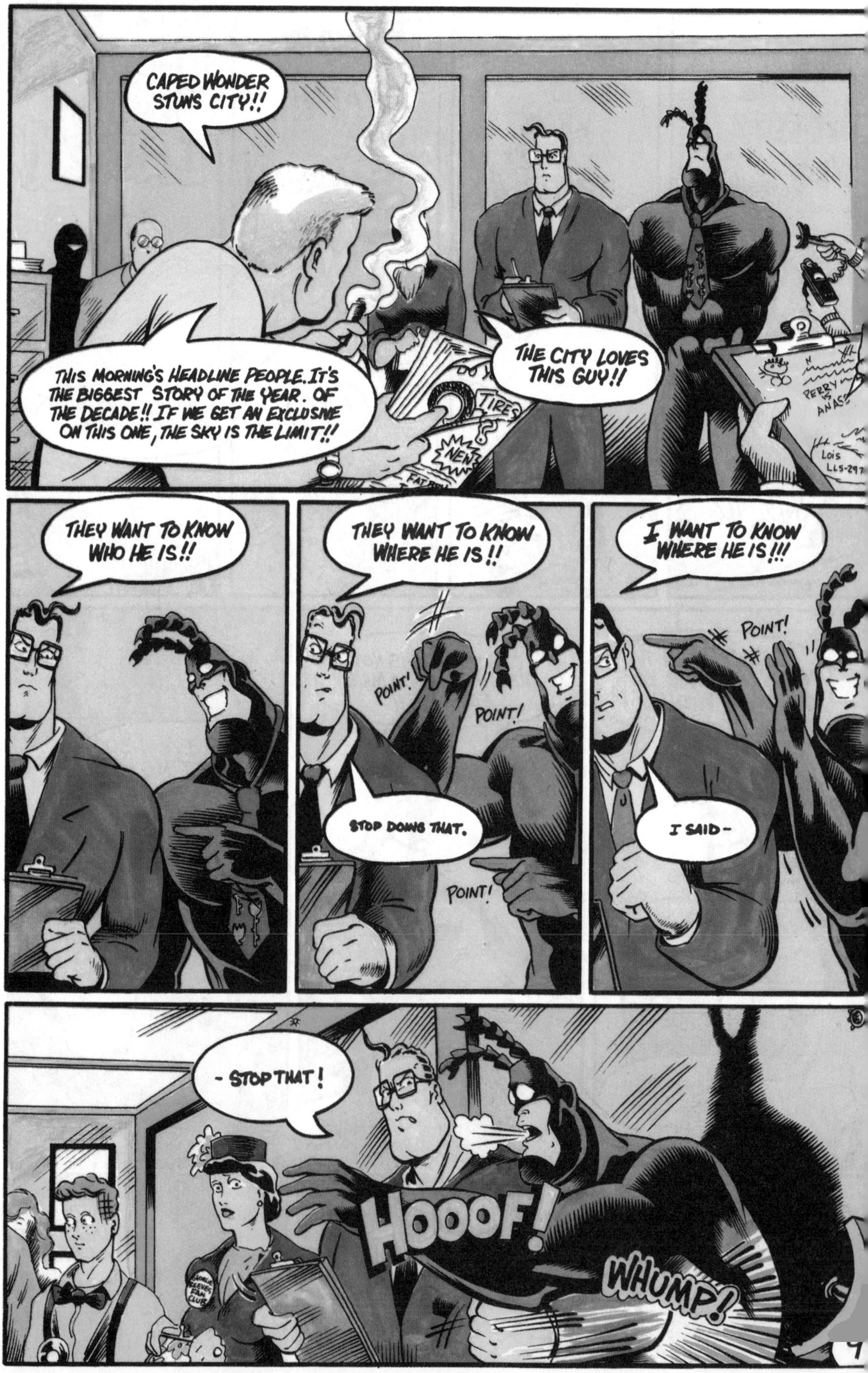

CAPED WONDER STUNS CITY!!
THIS MORNING'S HEADLINE PEOPLE. IT'S THE BIGGEST STORY OF THE YEAR. OF THE DECADE!! IF WE GET AN EXCLUSIVE ON THIS ONE, THE SKY IS THE LIMIT!!
THE CITY LOVES THIS GUY!!
THEY WANT TO KNOW WHO HE IS!!
THEY WANT TO KNOW WHERE HE IS!!
POINT!
POINT!
STOP DOING THAT.
POINT!
I WANT TO KNOW WHERE HE IS!!!
POINT!
I SAID-
- STOP THAT!
HOOOF!
WHUMP!

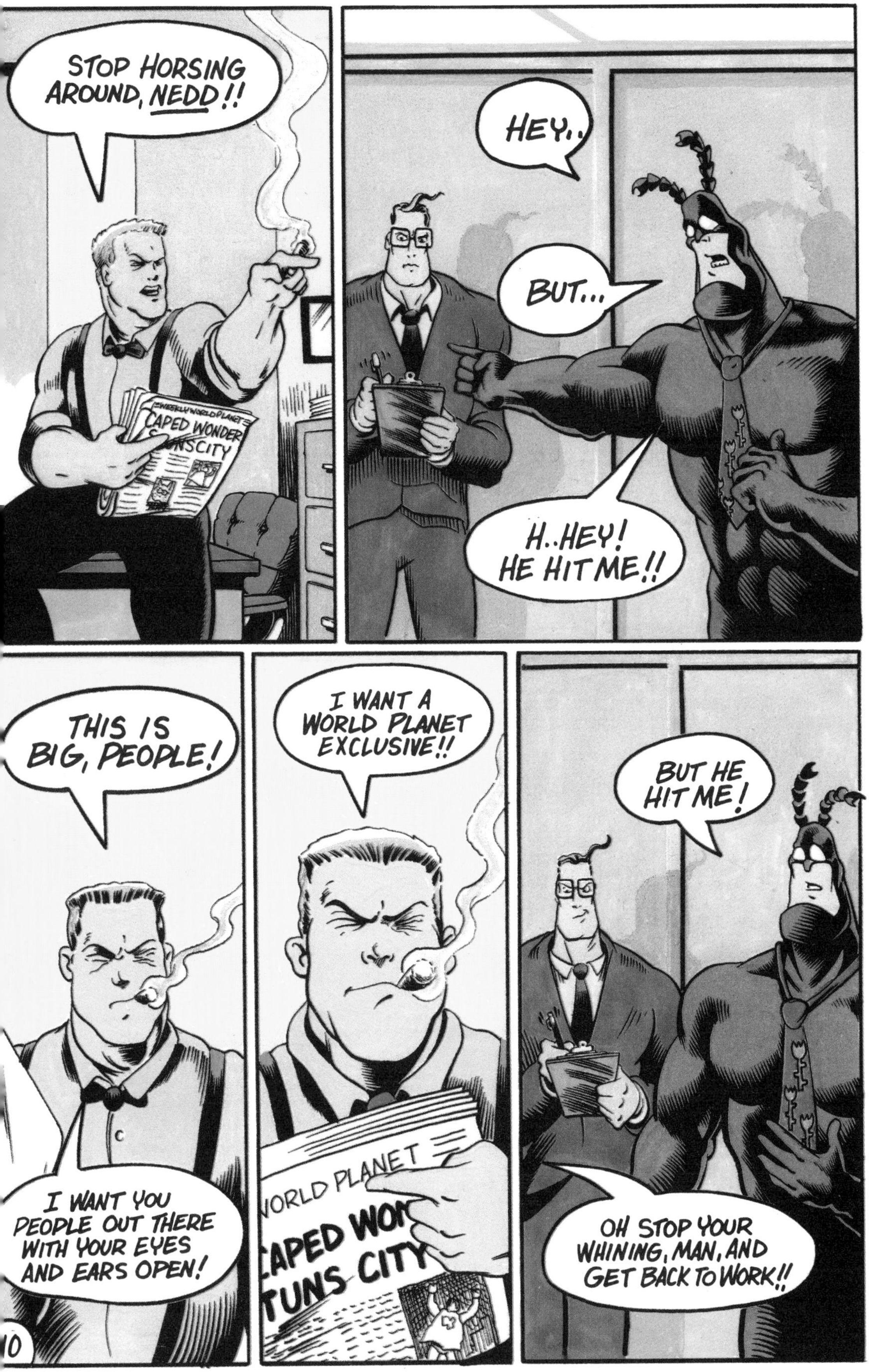
STOP HORSING AROUND, NEDD!!
WEEKLY WORLD PLANET
CAPED WONDER
HEY..
BUT...
H..HEY! HE HIT ME!!
THIS IS BIG, PEOPLE!
I WANT YOU PEOPLE OUT THERE WITH YOUR EYES AND EARS OPEN!
I WANT A WORLD PLANET EXCLUSIVE!!
WORLD PLANET
CAPED WON
TUNS CITY
BUT HE HIT ME!
OH STOP YOUR WHINING, MAN, AND GET BACK TO WORK!!

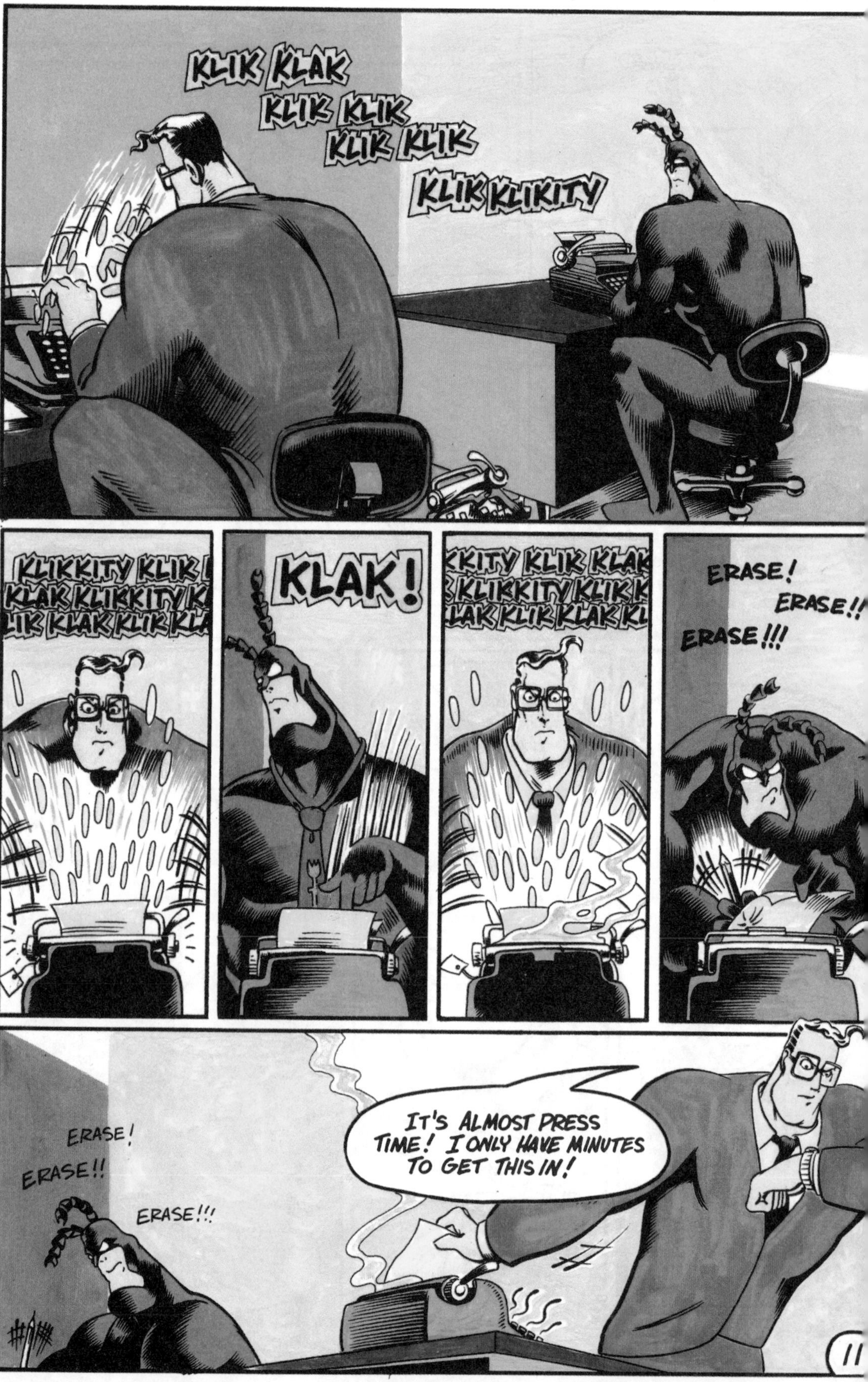

KLIK KLAK
KLIK KLIK
KLIK KLIK
KLIK KLIKITY
KLIKKITY KLIK
KLAK KLIKKITY
LIK KLAK KLIK KLA
KLAK!
KITY KLIK KLAK
KLIKKITY KLIK
LAK KLIK KLAK KL
ERASE!
ERASE!!
ERASE!!!
ERASE!
ERASE!!
ERASE!!!
IT'S ALMOST PRESS TIME! I ONLY HAVE MINUTES TO GET THIS IN!

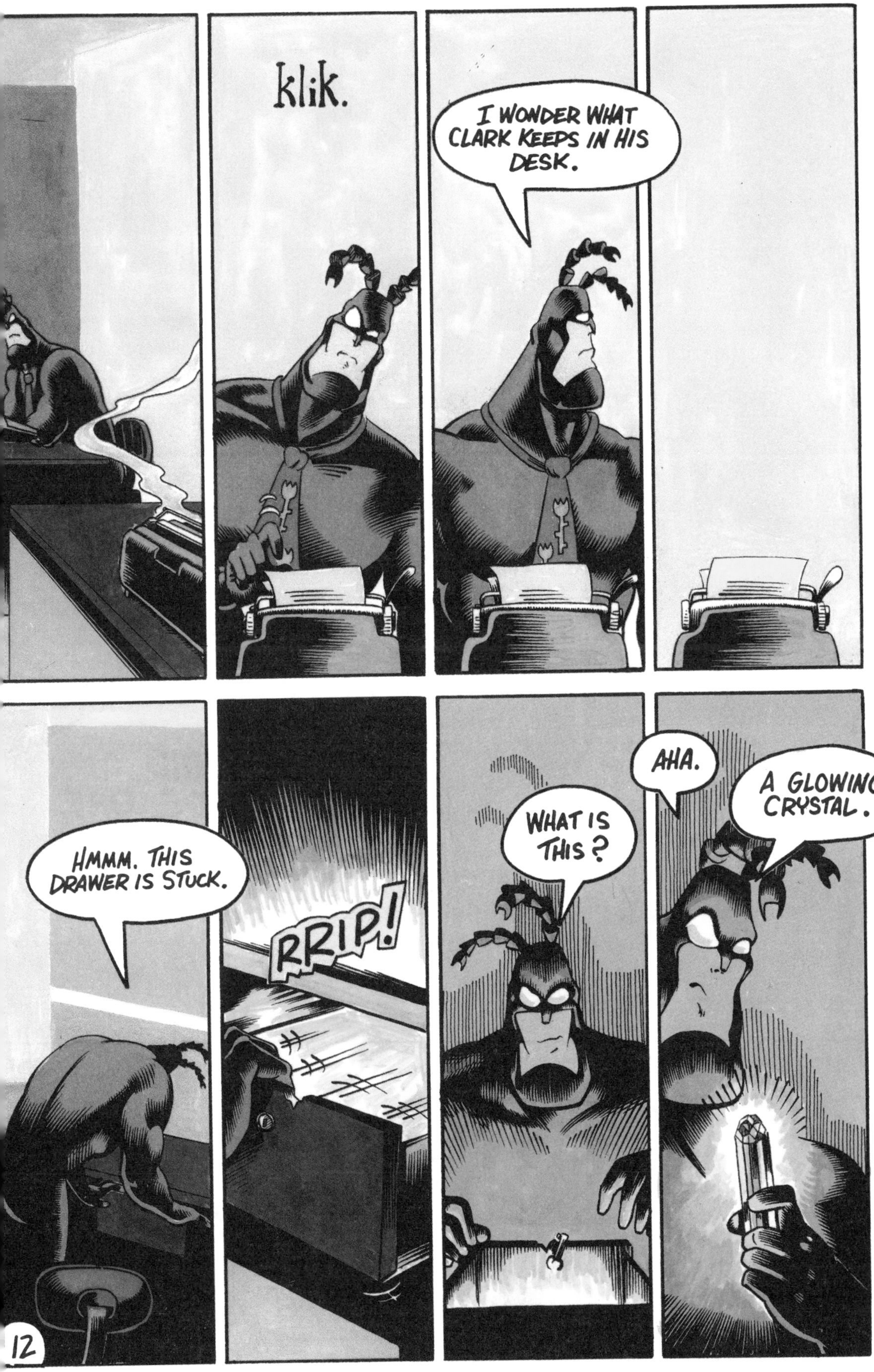
klik.
I WONDER WHAT CLARK KEEPS IN HIS DESK.
HMMM. THIS DRAWER IS STUCK.
RRIP!
WHAT IS THIS?
AHA.
A GLOWING CRYSTAL.

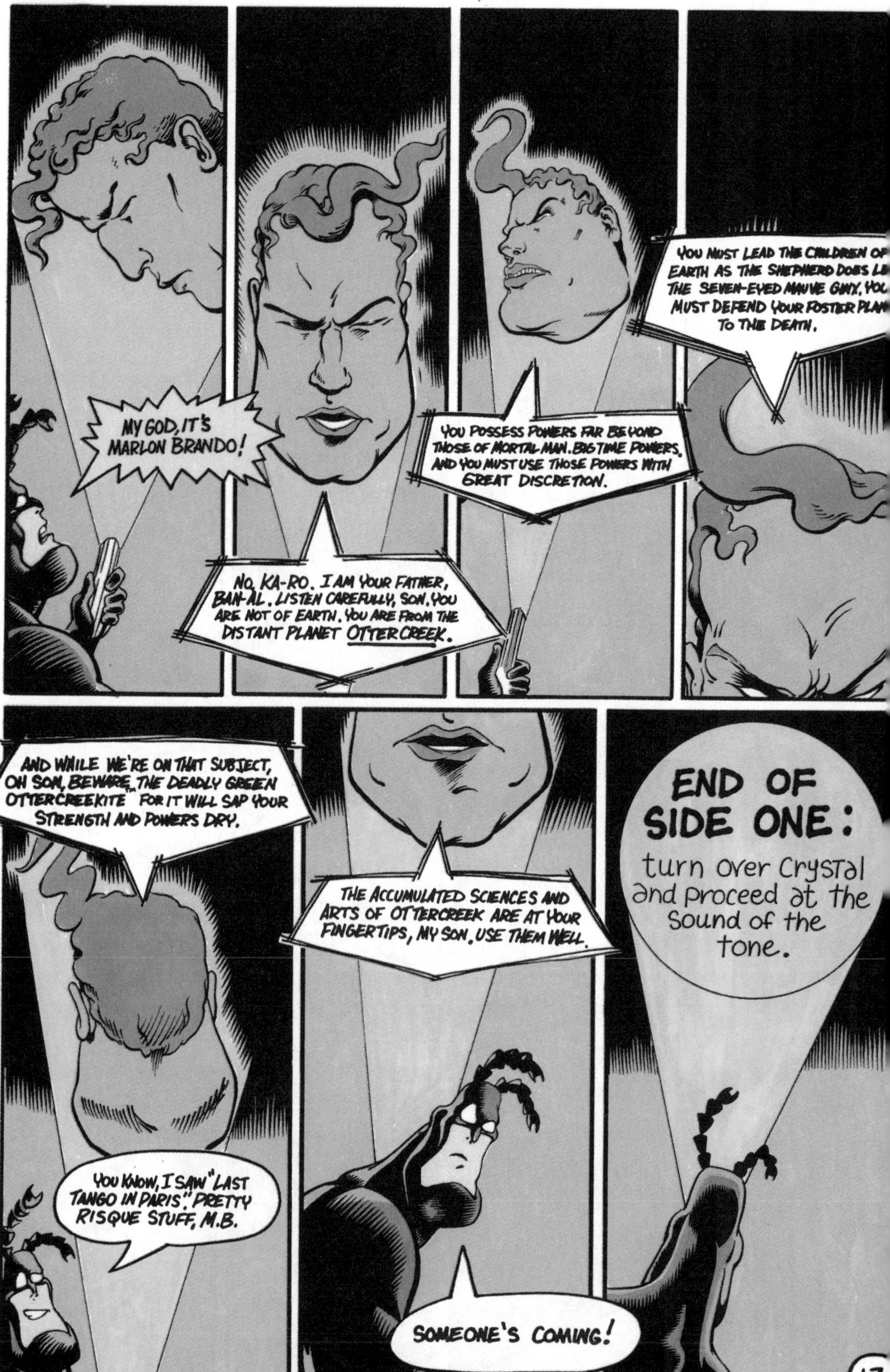
MY GOD, IT'S MARLON BRANDO!
NO, KA-RO. I AM YOUR FATHER, BAN-AL. LISTEN CAREFULLY, SON. YOU ARE NOT OF EARTH. YOU ARE FROM THE DISTANT PLANET OTTERCREEK.
YOU POSSESS POWERS FAR BEYOND THOSE OF MORTAL MAN. BIGTIME POWERS. AND YOU MUST USE THOSE POWERS WITH GREAT DISCRETION.
YOU MUST LEAD THE CHILDREN OF EARTH AS THE SHEPHERD DOES LE THE SEVEN-EYED MAUVE GNY. YOU MUST DEFEND YOUR FOSTER PLAN TO THE DEATH.
AND WHILE WE'RE ON THAT SUBJECT, OH SON, BEWARE,,, THE DEADLY GREEN OTTERCREEKITE FOR IT WILL SAP YOUR STRENGTH AND POWERS DRY.
YOU KNOW, I SAW "LAST TANGO IN PARIS". PRETTY RISQUE STUFF, M.B.
THE ACCUMULATED SCIENCES AND ARTS OF OTTERCREEK ARE AT YOUR FINGERTIPS, MY SON. USE THEM WELL.
SOMEONE'S COMING!
END OF SIDE ONE:
turn over crystal and proceed at the sound of the tone.

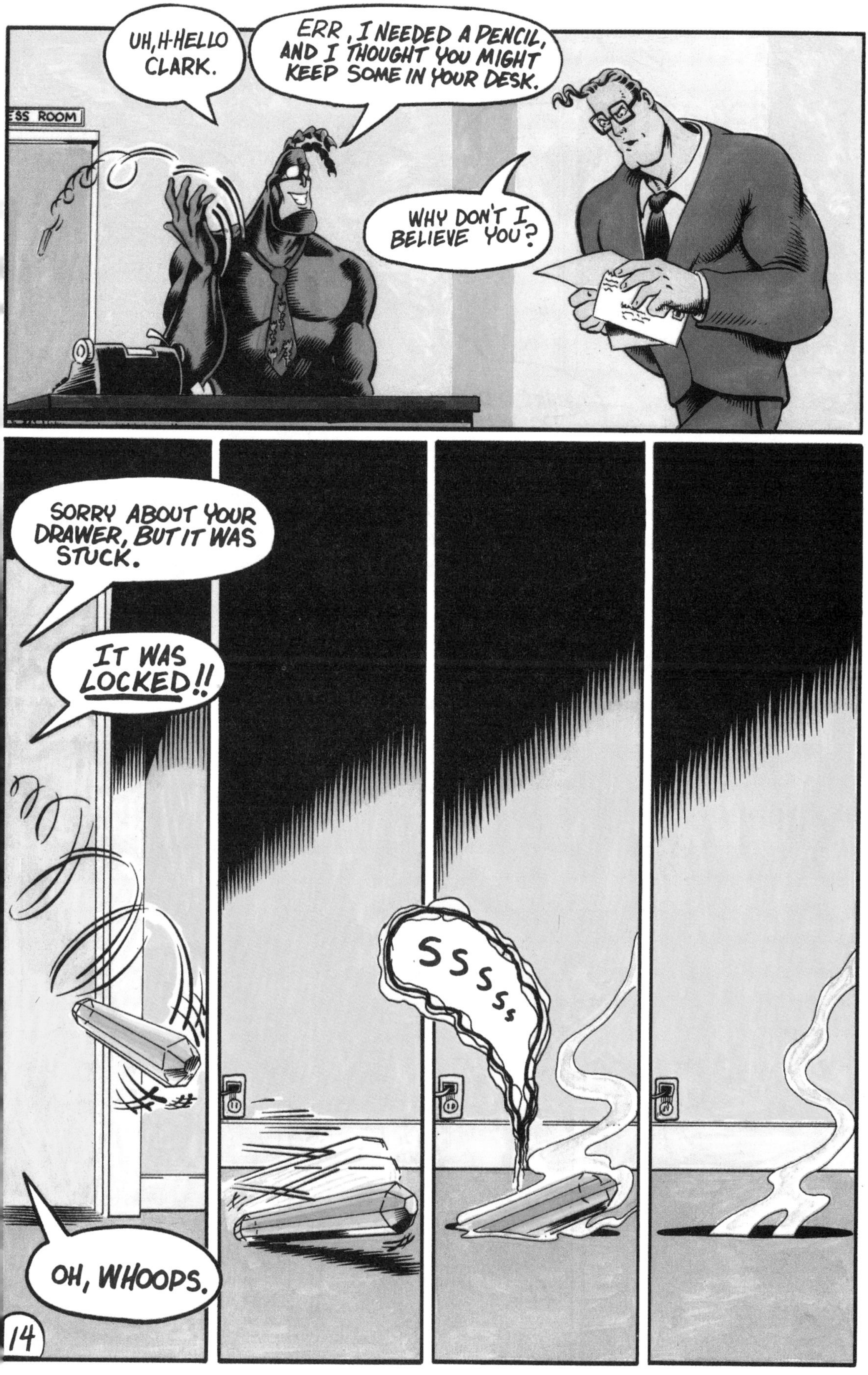

ESS ROOM
UH, H-HELLO CLARK.
ERR, I NEEDED A PENCIL, AND I THOUGHT YOU MIGHT KEEP SOME IN YOUR DESK.
WHY DON'T I BELIEVE YOU?
SORRY ABOUT YOUR DRAWER, BUT IT WAS STUCK.
IT WAS LOCKED!!
OH, WHOOPS.
SSSSS

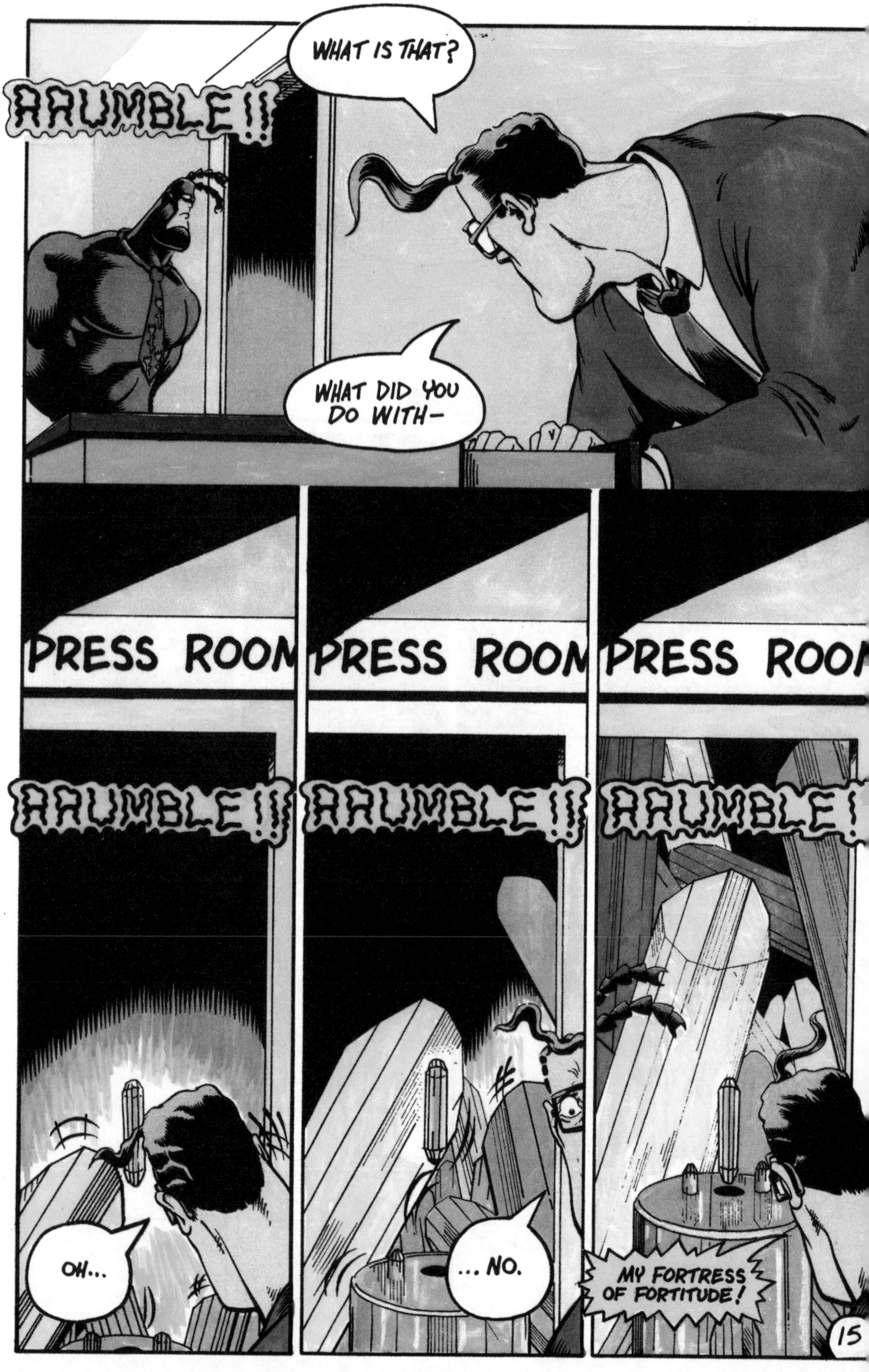

WHAT IS THAT?
RRUMBLE!!
WHAT DID YOU DO WITH-
PRESS ROOM
RRUMBLE!!
OH...
PRESS ROOM
RRUMBLE!!
... NO.
PRESS ROOM
RRUMBLE!
MY FORTRESS OF FORTITUDE!

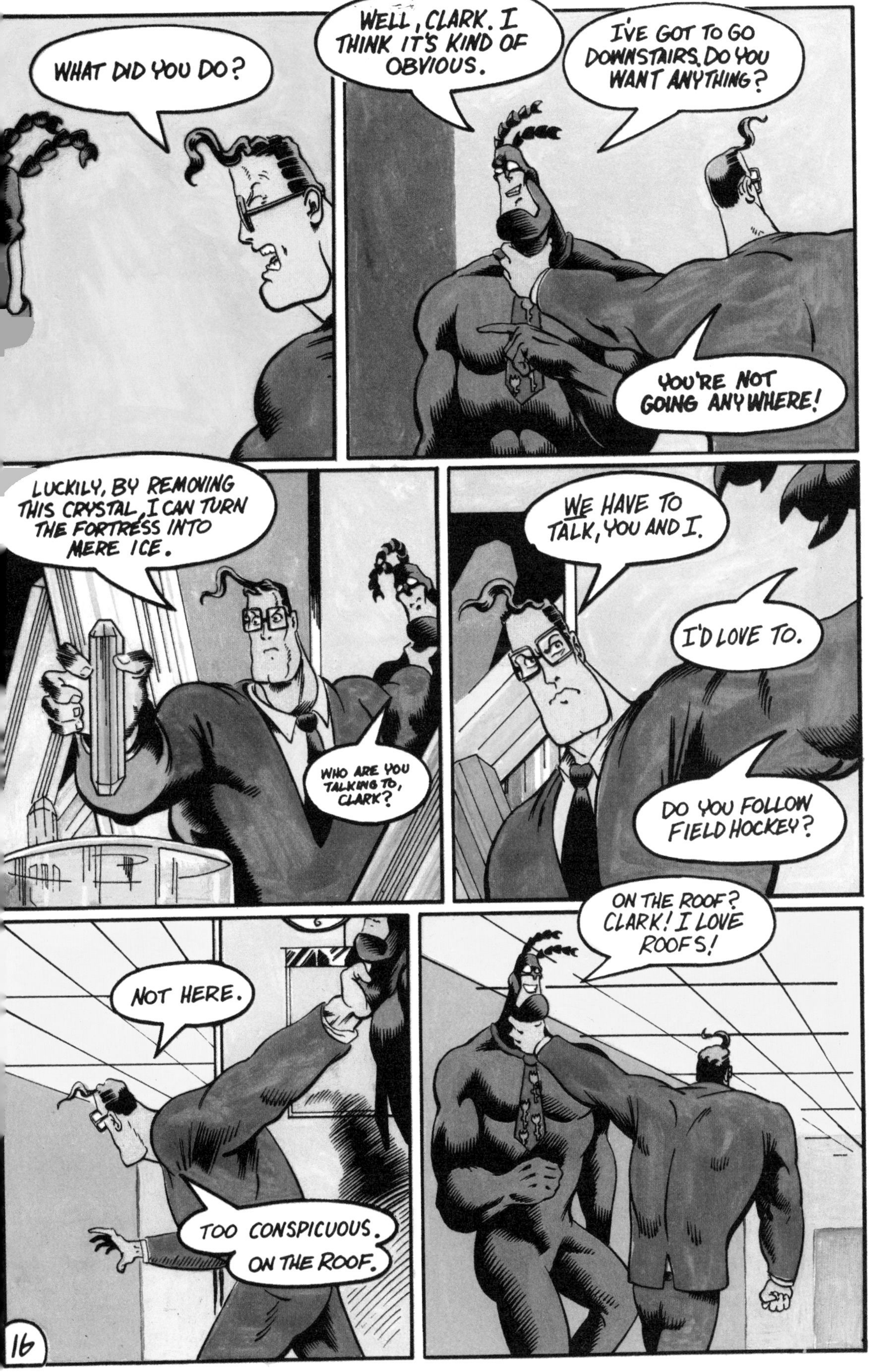
WHAT DID YOU DO?
WELL, CLARK. I THINK IT'S KIND OF OBVIOUS.
I'VE GOT TO GO DOWNSTAIRS. DO YOU WANT ANYTHING?
YOU'RE NOT GOING ANYWHERE!
LUCKILY, BY REMOVING THIS CRYSTAL, I CAN TURN THE FORTRESS INTO MERE ICE.
WHO ARE YOU TALKING TO, CLARK?
WE HAVE TO TALK, YOU AND I.
I'D LOVE TO.
DO YOU FOLLOW FIELD HOCKEY?
NOT HERE.
TOO CONSPICUOUS.
ON THE ROOF.
ON THE ROOF? CLARK! I LOVE ROOFS!

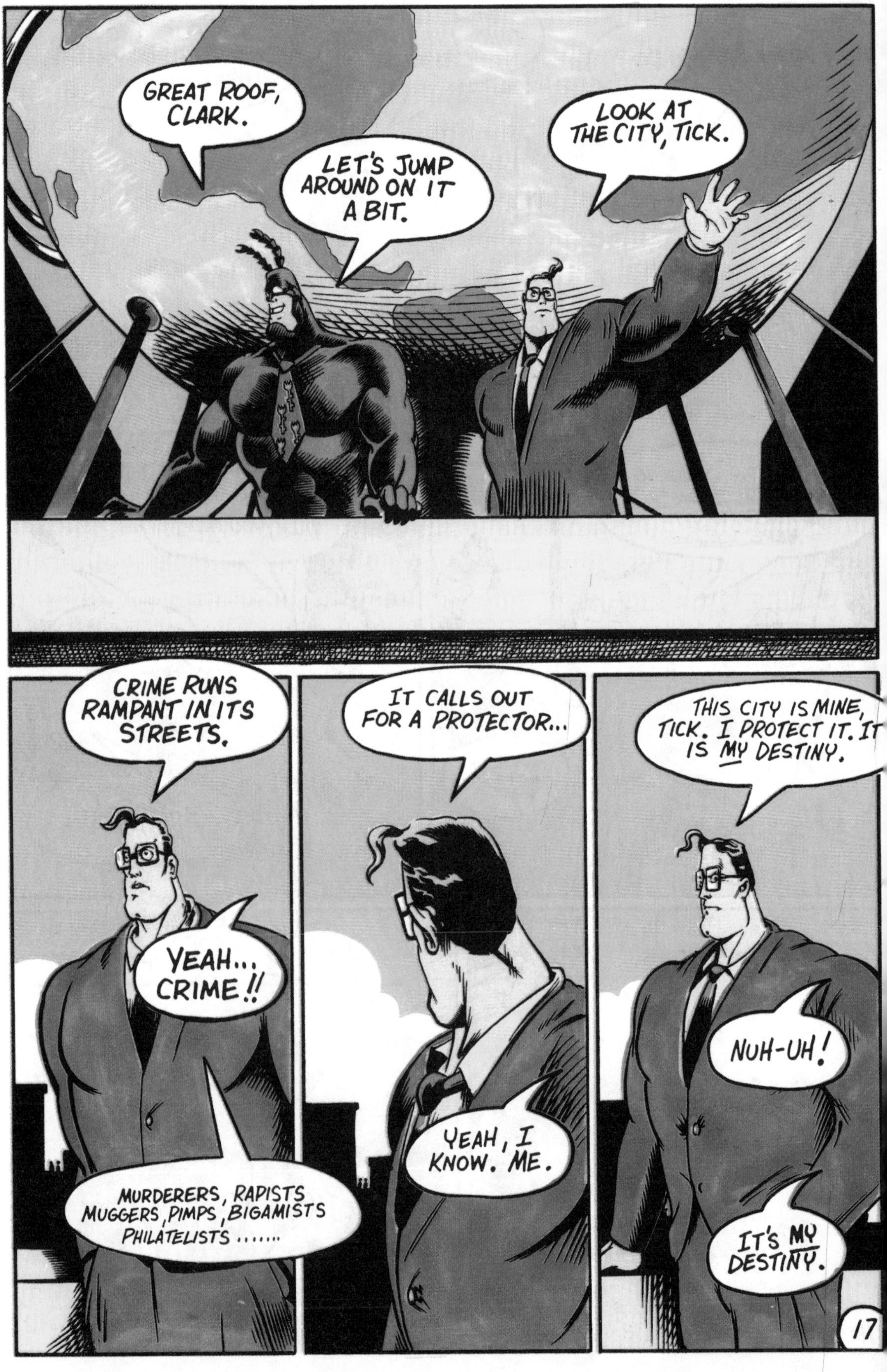
GREAT ROOF, CLARK.
LET'S JUMP AROUND ON IT A BIT.
LOOK AT THE CITY, TICK.
CRIME RUNS RAMPANT IN ITS STREETS.
YEAH... CRIME!!
MURDERERS, RAPISTS MUGGERS, PIMPS, BIGAMISTS PHILATELISTS ....
IT CALLS OUT FOR A PROTECTOR...
YEAH, I KNOW. ME.
THIS CITY IS MINE, TICK. I PROTECT IT. IT IS MY DESTINY.
NUH-UH!
IT'S MY DESTINY.

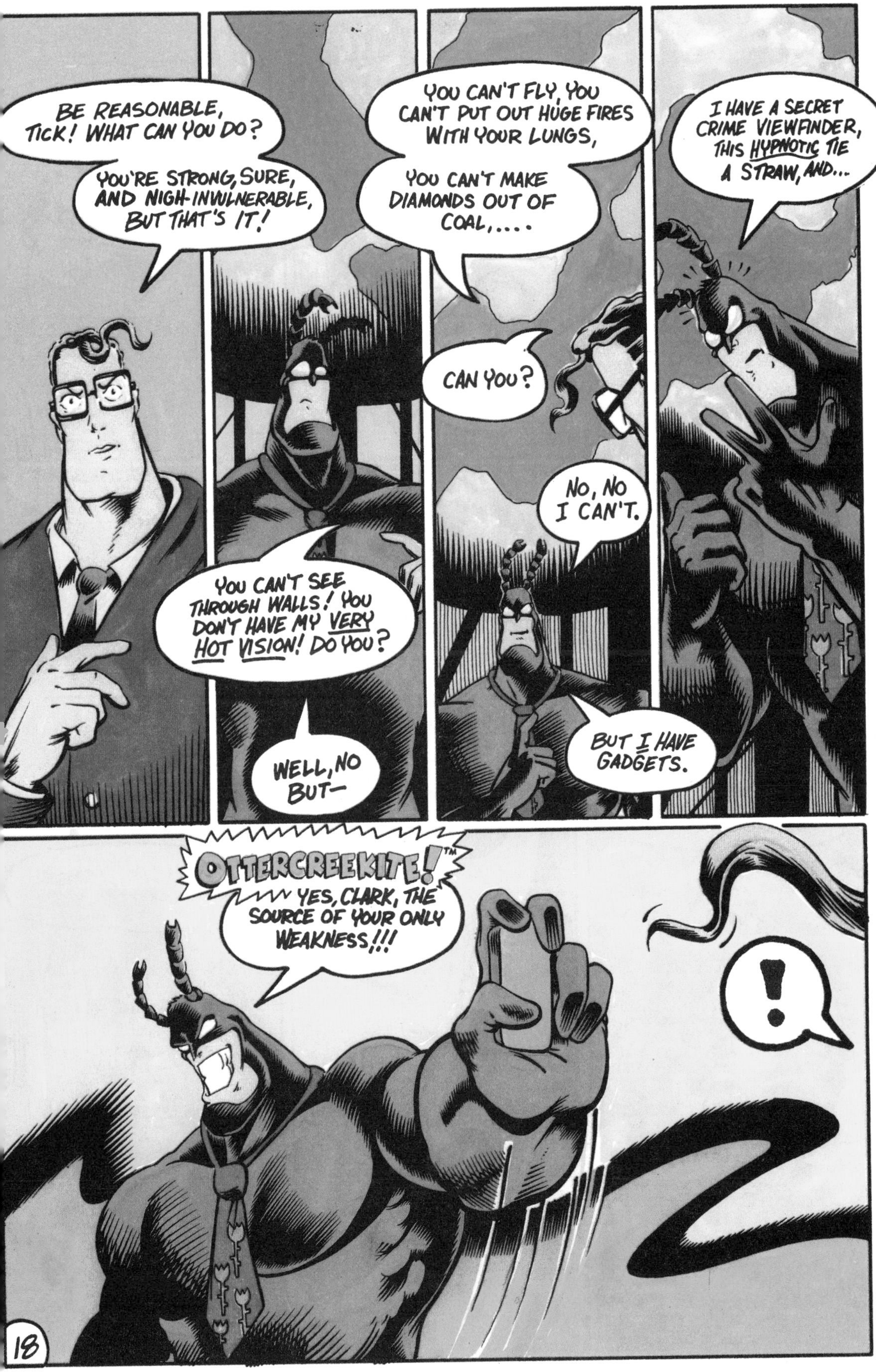

BE REASONABLE, TICK! WHAT CAN YOU DO?
YOU'RE STRONG, SURE, AND NIGH-INVULNERABLE, BUT THAT'S IT!
YOU CAN'T SEE THROUGH WALLS! YOU DON'T HAVE MY VERY HOT VISION! DO YOU?
WELL, NO BUT–
YOU CAN'T FLY, YOU CAN'T PUT OUT HUGE FIRES WITH YOUR LUNGS,
YOU CAN'T MAKE DIAMONDS OUT OF COAL,....
CAN YOU?
NO, NO I CAN'T.
BUT I HAVE GADGETS.
I HAVE A SECRET CRIME VIEWFINDER, THIS HYPNOTIC TIE A STRAW, AND...
OTTERCREEKITE!™
YES, CLARK, THE SOURCE OF YOUR ONLY WEAKNESS!!!
!

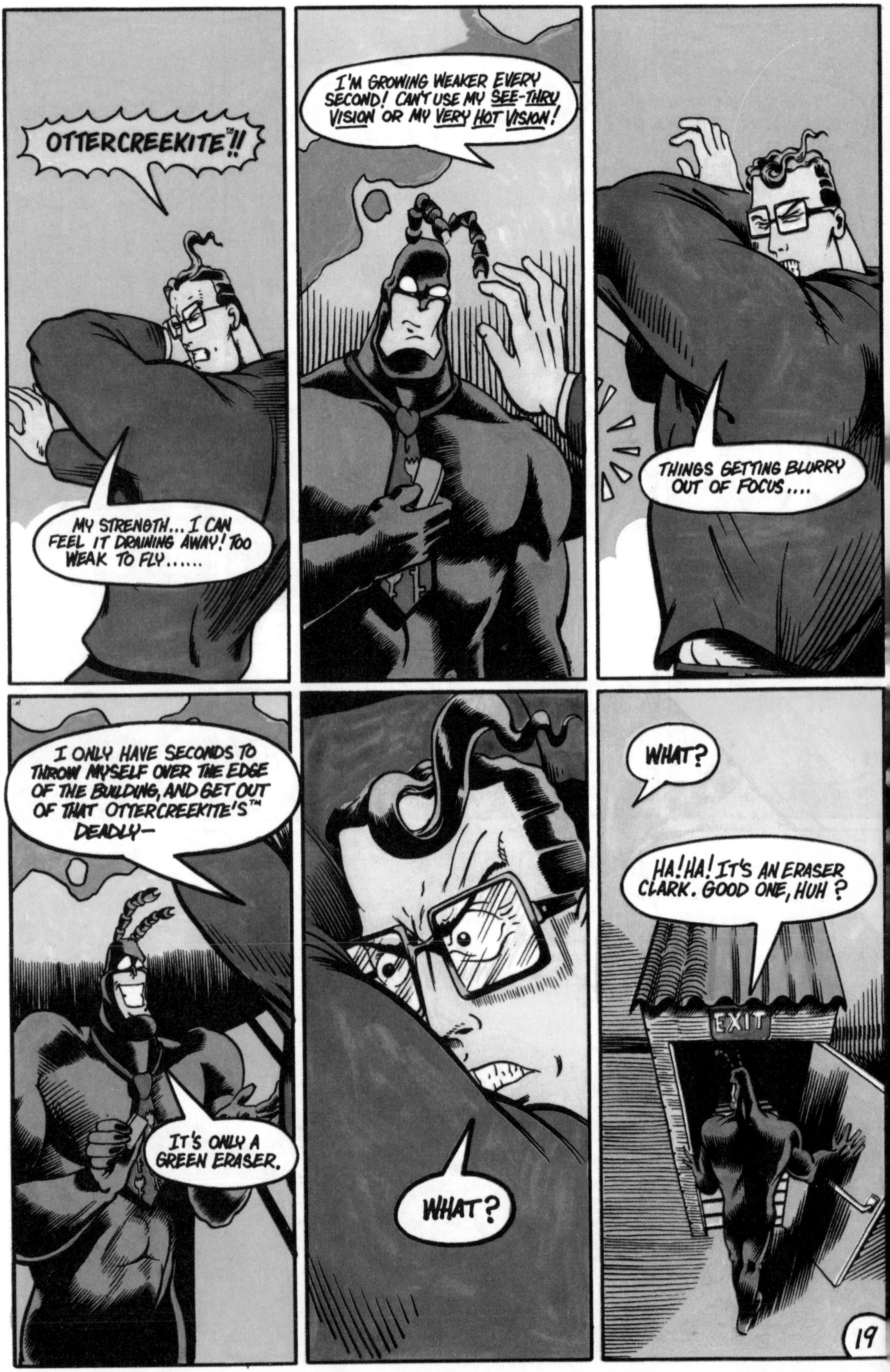
OTTERCREEKITE™!!
MY STRENGTH... I CAN FEEL IT DRAINING AWAY! TOO WEAK TO FLY......
I'M GROWING WEAKER EVERY SECOND! CAN'T USE MY SEE-THRU VISION OR MY VERY HOT VISION!
THINGS GETTING BLURRY OUT OF FOCUS....
I ONLY HAVE SECONDS TO THROW MYSELF OVER THE EDGE OF THE BUILDING, AND GET OUT OF THAT OTTERCREEKITE'S™ DEADLY—
IT'S ONLY A GREEN ERASER.
WHAT?
WHAT?
HA! HA! IT'S AN ERASER CLARK. GOOD ONE, HUH?
EXIT

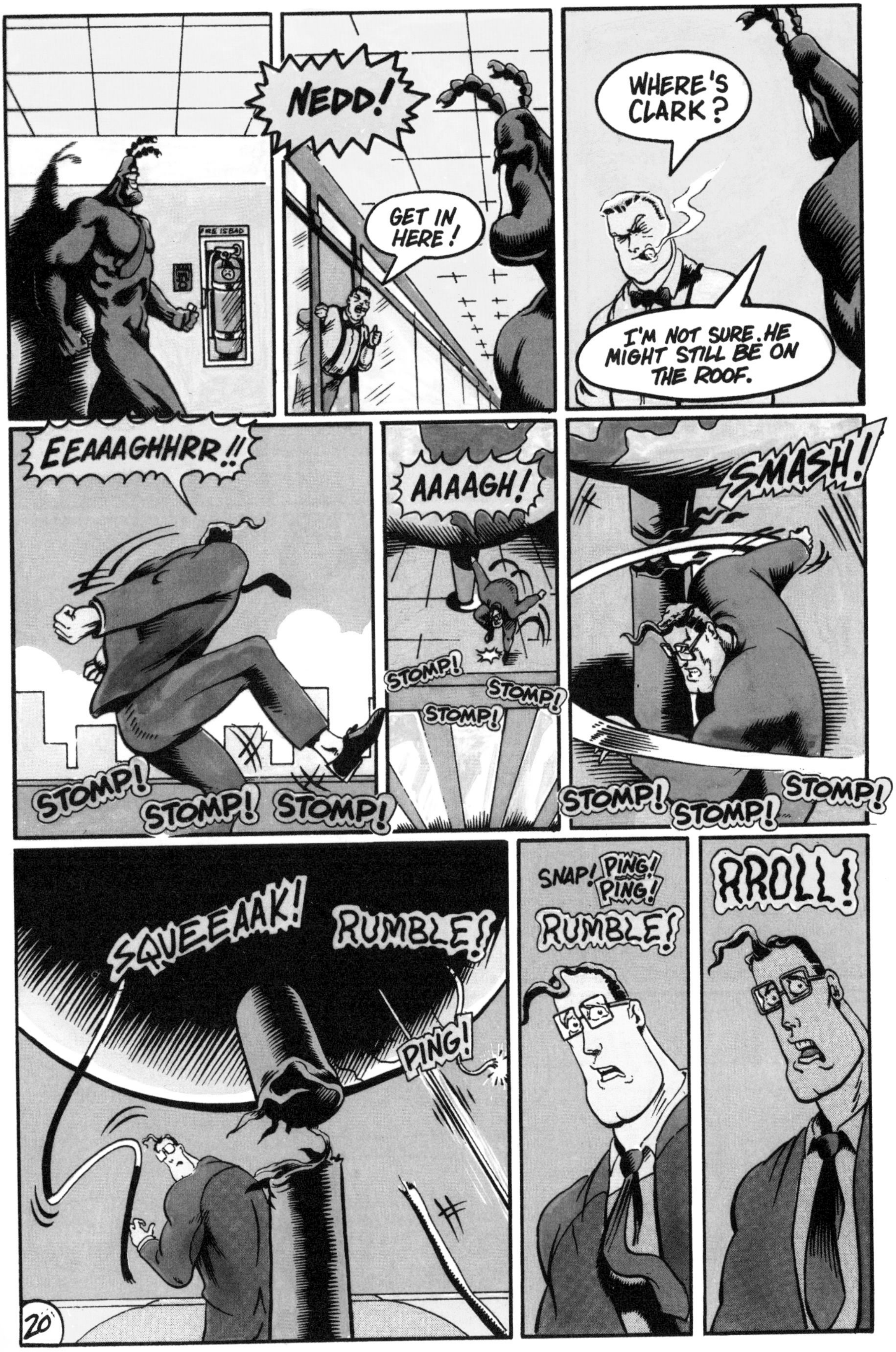
NEDD!
GET IN HERE!
WHERE'S CLARK?
I'M NOT SURE. HE MIGHT STILL BE ON THE ROOF.
EEAAAGHHRR!!
STOMP! STOMP! STOMP!
AAAAGH!
STOMP! STOMP! STOMP!
SMASH!
STOMP! STOMP! STOMP!
SQUEEEAAK! RUMBLE!
PING!
SNAP! PING! PING!
RUMBLE!
RROLL!

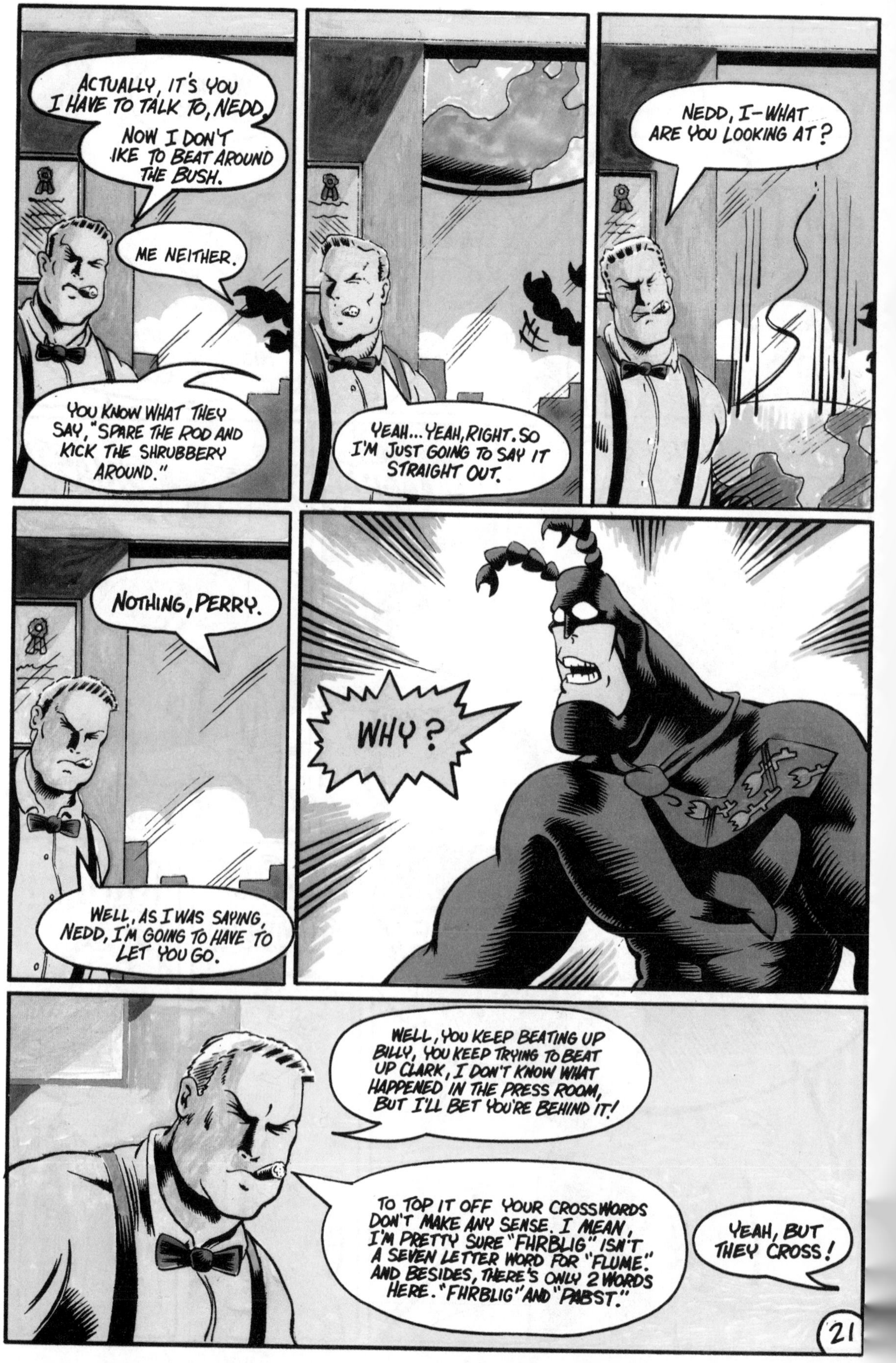

ACTUALLY, IT'S YOU I HAVE TO TALK TO, NEDD.
NOW I DON'T IKE TO BEAT AROUND THE BUSH.
ME NEITHER.
YOU KNOW WHAT THEY SAY, "SPARE THE ROD AND KICK THE SHRUBBERY AROUND."
YEAH... YEAH, RIGHT. SO I'M JUST GOING TO SAY IT STRAIGHT OUT.
NEDD, I—WHAT ARE YOU LOOKING AT?
NOTHING, PERRY.
WELL, AS I WAS SAYING, NEDD, I'M GOING TO HAVE TO LET YOU GO.
WHY?
WELL, YOU KEEP BEATING UP BILLY, YOU KEEP TRYING TO BEAT UP CLARK, I DON'T KNOW WHAT HAPPENED IN THE PRESS ROOM, BUT I'LL BET YOU'RE BEHIND IT!
TO TOP IT OFF YOUR CROSSWORDS DON'T MAKE ANY SENSE. I MEAN, I'M PRETTY SURE "FHRBLIG" ISN'T A SEVEN LETTER WORD FOR "FLUME." AND BESIDES, THERE'S ONLY 2 WORDS HERE. "FHRBLIG" AND "PABST."
YEAH, BUT THEY CROSS!

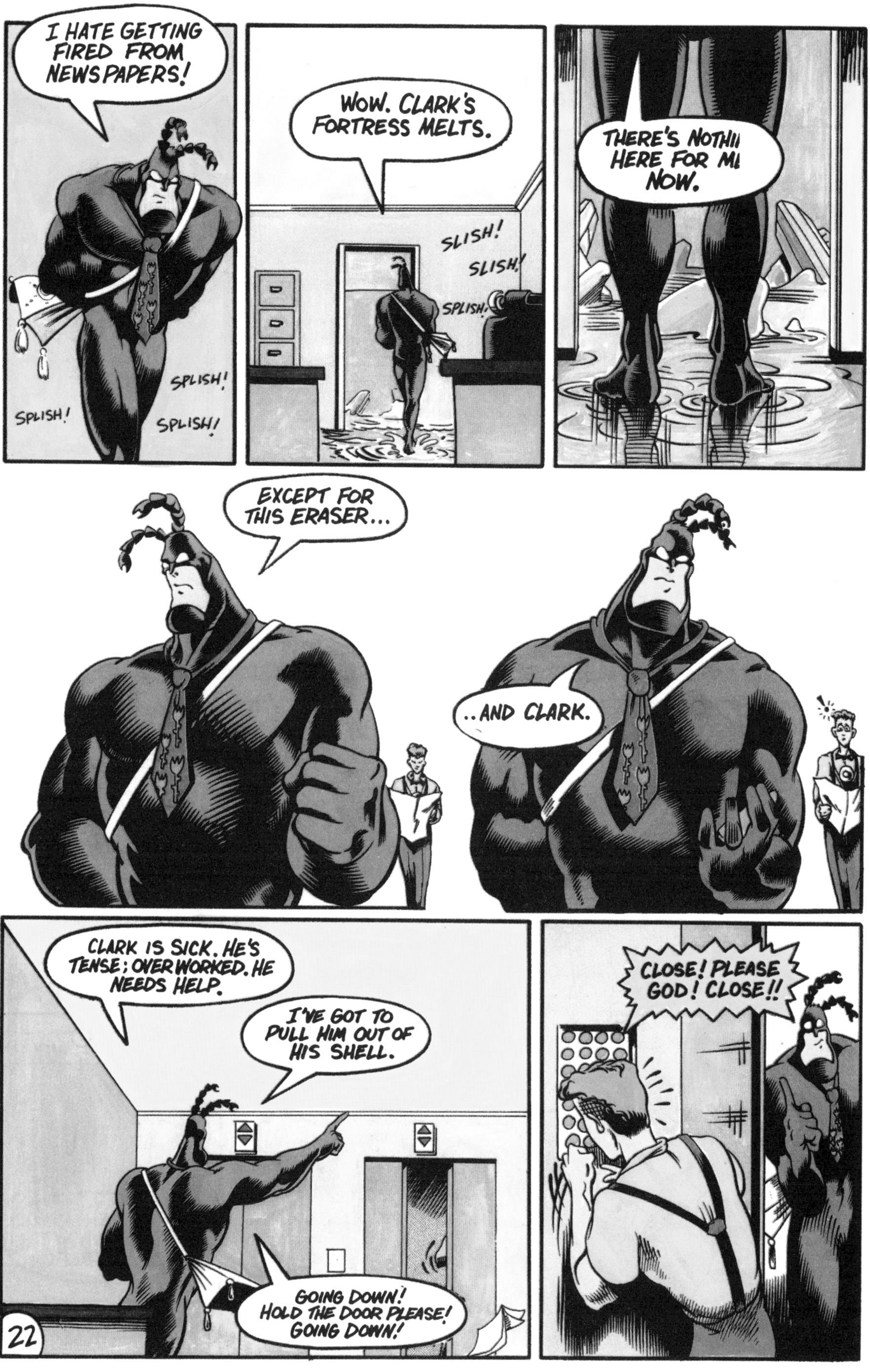
I HATE GETTING FIRED FROM NEWSPAPERS!
SPLISH!
SPLISH!
SPLISH!
WOW. CLARK'S FORTRESS MELTS.
SLISH!
SLISH!
SPLISH!
THERE'S NOTHI HERE FOR M NOW.
EXCEPT FOR THIS ERASER...
..AND CLARK.
CLARK IS SICK. HE'S TENSE; OVERWORKED. HE NEEDS HELP.
I'VE GOT TO PULL HIM OUT OF HIS SHELL.
GOING DOWN! HOLD THE DOOR PLEASE! GOING DOWN!
CLOSE! PLEASE GOD! CLOSE!!

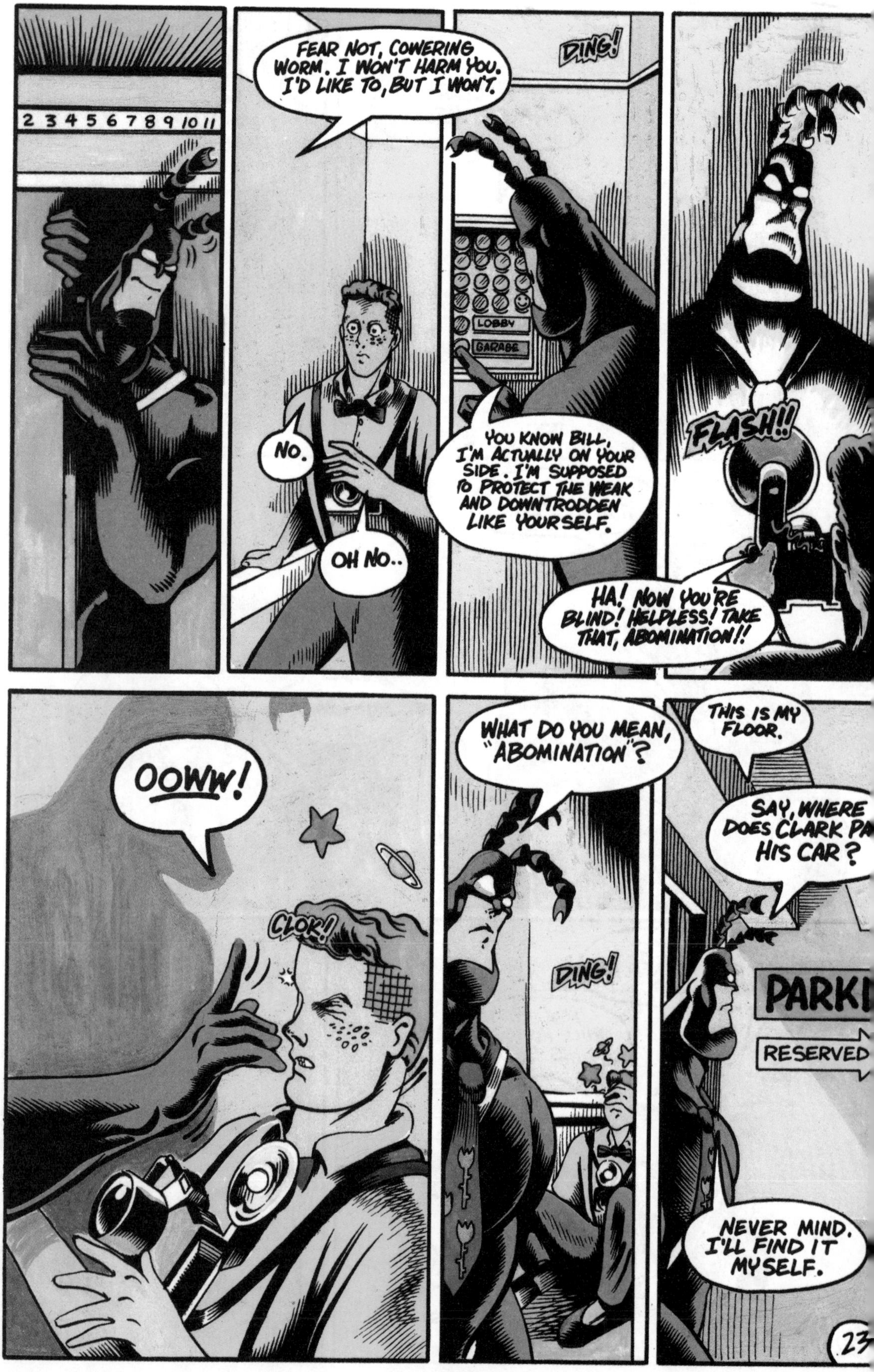
2 3 4 5 6 7 8 9 10 11
FEAR NOT, COWERING WORM. I WON'T HARM YOU. I'D LIKE TO, BUT I WON'T.
NO.
OH NO..
DING!
LOBBY
GARAGE
YOU KNOW BILL, I'M ACTUALLY ON YOUR SIDE. I'M SUPPOSED TO PROTECT THE WEAK AND DOWNTRODDEN LIKE YOURSELF.
FLASH!!
HA! NOW YOU'RE BLIND! HELPLESS! TAKE THAT, ABOMINATION!!
OOWW!
CLOK!
WHAT DO YOU MEAN, "ABOMINATION"?
DING!
THIS IS MY FLOOR.
SAY, WHERE DOES CLARK PA
HIS CAR?
PARKI
RESERVED
NEVER MIND. I'LL FIND IT MYSELF.

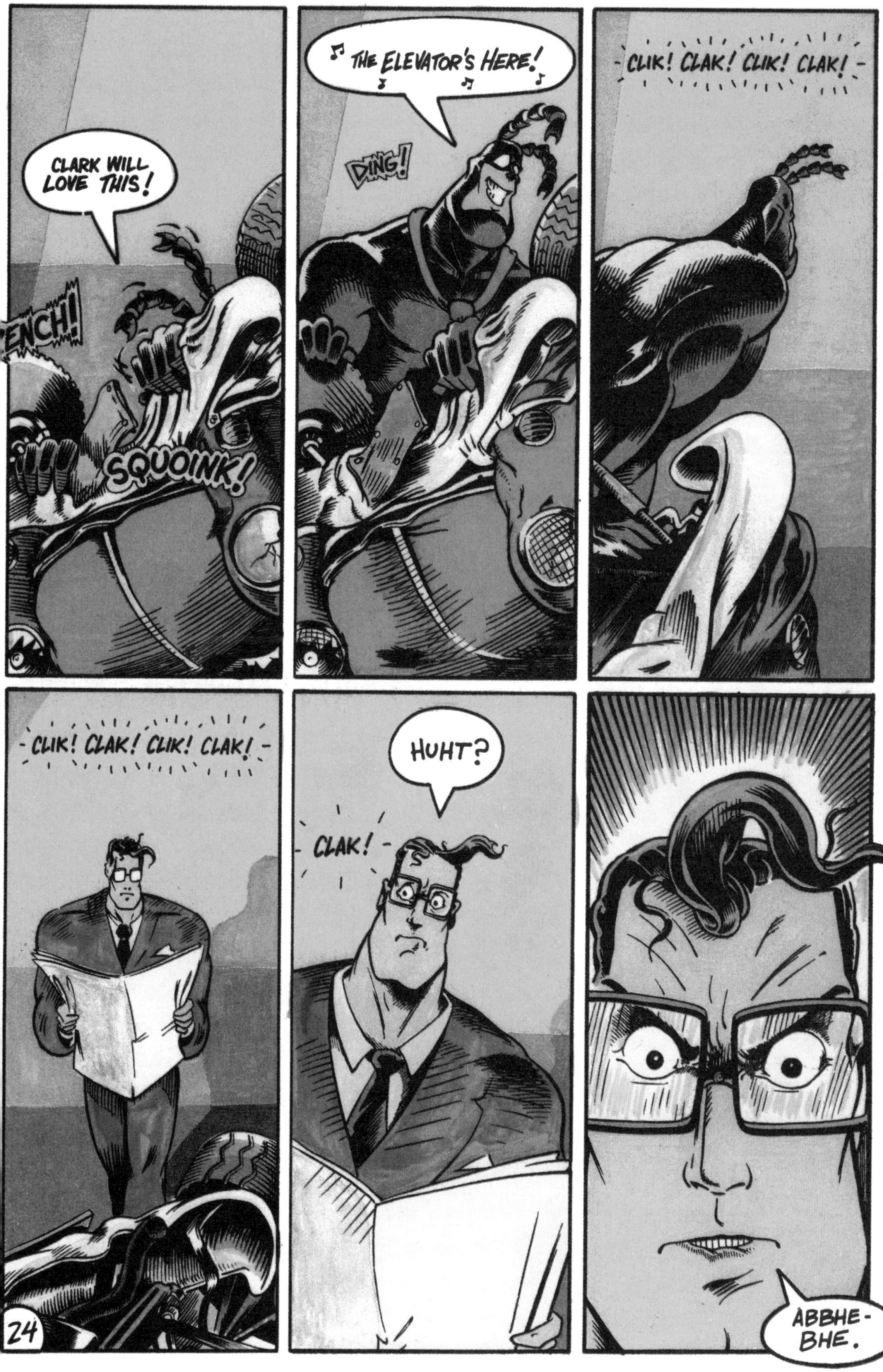
CLARK WILL LOVE THIS!
ENCH!
SQUOINK!
THE ELEVATOR'S HERE!
DING!
CLIK! CLAK! CLIK! CLAK!
CLIK! CLAK! CLIK! CLAK!
HUHT?
CLAK!
ABBHE-BHE.

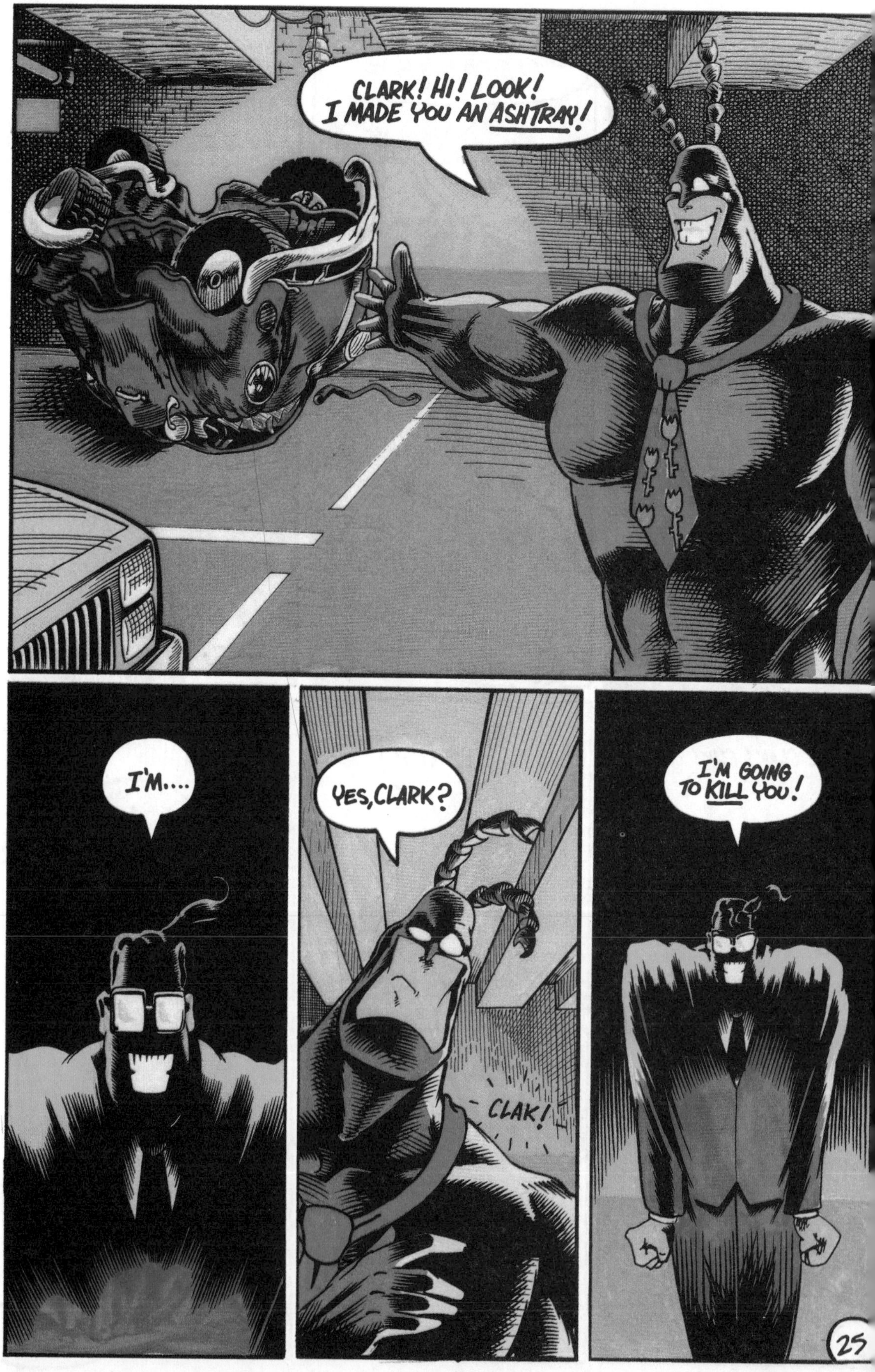
CLARK! HI! LOOK! I MADE YOU AN ASHTRAY!
I'M....
YES, CLARK?
CLAK!
I'M GOING TO KILL YOU!
25

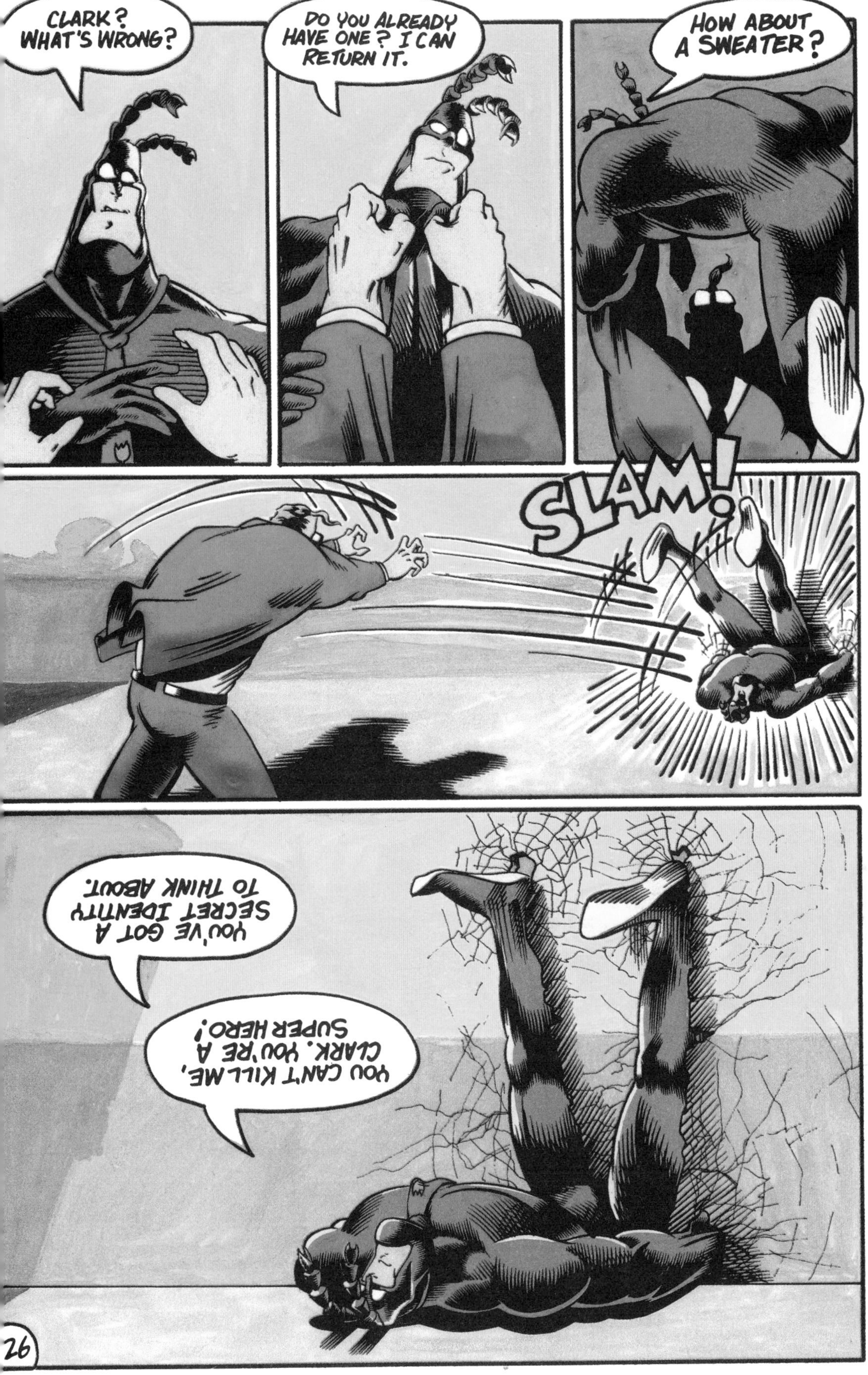
CLARK? WHAT'S WRONG?
DO YOU ALREADY HAVE ONE? I CAN RETURN IT.
HOW ABOUT A SWEATER?
SLAM!
YOU CAN'T KILL ME, CLARK. YOU'RE A SUPER HERO!
YOU'VE GOT A SECRET IDENTITY TO THINK ABOUT.

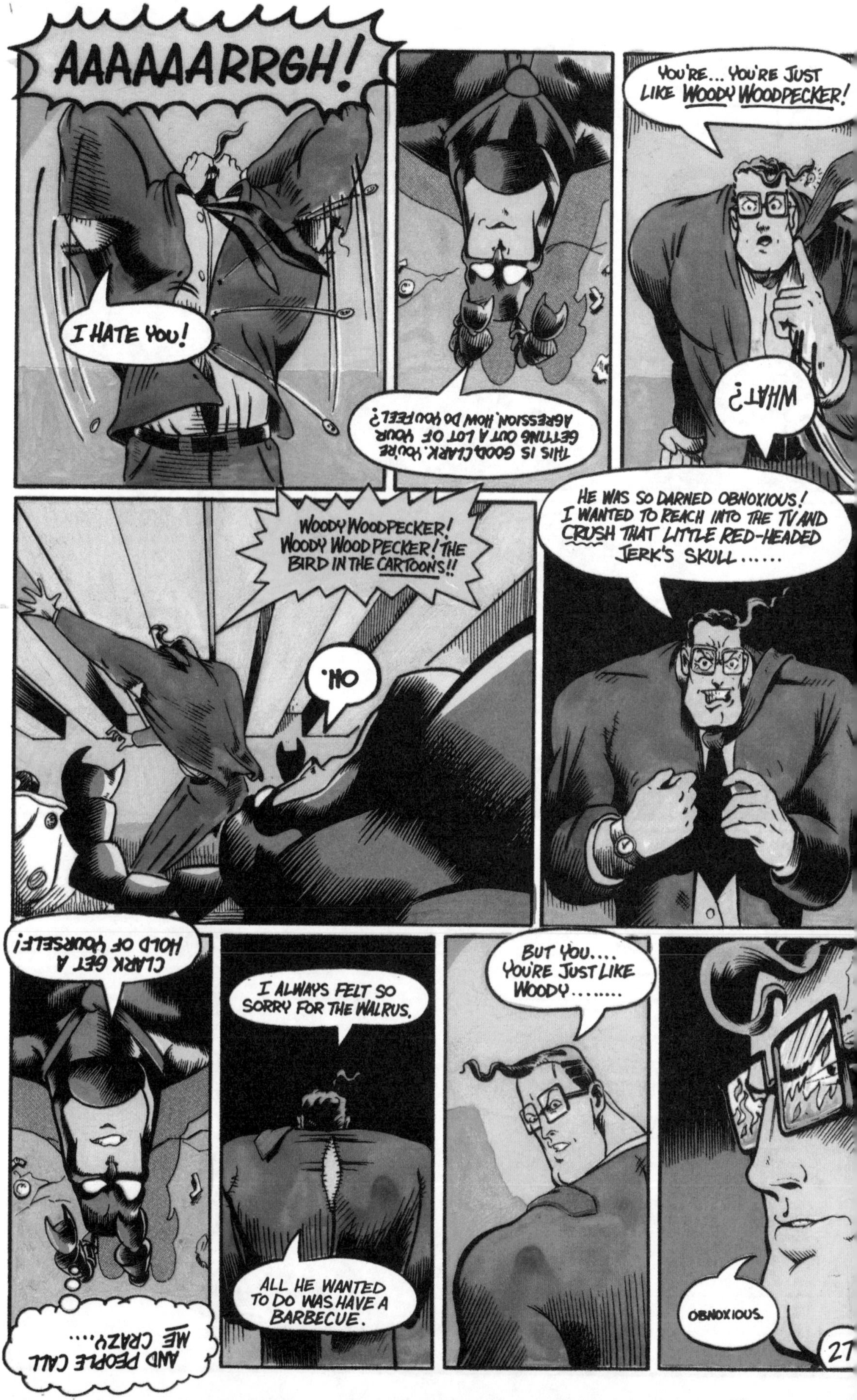
AAAAAARRGH!
I HATE YOU!
THIS IS GOOD, CLARK. YOU'RE GETTING OUT A LOT OF YOUR AGRESSION. HOW DO YOU FEEL?
YOU'RE... YOU'RE JUST LIKE WOODY WOODPECKER!
WHAT?
WOODY WOODPECKER! WOODY WOODPECKER! THE BIRD IN THE CARTOONS!!
OH.
HE WAS SO DARNED OBNOXIOUS! I WANTED TO REACH INTO THE TV AND CRUSH THAT LITTLE RED-HEADED JERK'S SKULL......
CLARK GET A HOLD OF YOURSELF!
AND PEOPLE CALL ME CRAZY....
I ALWAYS FELT SO SORRY FOR THE WALRUS.
ALL HE WANTED TO DO WAS HAVE A BARBECUE.
BUT YOU.... YOU'RE JUST LIKE WOODY........
OBNOXIOUS.

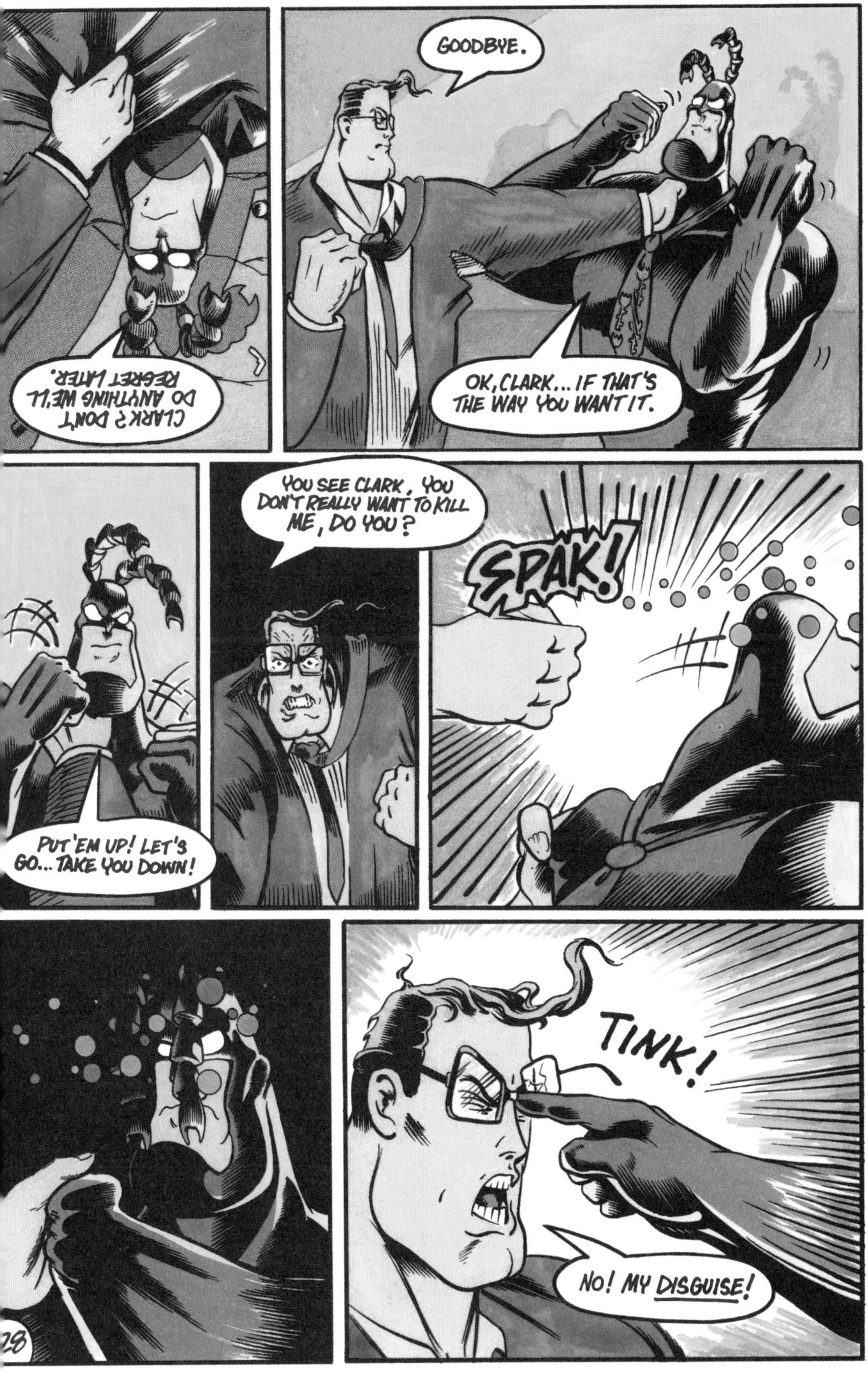

CLARK? DON'T DO ANYTHING WE'LL REGRET LATER.
GOODBYE.
OK, CLARK... IF THAT'S THE WAY YOU WANT IT.
PUT 'EM UP! LET'S GO... TAKE YOU DOWN!
YOU SEE CLARK, YOU DON'T REALLY WANT TO KILL ME, DO YOU?
SPAK!
TINK!
NO! MY DISGUISE!

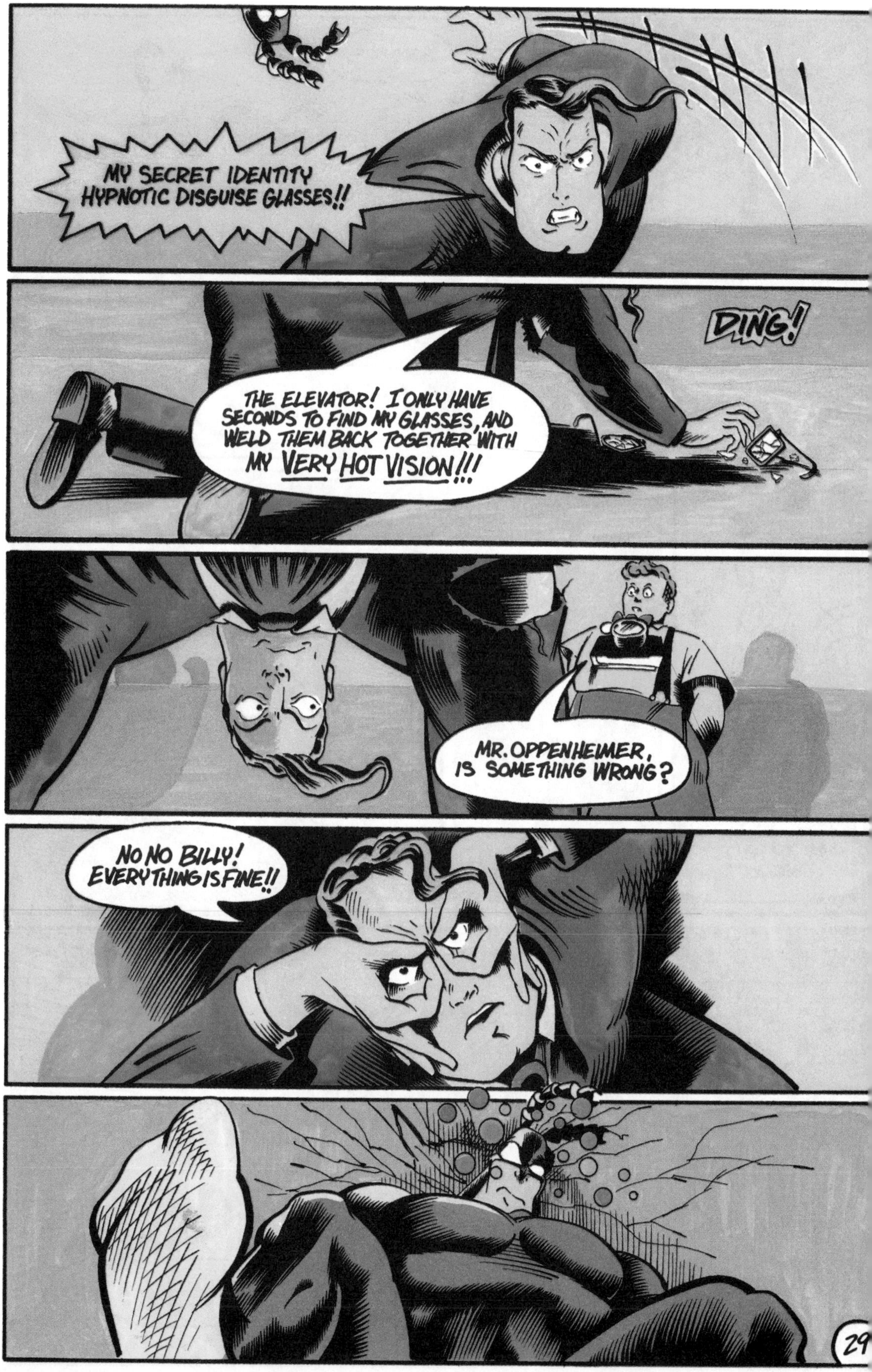
MY SECRET IDENTITY HYPNOTIC DISGUISE GLASSES!!
DING!
THE ELEVATOR! I ONLY HAVE SECONDS TO FIND MY GLASSES, AND WELD THEM BACK TOGETHER WITH MY VERY HOT VISION!!!
MR. OPPENHEIMER, IS SOMETHING WRONG?
NO NO BILLY! EVERYTHING IS FINE!!

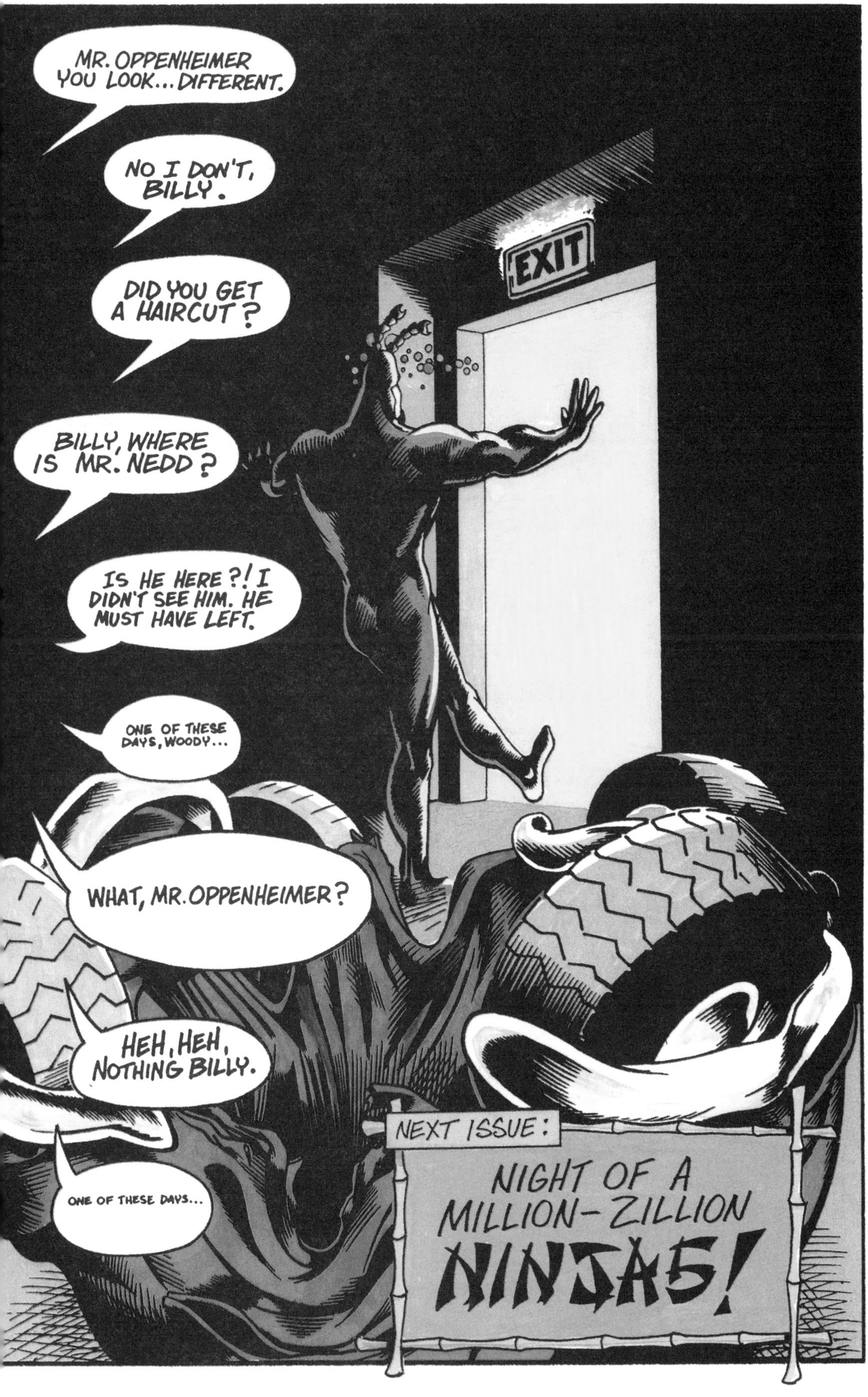
MR. OPPENHEIMER YOU LOOK... DIFFERENT.
NO I DON'T, BILLY.
DID YOU GET A HAIRCUT?
BILLY, WHERE IS MR. NEDD?
IS HE HERE?! I DIDN'T SEE HIM. HE MUST HAVE LEFT.
EXIT
ONE OF THESE DAYS, WOODY...
WHAT, MR. OPPENHEIMER?
HEH, HEH, NOTHING BILLY.
ONE OF THESE DAYS...
NEXT ISSUE:
NIGHT OF A MILLION-ZILLION NINJAS!

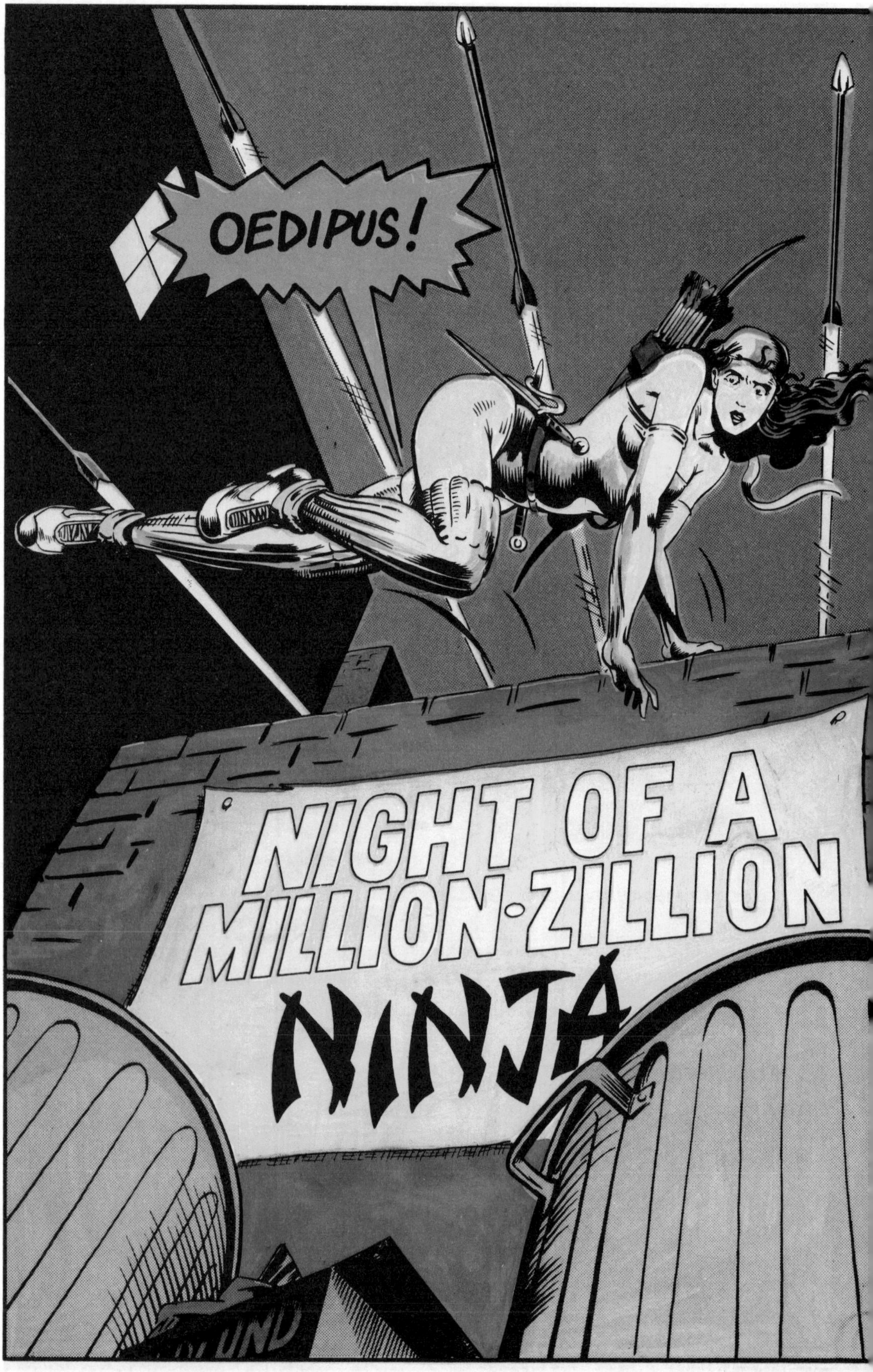
OEDIPUS!
NIGHT OF A MILLION-ZILLION NINJA

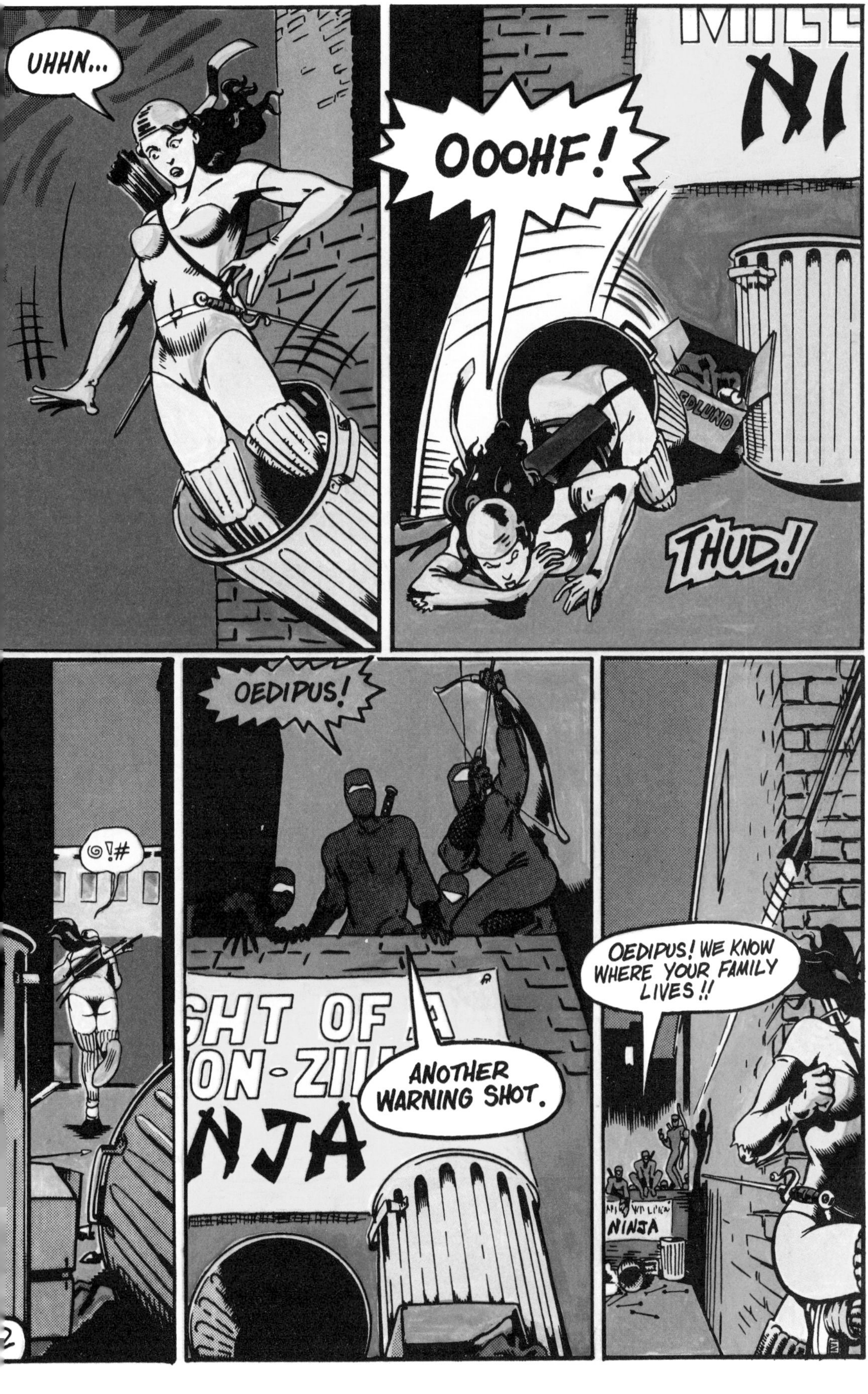
UHHN...
OOOHF!
EDLUND
THUD!
@!#
OEDIPUS!
ANOTHER WARNING SHOT.
OEDIPUS! WE KNOW WHERE YOUR FAMILY LIVES!!
NINJA

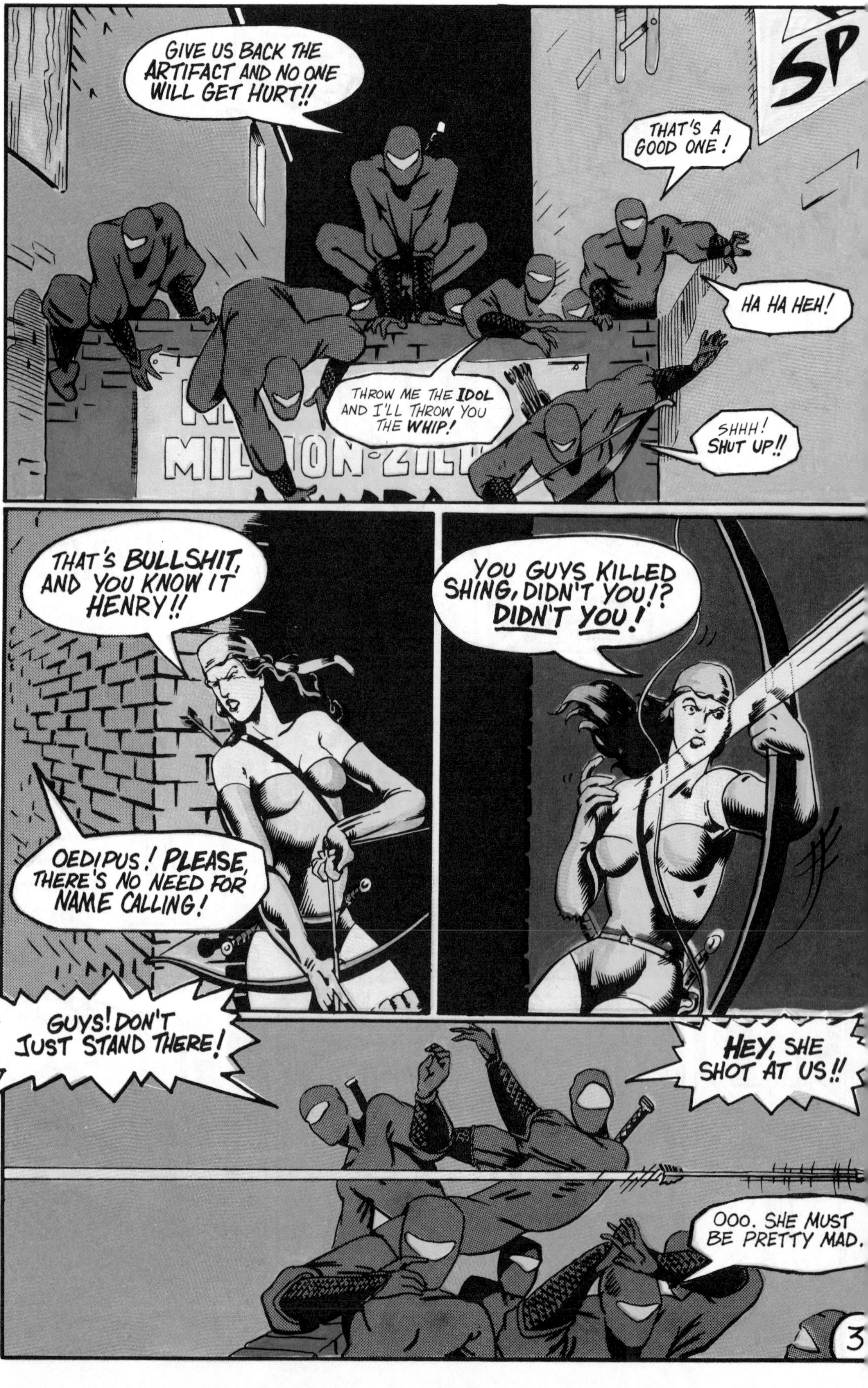
SP
GIVE US BACK THE ARTIFACT AND NO ONE WILL GET HURT!!
THAT'S A GOOD ONE!
HA HA HEH!
THROW ME THE IDOL AND I'LL THROW YOU THE WHIP!
SHHH! SHUT UP!!
THAT'S BULLSHIT, AND YOU KNOW IT HENRY!!
OEDIPUS! PLEASE, THERE'S NO NEED FOR NAME CALLING!
YOU GUYS KILLED SHING, DIDN'T YOU!? DIDN'T YOU!
GUYS! DON'T JUST STAND THERE!
HEY, SHE SHOT AT US!!
OOO. SHE MUST BE PRETTY MAD.

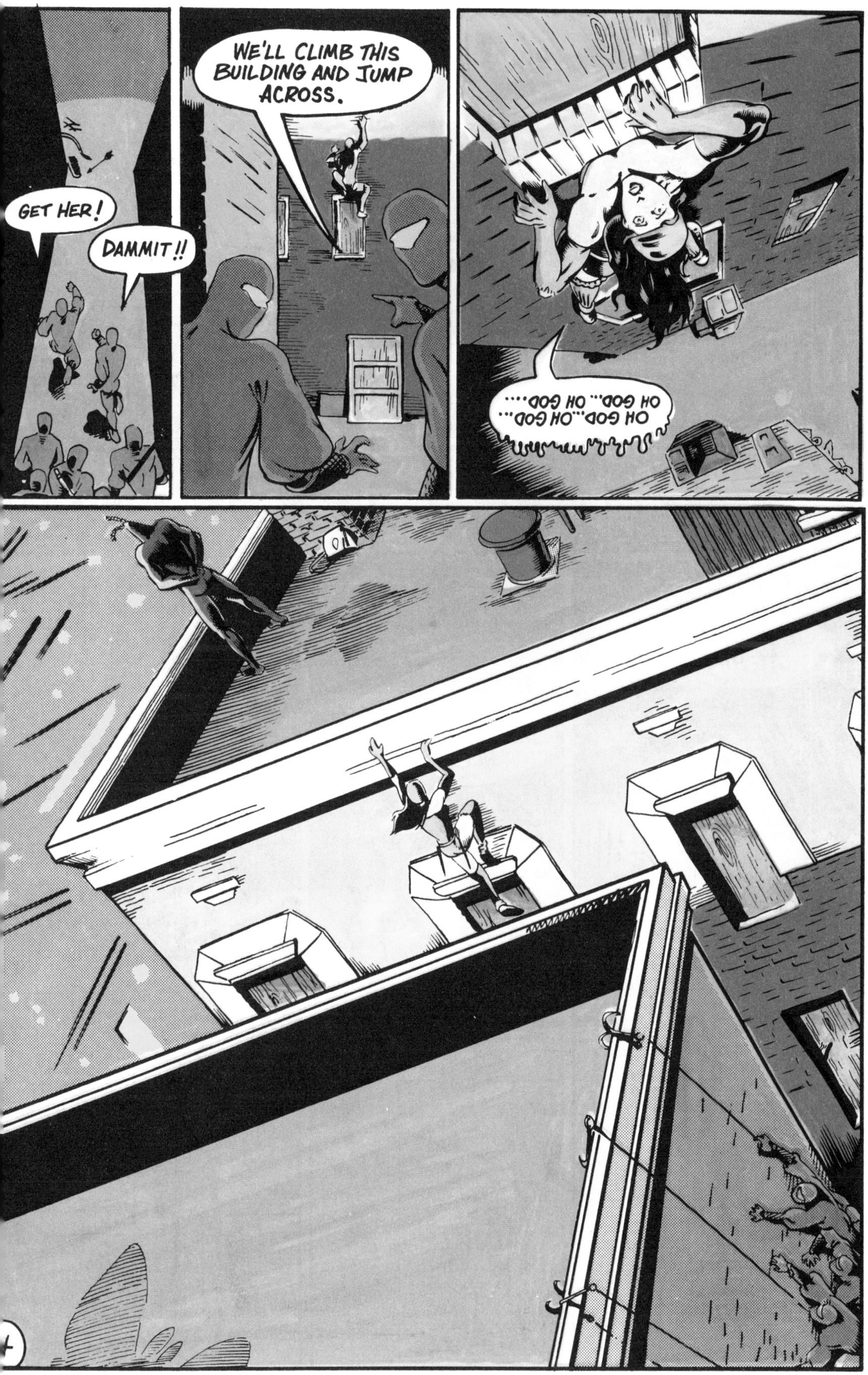
GET HER!
DAMMIT!!
WE'LL CLIMB THIS BUILDING AND JUMP ACROSS.
OH GOD...OH GOD...
OH GOD... OH GOD....

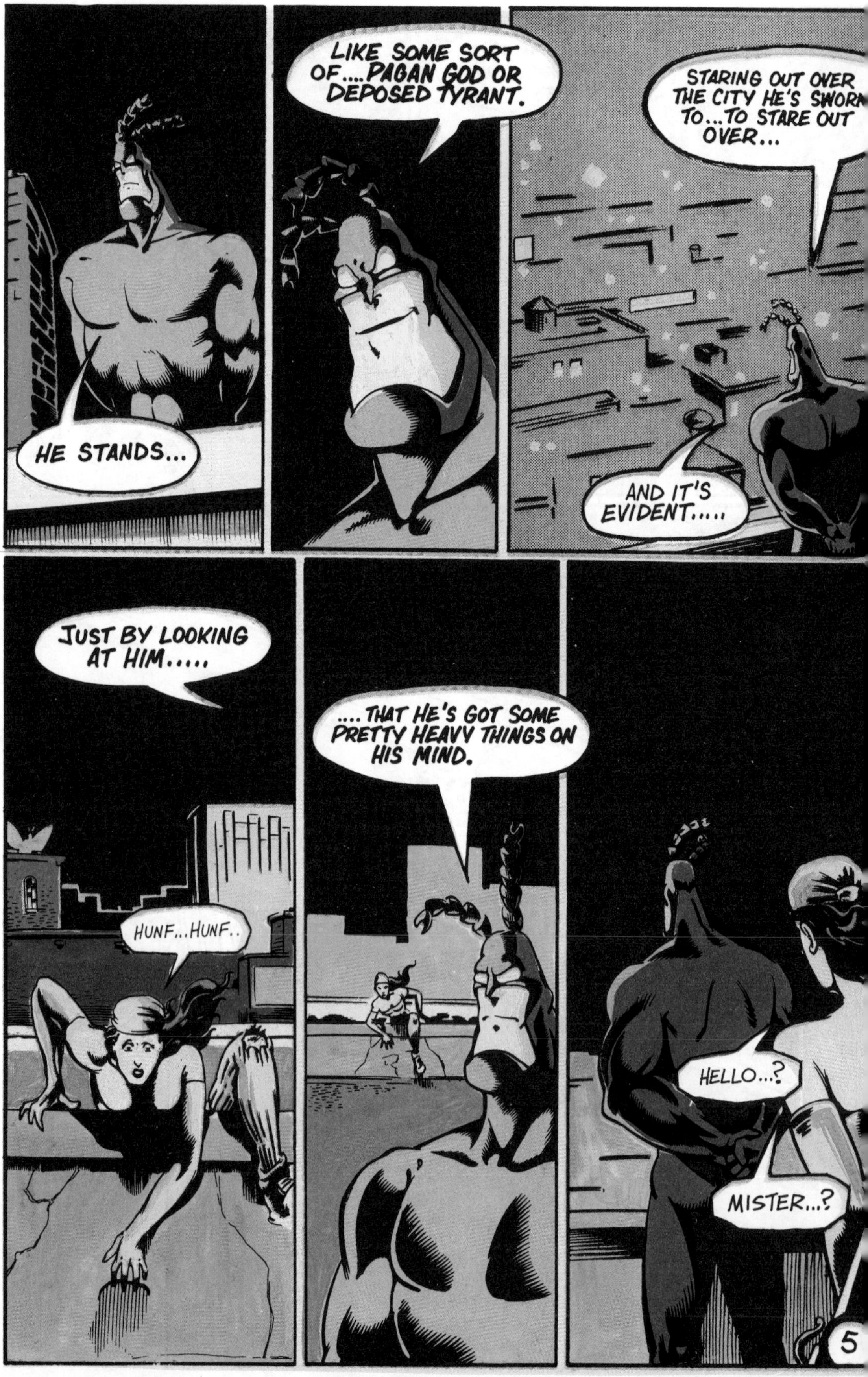

HE STANDS...
LIKE SOME SORT OF....PAGAN GOD OR DEPOSED TYRANT.
STARING OUT OVER THE CITY HE'S SWORN TO...TO STARE OUT OVER...
AND IT'S EVIDENT.....
JUST BY LOOKING AT HIM.....
HUNF...HUNF..
....THAT HE'S GOT SOME PRETTY HEAVY THINGS ON HIS MIND.
HELLO...?
MISTER...?

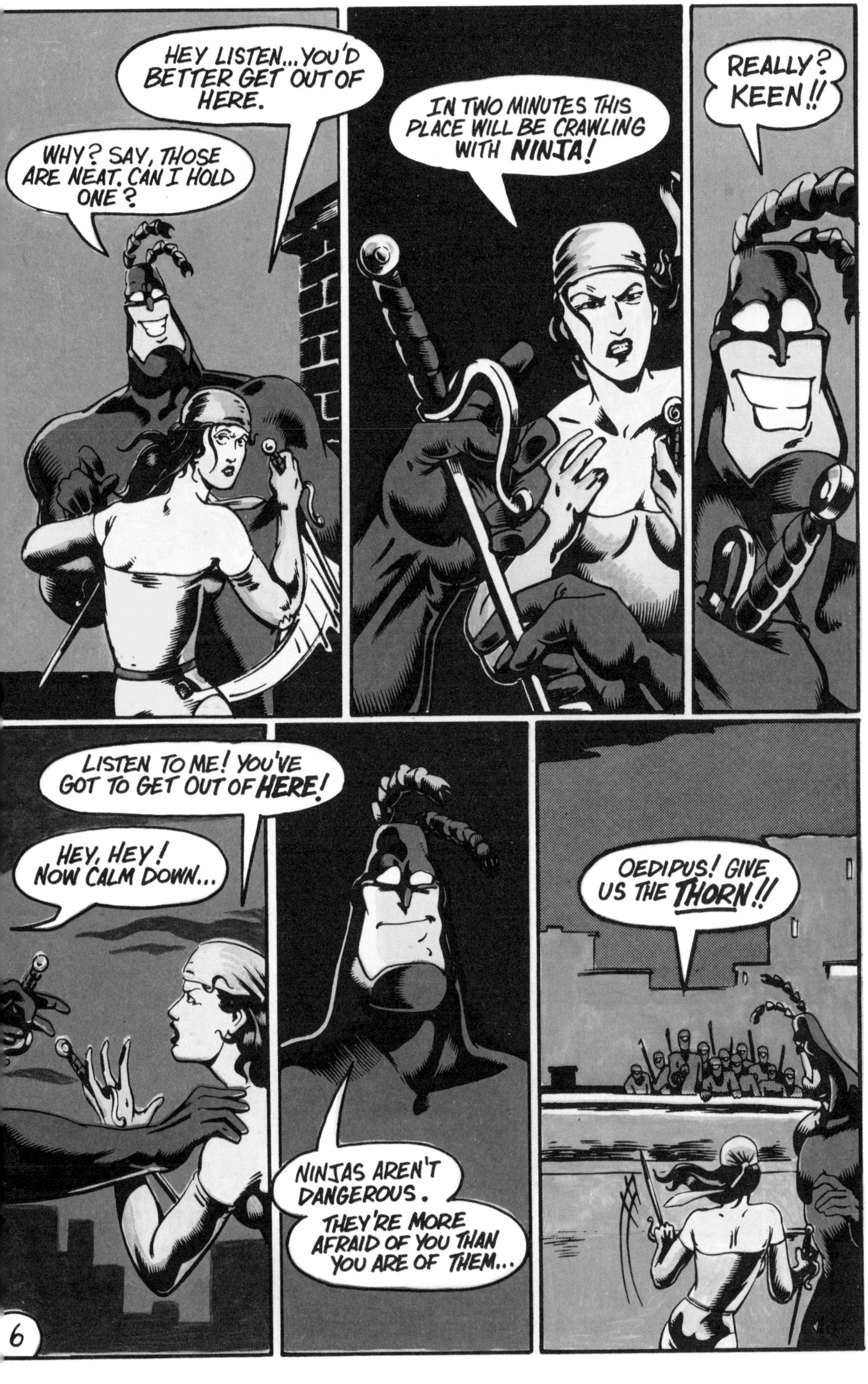
HEY LISTEN...YOU'D BETTER GET OUT OF HERE.
WHY? SAY, THOSE ARE NEAT. CAN I HOLD ONE?
IN TWO MINUTES THIS PLACE WILL BE CRAWLING WITH NINJA!
REALLY? KEEN!!
LISTEN TO ME! YOU'VE GOT TO GET OUT OF HERE!
HEY, HEY! NOW CALM DOWN...
NINJAS AREN'T DANGEROUS.
THEY'RE MORE AFRAID OF YOU THAN YOU ARE OF THEM...
OEDIPUS! GIVE US THE THORN!!

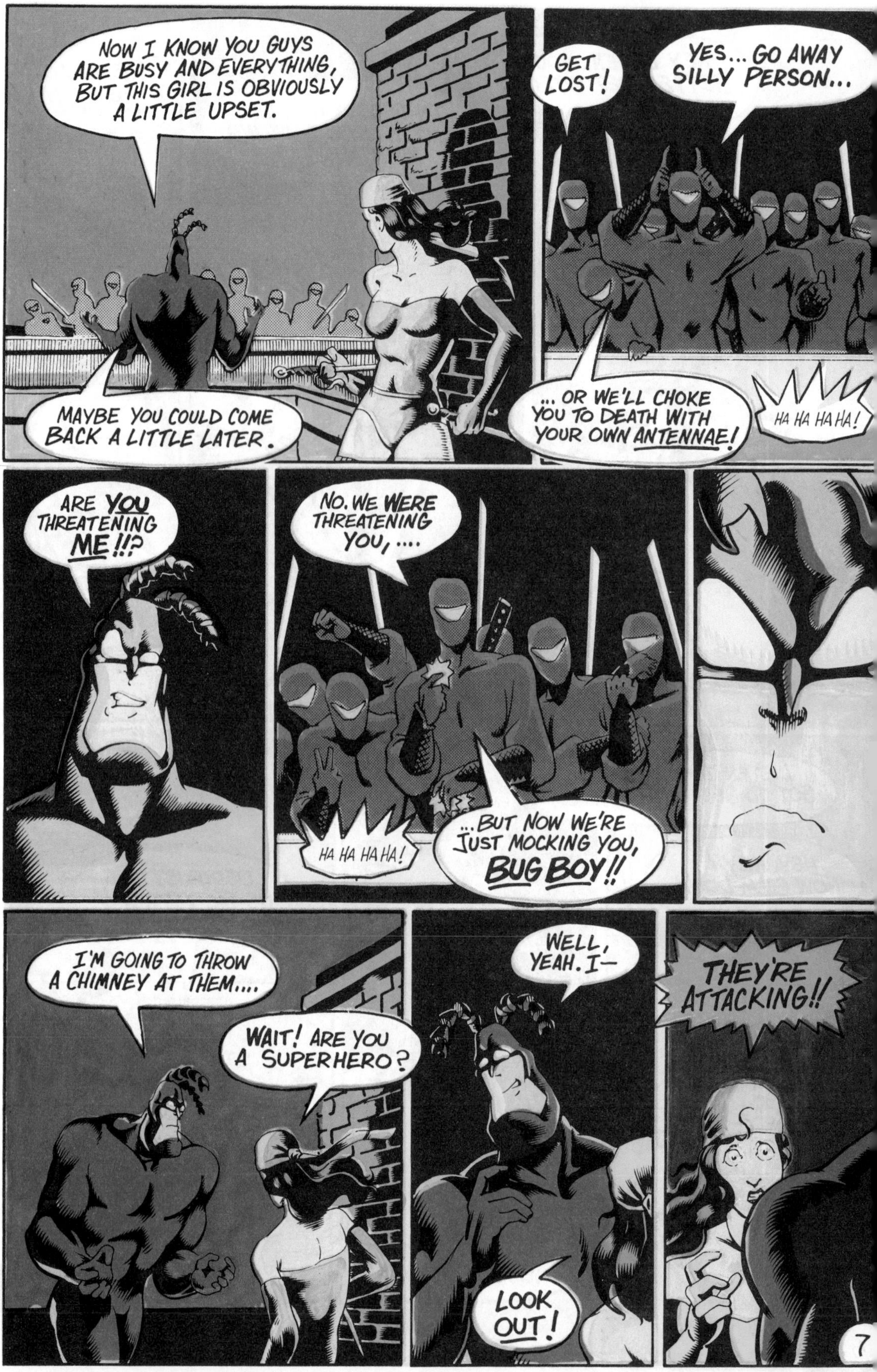
NOW I KNOW YOU GUYS ARE BUSY AND EVERYTHING, BUT THIS GIRL IS OBVIOUSLY A LITTLE UPSET.
MAYBE YOU COULD COME BACK A LITTLE LATER.
GET LOST!
YES... GO AWAY SILLY PERSON...
... OR WE'LL CHOKE YOU TO DEATH WITH YOUR OWN ANTENNAE!
HA HA HA HA!
ARE YOU THREATENING ME!!?
NO. WE WERE THREATENING YOU, ...
HA HA HA HA!
...BUT NOW WE'RE JUST MOCKING YOU, BUG BOY!!
I'M GOING TO THROW A CHIMNEY AT THEM....
WAIT! ARE YOU A SUPERHERO?
WELL, YEAH. I—
LOOK OUT!
THEY'RE ATTACKING!!

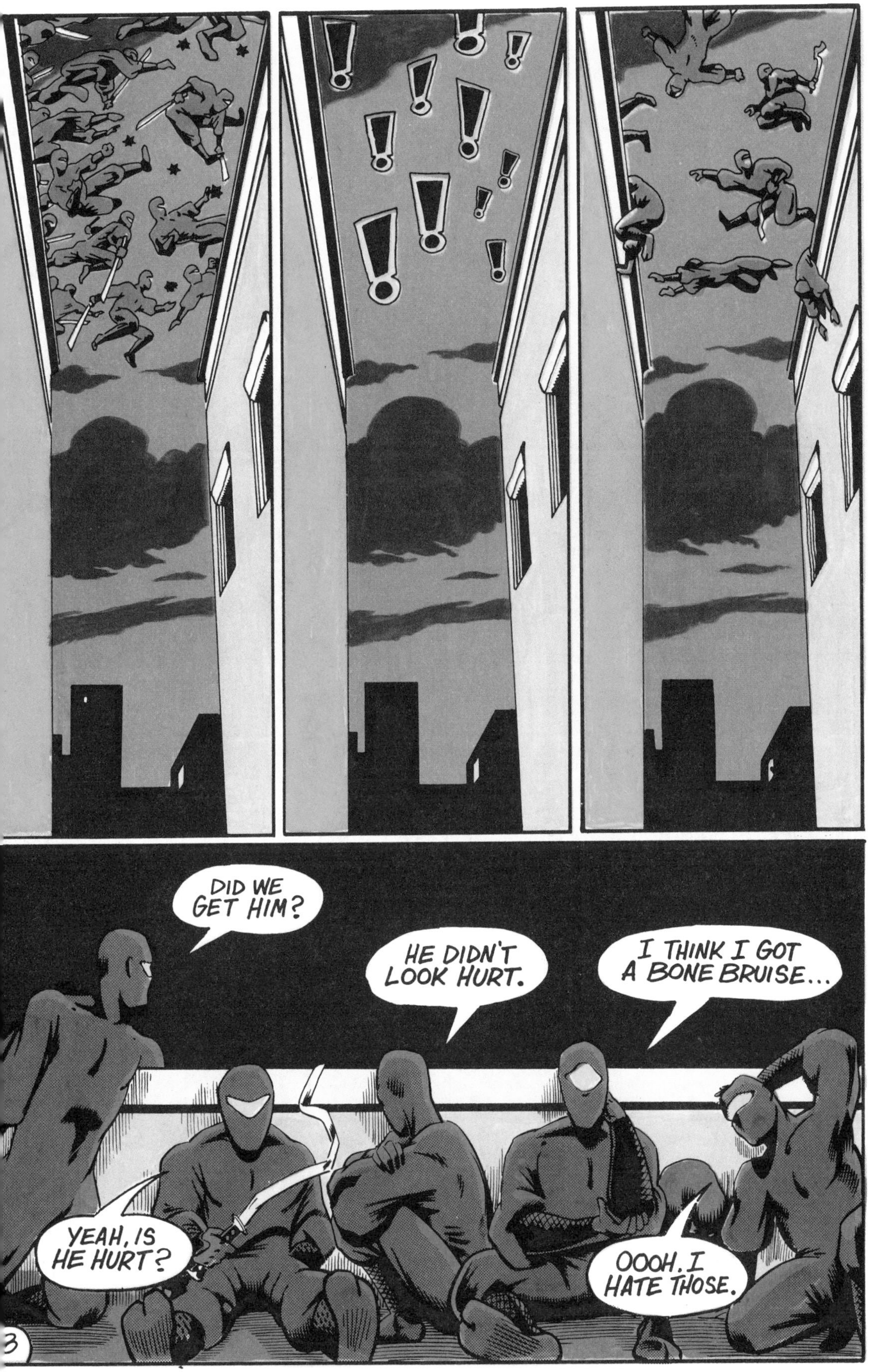
DID WE GET HIM?
YEAH, IS HE HURT?
HE DIDN'T LOOK HURT.
I THINK I GOT A BONE BRUISE...
OOOH. I HATE THOSE.

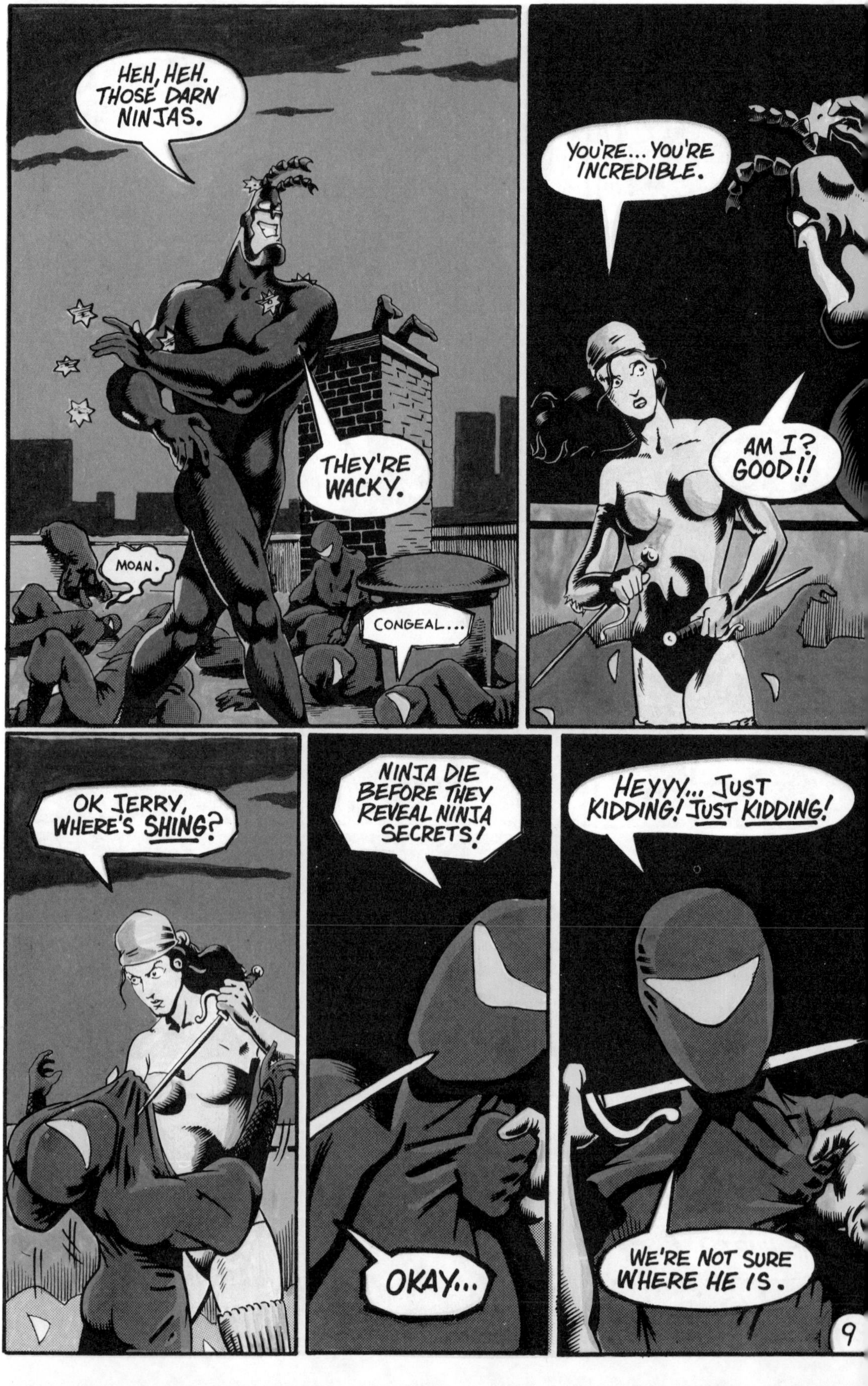
HEH, HEH. THOSE DARN NINJAS.
THEY'RE WACKY.
MOAN.
CONGEAL...
YOU'RE... YOU'RE INCREDIBLE.
AM I? GOOD!!
OK JERRY, WHERE'S SHING?
NINJA DIE BEFORE THEY REVEAL NINJA SECRETS!
OKAY...
HEYYY... JUST KIDDING! JUST KIDDING!
WE'RE NOT SURE WHERE HE IS.

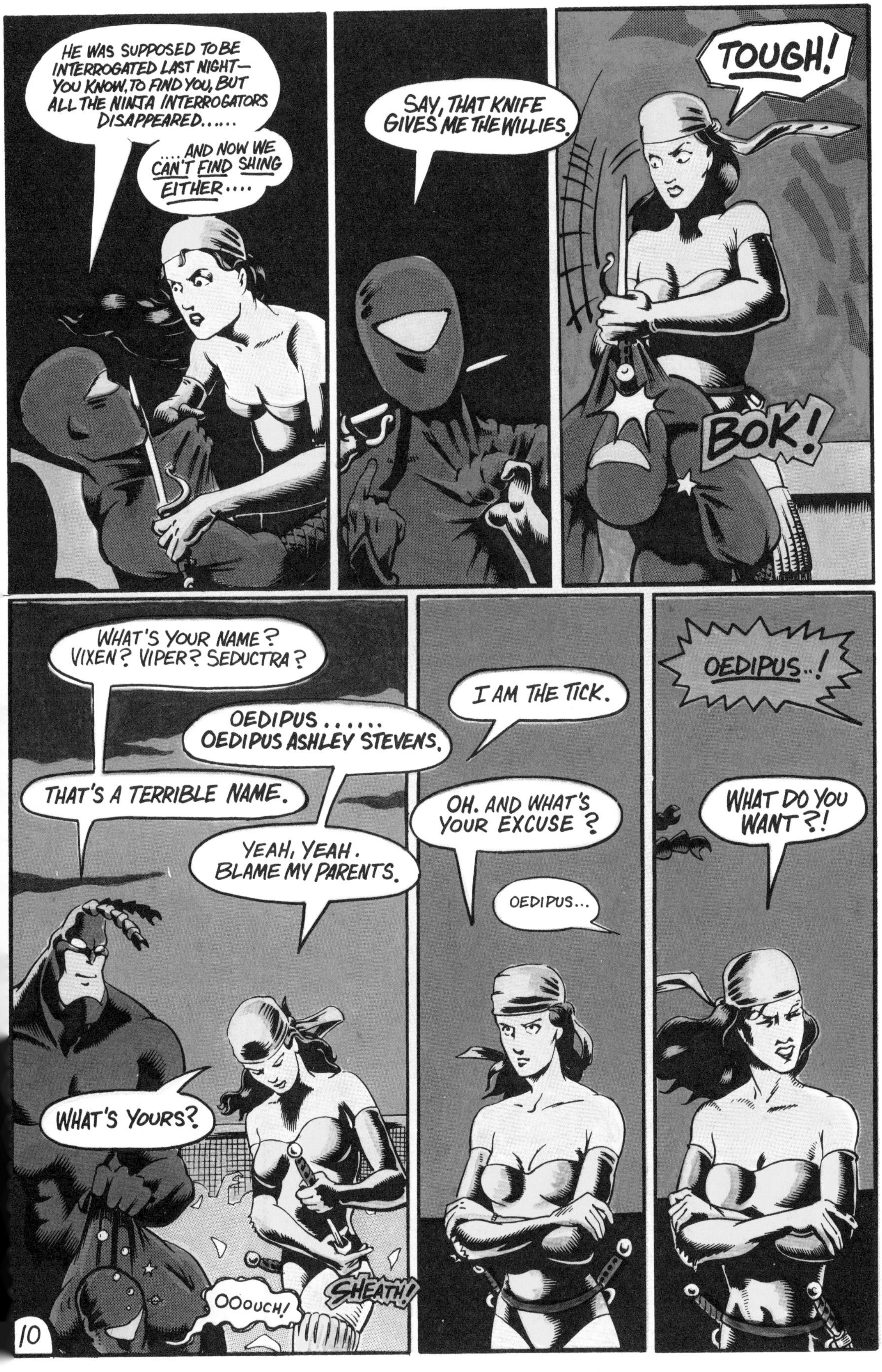
HE WAS SUPPOSED TO BE INTERROGATED LAST NIGHT— YOU KNOW, TO FIND YOU, BUT ALL THE NINJA INTERROGATORS DISAPPEARED......
....AND NOW WE CAN'T FIND SHING EITHER....
SAY, THAT KNIFE GIVES ME THE WILLIES.
TOUGH!
BOK!
WHAT'S YOUR NAME? VIXEN? VIPER? SEDUCTRA?
OEDIPUS...... OEDIPUS ASHLEY STEVENS.
THAT'S A TERRIBLE NAME.
YEAH, YEAH. BLAME MY PARENTS.
WHAT'S YOURS?
OOOUCH!
SHEATH!
I AM THE TICK.
OH. AND WHAT'S YOUR EXCUSE?
OEDIPUS...
OEDIPUS..!
WHAT DO YOU WANT?!

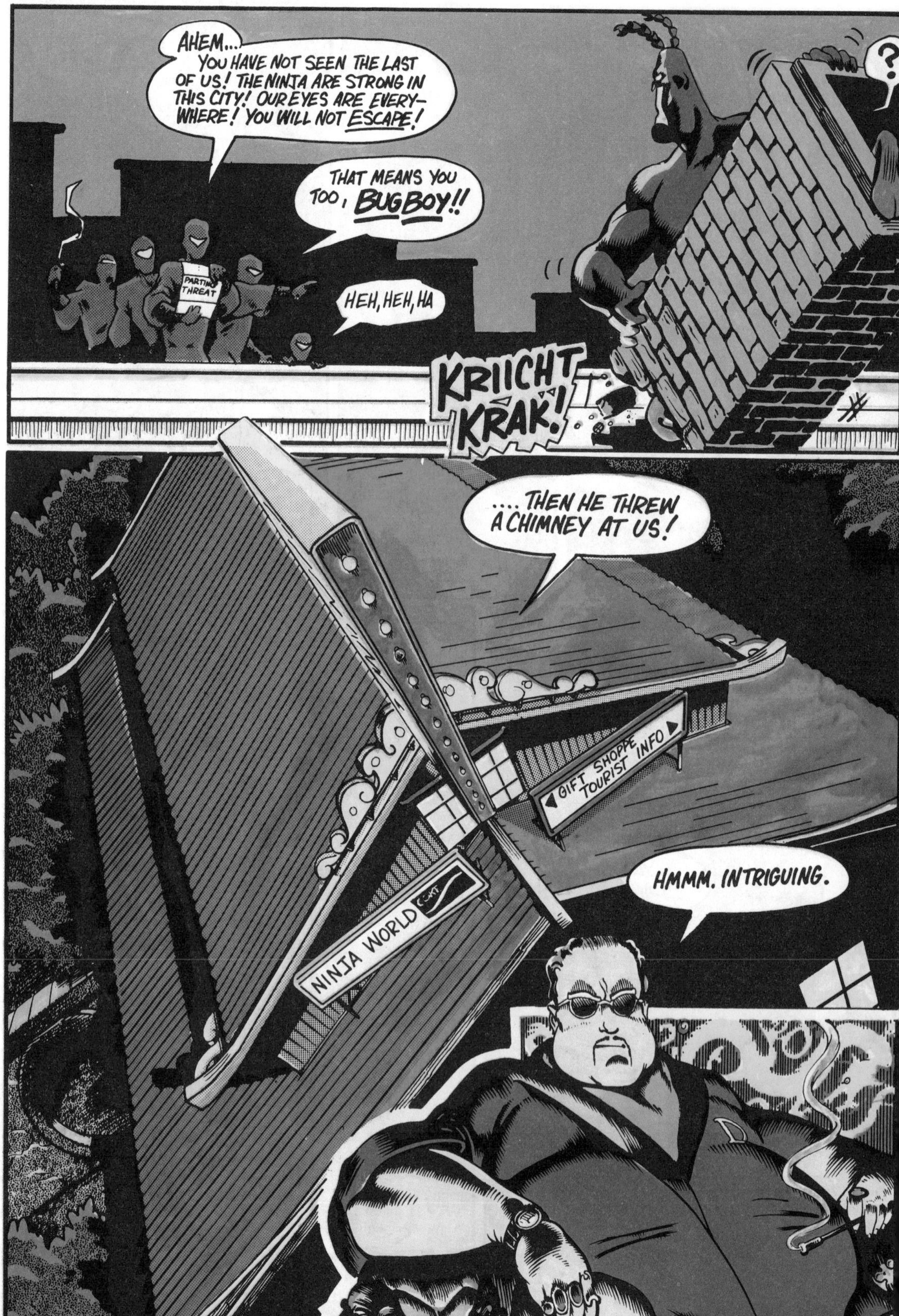
AHEM... YOU HAVE NOT SEEN THE LAST OF US! THE NINJA ARE STRONG IN THIS CITY! OUR EYES ARE EVERYWHERE! YOU WILL NOT ESCAPE!
PARTING THREAT
THAT MEANS YOU TOO, BUGBOY!!
HEH, HEH, HA
?
KRIICHT KRAK!
....THEN HE THREW A CHIMNEY AT US!
GIFT SHOPPE
TOURIST INFO
NINJA WORLD
HMMM. INTRIGUING.
11

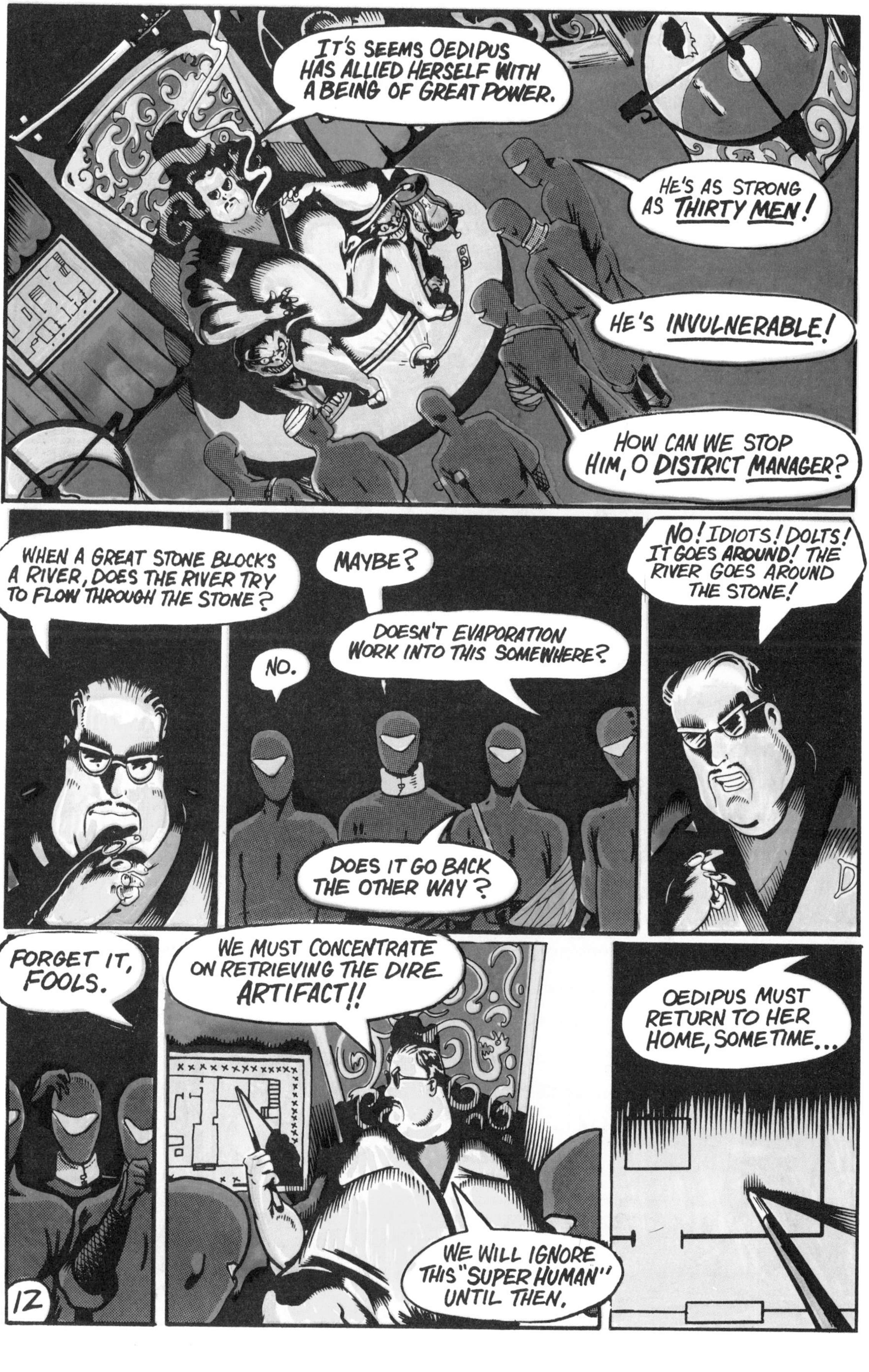
IT'S SEEMS OEDIPUS HAS ALLIED HERSELF WITH A BEING OF GREAT POWER.
HE'S AS STRONG AS THIRTY MEN!
HE'S INVULNERABLE!
HOW CAN WE STOP HIM, O DISTRICT MANAGER?
WHEN A GREAT STONE BLOCKS A RIVER, DOES THE RIVER TRY TO FLOW THROUGH THE STONE?
MAYBE?
DOESN'T EVAPORATION WORK INTO THIS SOMEWHERE?
NO.
DOES IT GO BACK THE OTHER WAY?
NO! IDIOTS! DOLTS! IT GOES AROUND! THE RIVER GOES AROUND THE STONE!
FORGET IT, FOOLS.
WE MUST CONCENTRATE ON RETRIEVING THE DIRE ARTIFACT!!
WE WILL IGNORE THIS "SUPER HUMAN" UNTIL THEN.
OEDIPUS MUST RETURN TO HER HOME, SOMETIME...

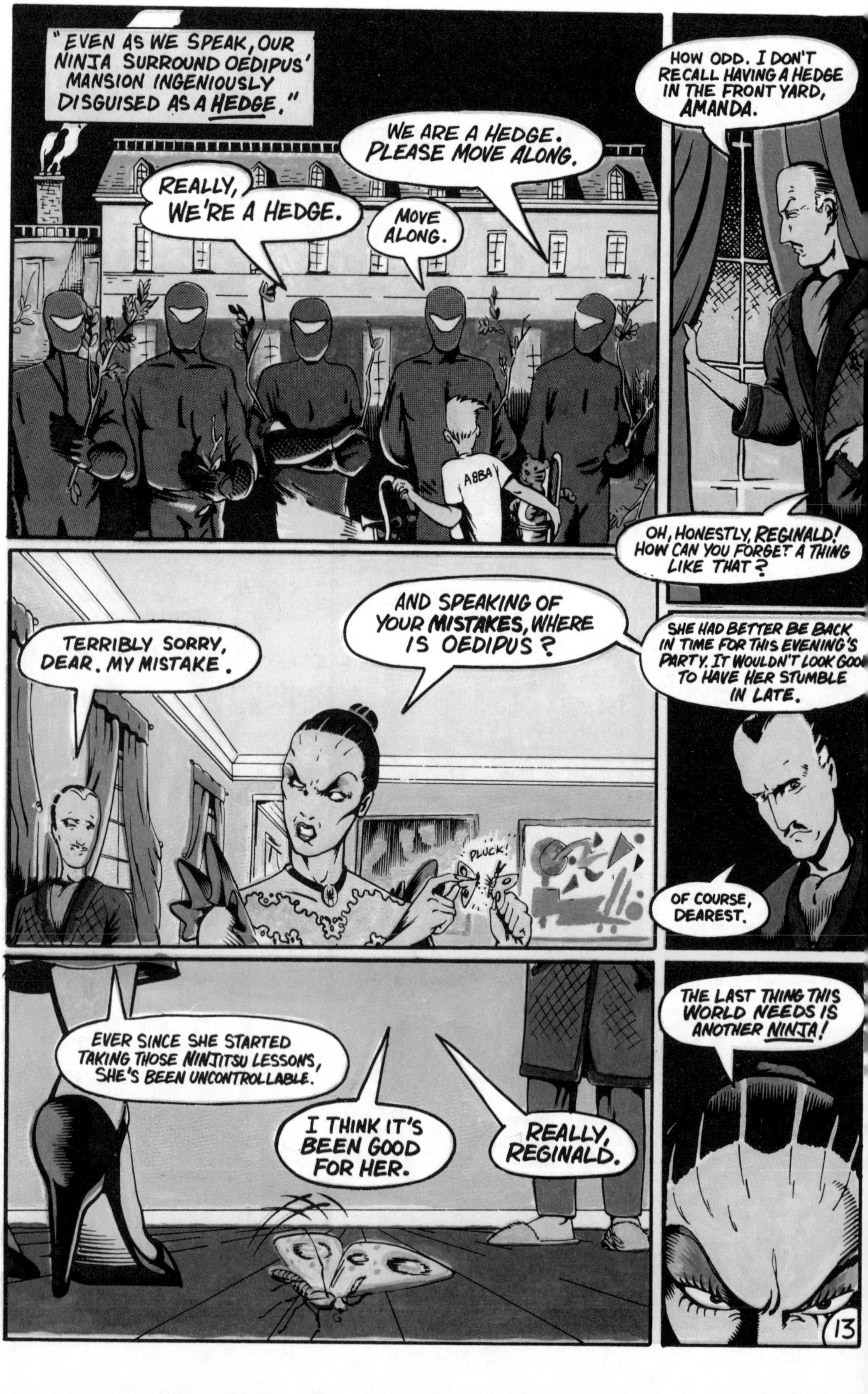
"EVEN AS WE SPEAK, OUR NINJA SURROUND OEDIPUS' MANSION INGENIOUSLY DISGUISED AS A HEDGE."
WE ARE A HEDGE. PLEASE MOVE ALONG.
REALLY, WE'RE A HEDGE.
MOVE ALONG.
ABBA
HOW ODD. I DON'T RECALL HAVING A HEDGE IN THE FRONT YARD, AMANDA.
OH, HONESTLY, REGINALD! HOW CAN YOU FORGET A THING LIKE THAT?
TERRIBLY SORRY, DEAR. MY MISTAKE.
AND SPEAKING OF YOUR MISTAKES, WHERE IS OEDIPUS?
PLUCK!
SHE HAD BETTER BE BACK IN TIME FOR THIS EVENING'S PARTY. IT WOULDN'T LOOK GOOD TO HAVE HER STUMBLE IN LATE.
OF COURSE, DEAREST.
EVER SINCE SHE STARTED TAKING THOSE NINJITSU LESSONS, SHE'S BEEN UNCONTROLLABLE.
I THINK IT'S BEEN GOOD FOR HER.
REALLY, REGINALD.
THE LAST THING THIS WORLD NEEDS IS ANOTHER NINJA!

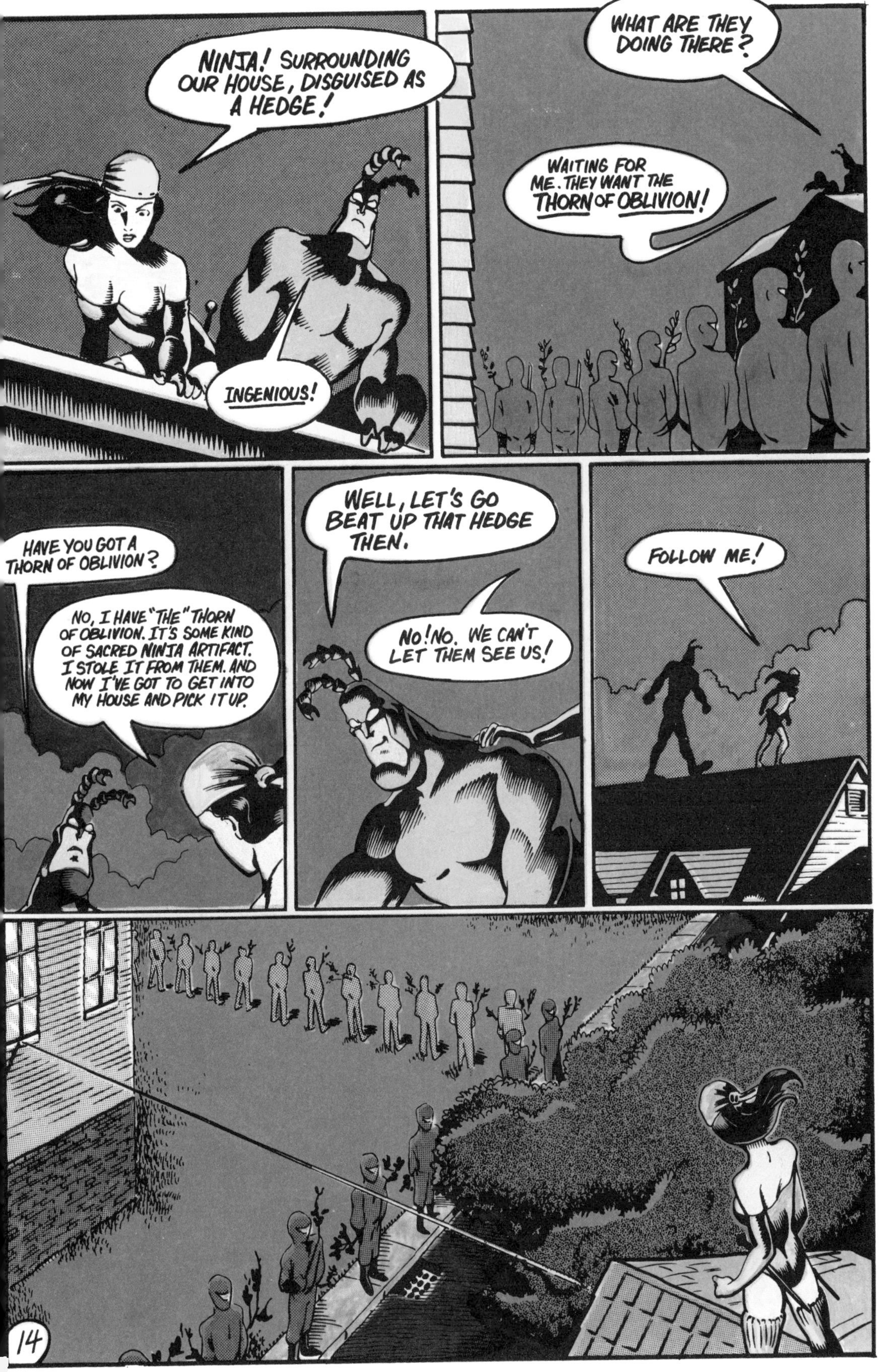
NINJA! SURROUNDING OUR HOUSE, DISGUISED AS A HEDGE!
INGENIOUS!
WHAT ARE THEY DOING THERE?
WAITING FOR ME. THEY WANT THE THORN OF OBLIVION!
HAVE YOU GOT A THORN OF OBLIVION?
NO, I HAVE "THE" THORN OF OBLIVION. IT'S SOME KIND OF SACRED NINJA ARTIFACT. I STOLE IT FROM THEM. AND NOW I'VE GOT TO GET INTO MY HOUSE AND PICK IT UP.
WELL, LET'S GO BEAT UP THAT HEDGE THEN.
NO! NO. WE CAN'T LET THEM SEE US!
FOLLOW ME!

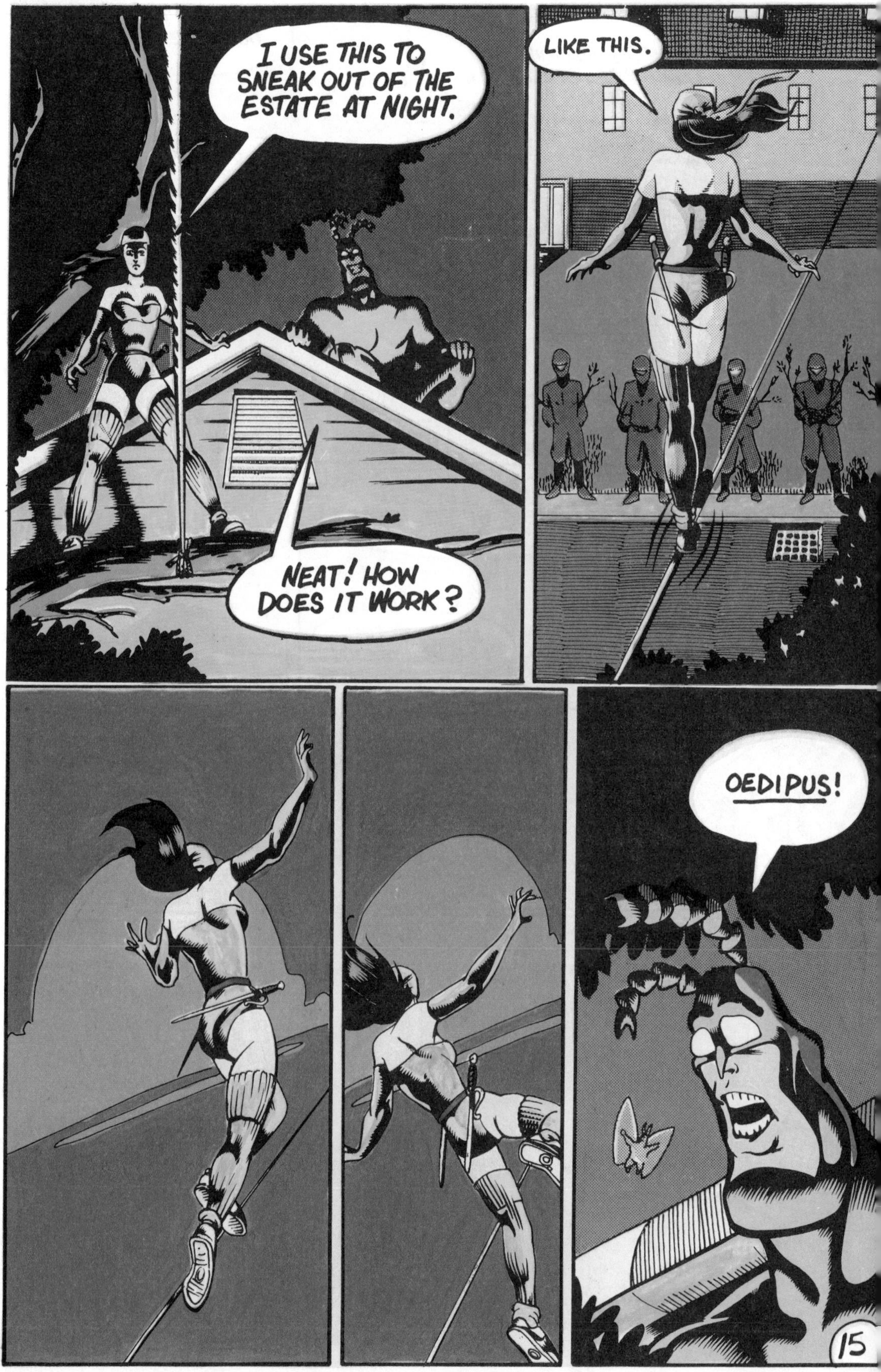
I USE THIS TO SNEAK OUT OF THE ESTATE AT NIGHT.
NEAT! HOW DOES IT WORK?
LIKE THIS.
OEDIPUS!

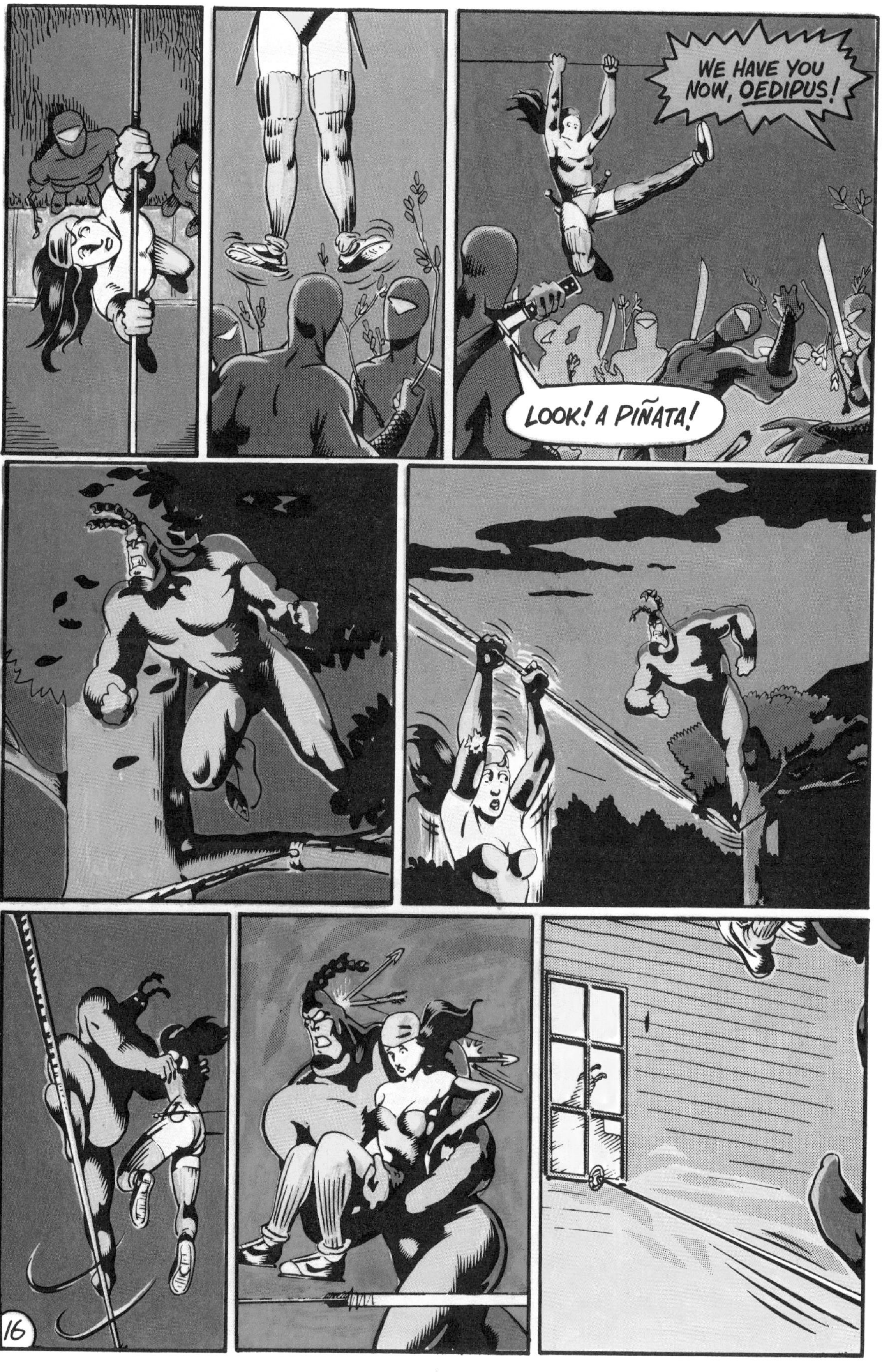
WE HAVE YOU NOW, OEDIPUS!
LOOK! A PIÑATA!
16

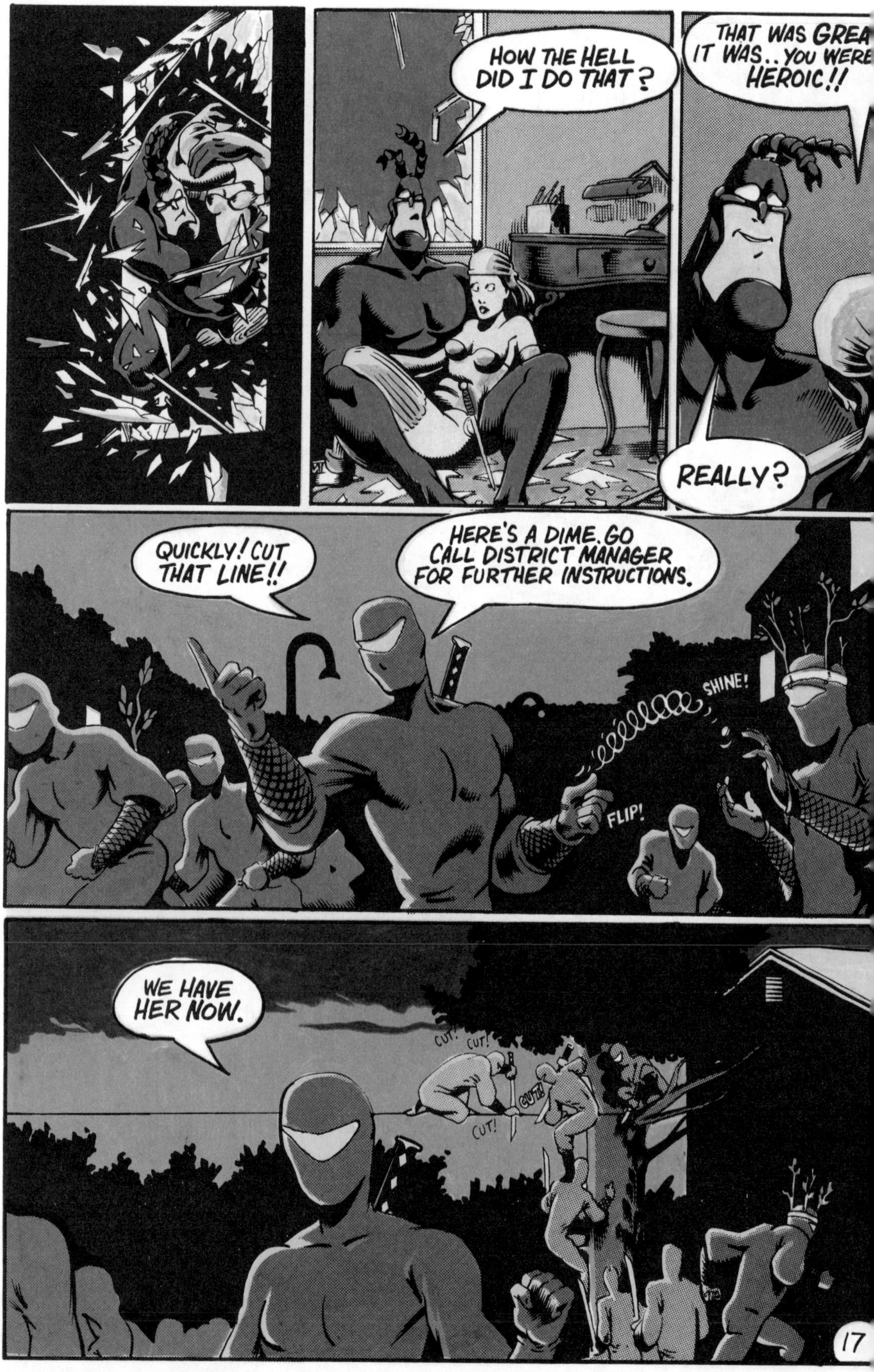
HOW THE HELL DID I DO THAT?
THAT WAS GREA
IT WAS.. YOU WERE
HEROIC!!
REALLY?
QUICKLY! CUT THAT LINE!!
HERE'S A DIME. GO CALL DISTRICT MANAGER FOR FURTHER INSTRUCTIONS.
SHINE!
FLIP!
WE HAVE HER NOW.
CUT!
CUT!
CUT!
CUT!

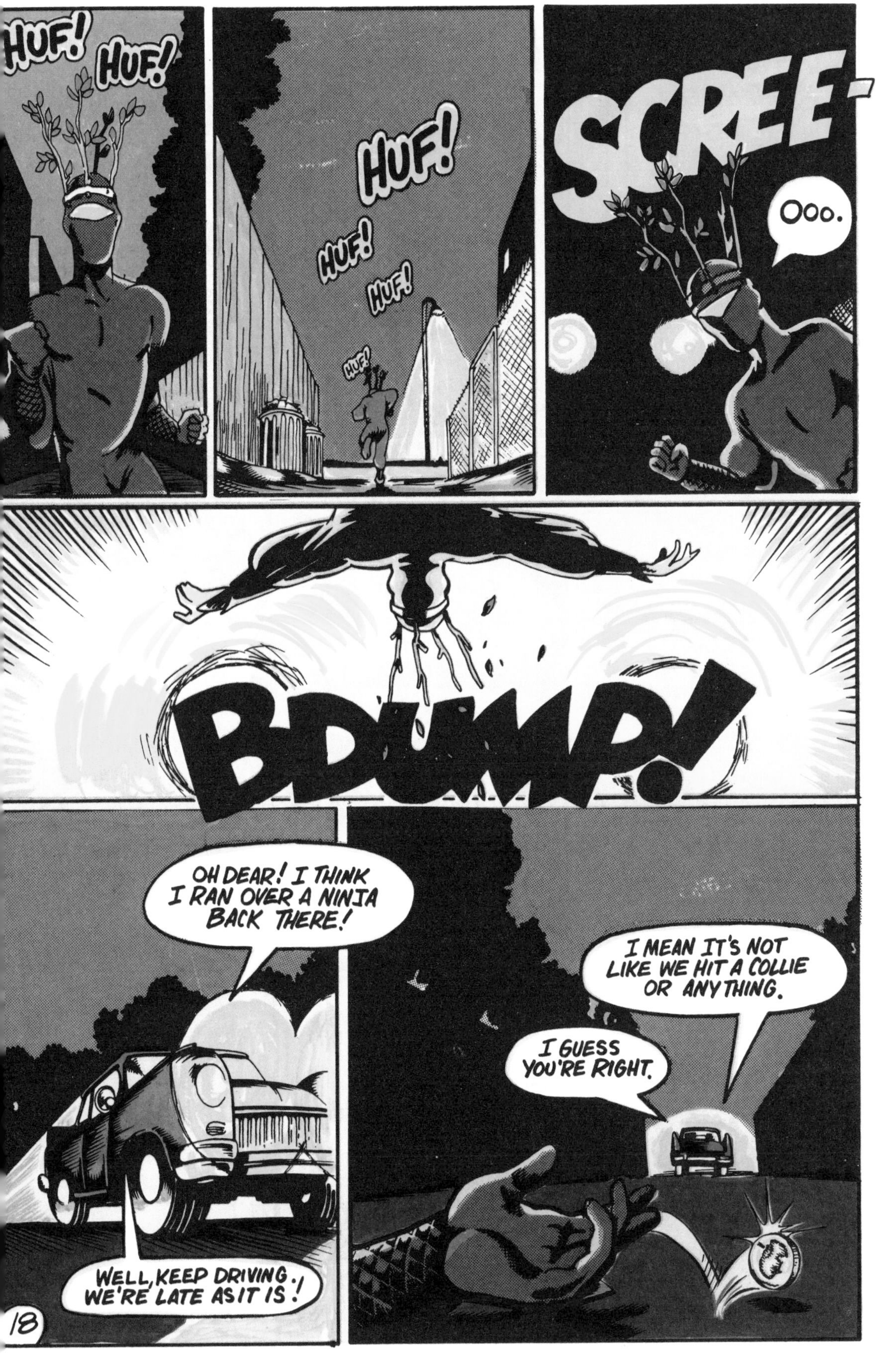
HUF! HUF!
HUF!
HUF!
HUF!
HUF!
SCREE-
Ooo.
BDUMP!
OH DEAR! I THINK I RAN OVER A NINJA BACK THERE!
WELL, KEEP DRIVING. WE'RE LATE AS IT IS!
I MEAN IT'S NOT LIKE WE HIT A COLLIE OR ANYTHING.
I GUESS YOU'RE RIGHT.

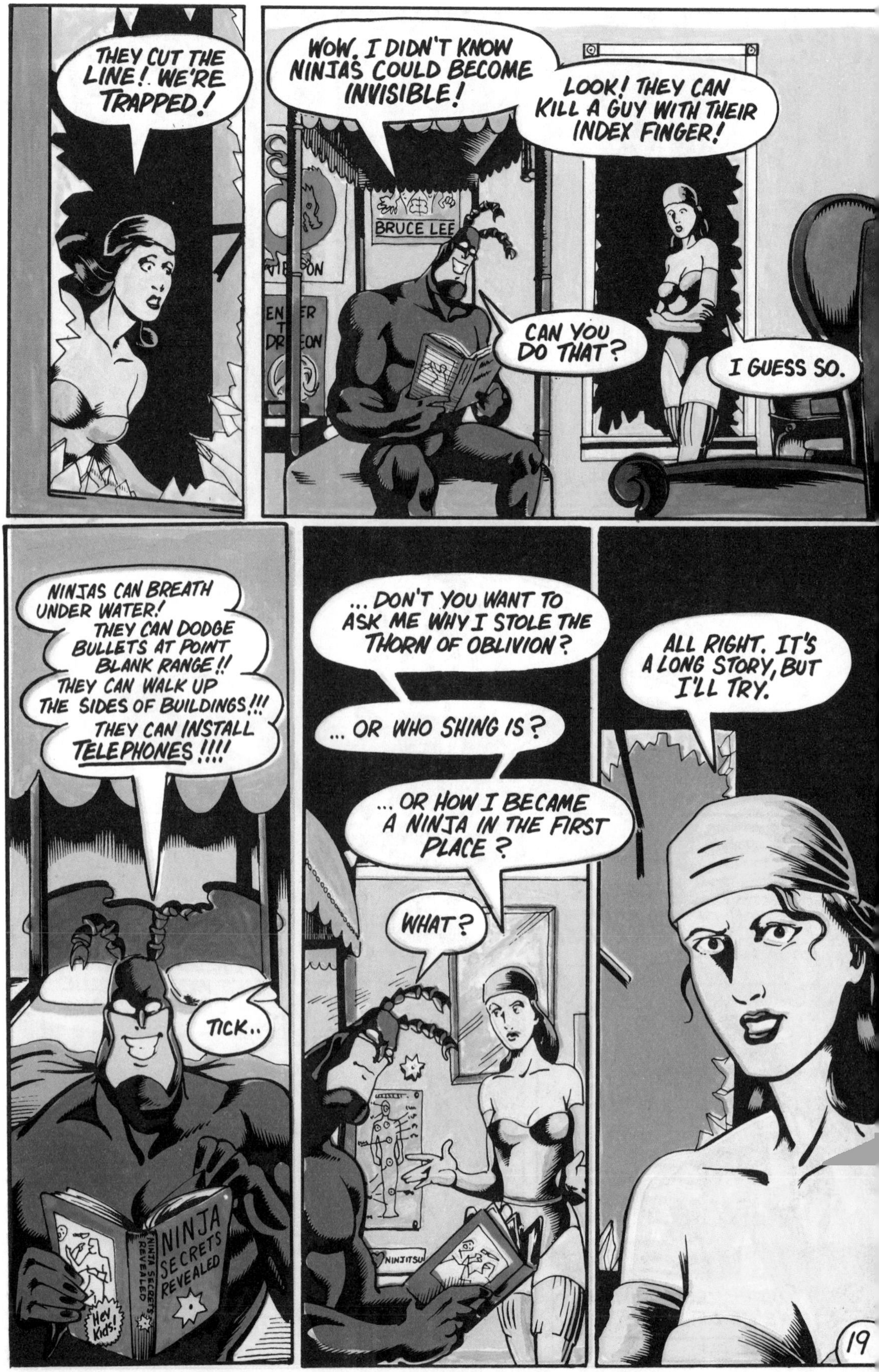
THEY CUT THE LINE! WE'RE TRAPPED!
WOW, I DIDN'T KNOW NINJAS COULD BECOME INVISIBLE!
LOOK! THEY CAN KILL A GUY WITH THEIR INDEX FINGER!
BRUCE LEE
CAN YOU DO THAT?
I GUESS SO.
NINJAS CAN BREATH UNDER WATER! THEY CAN DODGE BULLETS AT POINT BLANK RANGE!! THEY CAN WALK UP THE SIDES OF BUILDINGS!!! THEY CAN INSTALL TELEPHONES!!!!
TICK..
NINJA SECRETS REVEALED
Hey Kids!
... DON'T YOU WANT TO ASK ME WHY I STOLE THE THORN OF OBLIVION?
... OR WHO SHING IS?
... OR HOW I BECAME A NINJA IN THE FIRST PLACE?
WHAT?
NINJITSU
ALL RIGHT. IT'S A LONG STORY, BUT I'LL TRY.

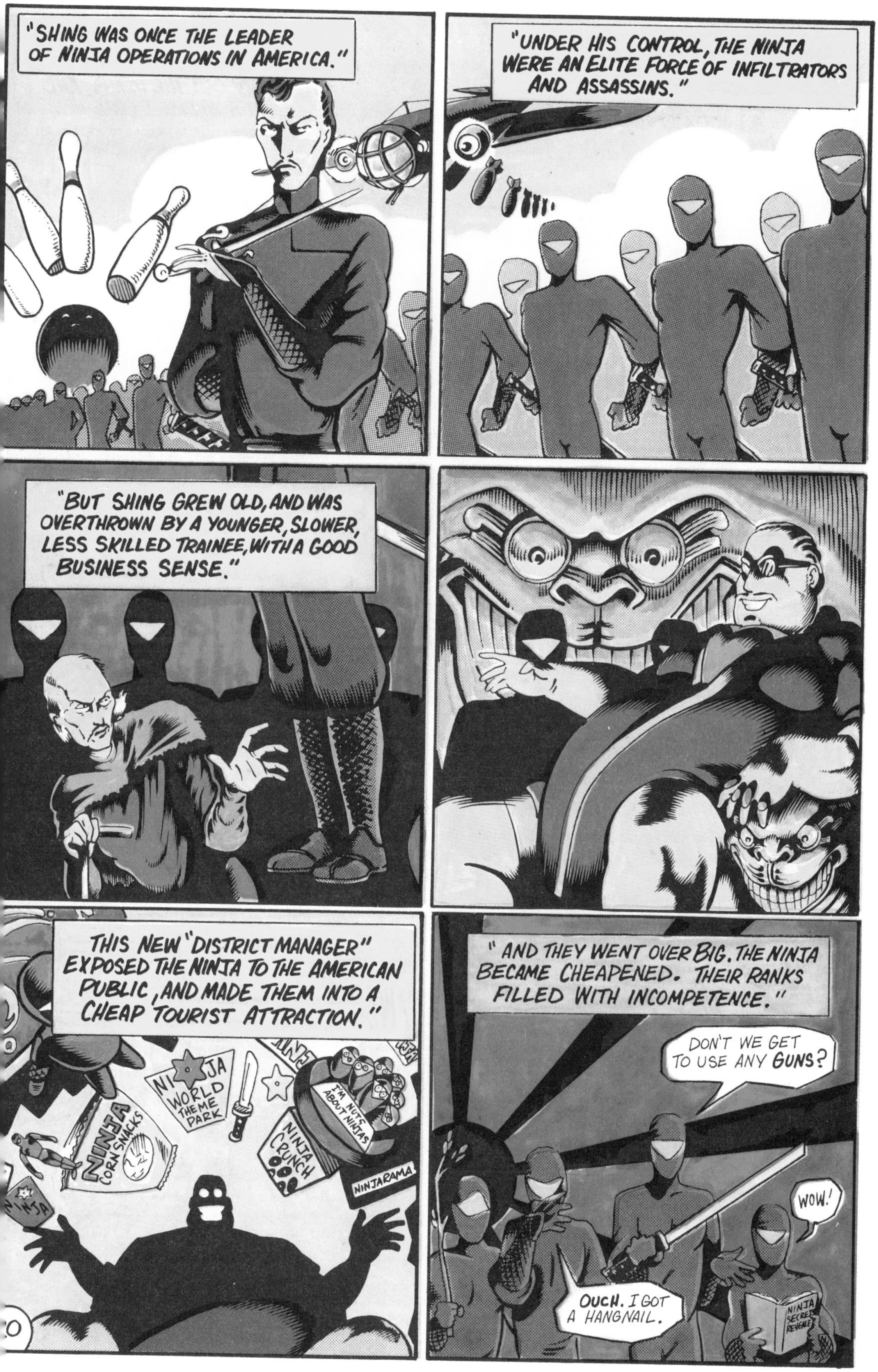
"SHING WAS ONCE THE LEADER OF NINJA OPERATIONS IN AMERICA."
"UNDER HIS CONTROL, THE NINJA WERE AN ELITE FORCE OF INFILTRATORS AND ASSASSINS."
"BUT SHING GREW OLD, AND WAS OVERTHROWN BY A YOUNGER, SLOWER, LESS SKILLED TRAINEE, WITH A GOOD BUSINESS SENSE."
THIS NEW "DISTRICT MANAGER" EXPOSED THE NINJA TO THE AMERICAN PUBLIC, AND MADE THEM INTO A CHEAP TOURIST ATTRACTION."
NI JA WORLD THEME PARK
NINJA CORN SNACKS
NINJA CRUNCH
I'M NUTS ABOUT NINJAS
NINJARAMA
NINJA
" AND THEY WENT OVER BIG. THE NINJA BECAME CHEAPENED. THEIR RANKS FILLED WITH INCOMPETENCE."
DON'T WE GET TO USE ANY GUNS?
WOW!
OUCH. I GOT A HANGNAIL.
NINJA

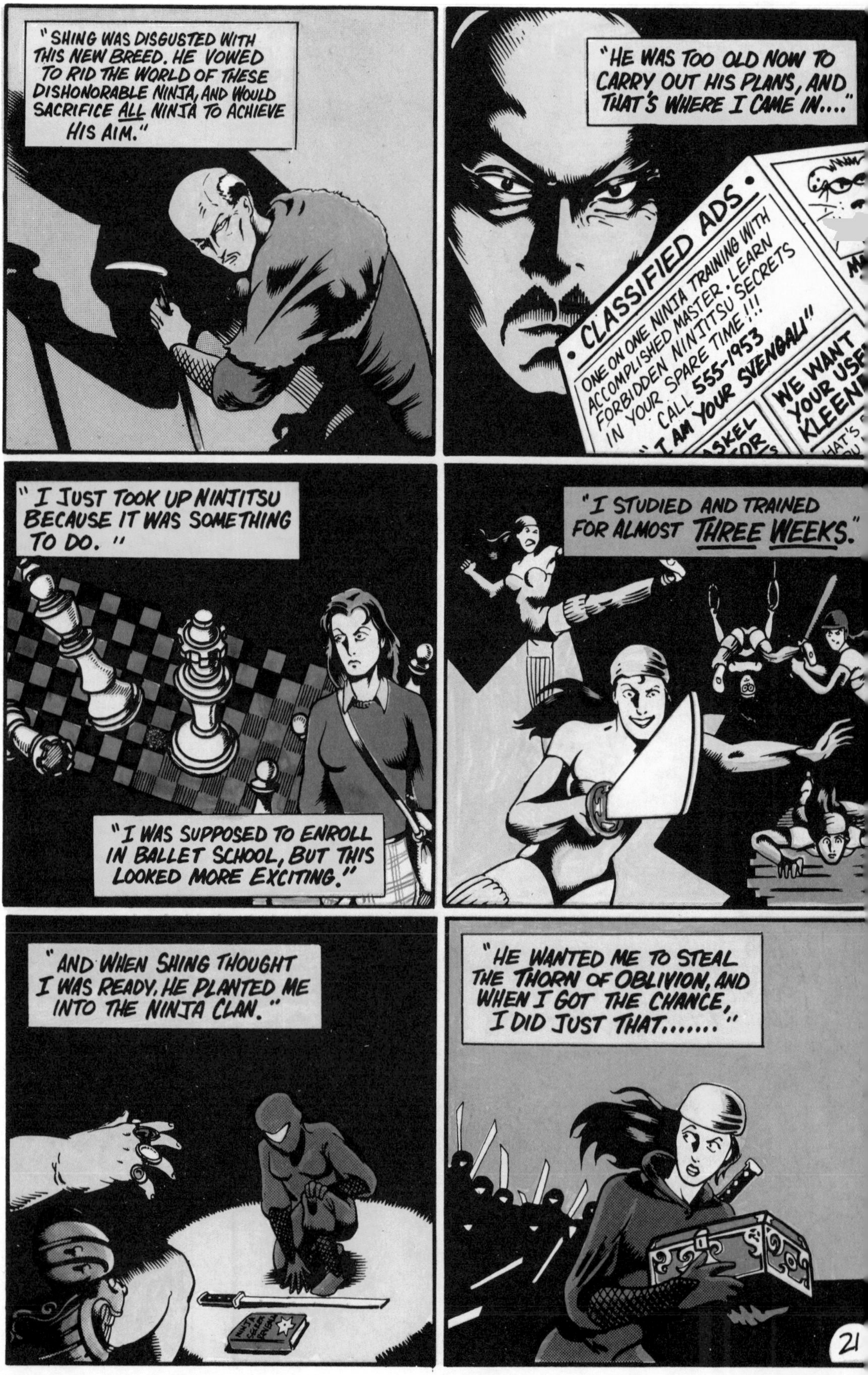
"SHING WAS DISGUSTED WITH THIS NEW BREED. HE VOWED TO RID THE WORLD OF THESE DISHONORABLE NINJA, AND WOULD SACRIFICE ALL NINJA TO ACHIEVE HIS AIM."
"HE WAS TOO OLD NOW TO CARRY OUT HIS PLANS, AND THAT'S WHERE I CAME IN...."
CLASSIFIED ADS
ONE ON ONE NINJA TRAINING WITH ACCOMPLISHED MASTER. LEARN FORBIDDEN NINITSU SECRETS IN YOUR SPARE TIME!!!
CALL 555-1953
"I AM YOUR SVENGALI"
WE WANT YOUR
"I JUST TOOK UP NINJITSU BECAUSE IT WAS SOMETHING TO DO."
"I WAS SUPPOSED TO ENROLL IN BALLET SCHOOL, BUT THIS LOOKED MORE EXCITING."
"I STUDIED AND TRAINED FOR ALMOST THREE WEEKS."
"AND WHEN SHING THOUGHT I WAS READY, HE PLANTED ME INTO THE NINJA CLAN."
"HE WANTED ME TO STEAL THE THORN OF OBLIVION, AND WHEN I GOT THE CHANCE, I DID JUST THAT......"

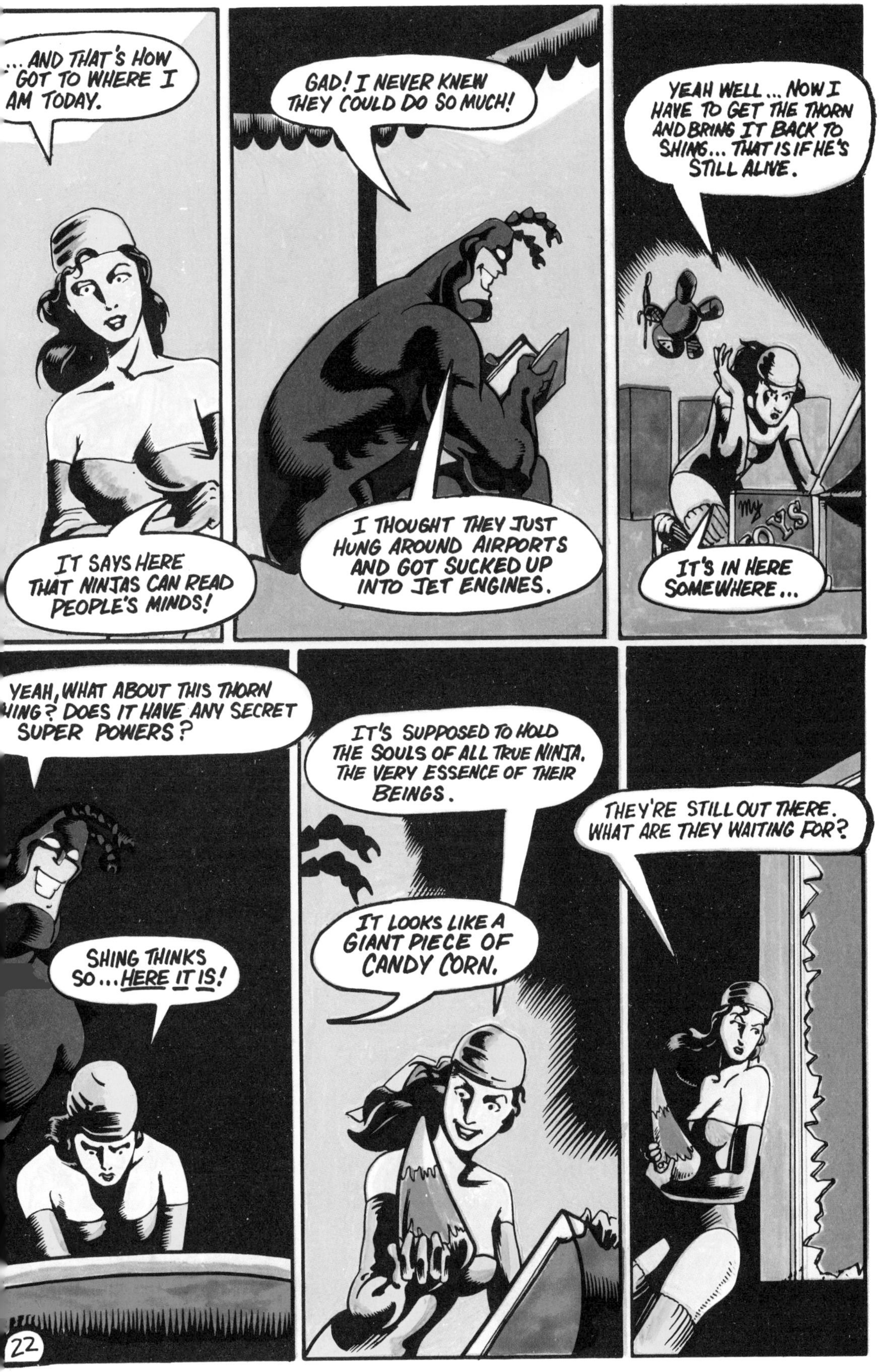
...AND THAT'S HOW
GOT TO WHERE I
AM TODAY.
IT SAYS HERE THAT NINJAS CAN READ PEOPLE'S MINDS!
GAD! I NEVER KNEW THEY COULD DO SO MUCH!
I THOUGHT THEY JUST HUNG AROUND AIRPORTS AND GOT SUCKED UP INTO JET ENGINES.
YEAH WELL... NOW I HAVE TO GET THE THORN AND BRING IT BACK TO SHING... THAT IS IF HE'S STILL ALIVE.
MY TOYS
IT'S IN HERE SOMEWHERE...
YEAH, WHAT ABOUT THIS THORN
HING? DOES IT HAVE ANY SECRET
SUPER POWERS?
SHING THINKS SO... HERE IT IS!
IT'S SUPPOSED TO HOLD THE SOULS OF ALL TRUE NINJA. THE VERY ESSENCE OF THEIR BEINGS.
IT LOOKS LIKE A GIANT PIECE OF CANDY CORN.
THEY'RE STILL OUT THERE. WHAT ARE THEY WAITING FOR?

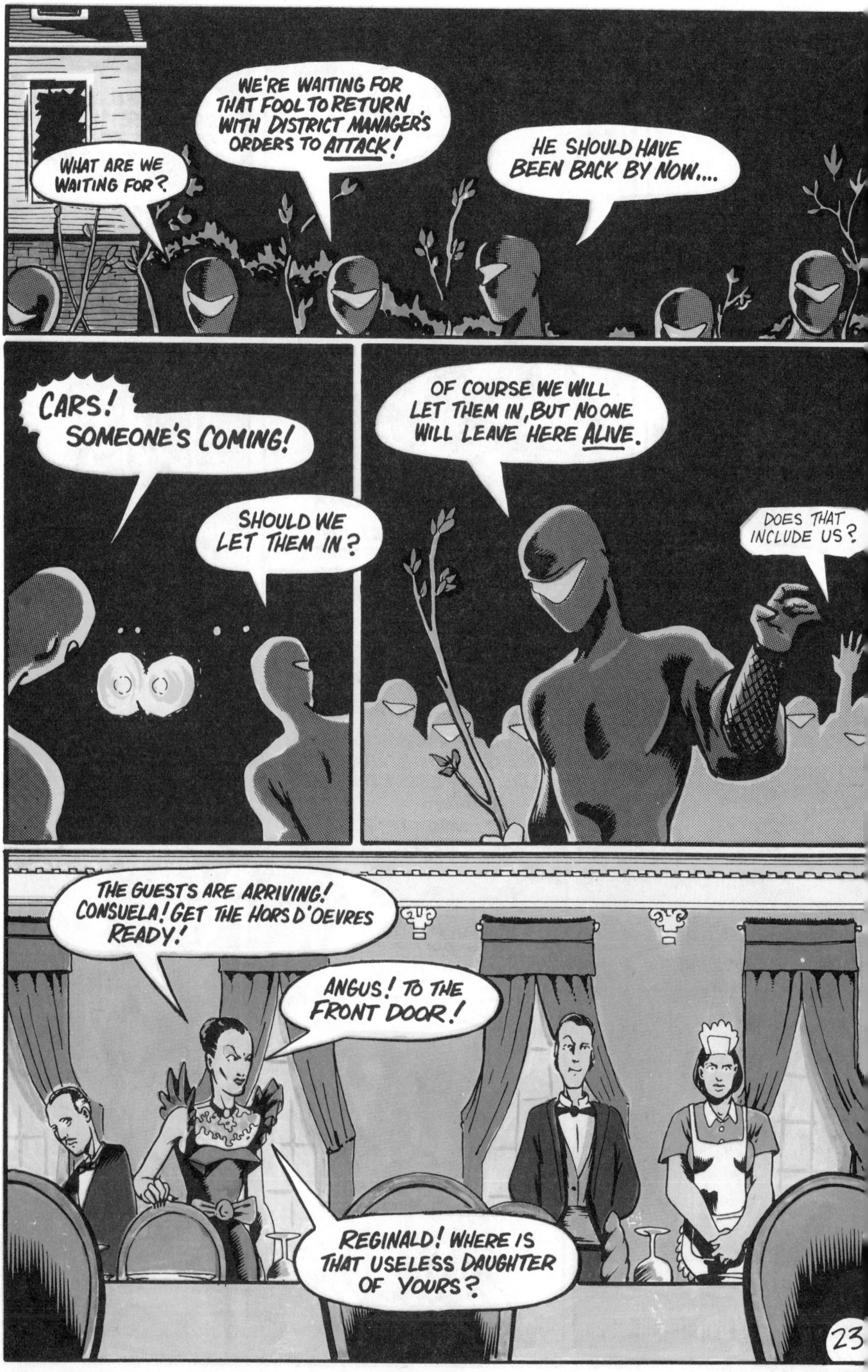
WHAT ARE WE WAITING FOR?
WE'RE WAITING FOR THAT FOOL TO RETURN WITH DISTRICT MANAGER'S ORDERS TO ATTACK!
HE SHOULD HAVE BEEN BACK BY NOW....
CARS! SOMEONE'S COMING!
SHOULD WE LET THEM IN?
OF COURSE WE WILL LET THEM IN, BUT NO ONE WILL LEAVE HERE ALIVE.
DOES THAT INCLUDE US?
THE GUESTS ARE ARRIVING! CONSUELA! GET THE HORS D'OEVRES READY!
ANGUS! TO THE FRONT DOOR!
REGINALD! WHERE IS THAT USELESS DAUGHTER OF YOURS?

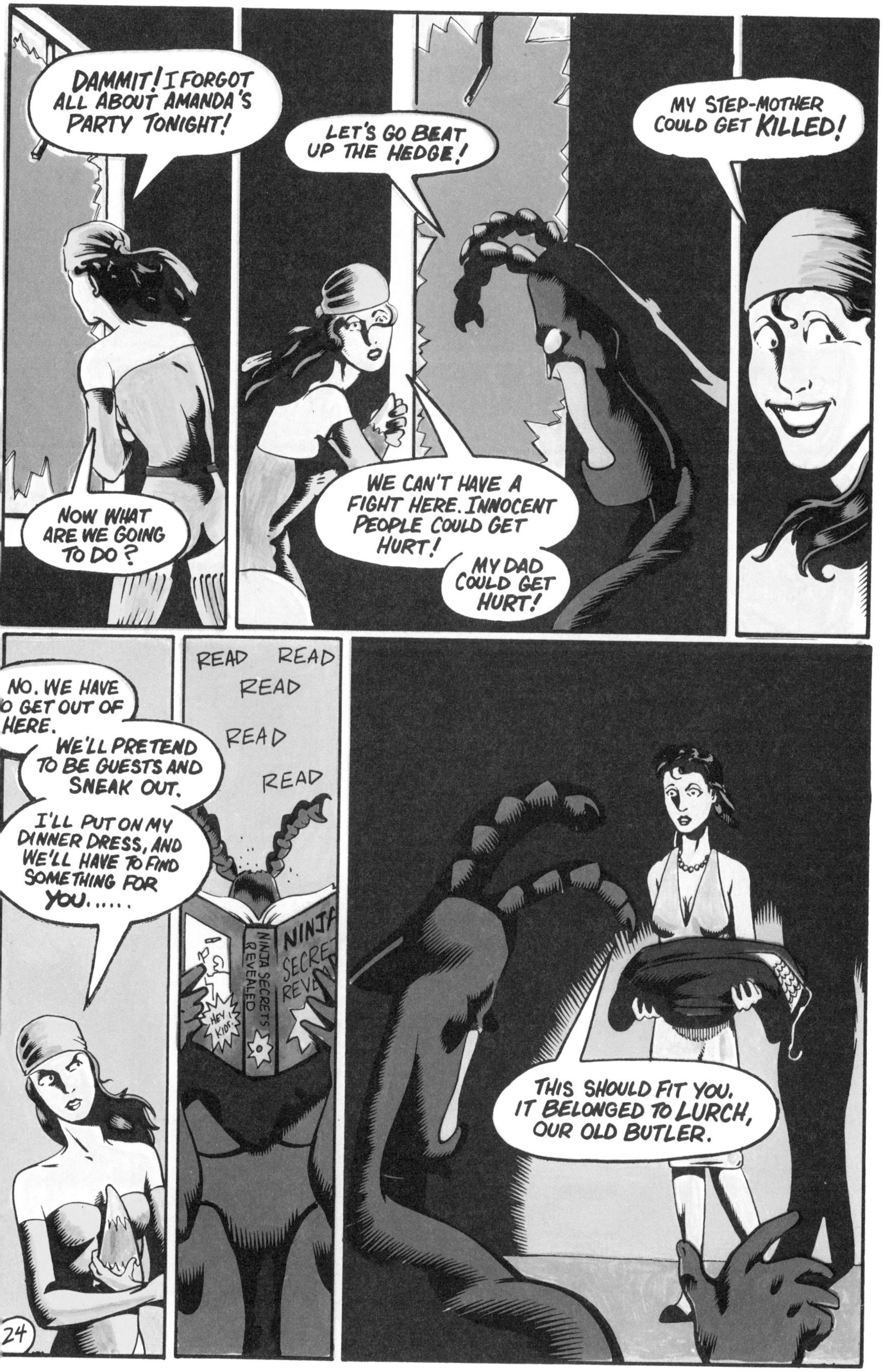
DAMMIT! I FORGOT ALL ABOUT AMANDA'S PARTY TONIGHT!
NOW WHAT ARE WE GOING TO DO?
LET'S GO BEAT UP THE HEDGE!
WE CAN'T HAVE A FIGHT HERE. INNOCENT PEOPLE COULD GET HURT!
MY DAD COULD GET HURT!
MY STEP-MOTHER COULD GET KILLED!
NO. WE HAVE TO GET OUT OF HERE.
WE'LL PRETEND TO BE GUESTS AND SNEAK OUT.
I'LL PUT ON MY DINNER DRESS, AND WE'LL HAVE TO FIND SOMETHING FOR YOU......
READ READ READ READ READ
NINJA SECRETS REVEALED
HEY KIDS!
THIS SHOULD FIT YOU. IT BELONGED TO LURCH, OUR OLD BUTLER.

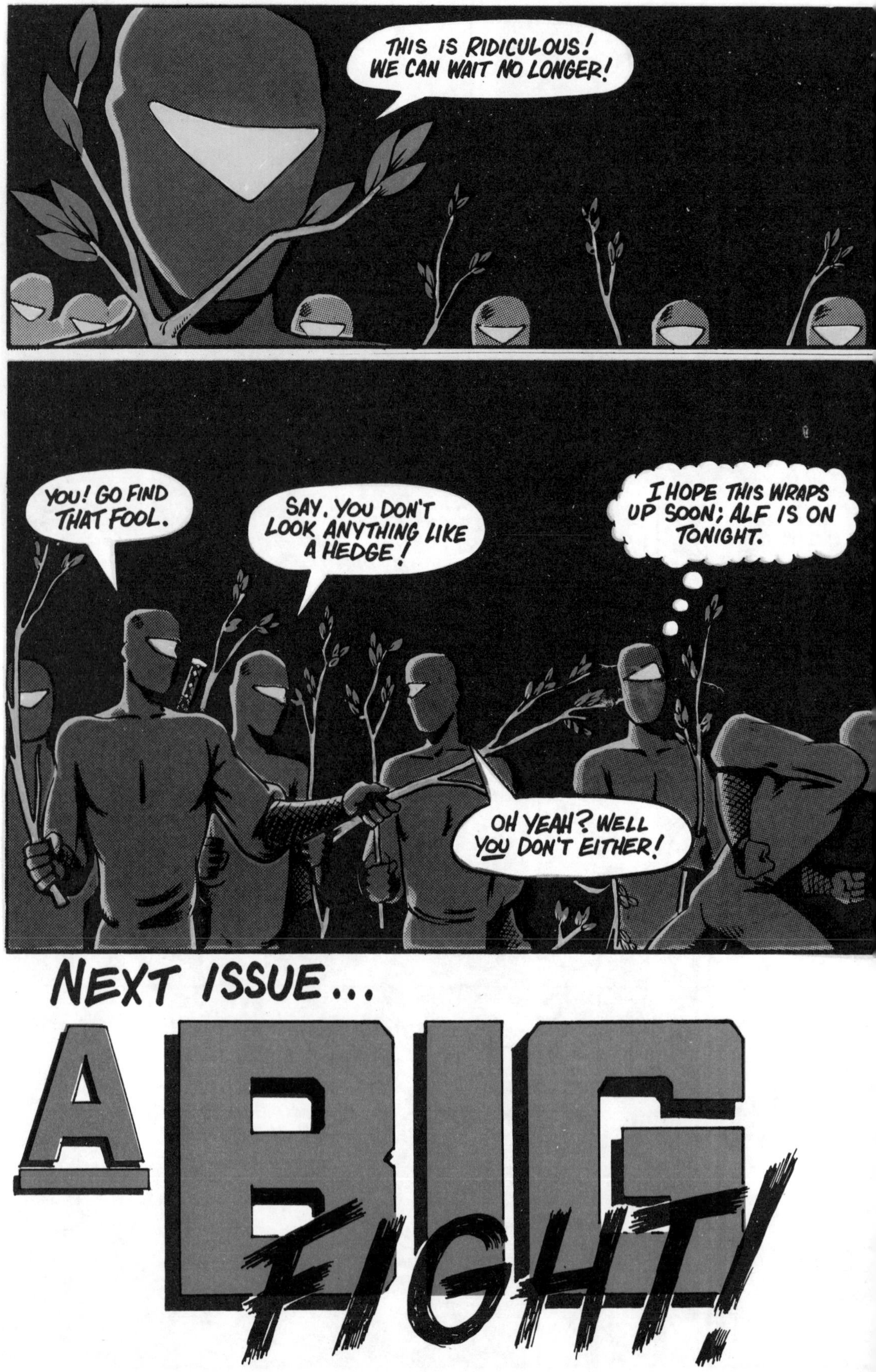
THIS IS RIDICULOUS! WE CAN WAIT NO LONGER!
YOU! GO FIND THAT FOOL.
SAY. YOU DON'T LOOK ANYTHING LIKE A HEDGE!
OH YEAH? WELL YOU DON'T EITHER!
I HOPE THIS WRAPS UP SOON; ALF IS ON TONIGHT.

NEXT ISSUE...

A BIG FIGHT!

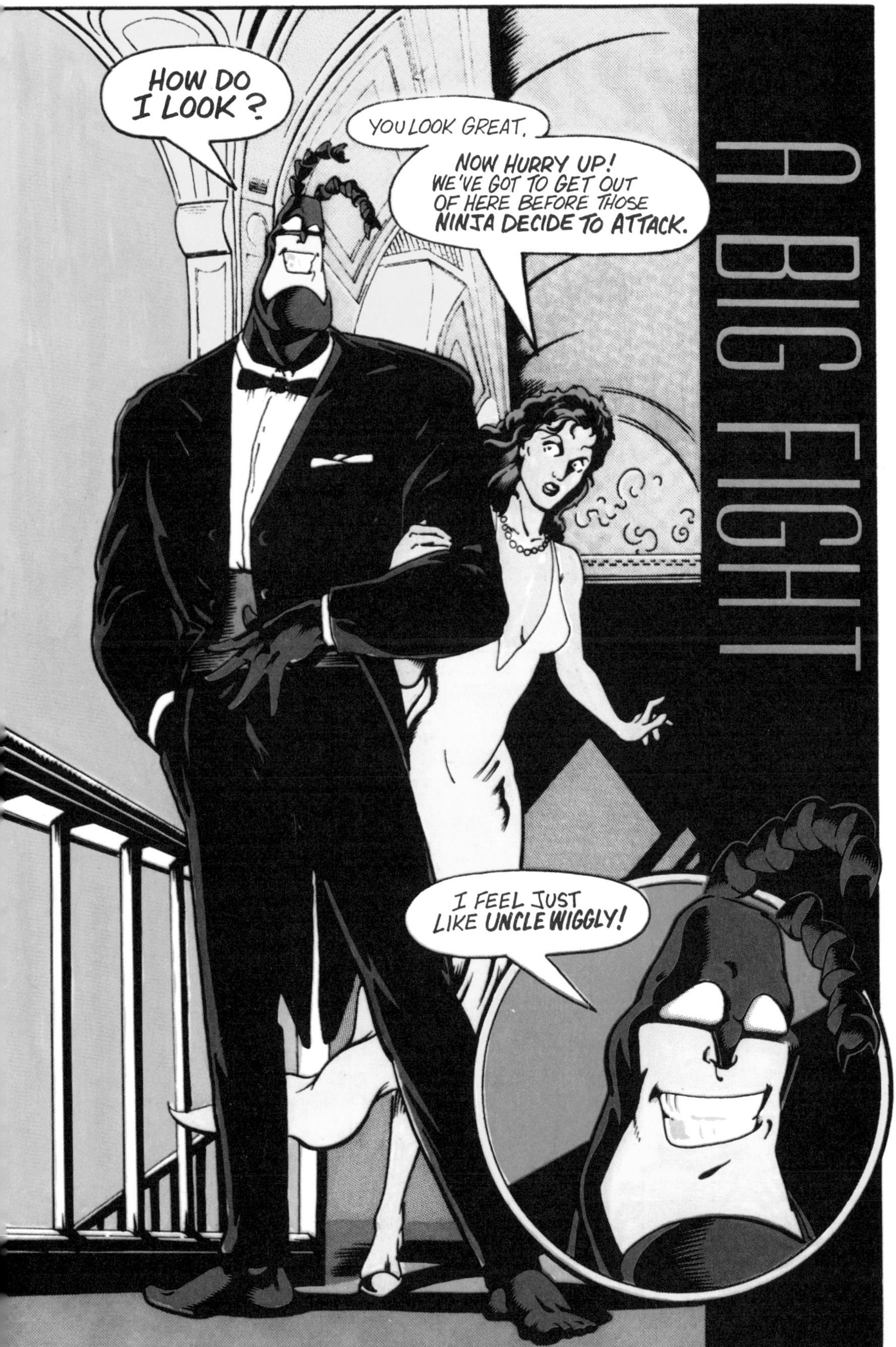
A BIG FIGHT
HOW DO I LOOK?
YOU LOOK GREAT.
NOW HURRY UP! WE'VE GOT TO GET OUT OF HERE BEFORE THOSE NINJA DECIDE TO ATTACK.
I FEEL JUST LIKE UNCLE WIGGLY!

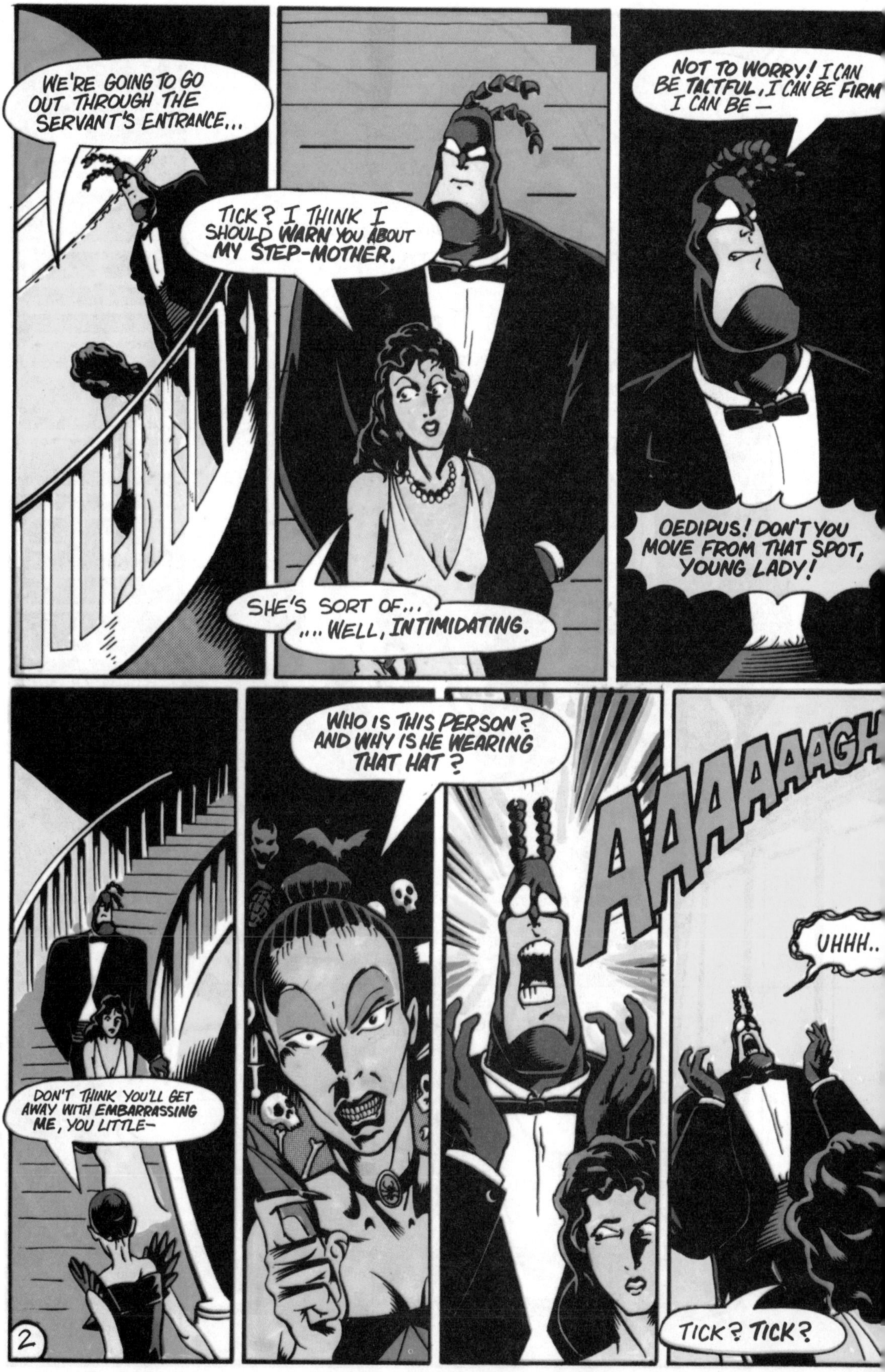
WE'RE GOING TO GO OUT THROUGH THE SERVANT'S ENTRANCE...
TICK? I THINK I SHOULD WARN YOU ABOUT MY STEP-MOTHER.
SHE'S SORT OF... ....WELL, INTIMIDATING.
NOT TO WORRY! I CAN BE TACTFUL, I CAN BE FIRM I CAN BE—
OEDIPUS! DON'T YOU MOVE FROM THAT SPOT, YOUNG LADY!
DON'T THINK YOU'LL GET AWAY WITH EMBARRASSING ME, YOU LITTLE-
WHO IS THIS PERSON? AND WHY IS HE WEARING THAT HAT?
AAAAAAGH
UHHH..
TICK? TICK?
2

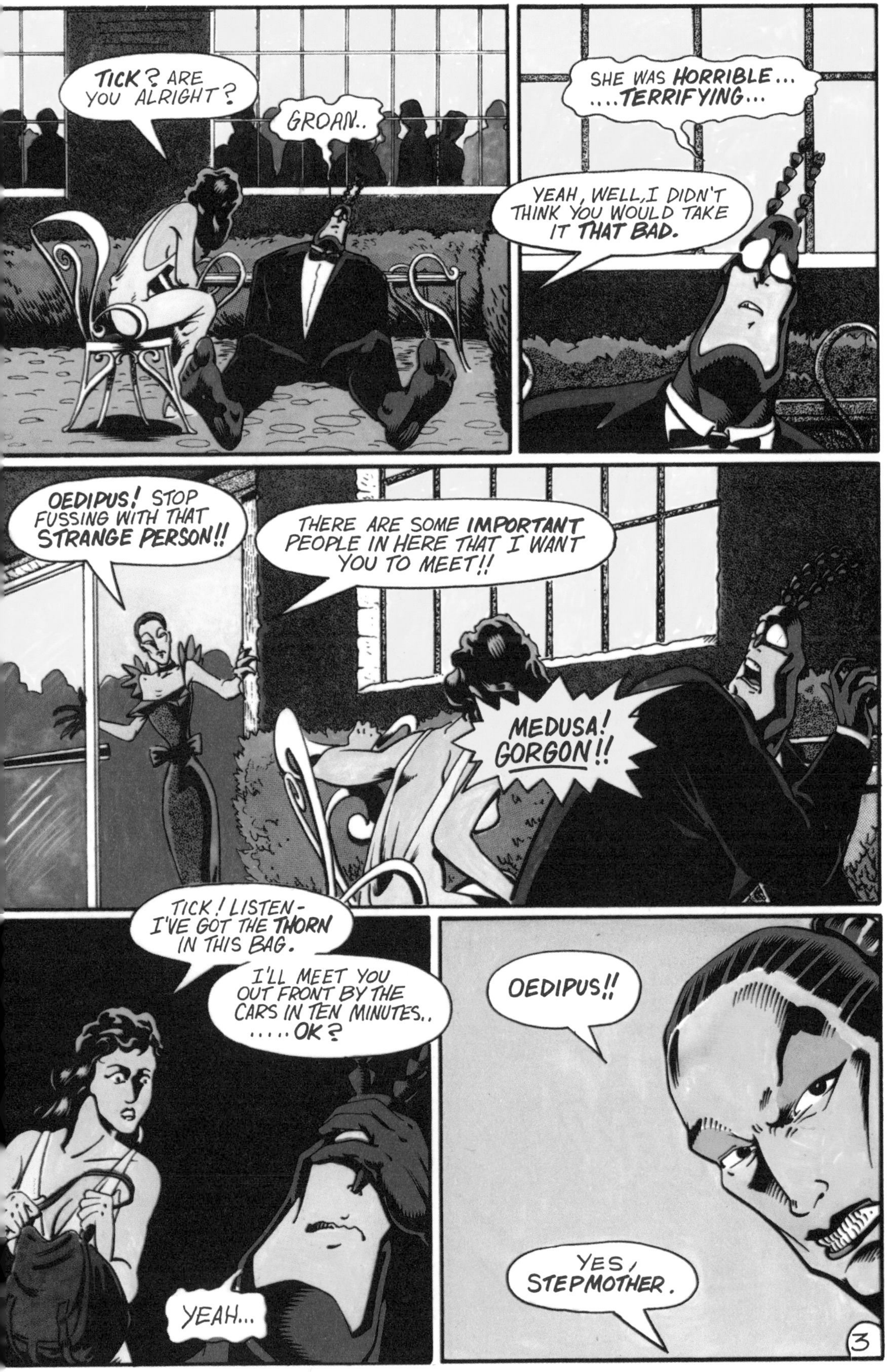
TICK? ARE YOU ALRIGHT?
GROAN..
SHE WAS HORRIBLE... ....TERRIFYING...
YEAH, WELL, I DIDN'T THINK YOU WOULD TAKE IT THAT BAD.
OEDIPUS! STOP FUSSING WITH THAT STRANGE PERSON!!
THERE ARE SOME IMPORTANT PEOPLE IN HERE THAT I WANT YOU TO MEET!!
MEDUSA! GORGON!!
TICK! LISTEN- I'VE GOT THE THORN IN THIS BAG.
I'LL MEET YOU OUT FRONT BY THE CARS IN TEN MINUTES.. .....OK?
YEAH...
OEDIPUS!!
YES, STEPMOTHER.
3

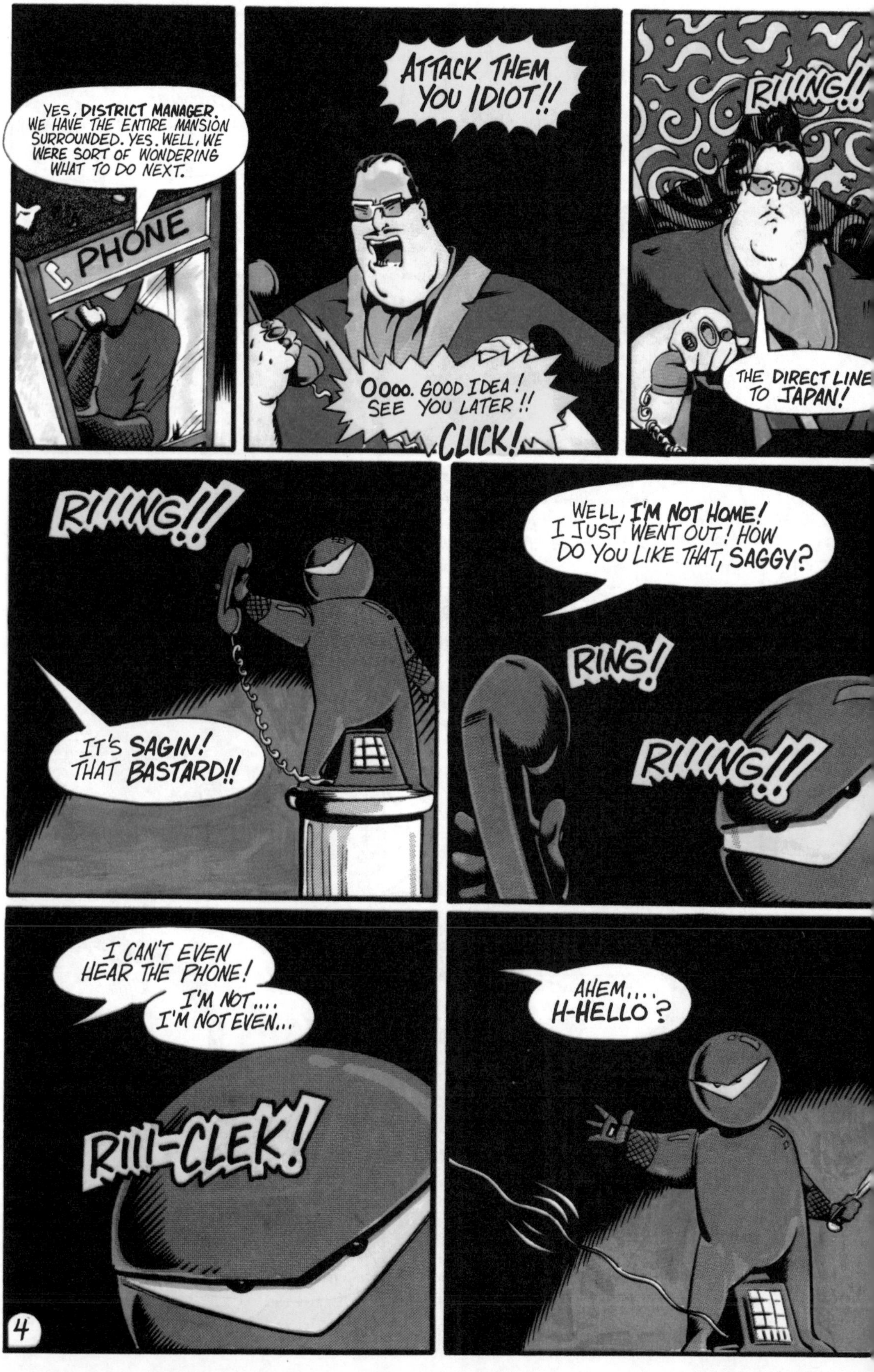

YES, DISTRICT MANAGER. WE HAVE THE ENTIRE MANSION SURROUNDED. YES. WELL, WE WERE SORT OF WONDERING WHAT TO DO NEXT.
PHONE
ATTACK THEM YOU IDIOT!!
Oooo. GOOD IDEA! SEE YOU LATER!!
CLICK!
RIIING!!
THE DIRECT LINE TO JAPAN!
RIIING!!
IT'S SAGIN! THAT BASTARD!!
WELL, I'M NOT HOME! I JUST WENT OUT! HOW DO YOU LIKE THAT, SAGGY?
RING!
RIIING!!
I CAN'T EVEN HEAR THE PHONE!
I'M NOT.... I'M NOT EVEN...
RIII-CLEK!
AHEM.... H-HELLO?

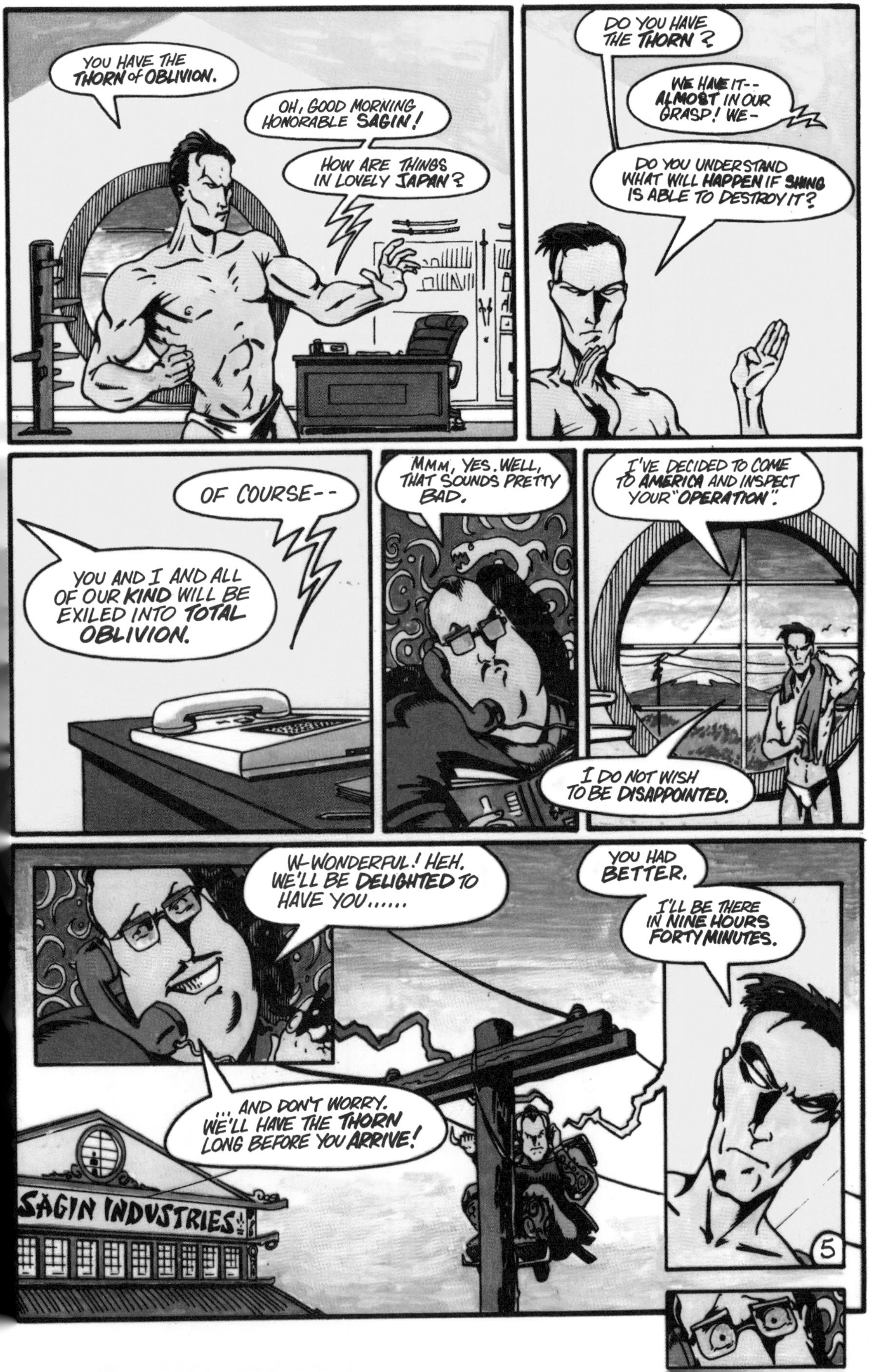
YOU HAVE THE THORN of OBLIVION.
OH, GOOD MORNING HONORABLE SAGIN!
HOW ARE THINGS IN LOVELY JAPAN?
DO YOU HAVE THE THORN?
WE HAVE IT-- ALMOST IN OUR GRASP! WE-
DO YOU UNDERSTAND WHAT WILL HAPPEN IF SHING IS ABLE TO DESTROY IT?
OF COURSE--
YOU AND I AND ALL OF OUR KIND WILL BE EXILED INTO TOTAL OBLIVION.
MMM, YES. WELL, THAT SOUNDS PRETTY BAD.
I'VE DECIDED TO COME TO AMERICA AND INSPECT YOUR "OPERATION".
I DO NOT WISH TO BE DISAPPOINTED.
W-WONDERFUL! HEH. WE'LL BE DELIGHTED TO HAVE YOU......
YOU HAD BETTER.
I'LL BE THERE IN NINE HOURS FORTY MINUTES.
... AND DON'T WORRY. WE'LL HAVE THE THORN LONG BEFORE YOU ARRIVE!
SAGIN INDUSTRIES
5

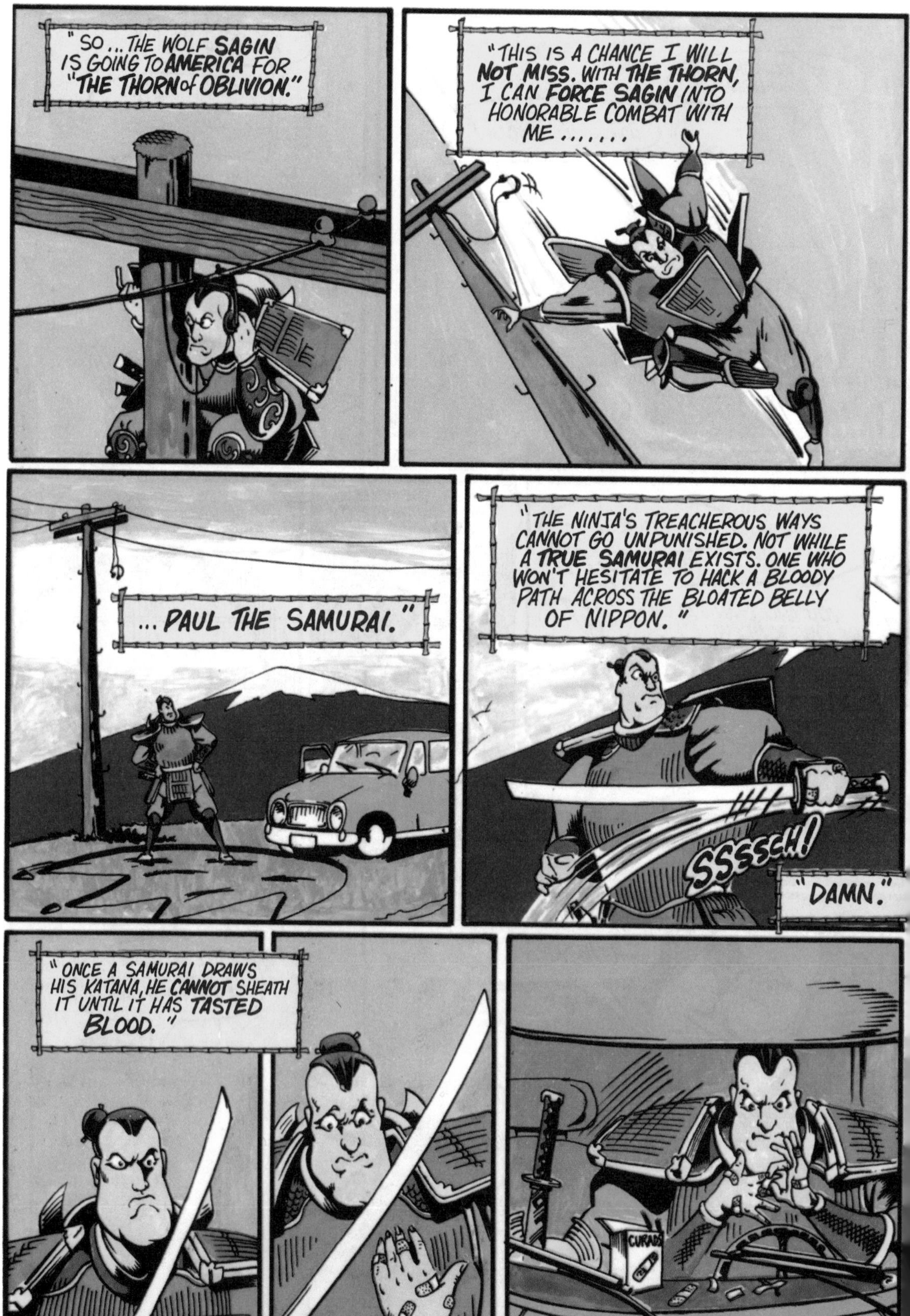
"SO... THE WOLF SAGIN IS GOING TO AMERICA FOR "THE THORN of OBLIVION."
"THIS IS A CHANCE I WILL NOT MISS. WITH THE THORN, I CAN FORCE SAGIN INTO HONORABLE COMBAT WITH ME.......
...PAUL THE SAMURAI."
"THE NINJA'S TREACHEROUS WAYS CANNOT GO UNPUNISHED. NOT WHILE A TRUE SAMURAI EXISTS. ONE WHO WON'T HESITATE TO HACK A BLOODY PATH ACROSS THE BLOATED BELLY OF NIPPON."
SSSSCH!
"DAMN."
"ONCE A SAMURAI DRAWS HIS KATANA, HE CANNOT SHEATH IT UNTIL IT HAS TASTED BLOOD."
CURADS

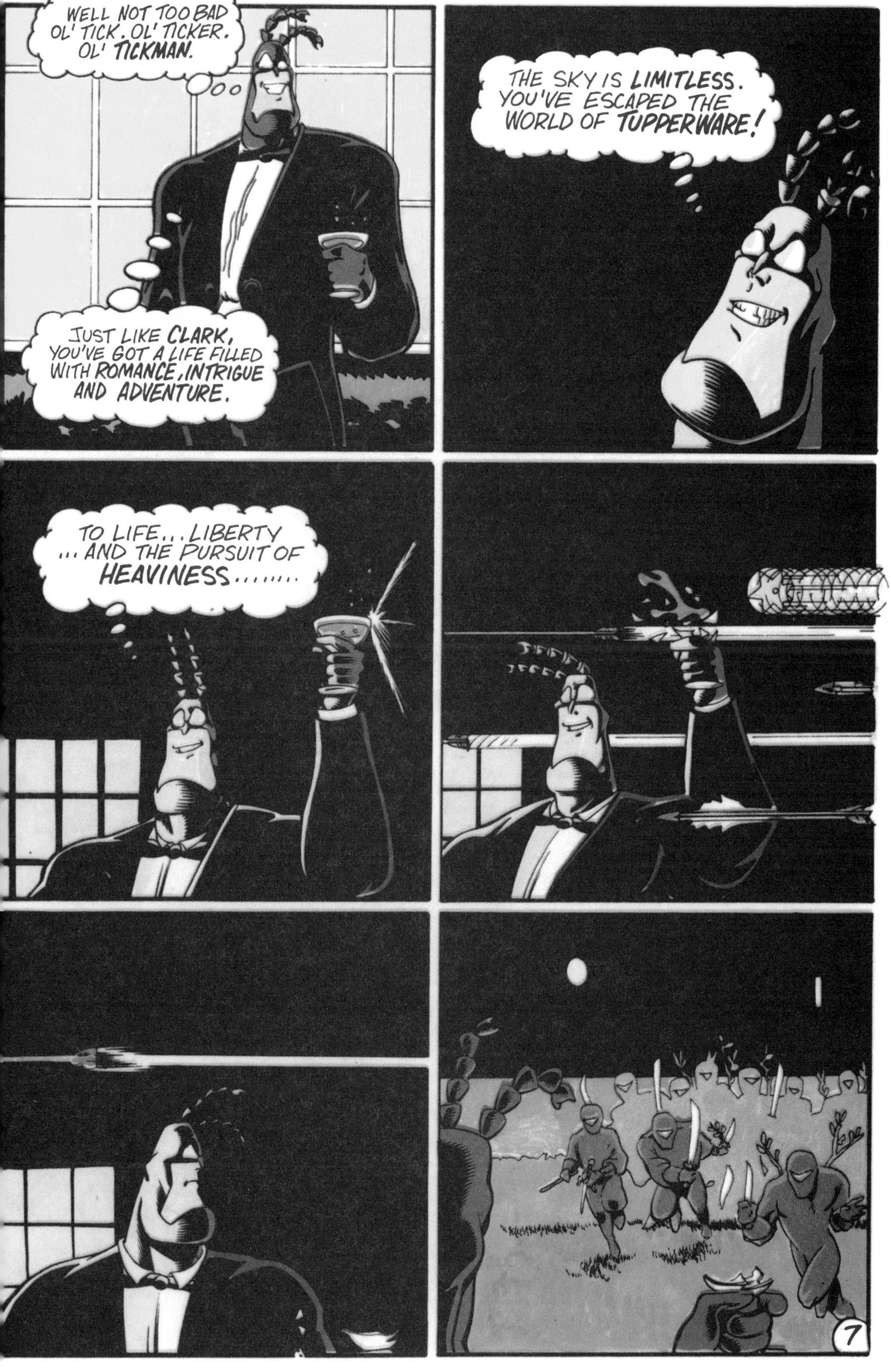
WELL NOT TOO BAD OL' TICK. OL' TICKER. OL' TICKMAN.
JUST LIKE CLARK, YOU'VE GOT A LIFE FILLED WITH ROMANCE, INTRIGUE AND ADVENTURE.
THE SKY IS LIMITLESS. YOU'VE ESCAPED THE WORLD OF TUPPERWARE!
TO LIFE... LIBERTY ... AND THE PURSUIT OF HEAVINESS........
7

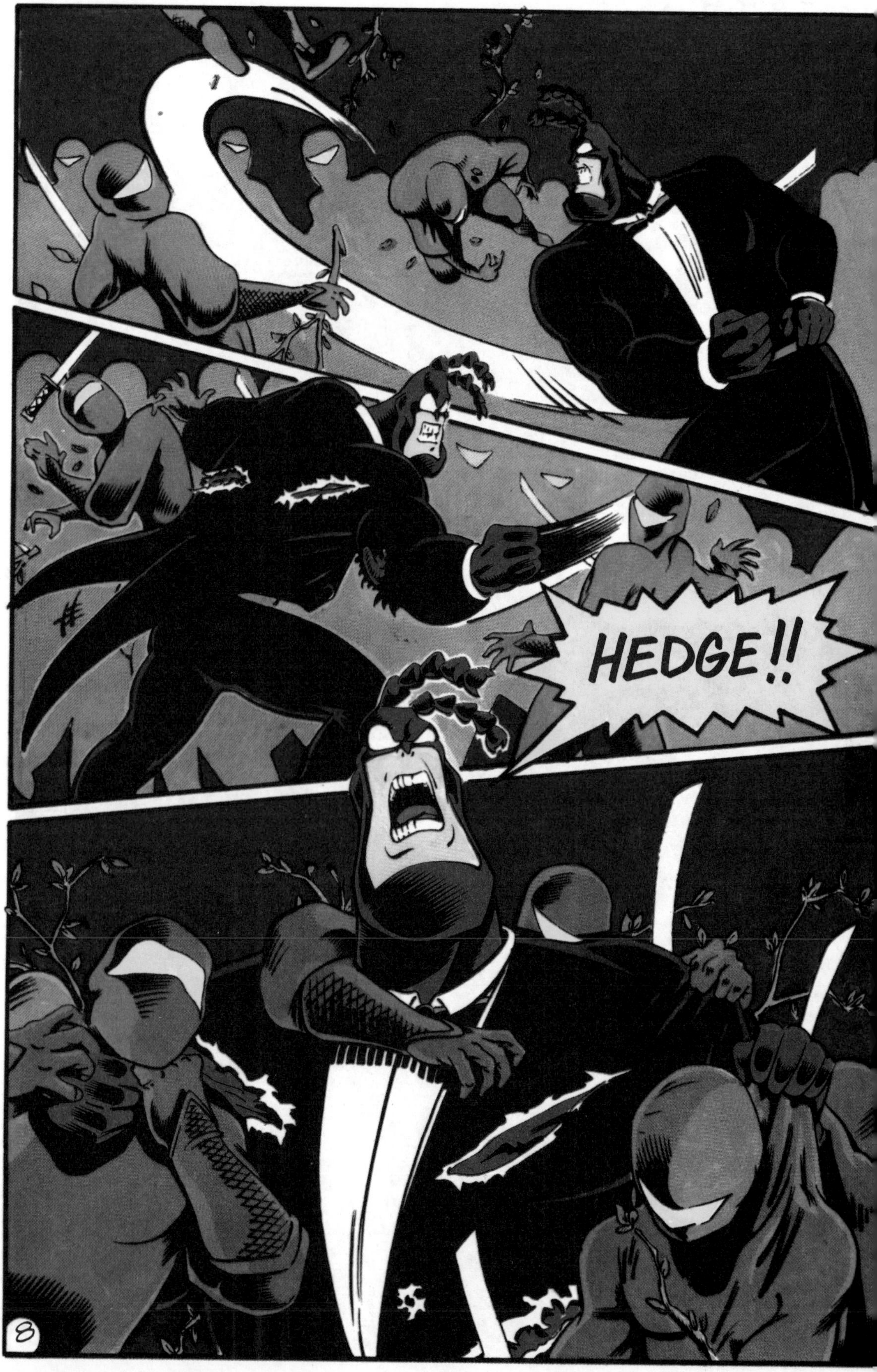
HEDGE!!

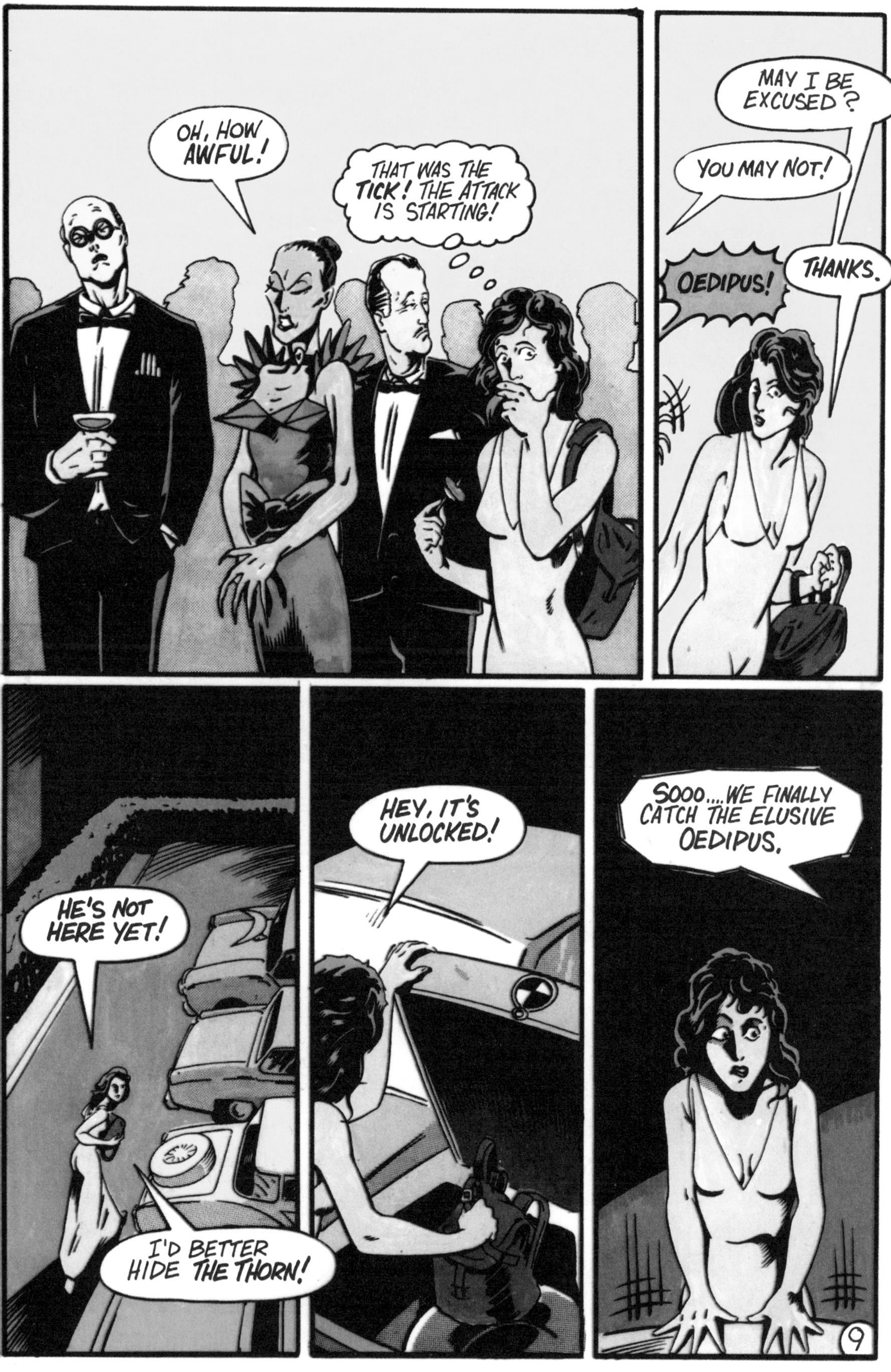
OH, HOW AWFUL!
THAT WAS THE TICK! THE ATTACK IS STARTING!
MAY I BE EXCUSED?
YOU MAY NOT!
OEDIPUS!
THANKS.
HE'S NOT HERE YET!
I'D BETTER HIDE THE THORN!
HEY, IT'S UNLOCKED!
SOOO....WE FINALLY CATCH THE ELUSIVE OEDIPUS.
9

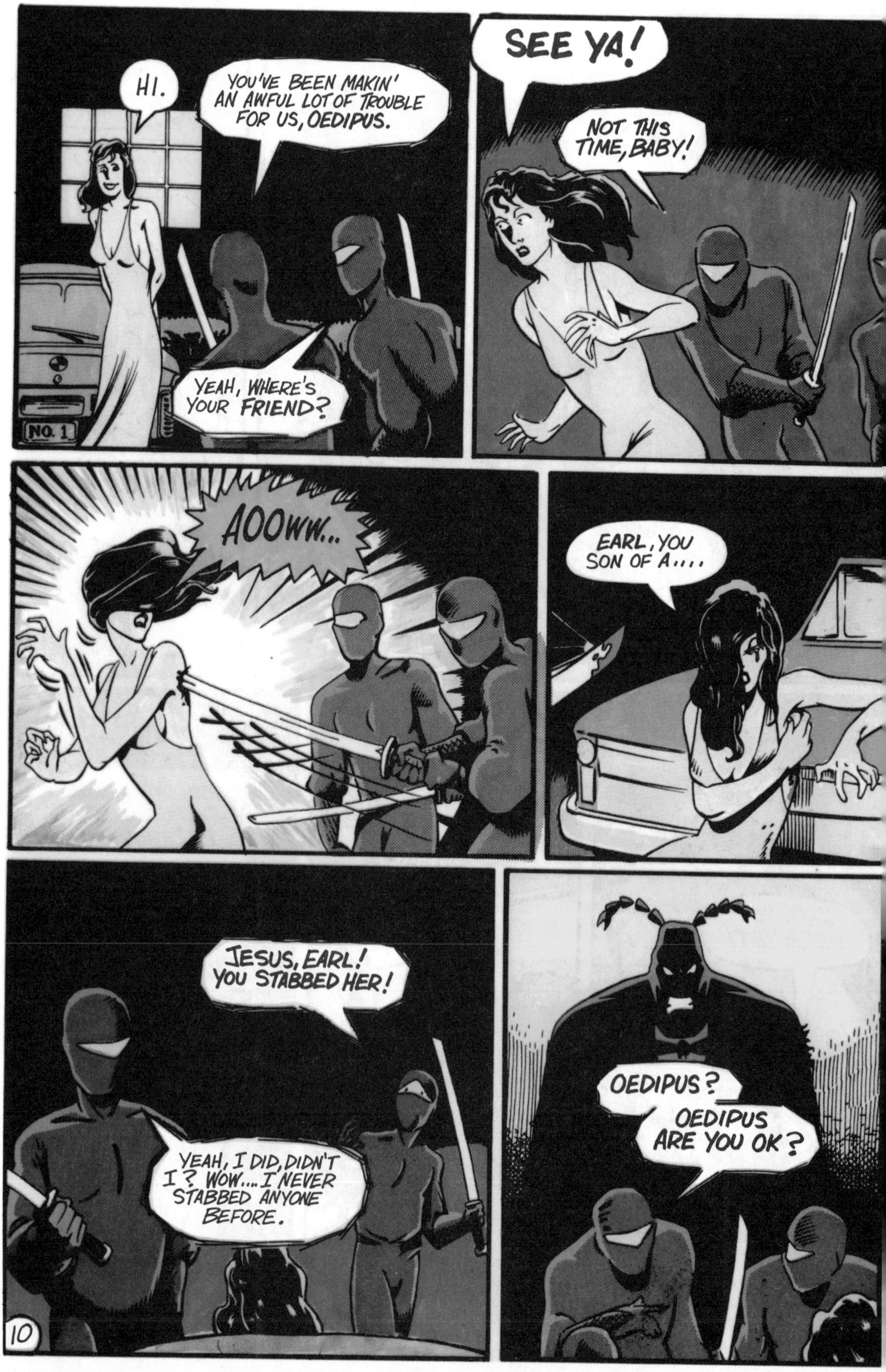
HI.
YOU'VE BEEN MAKIN' AN AWFUL LOT OF TROUBLE FOR US, OEDIPUS.
YEAH, WHERE'S YOUR FRIEND?
NO. 1
SEE YA!
NOT THIS TIME, BABY!
AOOWW...
EARL, YOU SON OF A....
JESUS, EARL! YOU STABBED HER!
YEAH, I DID, DIDN'T I? WOW.... I NEVER STABBED ANYONE BEFORE.
OEDIPUS?
OEDIPUS ARE YOU OK?

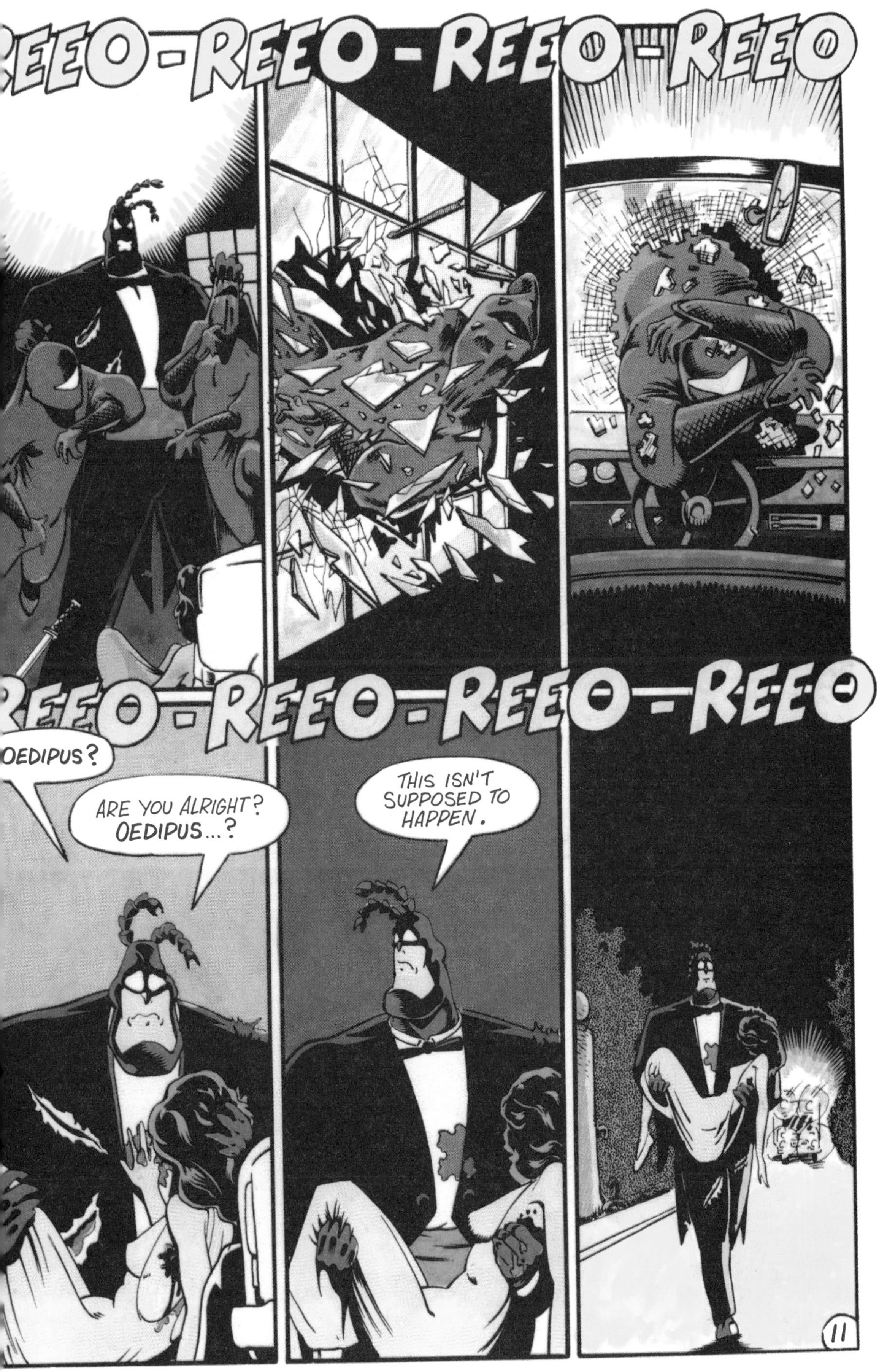
REEO-REEO-REEO-REEO
REEO-REEO-REEO-REEO
OEDIPUS?
ARE YOU ALRIGHT? OEDIPUS...?
THIS ISN'T SUPPOSED TO HAPPEN.
11

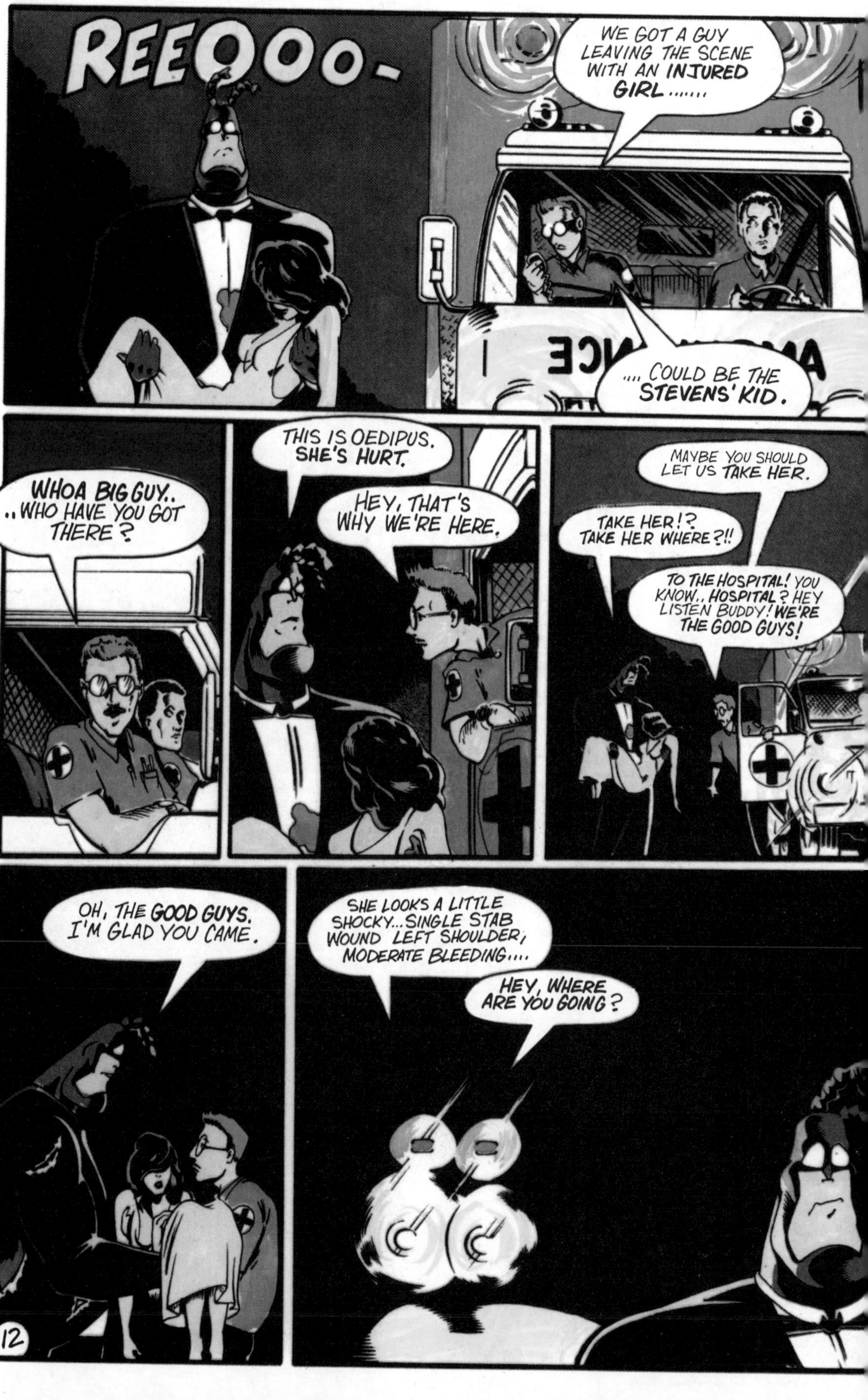
REEOOo-
WE GOT A GUY LEAVING THE SCENE WITH AN INJURED GIRL.......
....COULD BE THE STEVENS' KID.
WHOA BIG GUY.. ..WHO HAVE YOU GOT THERE?
THIS IS OEDIPUS. SHE'S HURT.
HEY, THAT'S WHY WE'RE HERE.
MAYBE YOU SHOULD LET US TAKE HER.
TAKE HER!? TAKE HER WHERE?!!
TO THE HOSPITAL! YOU KNOW.. HOSPITAL? HEY LISTEN BUDDY! WE'RE THE GOOD GUYS!
OH, THE GOOD GUYS. I'M GLAD YOU CAME.
SHE LOOKS A LITTLE SHOCKY...SINGLE STAB WOUND LEFT SHOULDER, MODERATE BLEEDING....
HEY, WHERE ARE YOU GOING?

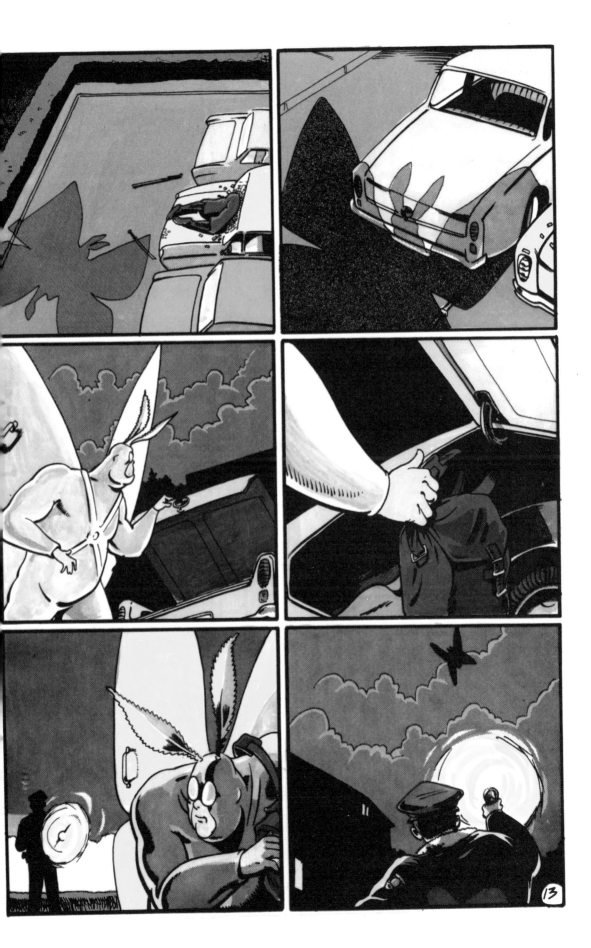

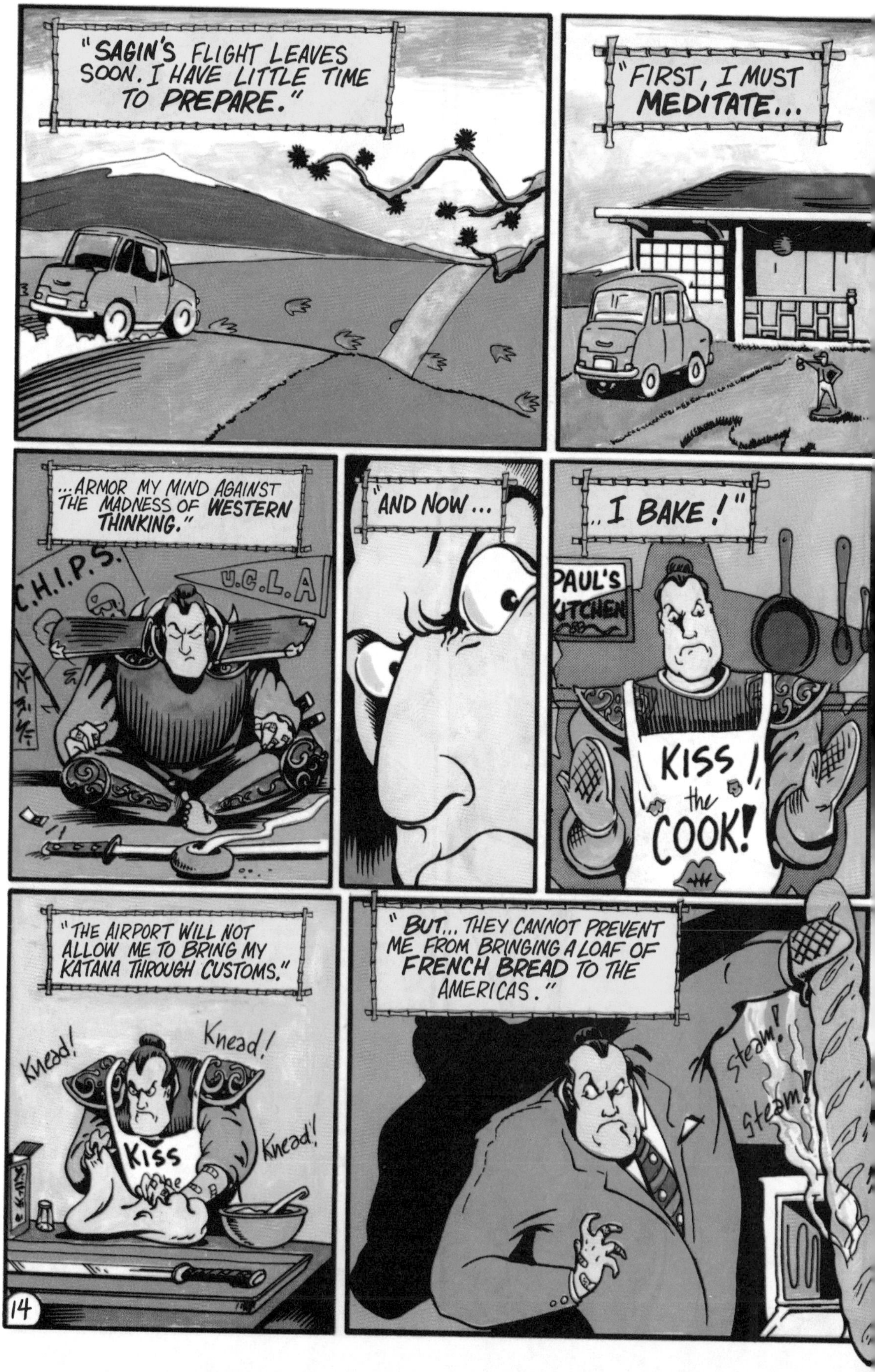
"SAGIN'S FLIGHT LEAVES SOON. I HAVE LITTLE TIME TO PREPARE."
"FIRST, I MUST MEDITATE...
...ARMOR MY MIND AGAINST THE MADNESS OF WESTERN THINKING."
C.H.I.P.S.
U.C.L.A
"AND NOW...
...I BAKE!"
PAUL'S KITCHEN
KISS the COOK!
"THE AIRPORT WILL NOT ALLOW ME TO BRING MY KATANA THROUGH CUSTOMS."
Knead!
Knead!
Knead!
KISS
"BUT... THEY CANNOT PREVENT ME FROM BRINGING A LOAF OF FRENCH BREAD TO THE AMERICAS."
steam!
steam!

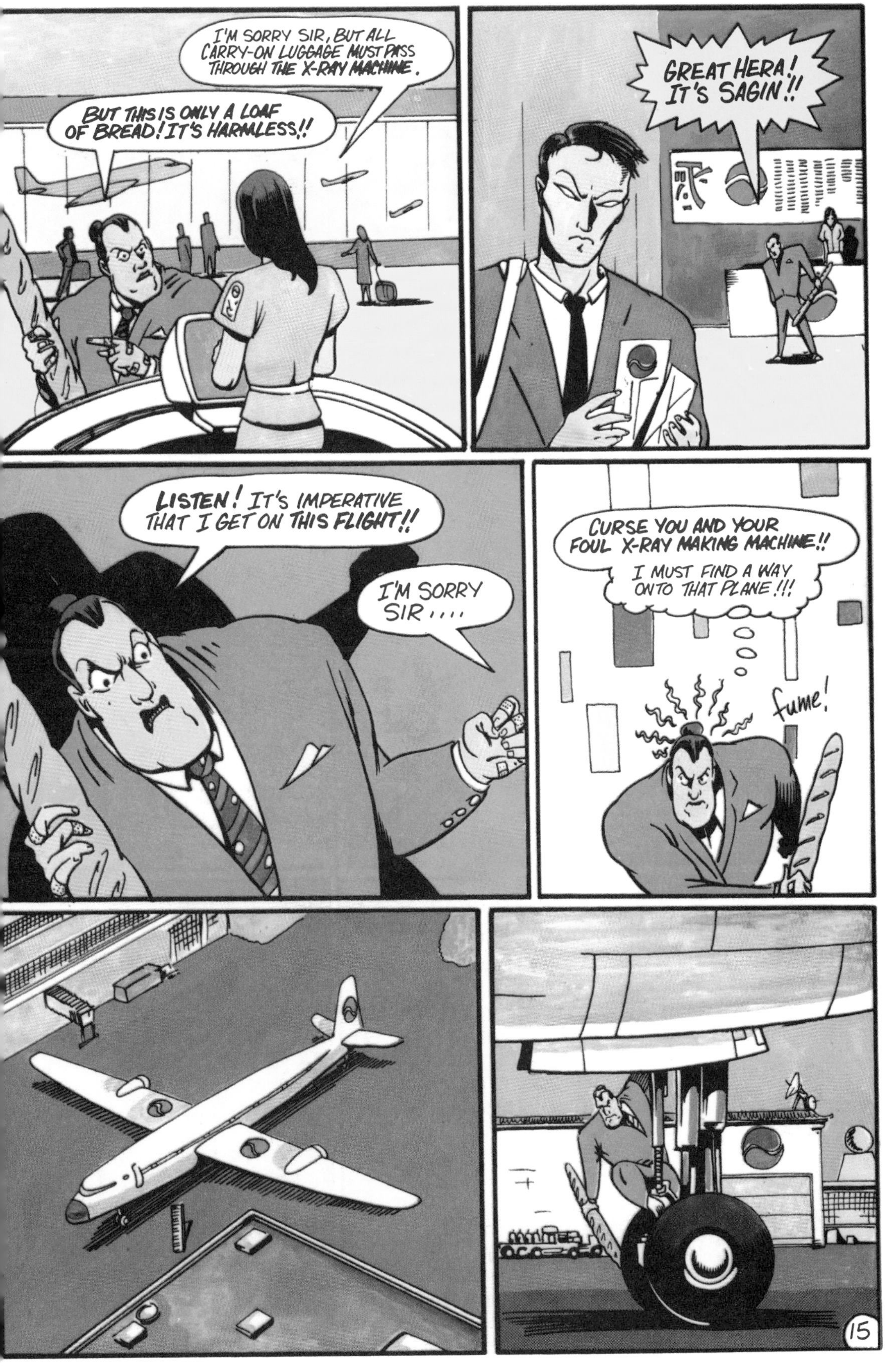
I'M SORRY SIR, BUT ALL CARRY-ON LUGGAGE MUST PASS THROUGH THE X-RAY MACHINE.
BUT THIS IS ONLY A LOAF OF BREAD! IT'S HARMLESS!!
GREAT HERA! IT'S SAGIN!!
LISTEN! IT'S IMPERATIVE THAT I GET ON THIS FLIGHT!!
I'M SORRY SIR....
CURSE YOU AND YOUR FOUL X-RAY MAKING MACHINE!!
I MUST FIND A WAY ONTO THAT PLANE!!!
fume!

"TIME IS MEANINGLESS. I'VE BEEN AT THIS FOR HOURS. JUMPING, JUMPING, JUMPING."

"I CAN'T SEEM TO CONCENTRATE. CAN'T FOCUS. BUT I KNOW THIS:

THE WORLD ISN'T WHAT I WANT IT TO BE ANYMORE."

"IT USED TO BE SO EASY...

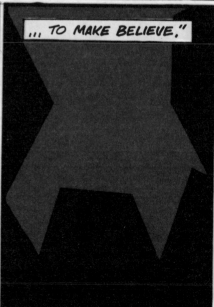

"... TO MAKE BELIEVE."

16

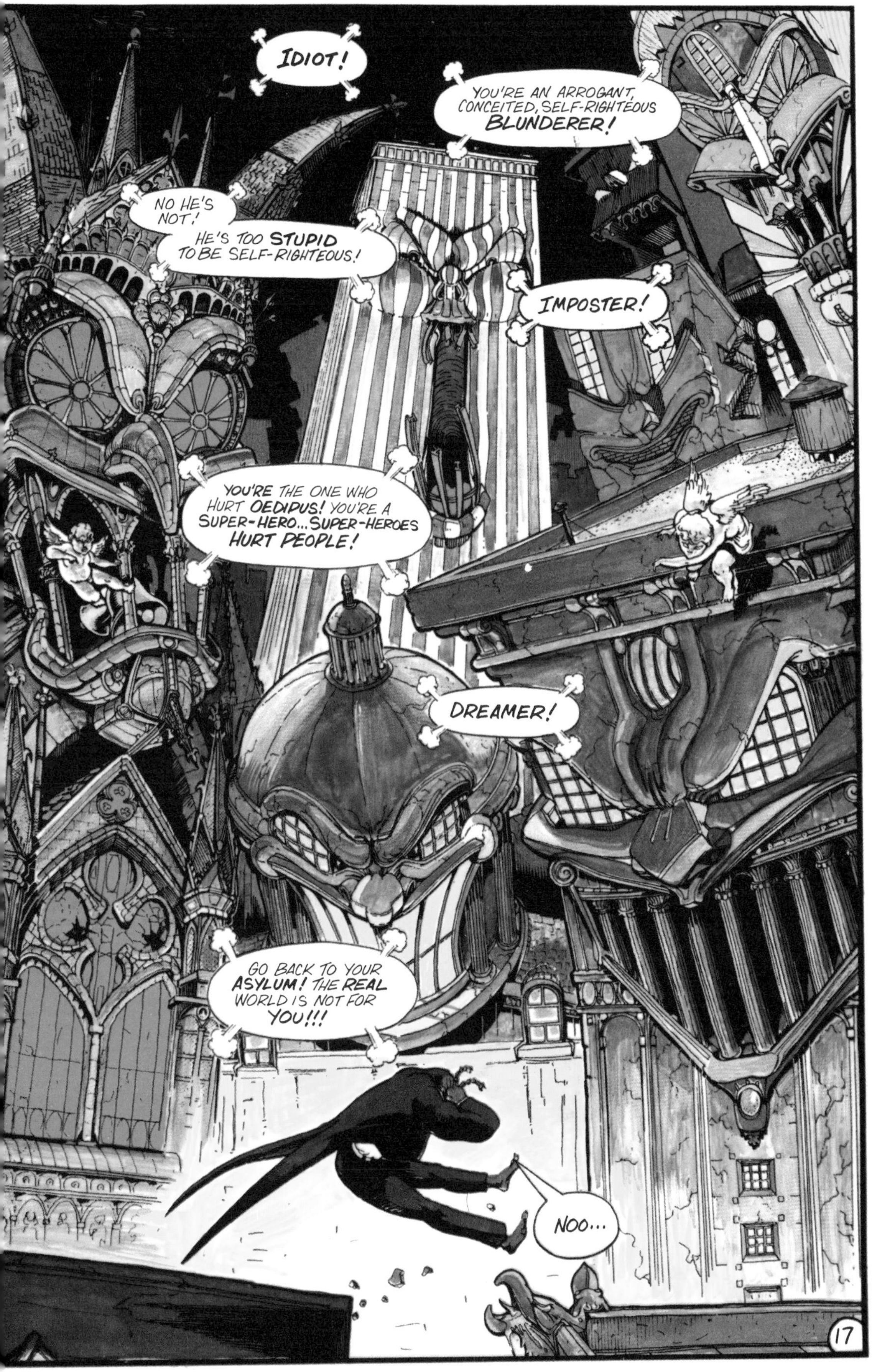
IDIOT!
YOU'RE AN ARROGANT, CONCEITED, SELF-RIGHTEOUS BLUNDERER!
NO HE'S NOT!
HE'S TOO STUPID TO BE SELF-RIGHTEOUS!
IMPOSTER!
YOU'RE THE ONE WHO HURT OEDIPUS! YOU'RE A SUPER-HERO... SUPER-HEROES HURT PEOPLE!
DREAMER!
GO BACK TO YOUR ASYLUM! THE REAL WORLD IS NOT FOR YOU!!!
NOO...

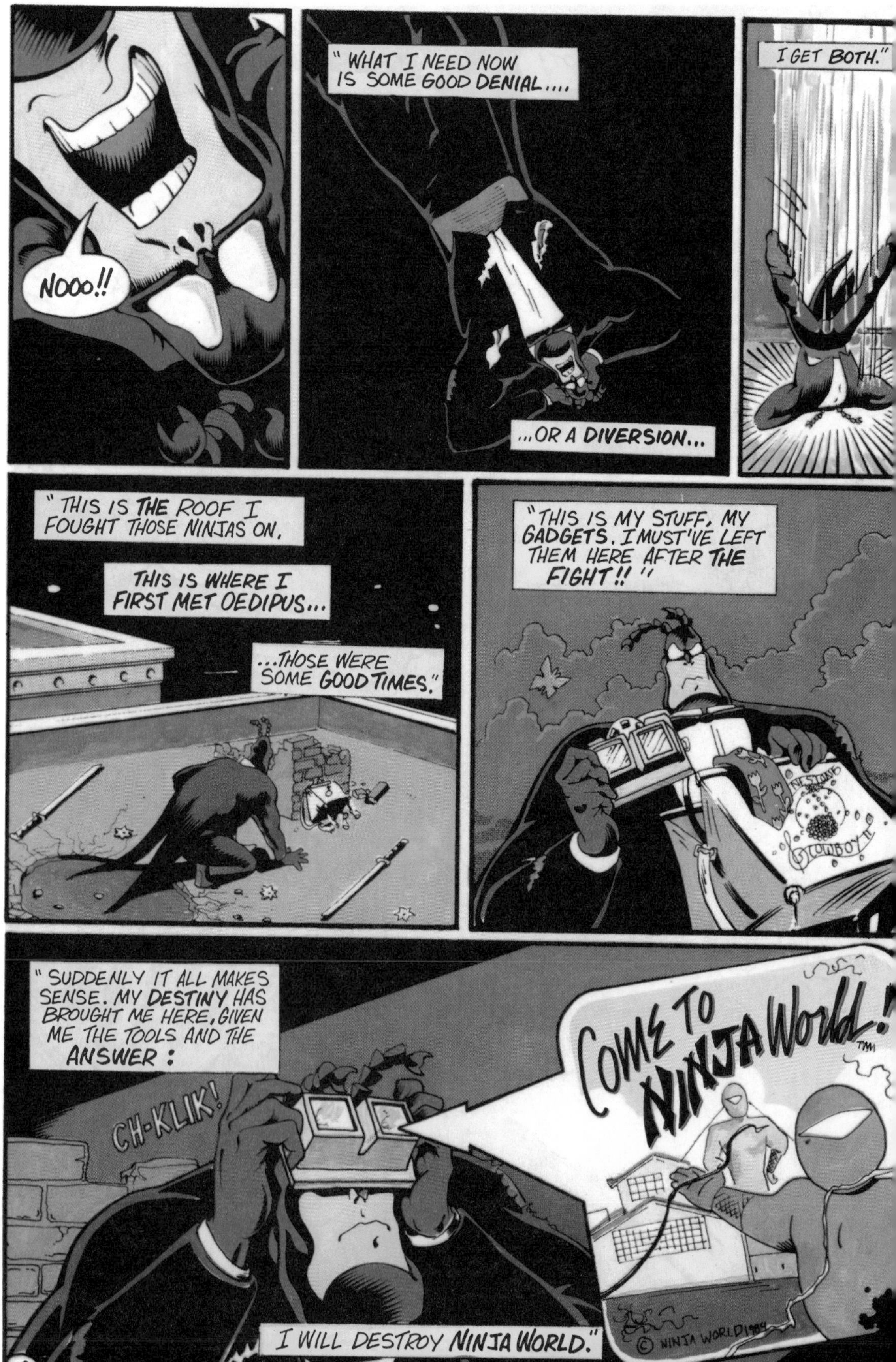
NOOO!!
"WHAT I NEED NOW IS SOME GOOD DENIAL....
...OR A DIVERSION...
I GET BOTH."
"THIS IS THE ROOF I FOUGHT THOSE NINJAS ON.
THIS IS WHERE I FIRST MET OEDIPUS...
...THOSE WERE SOME GOOD TIMES."
"THIS IS MY STUFF, MY GADGETS. I MUST'VE LEFT THEM HERE AFTER THE FIGHT!!"
"SUDDENLY IT ALL MAKES SENSE. MY DESTINY HAS BROUGHT ME HERE, GIVEN ME THE TOOLS AND THE ANSWER:
CH-KLIK!
COME TO NINJA WORLD!™
© NINJA WORLD 1984
I WILL DESTROY NINJA WORLD."

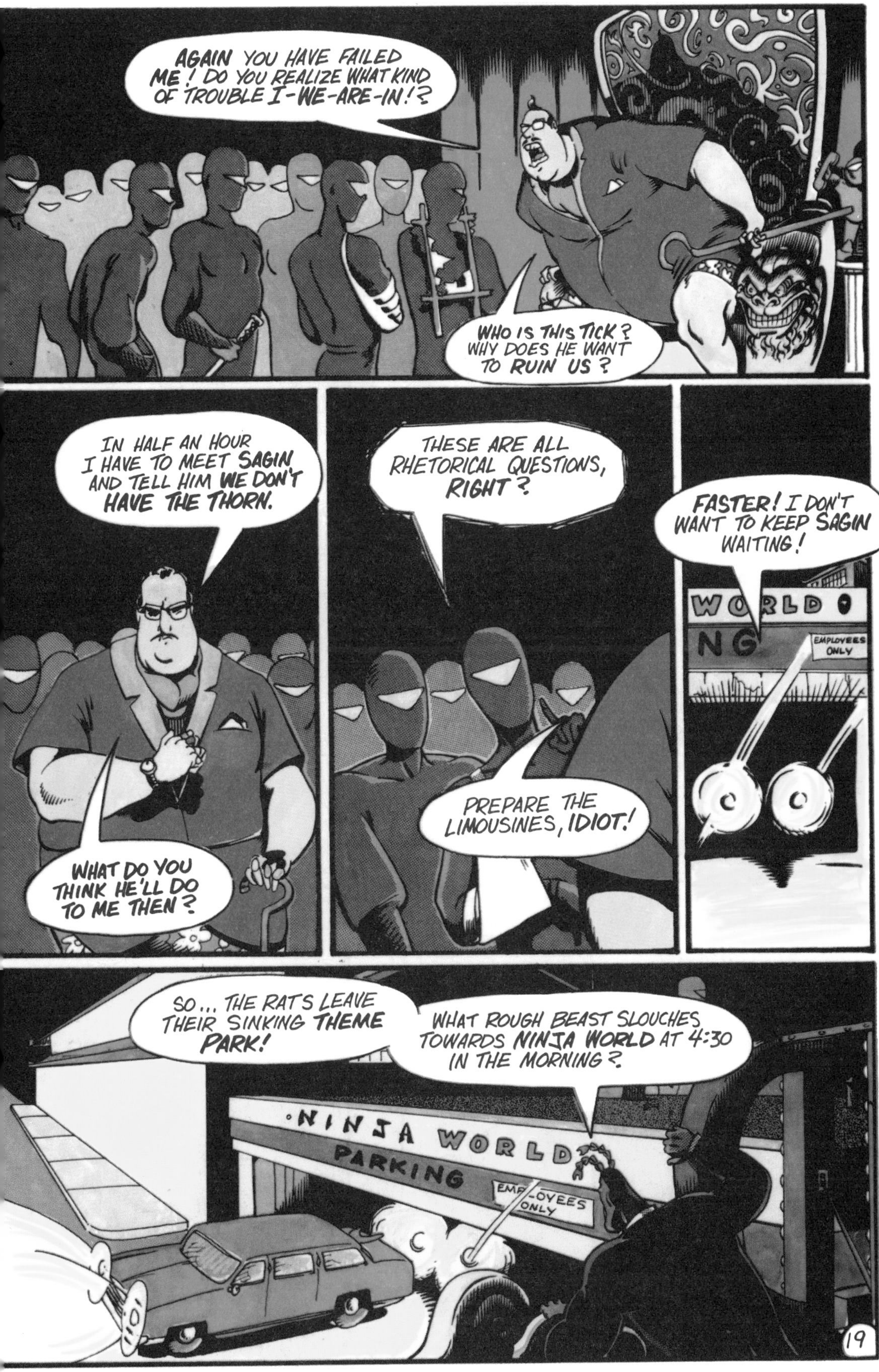
AGAIN YOU HAVE FAILED ME! DO YOU REALIZE WHAT KIND OF TROUBLE I-WE-ARE-IN!?
WHO IS THIS TICK? WHY DOES HE WANT TO RUIN US?
IN HALF AN HOUR I HAVE TO MEET SAGIN AND TELL HIM WE DON'T HAVE THE THORN.
WHAT DO YOU THINK HE'LL DO TO ME THEN?
THESE ARE ALL RHETORICAL QUESTIONS, RIGHT?
PREPARE THE LIMOUSINES, IDIOT!
FASTER! I DON'T WANT TO KEEP SAGIN WAITING!
WORLD
NG
EMPLOYEES ONLY
SO... THE RAT'S LEAVE THEIR SINKING THEME PARK!
WHAT ROUGH BEAST SLOUCHES TOWARDS NINJA WORLD AT 4:30 IN THE MORNING?
NINJA WORLD
PARKING
EMPLOYEES ONLY

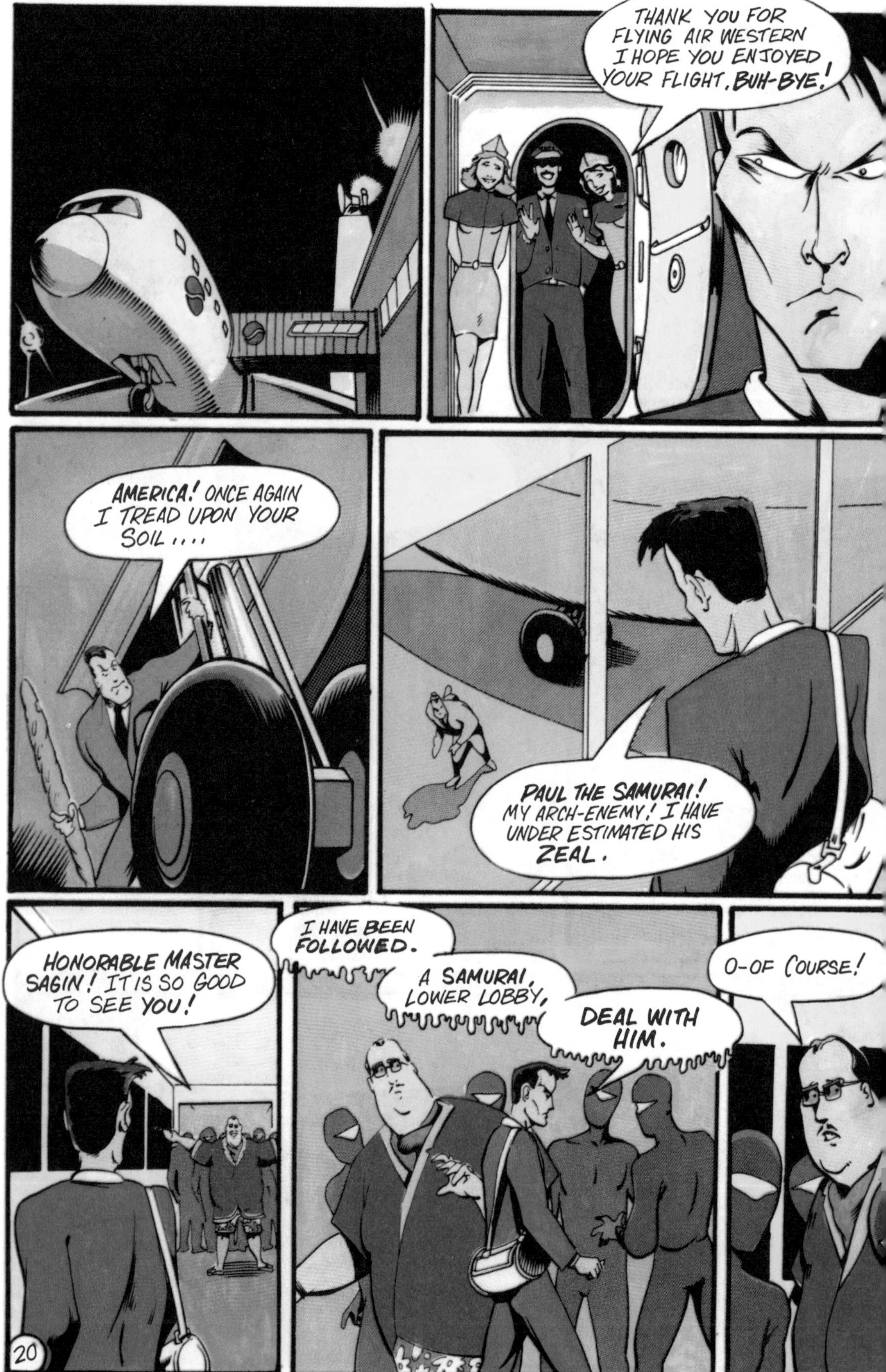
THANK YOU FOR FLYING AIR WESTERN I HOPE YOU ENJOYED YOUR FLIGHT. BUH-BYE!
AMERICA! ONCE AGAIN I TREAD UPON YOUR SOIL....
PAUL THE SAMURAI! MY ARCH-ENEMY! I HAVE UNDER ESTIMATED HIS ZEAL.
HONORABLE MASTER SAGIN! IT IS SO GOOD TO SEE YOU!
I HAVE BEEN FOLLOWED.
A SAMURAI, LOWER LOBBY,
DEAL WITH HIM.
O-OF COURSE!
20

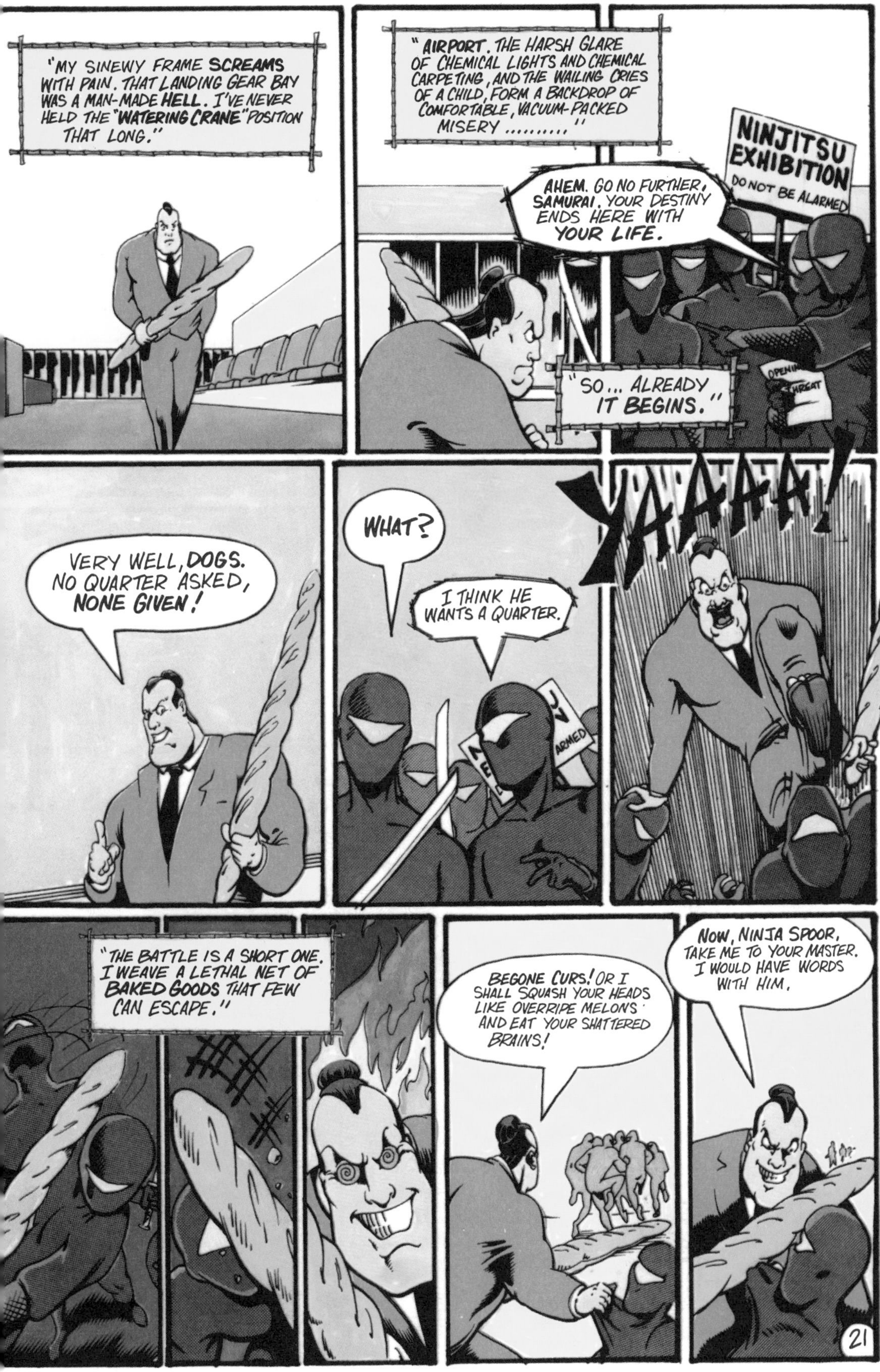
"MY SINEWY FRAME SCREAMS WITH PAIN. THAT LANDING GEAR BAY WAS A MAN-MADE HELL. I'VE NEVER HELD THE "WATERING CRANE" POSITION THAT LONG."
"AIRPORT. THE HARSH GLARE OF CHEMICAL LIGHTS AND CHEMICAL CARPETING, AND THE WAILING CRIES OF A CHILD, FORM A BACKDROP OF COMFORTABLE, VACUUM-PACKED MISERY ...."
NINJITSU EXHIBITION
DO NOT BE ALARMED
AHEM. GO NO FURTHER, SAMURAI, YOUR DESTINY ENDS HERE WITH YOUR LIFE.
"SO... ALREADY IT BEGINS."
VERY WELL, DOGS. NO QUARTER ASKED, NONE GIVEN!
WHAT?
I THINK HE WANTS A QUARTER.
YAAAA!
"THE BATTLE IS A SHORT ONE. I WEAVE A LETHAL NET OF BAKED GOODS THAT FEW CAN ESCAPE."
BEGONE CURS! OR I SHALL SQUASH YOUR HEADS LIKE OVERRIPE MELONS AND EAT YOUR SHATTERED BRAINS!
NOW, NINJA SPOOR, TAKE ME TO YOUR MASTER. I WOULD HAVE WORDS WITH HIM.

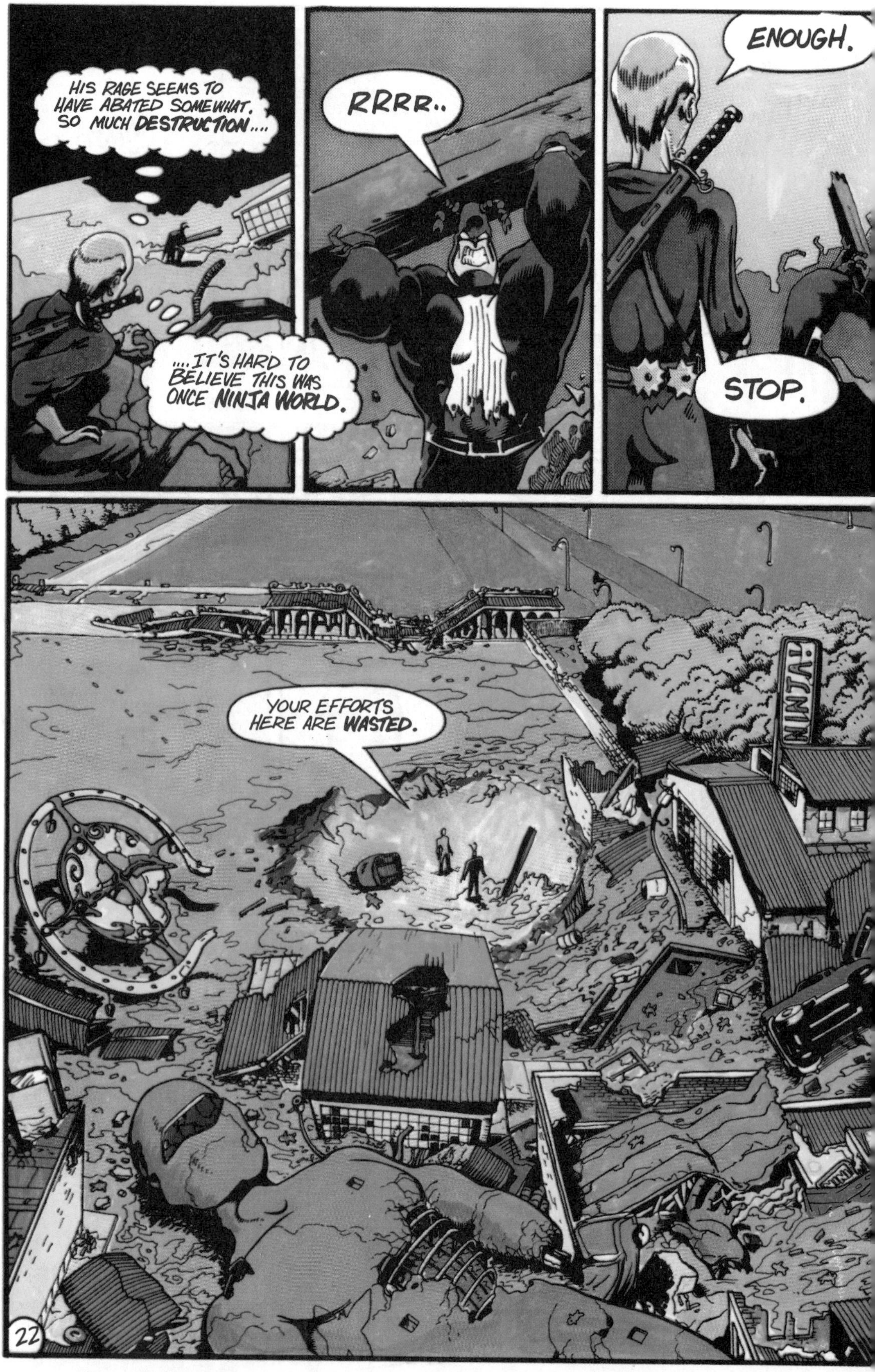

HIS RAGE SEEMS TO HAVE ABATED SOMEWHAT. SO MUCH DESTRUCTION....
....IT'S HARD TO BELIEVE THIS WAS ONCE NINJA WORLD.
RRRR..
ENOUGH.
STOP.
YOUR EFFORTS HERE ARE WASTED.

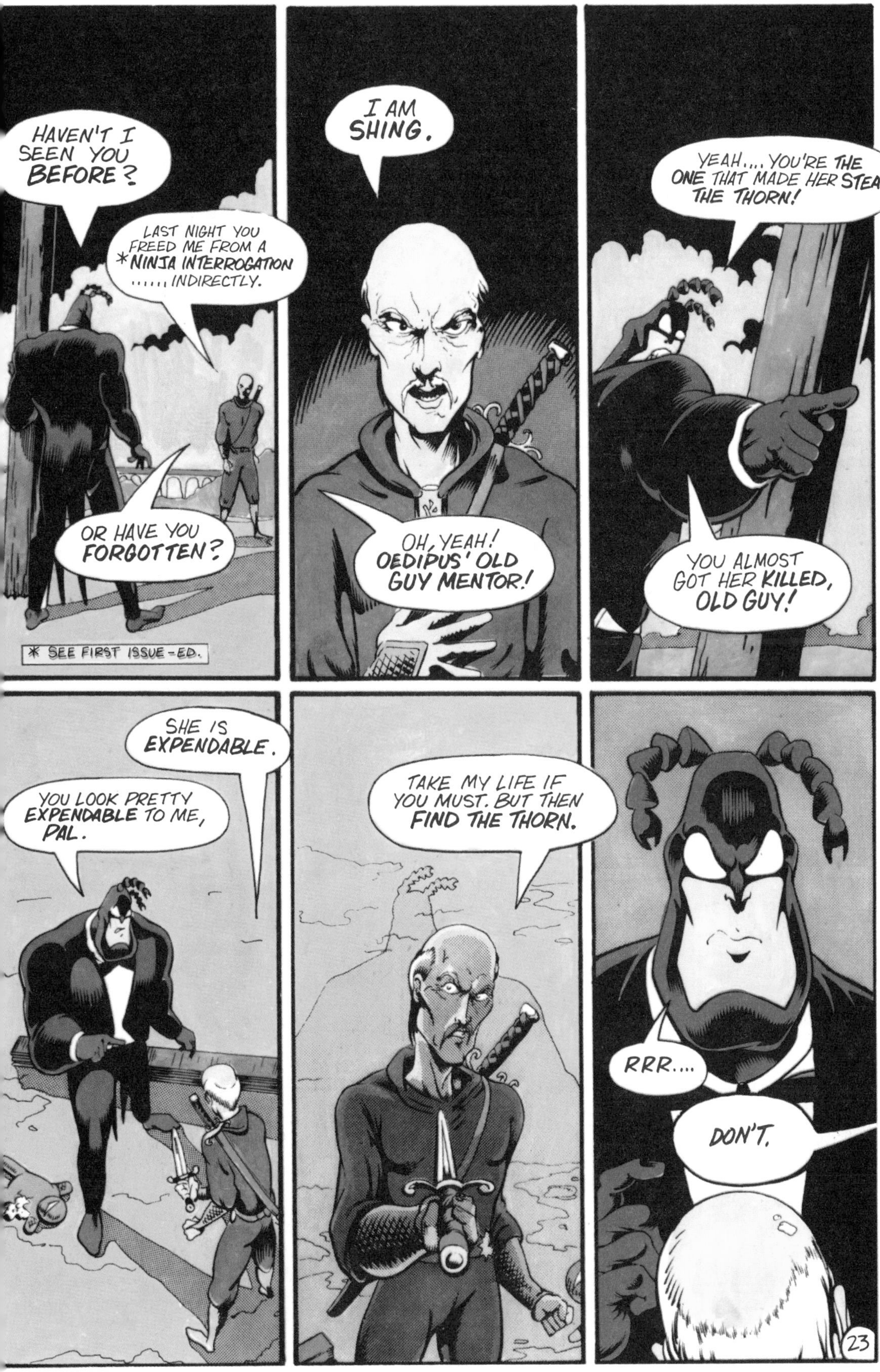
HAVEN'T I SEEN YOU BEFORE?
LAST NIGHT YOU FREED ME FROM A *NINJA INTERROGATION ...... INDIRECTLY.
OR HAVE YOU FORGOTTEN?
* SEE FIRST ISSUE - ED.
I AM SHING.
OH, YEAH! OEDIPUS' OLD GUY MENTOR!
YEAH.... YOU'RE THE ONE THAT MADE HER STEAL THE THORN!
YOU ALMOST GOT HER KILLED, OLD GUY!
SHE IS EXPENDABLE.
YOU LOOK PRETTY EXPENDABLE TO ME, PAL.
TAKE MY LIFE IF YOU MUST. BUT THEN FIND THE THORN.
RRR....
DON'T.

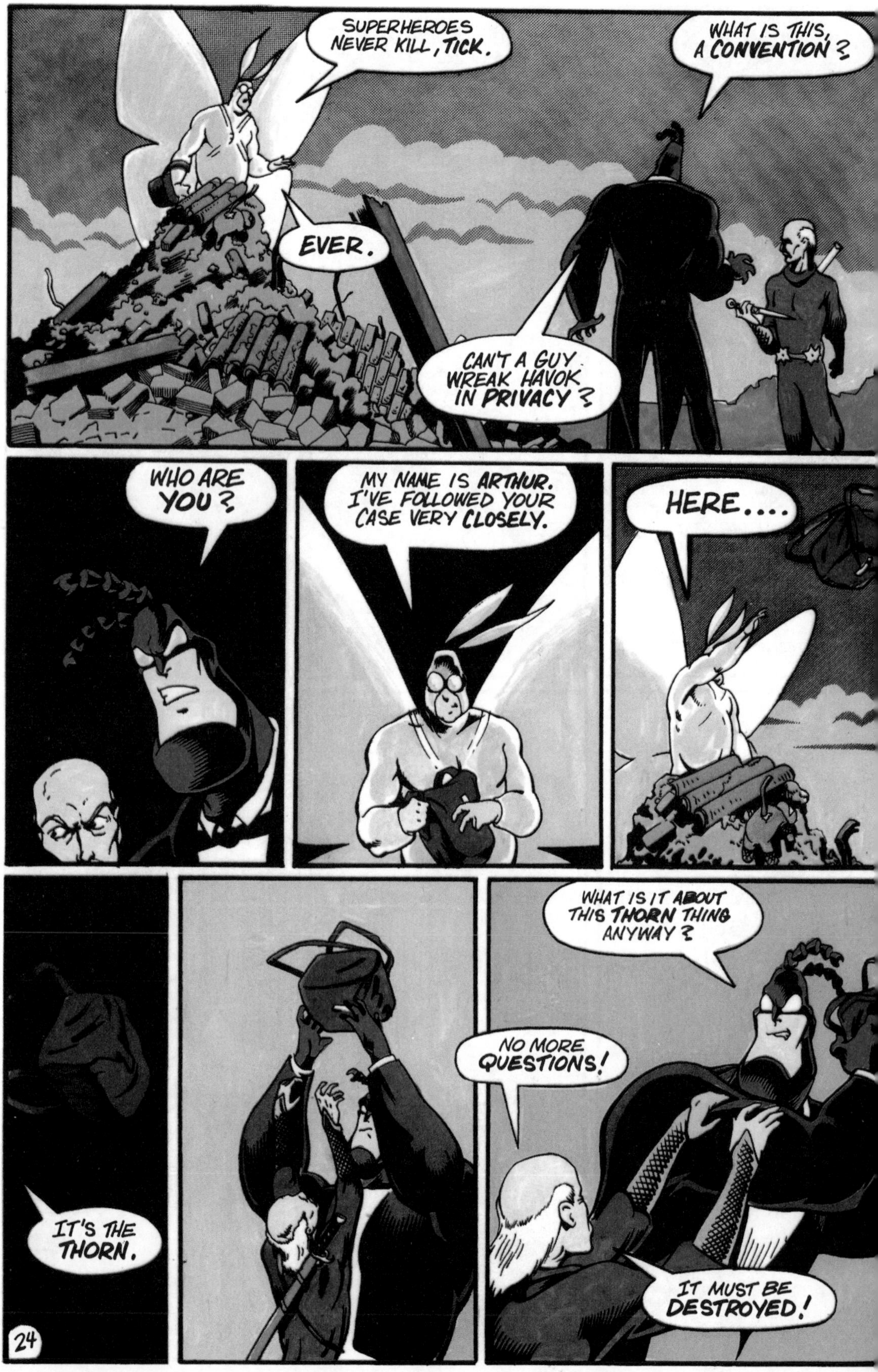
SUPERHEROES NEVER KILL, TICK.
EVER.
WHAT IS THIS, A CONVENTION?
CAN'T A GUY WREAK HAVOK IN PRIVACY?
WHO ARE YOU?
MY NAME IS ARTHUR. I'VE FOLLOWED YOUR CASE VERY CLOSELY.
HERE....
IT'S THE THORN.
WHAT IS IT ABOUT THIS THORN THING ANYWAY?
NO MORE QUESTIONS!
IT MUST BE DESTROYED!

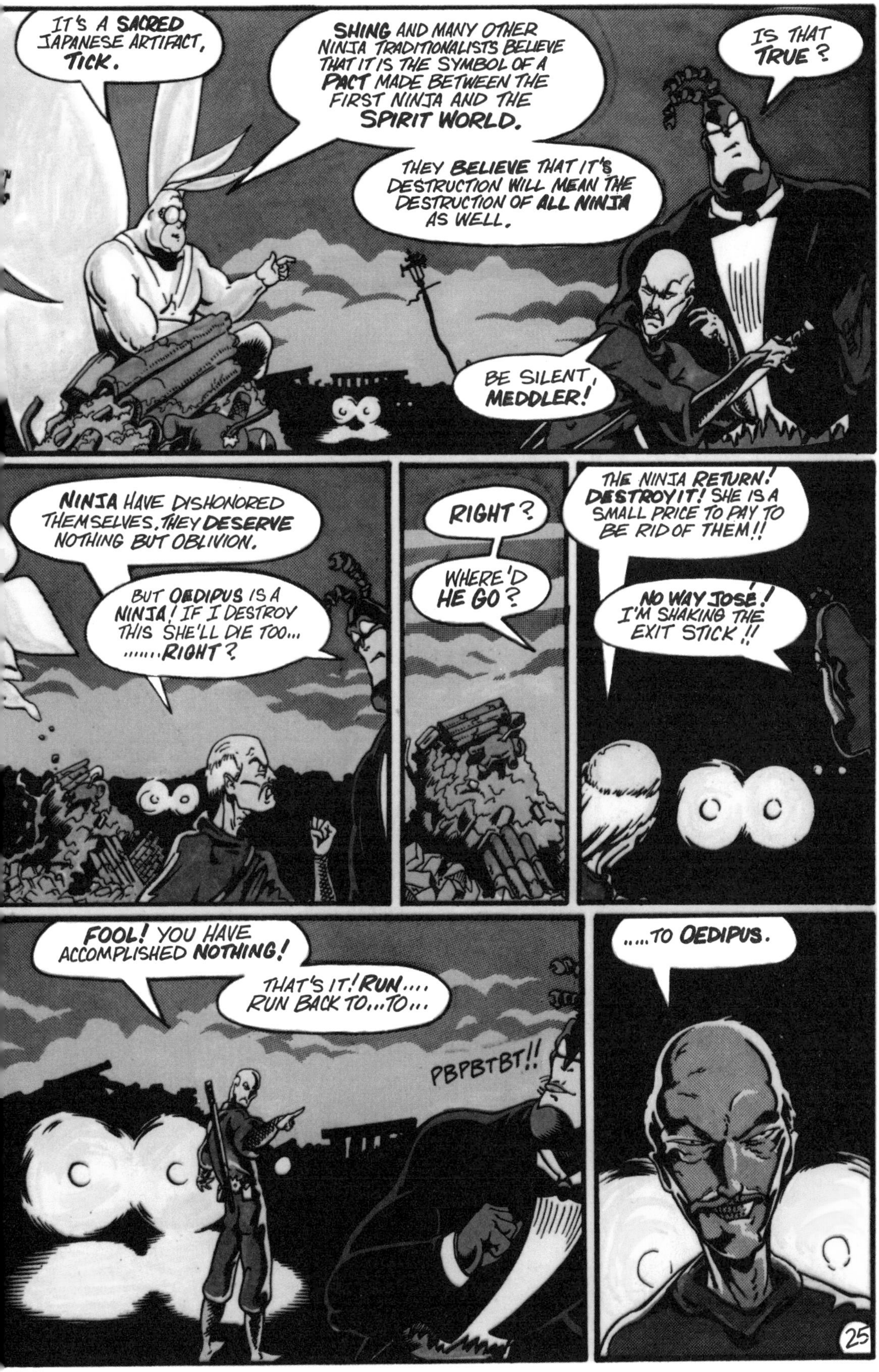
IT'S A SACRED JAPANESE ARTIFACT, TICK.
SHING AND MANY OTHER NINJA TRADITIONALISTS BELIEVE THAT IT IS THE SYMBOL OF A PACT MADE BETWEEN THE FIRST NINJA AND THE SPIRIT WORLD.
THEY BELIEVE THAT IT'S DESTRUCTION WILL MEAN THE DESTRUCTION OF ALL NINJA AS WELL.
IS THAT TRUE?
BE SILENT, MEDDLER!
NINJA HAVE DISHONORED THEMSELVES, THEY DESERVE NOTHING BUT OBLIVION.
BUT OEDIPUS IS A NINJA! IF I DESTROY THIS SHE'LL DIE TOO... ....RIGHT?
RIGHT?
WHERE'D HE GO?
THE NINJA RETURN! DESTROY IT! SHE IS A SMALL PRICE TO PAY TO BE RID OF THEM!!
NO WAY JOSÉ! I'M SHAKING THE EXIT STICK!!
FOOL! YOU HAVE ACCOMPLISHED NOTHING!
THAT'S IT! RUN.... RUN BACK TO...TO...
PBPBTBT!!
.....TO OEDIPUS.

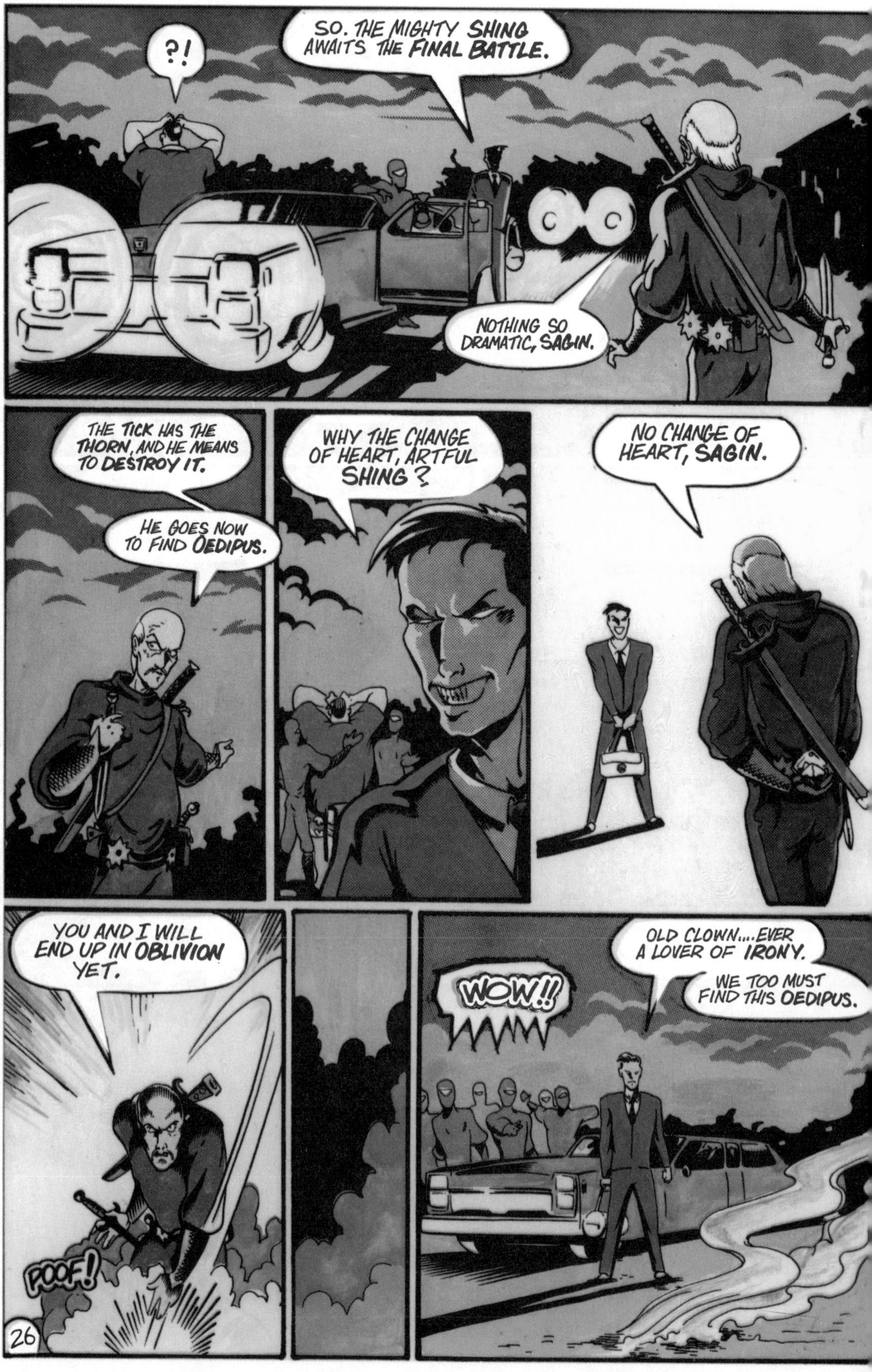
?!
SO. THE MIGHTY SHING AWAITS THE FINAL BATTLE.
NOTHING SO DRAMATIC, SAGIN.
THE TICK HAS THE THORN, AND HE MEANS TO DESTROY IT.
HE GOES NOW TO FIND OEDIPUS.
WHY THE CHANGE OF HEART, ARTFUL SHING?
NO CHANGE OF HEART, SAGIN.
YOU AND I WILL END UP IN OBLIVION YET.
POOF!
WOW!!
OLD CLOWN....EVER A LOVER OF IRONY.
WE TOO MUST FIND THIS OEDIPUS.

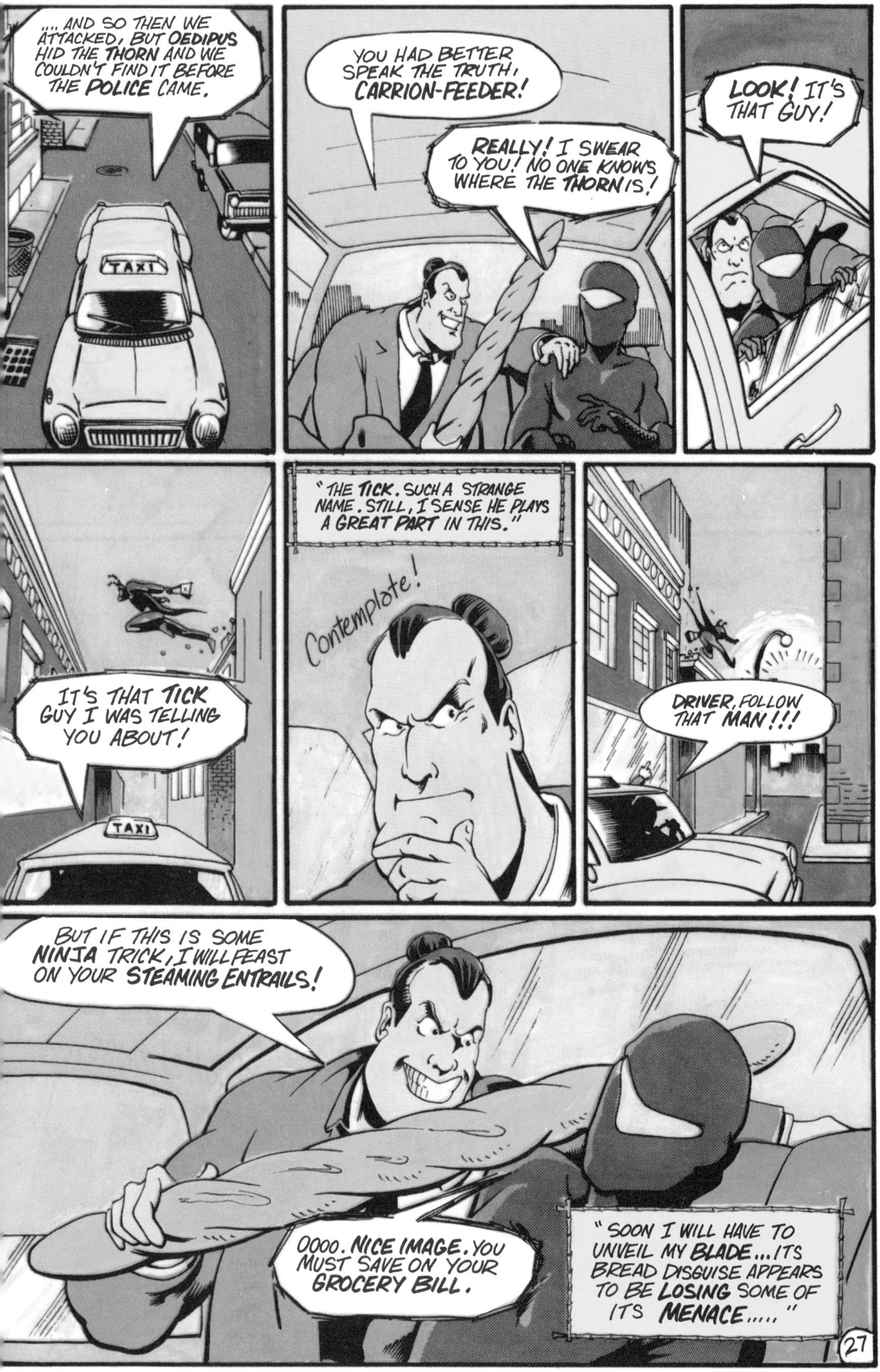
....AND SO THEN WE ATTACKED, BUT OEDIPUS HID THE THORN AND WE COULDN'T FIND IT BEFORE THE POLICE CAME.
TAXI
YOU HAD BETTER SPEAK THE TRUTH, CARRION-FEEDER!
REALLY! I SWEAR TO YOU! NO ONE KNOWS WHERE THE THORN IS!
LOOK! IT'S THAT GUY!
IT'S THAT TICK GUY I WAS TELLING YOU ABOUT!
TAXI
"THE TICK. SUCH A STRANGE NAME. STILL, I SENSE HE PLAYS A GREAT PART IN THIS."
Contemplate!
DRIVER, FOLLOW THAT MAN!!!
BUT IF THIS IS SOME NINJA TRICK, I WILL FEAST ON YOUR STEAMING ENTRAILS!
OOOO. NICE IMAGE. YOU MUST SAVE ON YOUR GROCERY BILL.
"SOON I WILL HAVE TO UNVEIL MY BLADE... ITS BREAD DISGUISE APPEARS TO BE LOSING SOME OF ITS MENACE....."

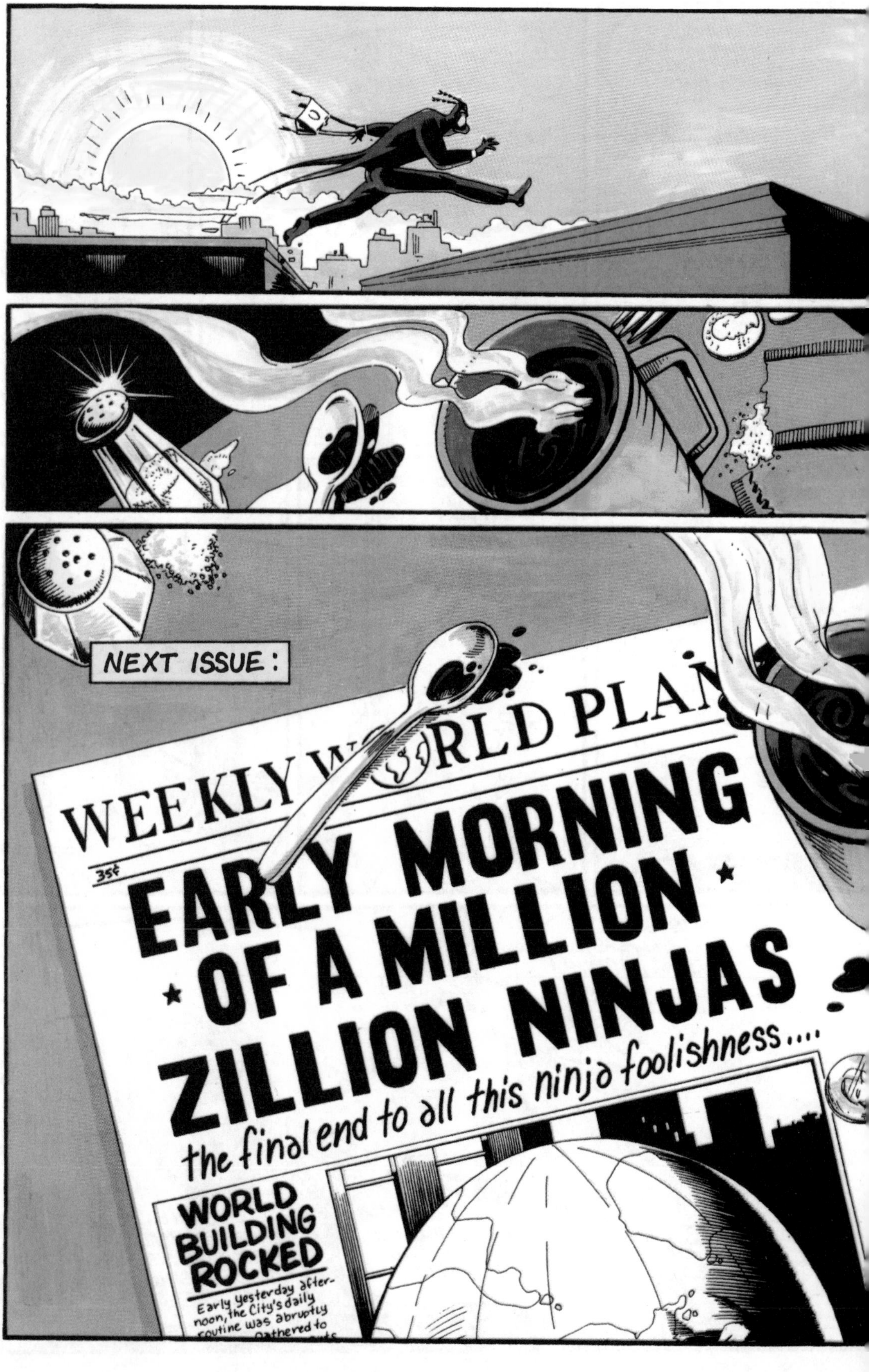
NEXT ISSUE:
WEEKLY WORLD PLAN
35¢
EARLY MORNING OF A MILLION ZILLION NINJAS
the final end to all this ninja foolishness....
WORLD BUILDING ROCKED
Early yesterday after-
noon, the City's daily
routine was abruptly

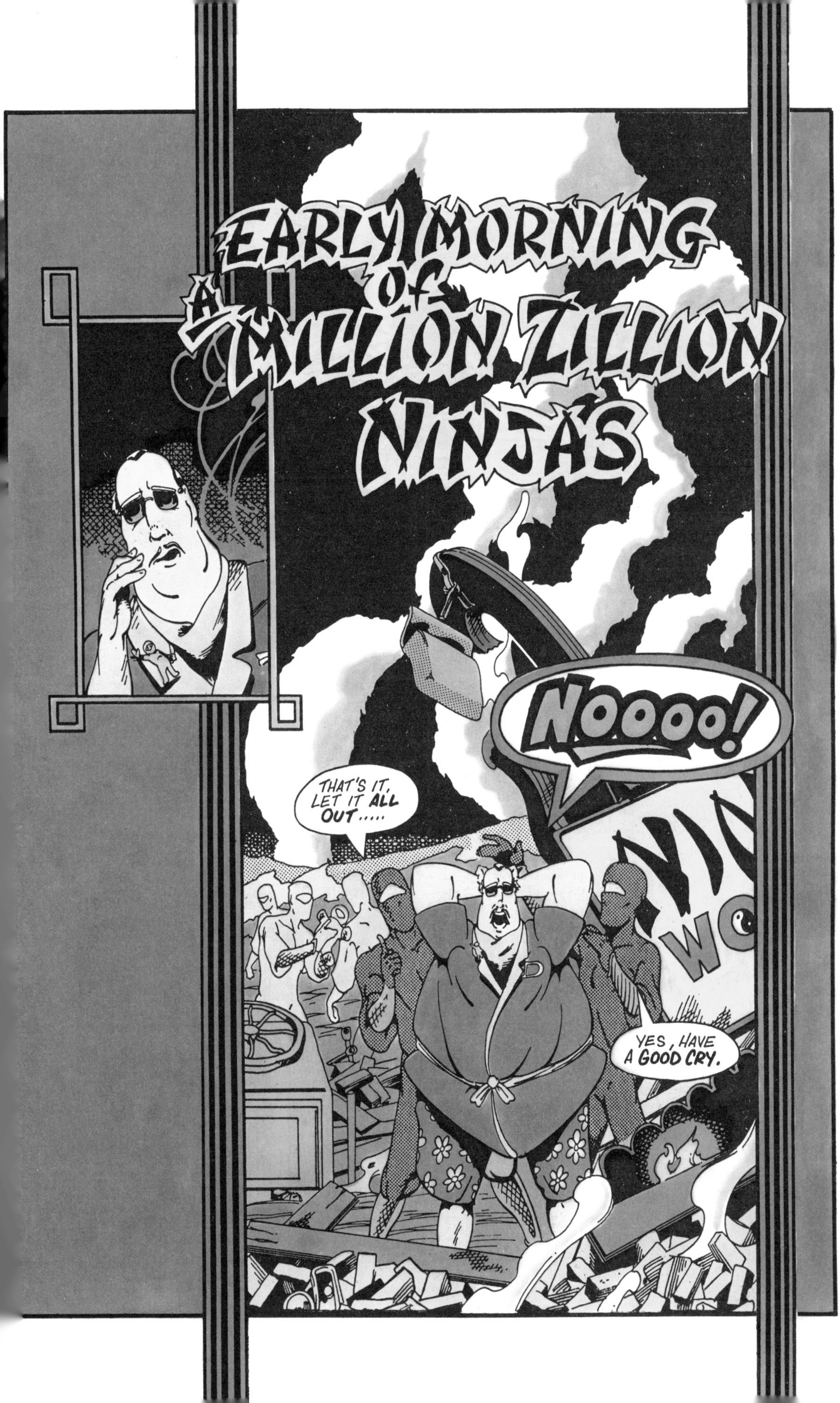

EARLY MORNING of A MILLION ZILLION NINJAS
NOOOO!
THAT'S IT, LET IT ALL OUT.....
YES, HAVE A GOOD CRY.

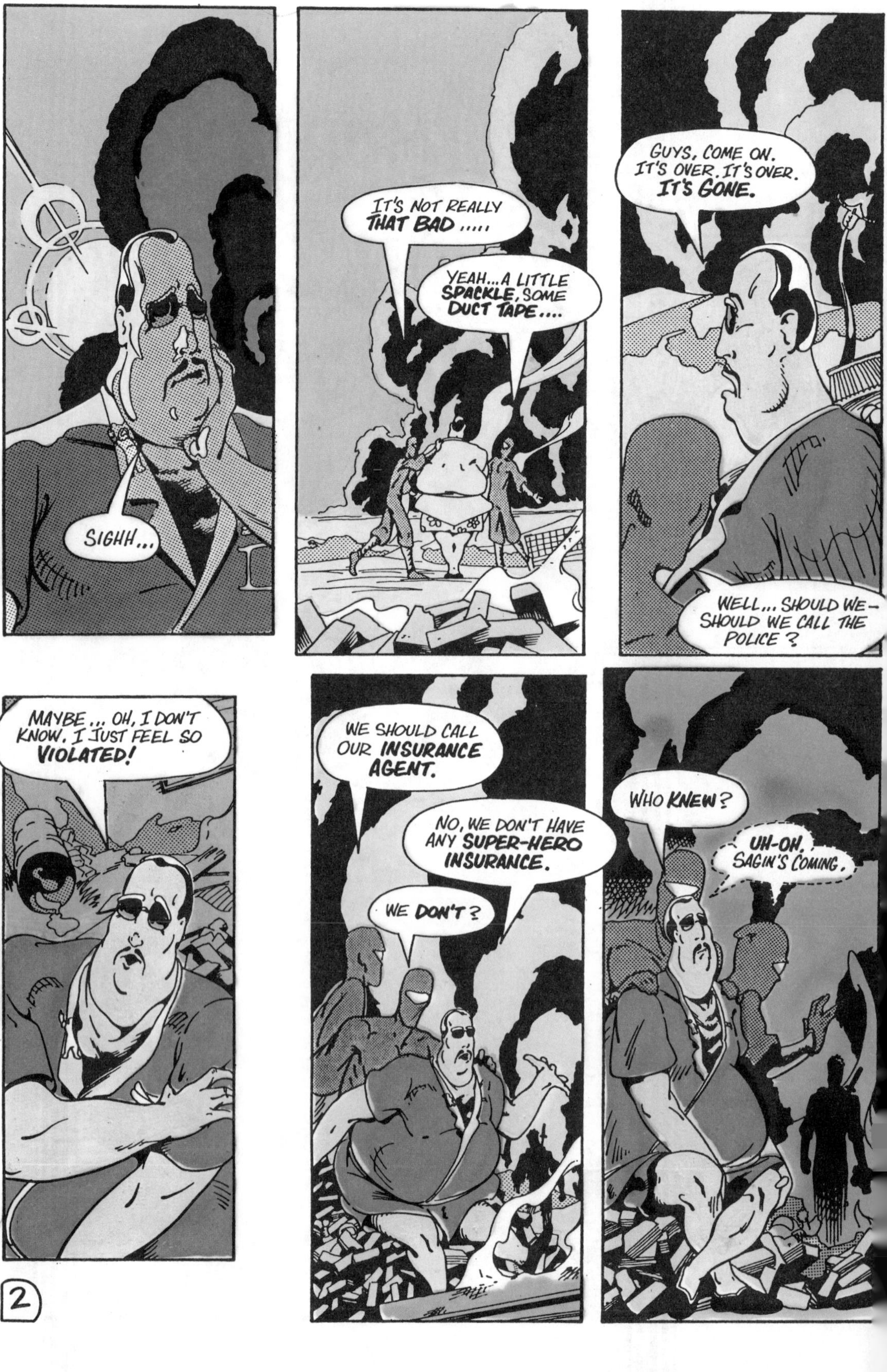
SIGHH...
IT'S NOT REALLY THAT BAD .....
YEAH... A LITTLE SPACKLE, SOME DUCT TAPE....
GUYS, COME ON. IT'S OVER. IT'S OVER. IT'S GONE.
WELL... SHOULD WE- SHOULD WE CALL THE POLICE ?
MAYBE... OH, I DON'T KNOW. I JUST FEEL SO VIOLATED!
WE SHOULD CALL OUR INSURANCE AGENT.
NO, WE DON'T HAVE ANY SUPER-HERO INSURANCE.
WE DON'T ?
WHO KNEW ?
UH-OH. SAGIN'S COMING.

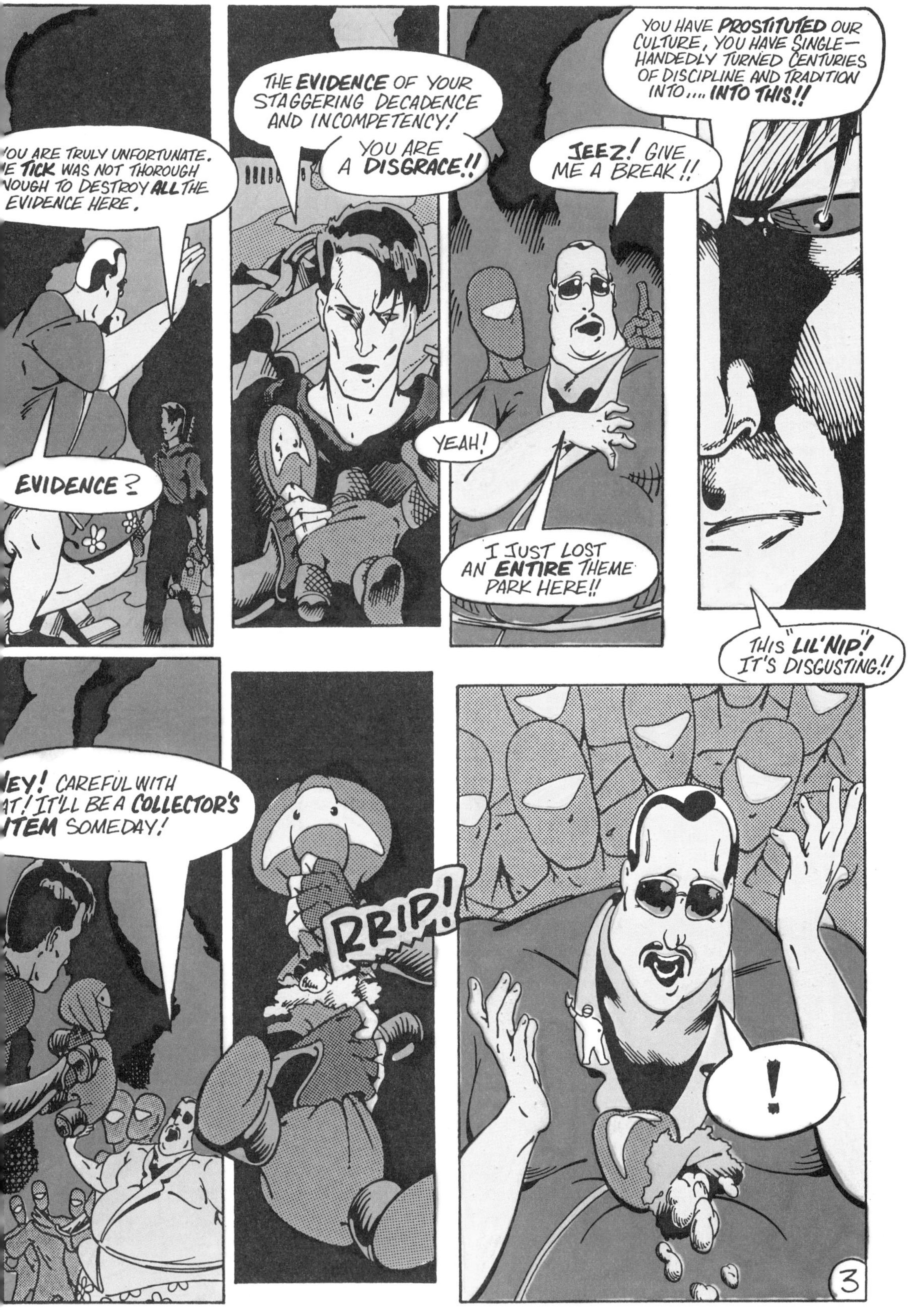

OU ARE TRULY UNFORTUNATE. E TICK WAS NOT THOROUGH NOUGH TO DESTROY ALL THE EVIDENCE HERE.
EVIDENCE?
THE EVIDENCE OF YOUR STAGGERING DECADENCE AND INCOMPETENCY!
YOU ARE A DISGRACE!!
JEEZ! GIVE ME A BREAK!!
YEAH!
I JUST LOST AN ENTIRE THEME PARK HERE!!
YOU HAVE PROSTITUTED OUR CULTURE, YOU HAVE SINGLE-HANDEDLY TURNED CENTURIES OF DISCIPLINE AND TRADITION INTO.... INTO THIS!!
THIS "LIL' NIP"! IT'S DISGUSTING!!
EY! CAREFUL WITH AT! IT'LL BE A COLLECTOR'S ITEM SOMEDAY!
RRIP!
!

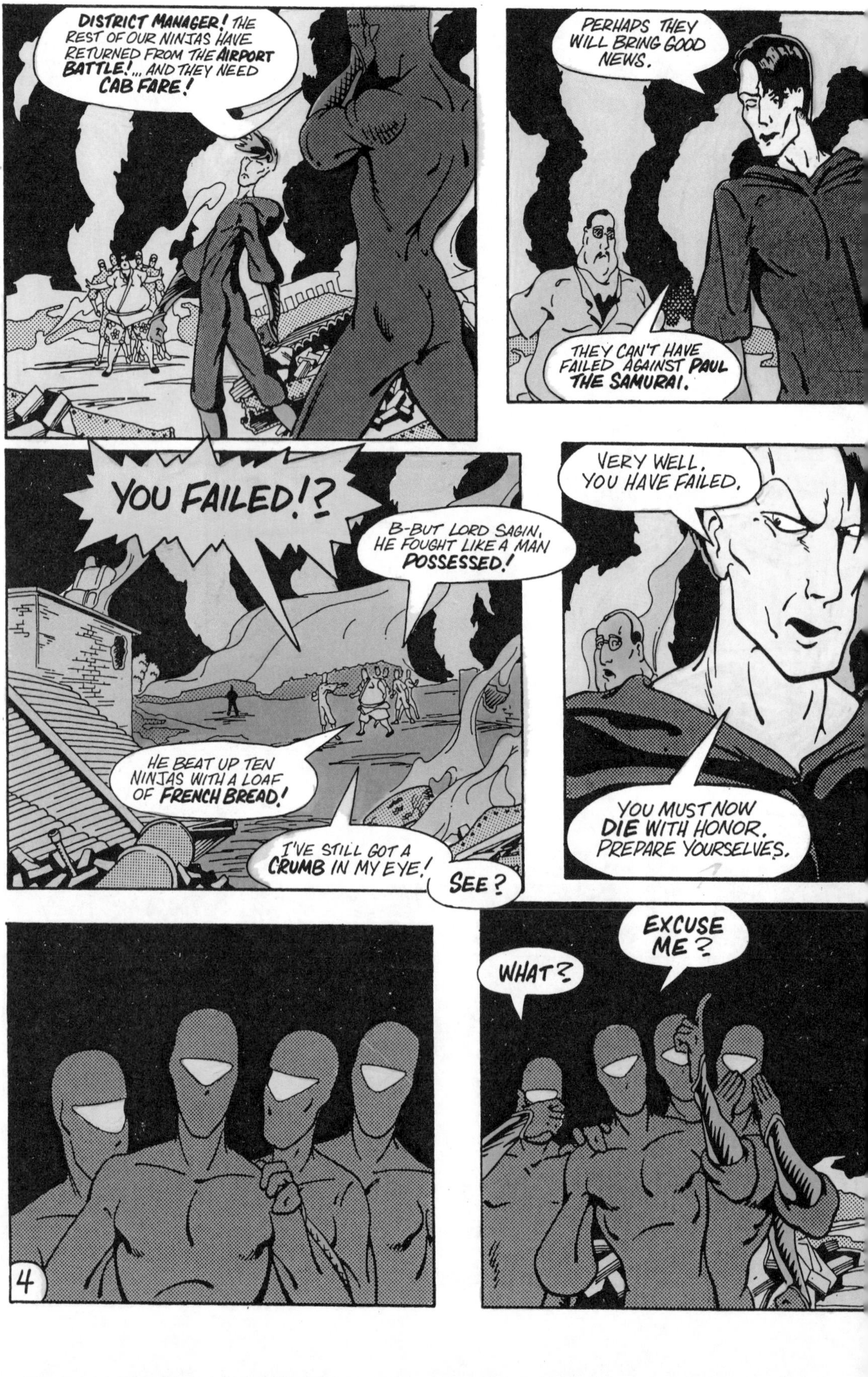
DISTRICT MANAGER! THE REST OF OUR NINJAS HAVE RETURNED FROM THE AIRPORT BATTLE!... AND THEY NEED CAB FARE!
PERHAPS THEY WILL BRING GOOD NEWS.
THEY CAN'T HAVE FAILED AGAINST PAUL THE SAMURAI.
YOU FAILED!?
B-BUT LORD SAGIN, HE FOUGHT LIKE A MAN POSSESSED!
HE BEAT UP TEN NINJAS WITH A LOAF OF FRENCH BREAD!
I'VE STILL GOT A CRUMB IN MY EYE!
SEE?
VERY WELL. YOU HAVE FAILED.
YOU MUST NOW DIE WITH HONOR. PREPARE YOURSELVES.
WHAT?
EXCUSE ME?

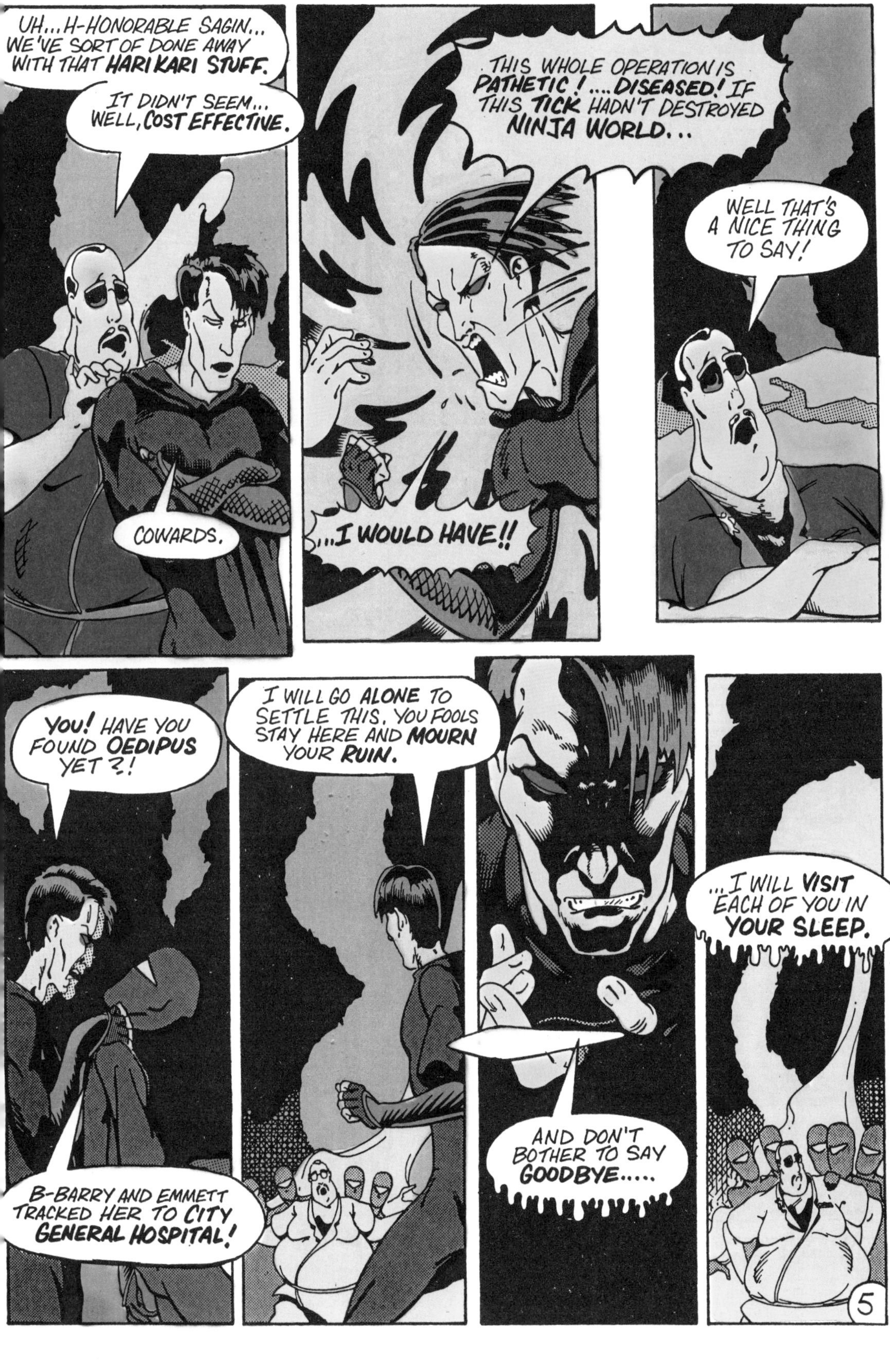
UH... H-HONORABLE SAGIN... WE'VE SORT OF DONE AWAY WITH THAT HARI KARI STUFF.
IT DIDN'T SEEM... WELL, COST EFFECTIVE.
COWARDS.
THIS WHOLE OPERATION IS PATHETIC! ....DISEASED! IF THIS TICK HADN'T DESTROYED NINJA WORLD...
...I WOULD HAVE!!
WELL THAT'S A NICE THING TO SAY!
YOU! HAVE YOU FOUND OEDIPUS YET?!
B-BARRY AND EMMETT TRACKED HER TO CITY GENERAL HOSPITAL!
I WILL GO ALONE TO SETTLE THIS. YOU FOOLS STAY HERE AND MOURN YOUR RUIN.
AND DON'T BOTHER TO SAY GOODBYE.....
...I WILL VISIT EACH OF YOU IN YOUR SLEEP.

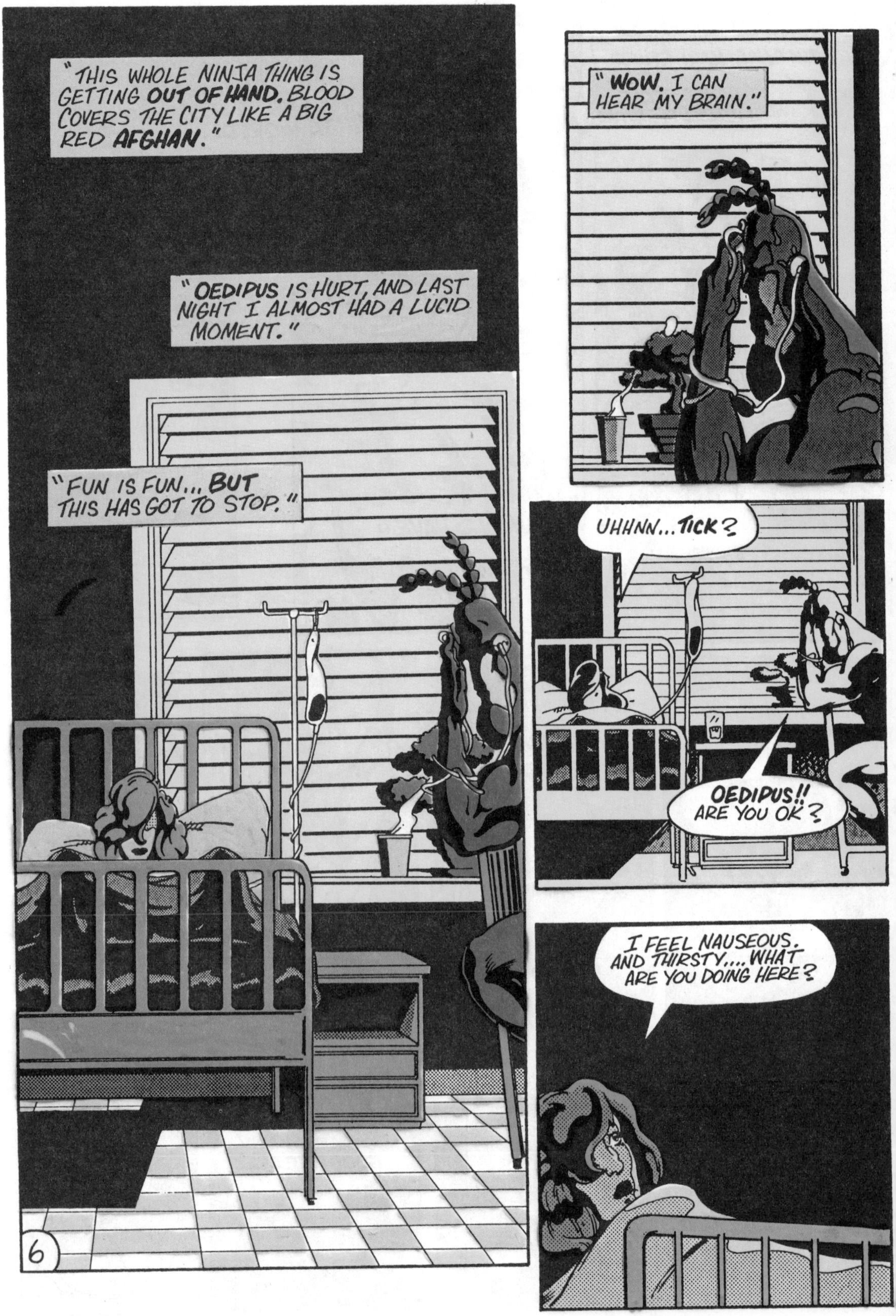
"THIS WHOLE NINJA THING IS GETTING **OUT OF HAND.** BLOOD COVERS THE CITY LIKE A BIG RED **AFGHAN**."
"**OEDIPUS** IS HURT, AND LAST NIGHT I ALMOST HAD A LUCID MOMENT."
"FUN IS FUN... **BUT** THIS HAS GOT TO STOP."
"**WOW.** I CAN HEAR MY BRAIN."
UHHNN... **TICK**?
OEDIPUS!! ARE YOU OK?
I FEEL NAUSEOUS. AND THIRSTY.... WHAT ARE YOU DOING HERE?
6

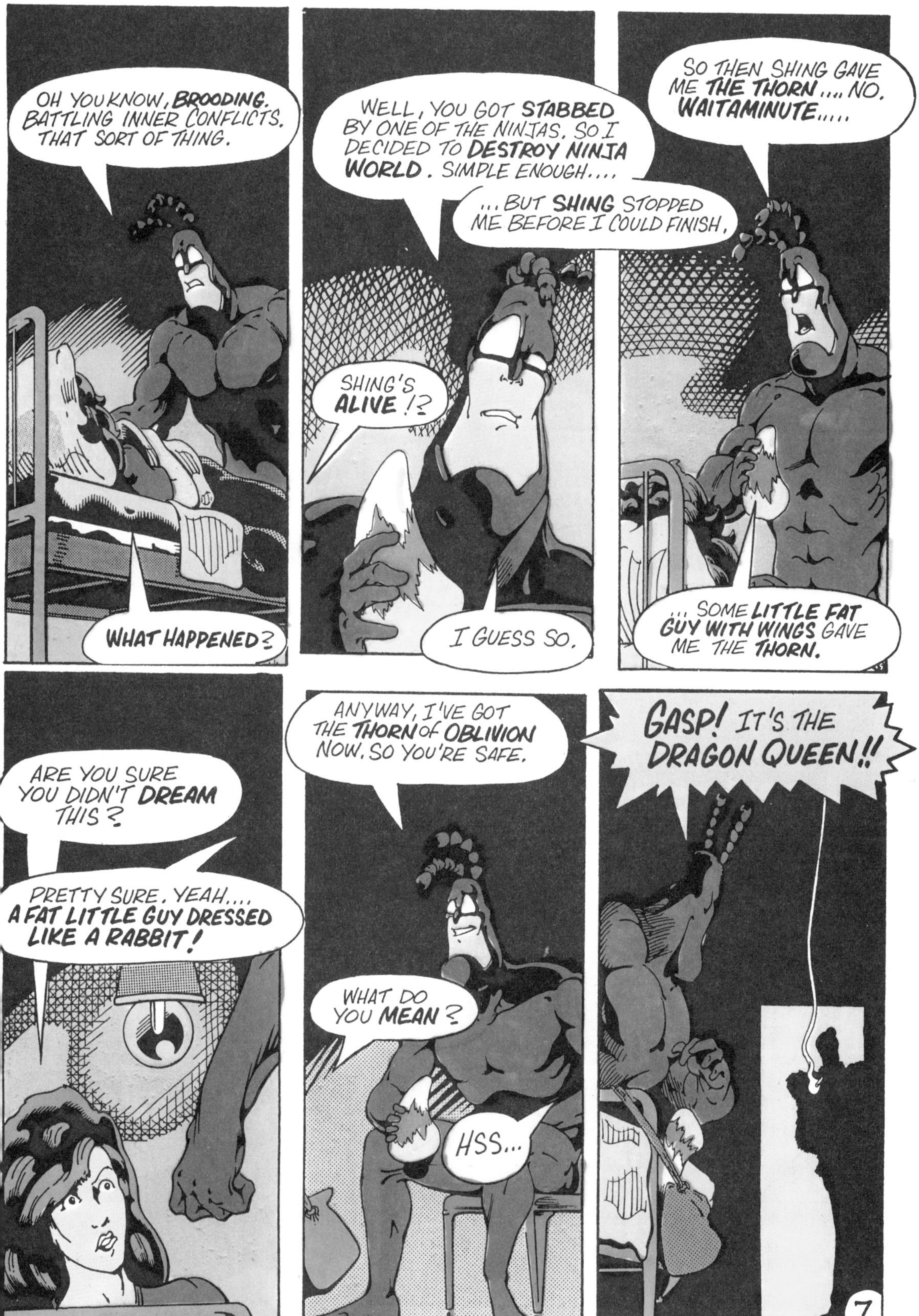
OH YOU KNOW, BROODING. BATTLING INNER CONFLICTS. THAT SORT OF THING.
WHAT HAPPENED?
WELL, YOU GOT STABBED BY ONE OF THE NINJAS, SO I DECIDED TO DESTROY NINJA WORLD. SIMPLE ENOUGH....
...BUT SHING STOPPED ME BEFORE I COULD FINISH.
SHING'S ALIVE!?
I GUESS SO.
SO THEN SHING GAVE ME THE THORN.... NO, WAITAMINUTE.....
...SOME LITTLE FAT GUY WITH WINGS GAVE ME THE THORN.
ARE YOU SURE YOU DIDN'T DREAM THIS?
PRETTY SURE, YEAH.... A FAT LITTLE GUY DRESSED LIKE A RABBIT!
ANYWAY, I'VE GOT THE THORN OF OBLIVION NOW, SO YOU'RE SAFE.
WHAT DO YOU MEAN?
HSS...
GASP! IT'S THE DRAGON QUEEN!!

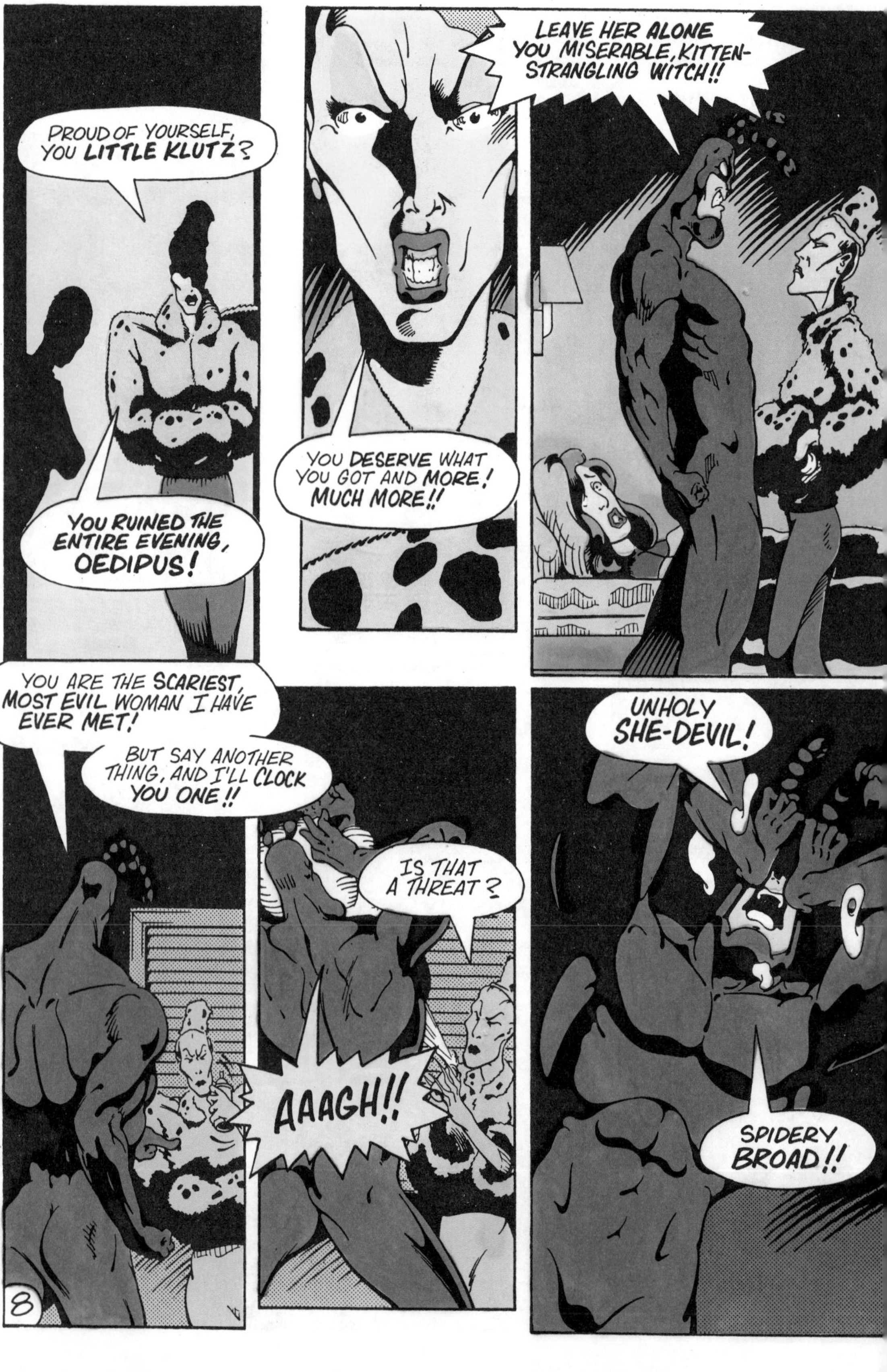

PROUD OF YOURSELF, YOU LITTLE KLUTZ?
YOU RUINED THE ENTIRE EVENING, OEDIPUS!
YOU DESERVE WHAT YOU GOT AND MORE! MUCH MORE!!
LEAVE HER ALONE YOU MISERABLE, KITTEN-STRANGLING WITCH!!
YOU ARE THE SCARIEST, MOST EVIL WOMAN I HAVE EVER MET!
BUT SAY ANOTHER THING, AND I'LL CLOCK YOU ONE!!
IS THAT A THREAT?
AAAGH!!
UNHOLY SHE-DEVIL!
SPIDERY BROAD!!
8

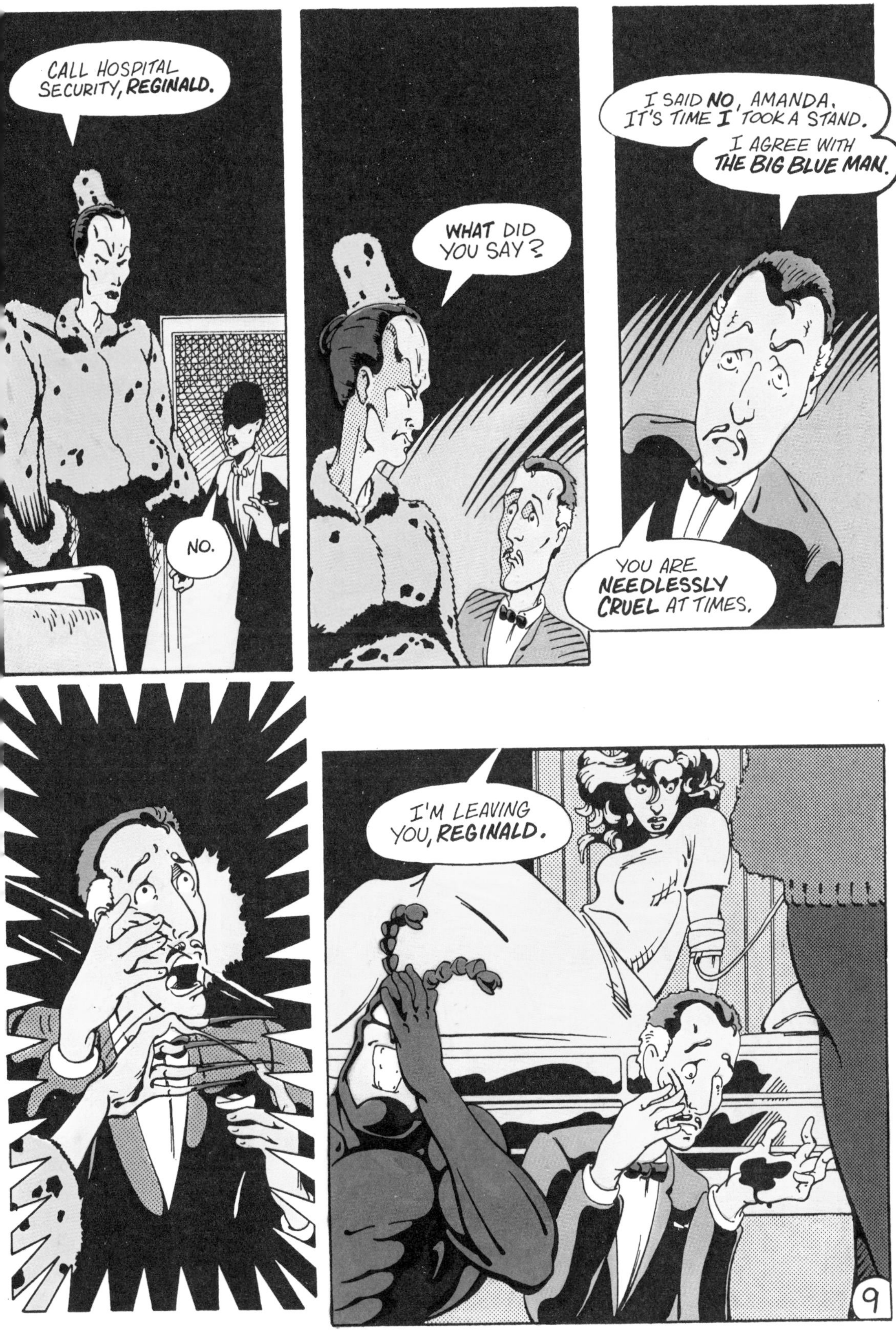

CALL HOSPITAL SECURITY, REGINALD.
NO.
WHAT DID YOU SAY?
I SAID NO, AMANDA. IT'S TIME I TOOK A STAND.
I AGREE WITH THE BIG BLUE MAN.
YOU ARE NEEDLESSLY CRUEL AT TIMES.
I'M LEAVING YOU, REGINALD.

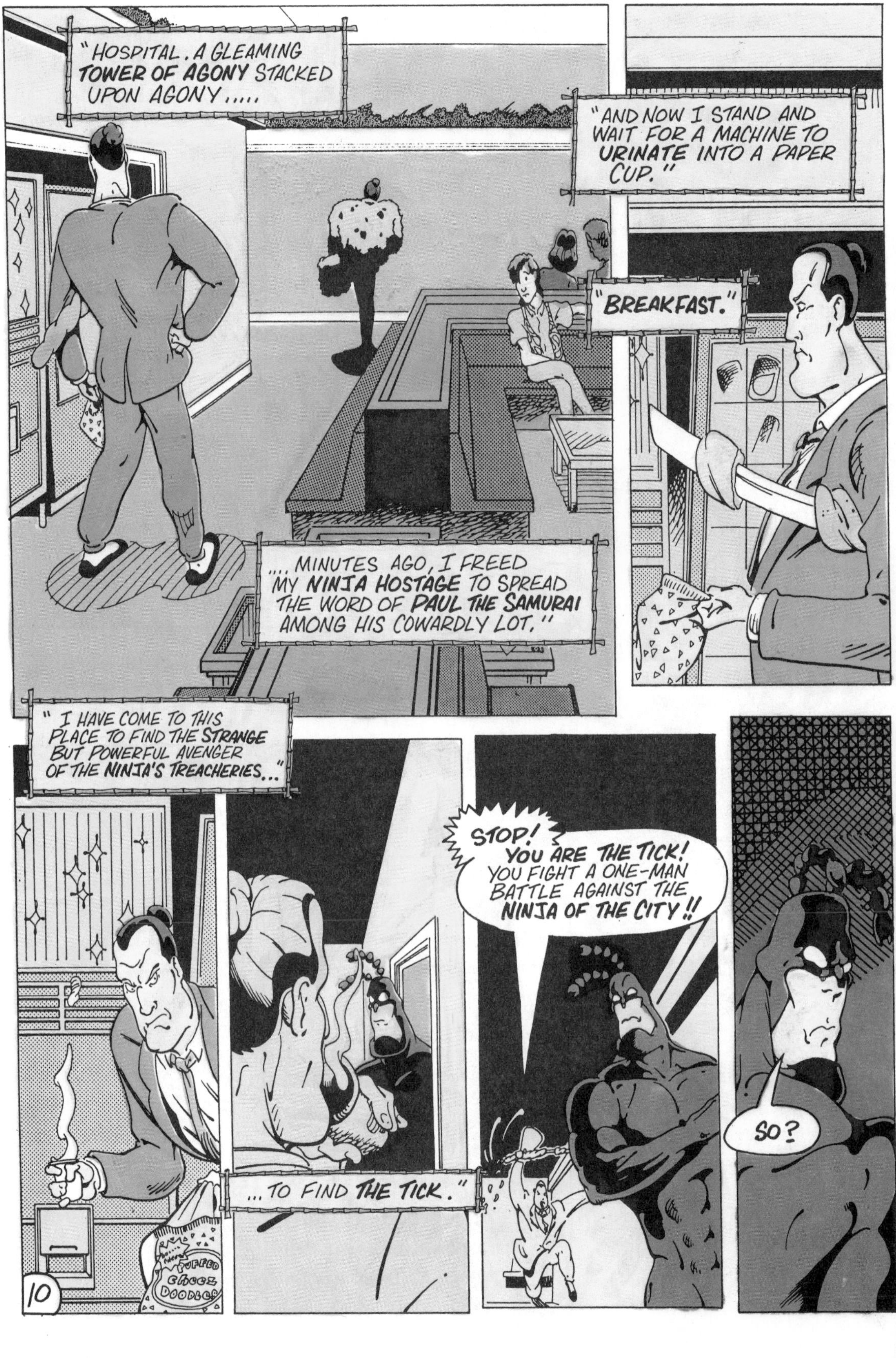
"HOSPITAL. A GLEAMING TOWER OF AGONY STACKED UPON AGONY.....
"AND NOW I STAND AND WAIT FOR A MACHINE TO URINATE INTO A PAPER CUP."
"BREAKFAST."
"...MINUTES AGO, I FREED MY NINJA HOSTAGE TO SPREAD THE WORD OF PAUL THE SAMURAI AMONG HIS COWARDLY LOT."
"I HAVE COME TO THIS PLACE TO FIND THE STRANGE BUT POWERFUL AVENGER OF THE NINJA'S TREACHERIES..."
PUFFED CHEEZ DOODLES
...TO FIND THE TICK."
STOP!
YOU ARE THE TICK! YOU FIGHT A ONE-MAN BATTLE AGAINST THE NINJA OF THE CITY!!
SO?

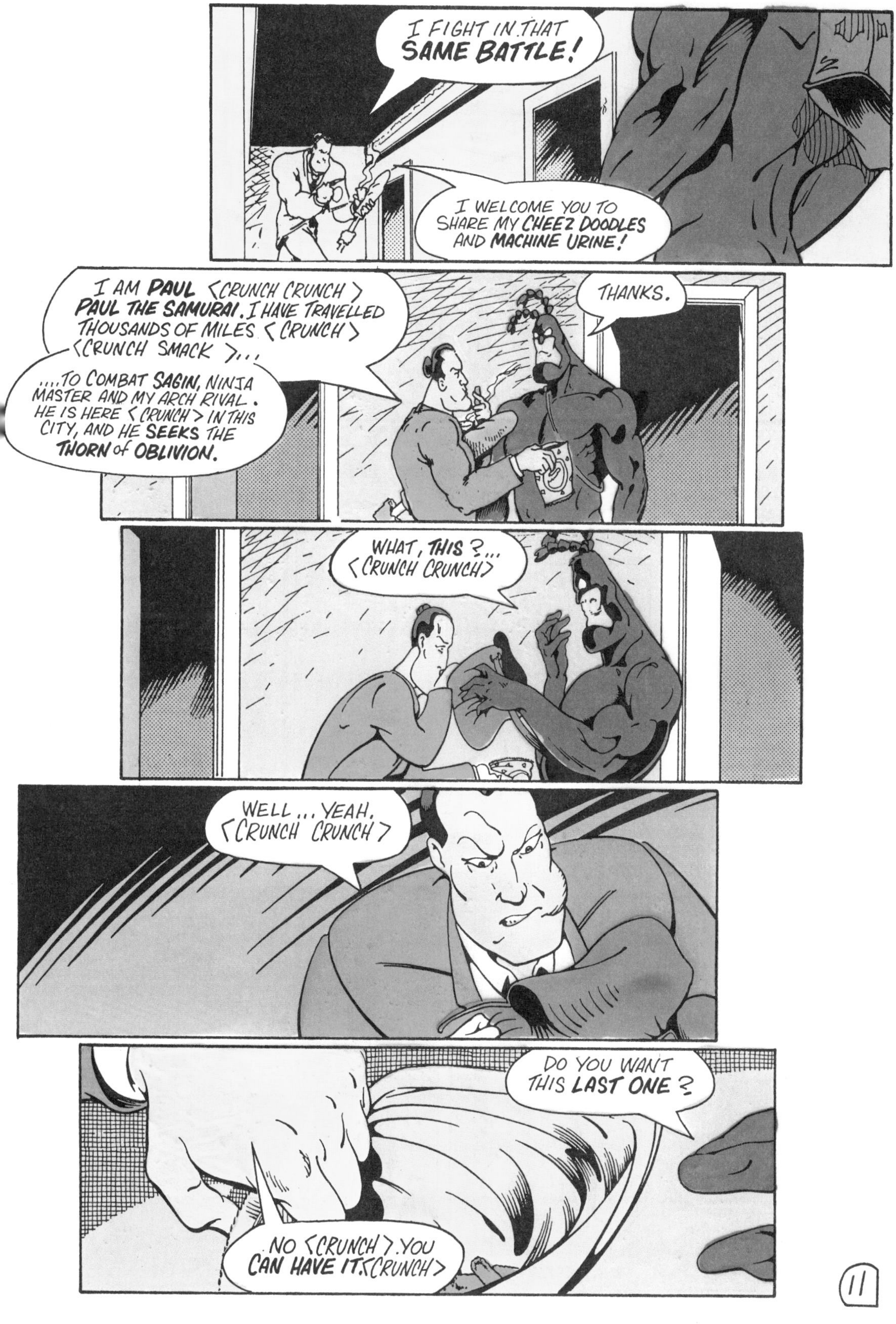
I FIGHT IN THAT SAME BATTLE!
I WELCOME YOU TO SHARE MY CHEEZ DOODLES AND MACHINE URINE!
I AM PAUL <CRUNCH CRUNCH> PAUL THE SAMURAI. I HAVE TRAVELLED THOUSANDS OF MILES <CRUNCH> <CRUNCH SMACK>...
THANKS.
....TO COMBAT SAGIN, NINJA MASTER AND MY ARCH RIVAL. HE IS HERE <CRUNCH> IN THIS CITY, AND HE SEEKS THE THORN of OBLIVION.
WHAT, THIS?... <CRUNCH CRUNCH>
WELL... YEAH. <CRUNCH CRUNCH>
DO YOU WANT THIS LAST ONE?
NO <CRUNCH>. YOU CAN HAVE IT. <CRUNCH>

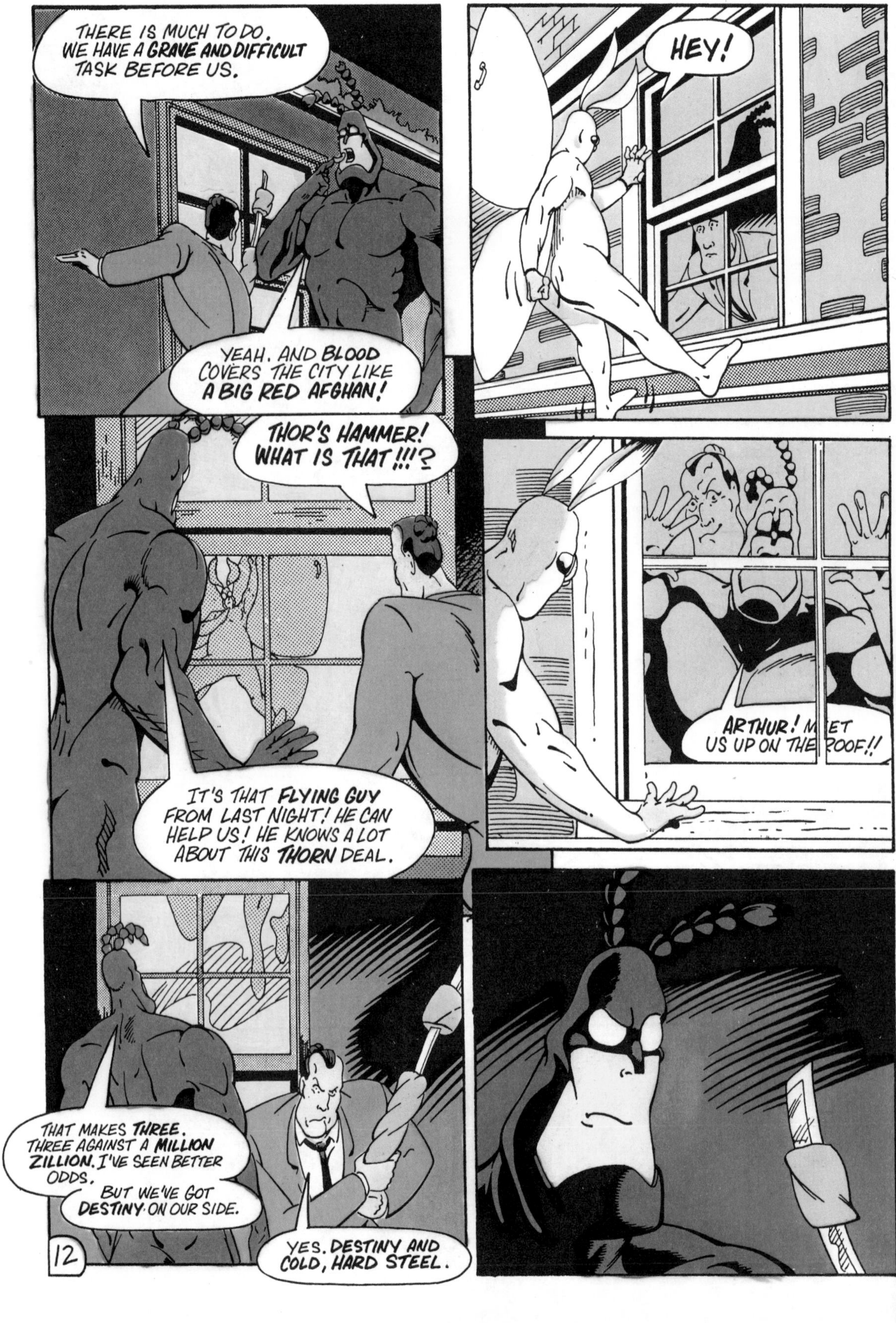
THERE IS MUCH TO DO. WE HAVE A GRAVE AND DIFFICULT TASK BEFORE US.
YEAH. AND BLOOD COVERS THE CITY LIKE A BIG RED AFGHAN!
HEY!
THOR'S HAMMER! WHAT IS THAT!!!?
IT'S THAT FLYING GUY FROM LAST NIGHT! HE CAN HELP US! HE KNOWS A LOT ABOUT THIS THORN DEAL.
ARTHUR! MEET US UP ON THE ROOF!!
THAT MAKES THREE. THREE AGAINST A MILLION ZILLION. I'VE SEEN BETTER ODDS.
BUT WE'VE GOT DESTINY ON OUR SIDE.
YES. DESTINY AND COLD, HARD STEEL.

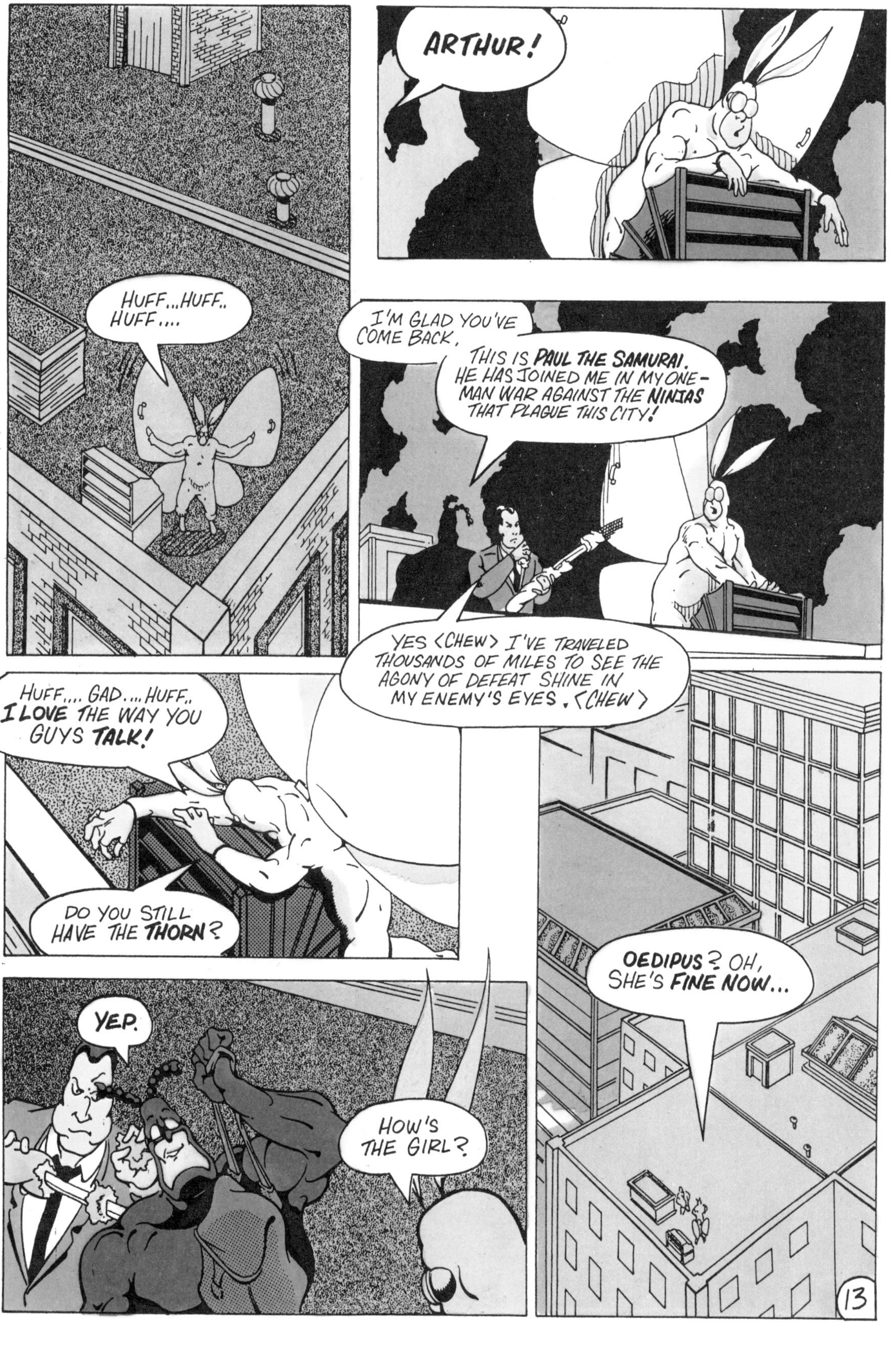
HUFF... HUFF.. HUFF....
ARTHUR!
I'M GLAD YOU'VE COME BACK.
THIS IS PAUL THE SAMURAI. HE HAS JOINED ME IN MY ONE-MAN WAR AGAINST THE NINJAS THAT PLAGUE THIS CITY!
YES <CHEW> I'VE TRAVELED THOUSANDS OF MILES TO SEE THE AGONY OF DEFEAT SHINE IN MY ENEMY'S EYES. <CHEW>
HUFF.... GAD.... HUFF.. I LOVE THE WAY YOU GUYS TALK!
DO YOU STILL HAVE THE THORN?
YEP.
HOW'S THE GIRL?
OEDIPUS? OH, SHE'S FINE NOW...
13

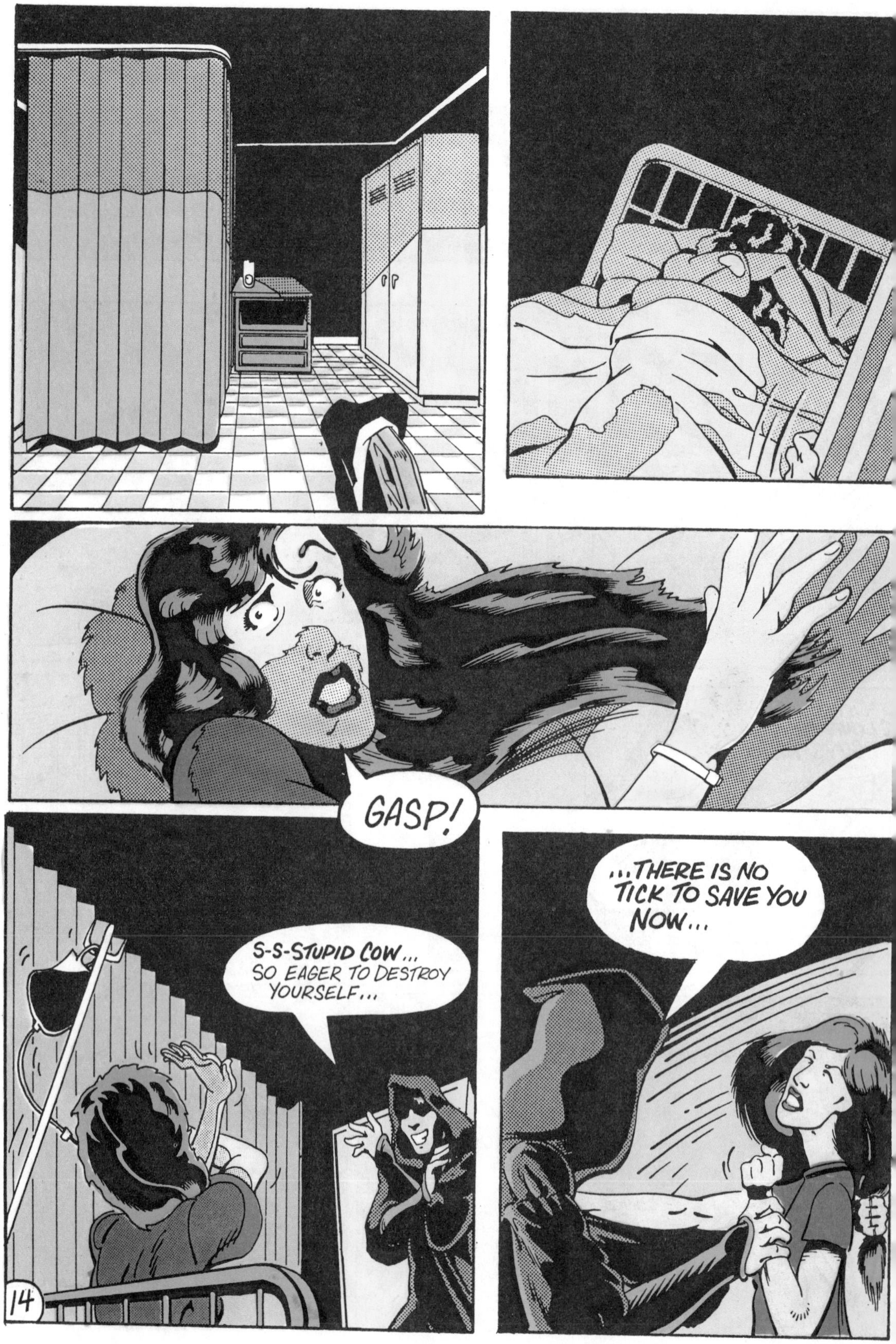
GASP!
S-S-STUPID COW... SO EAGER TO DESTROY YOURSELF...
...THERE IS NO TICK TO SAVE YOU NOW...
14

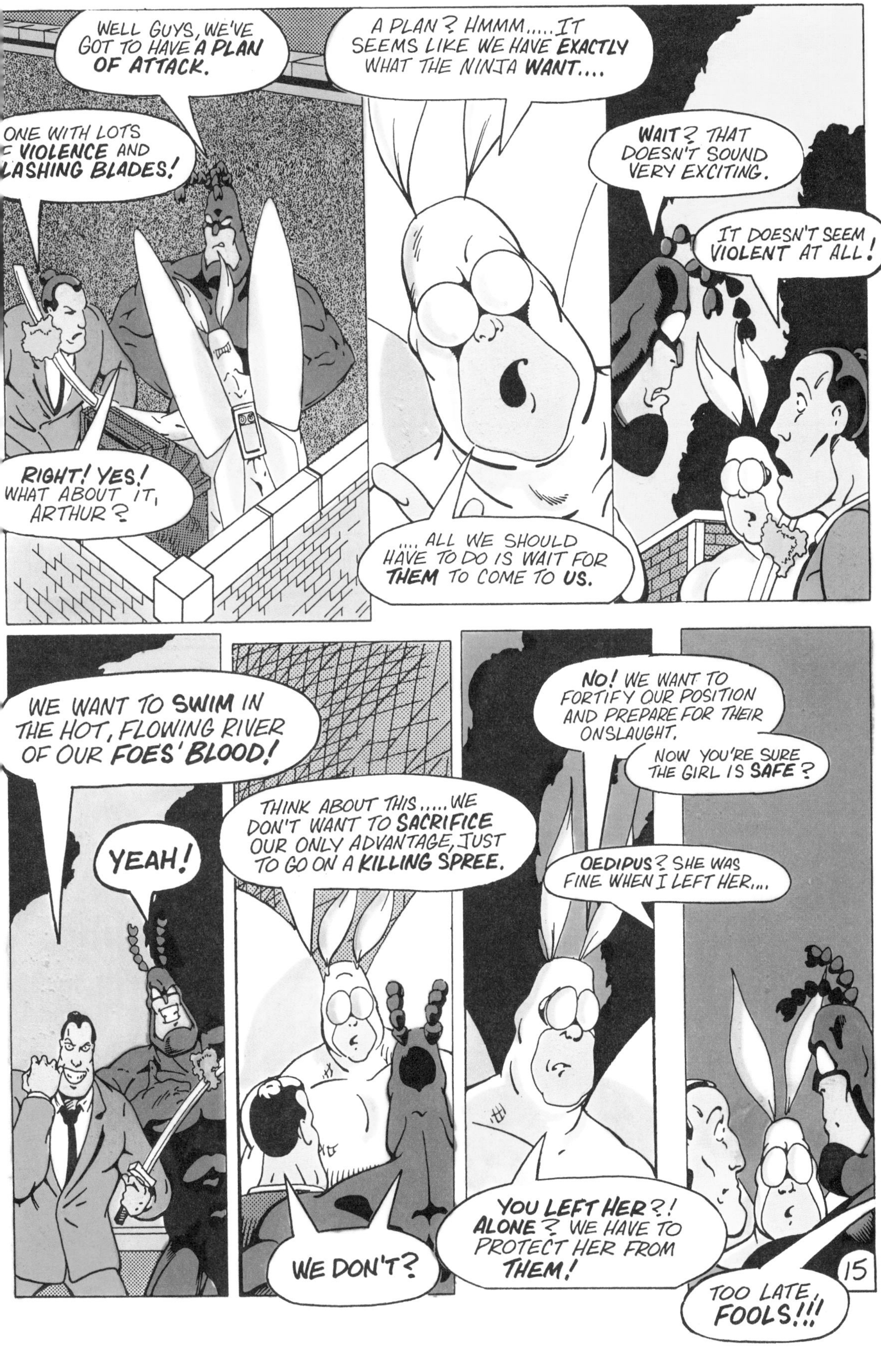
WELL GUYS, WE'VE GOT TO HAVE A PLAN OF ATTACK.
ONE WITH LOTS OF VIOLENCE AND SLASHING BLADES!
RIGHT! YES! WHAT ABOUT IT, ARTHUR?
A PLAN? HMMM..... IT SEEMS LIKE WE HAVE EXACTLY WHAT THE NINJA WANT....
.... ALL WE SHOULD HAVE TO DO IS WAIT FOR THEM TO COME TO US.
WAIT? THAT DOESN'T SOUND VERY EXCITING.
IT DOESN'T SEEM VIOLENT AT ALL!
WE WANT TO SWIM IN THE HOT, FLOWING RIVER OF OUR FOES' BLOOD!
YEAH!
THINK ABOUT THIS..... WE DON'T WANT TO SACRIFICE OUR ONLY ADVANTAGE, JUST TO GO ON A KILLING SPREE.
WE DON'T?
NO! WE WANT TO FORTIFY OUR POSITION AND PREPARE FOR THEIR ONSLAUGHT.
NOW YOU'RE SURE THE GIRL IS SAFE?
OEDIPUS? SHE WAS FINE WHEN I LEFT HER....
YOU LEFT HER?! ALONE? WE HAVE TO PROTECT HER FROM THEM!
TOO LATE, FOOLS!!!

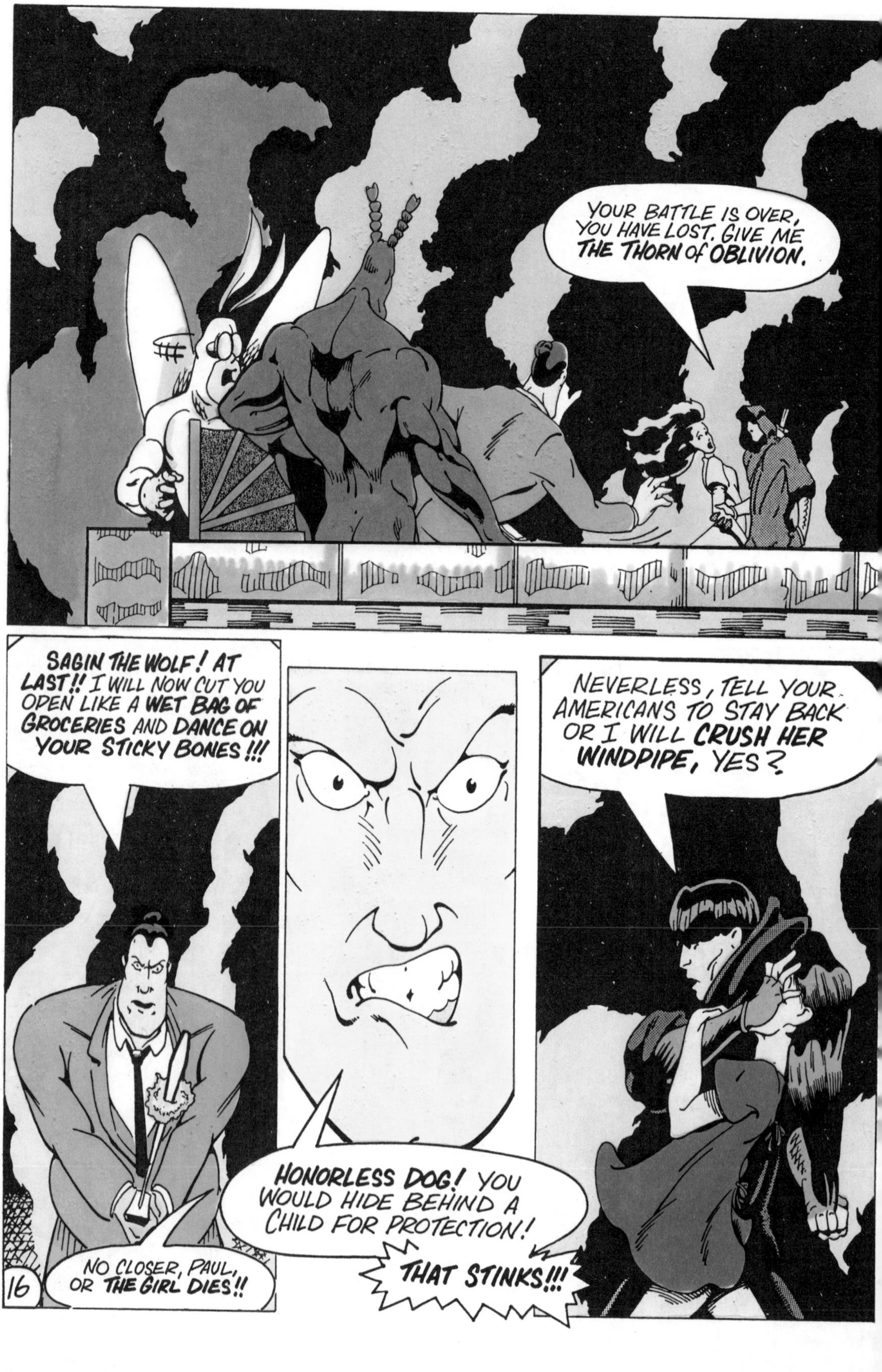

YOUR BATTLE IS OVER, YOU HAVE LOST. GIVE ME THE THORN of OBLIVION.
SAGIN THE WOLF! AT LAST!! I WILL NOW CUT YOU OPEN LIKE A WET BAG OF GROCERIES AND DANCE ON YOUR STICKY BONES!!!
NEVERLESS, TELL YOUR AMERICANS TO STAY BACK OR I WILL CRUSH HER WINDPIPE, YES?
NO CLOSER, PAUL, OR THE GIRL DIES!!
HONORLESS DOG! YOU WOULD HIDE BEHIND A CHILD FOR PROTECTION!
THAT STINKS!!!

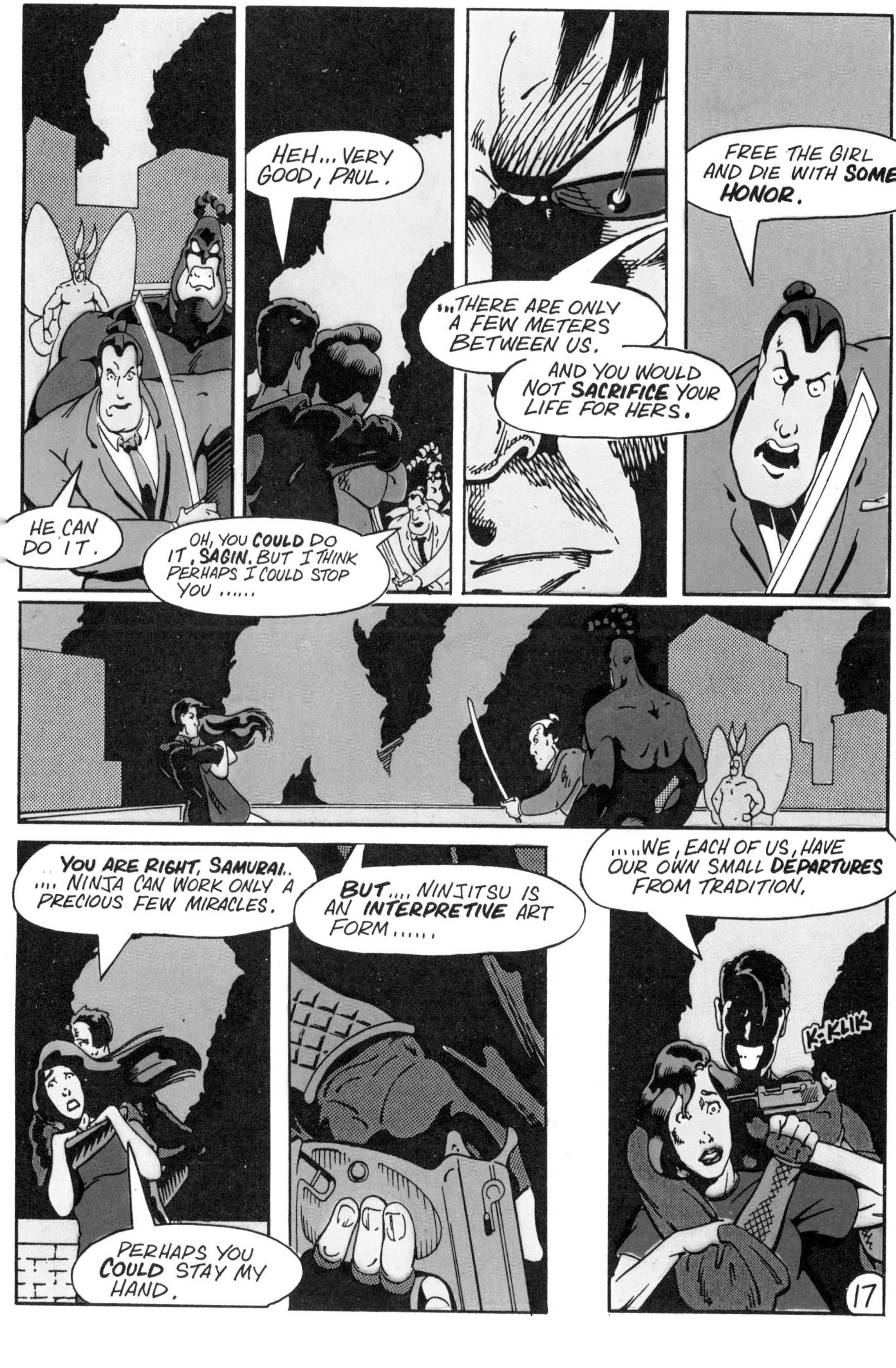

HE CAN DO IT.
HEH... VERY GOOD, PAUL.
OH, YOU COULD DO IT, SAGIN. BUT I THINK PERHAPS I COULD STOP YOU ......
...THERE ARE ONLY A FEW METERS BETWEEN US.
AND YOU WOULD NOT SACRIFICE YOUR LIFE FOR HERS.
FREE THE GIRL AND DIE WITH SOME HONOR.
.. YOU ARE RIGHT, SAMURAI.. .... NINJA CAN WORK ONLY A PRECIOUS FEW MIRACLES.
PERHAPS YOU COULD STAY MY HAND.
BUT.... NINJITSU IS AN INTERPRETIVE ART FORM......
.....WE, EACH OF US, HAVE OUR OWN SMALL DEPARTURES FROM TRADITION.
K-KLIK

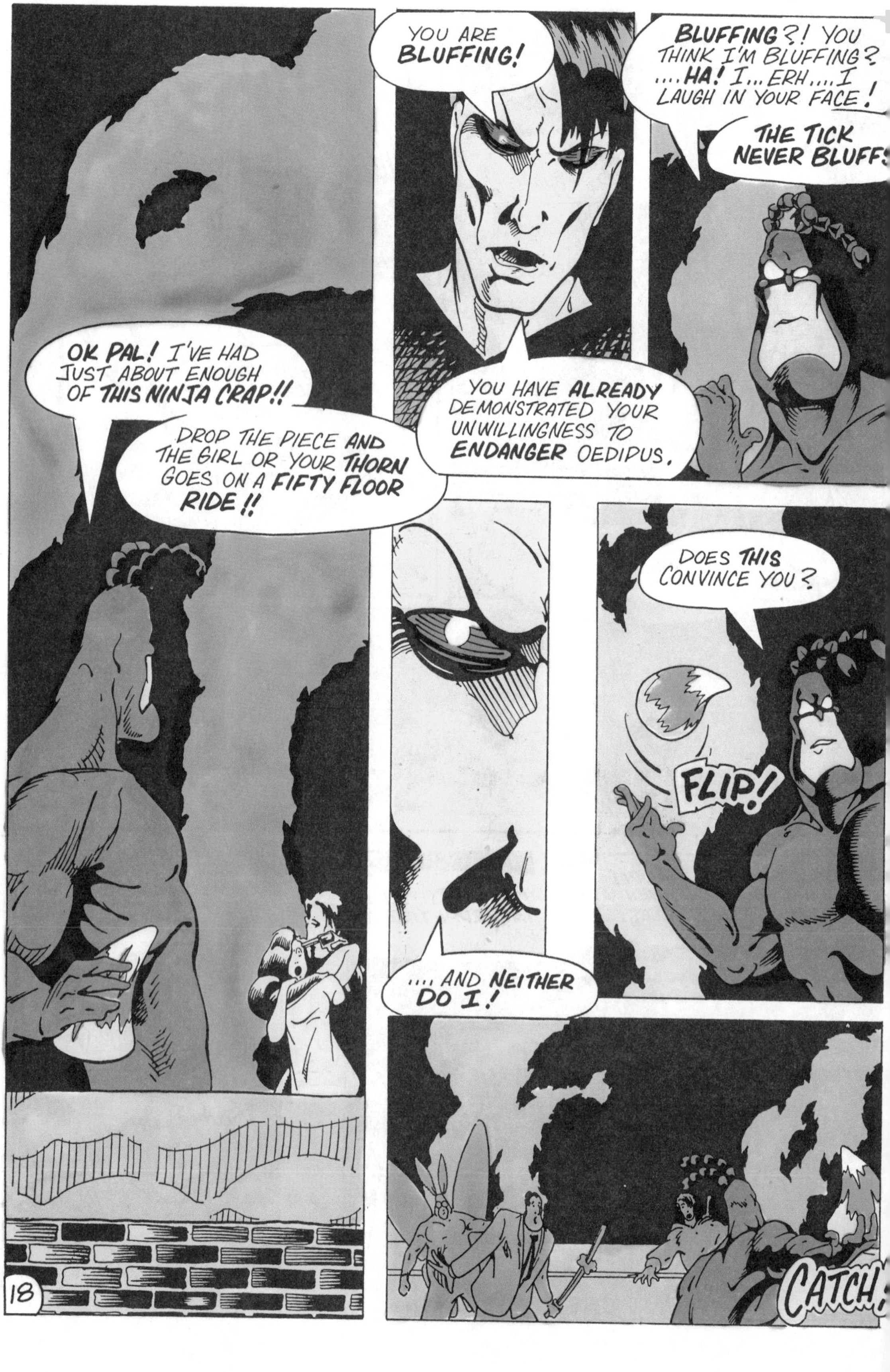
OK PAL! I'VE HAD JUST ABOUT ENOUGH OF THIS NINJA CRAP!!
DROP THE PIECE AND THE GIRL OR YOUR THORN GOES ON A FIFTY FLOOR RIDE!!
YOU ARE BLUFFING!
YOU HAVE ALREADY DEMONSTRATED YOUR UNWILLINGNESS TO ENDANGER OEDIPUS.
BLUFFING?! YOU THINK I'M BLUFFING? ....HA! I...ERH....I LAUGH IN YOUR FACE!
THE TICK NEVER BLUFFS
....AND NEITHER DO I!
DOES THIS CONVINCE YOU?
FLIP!
CATCH!

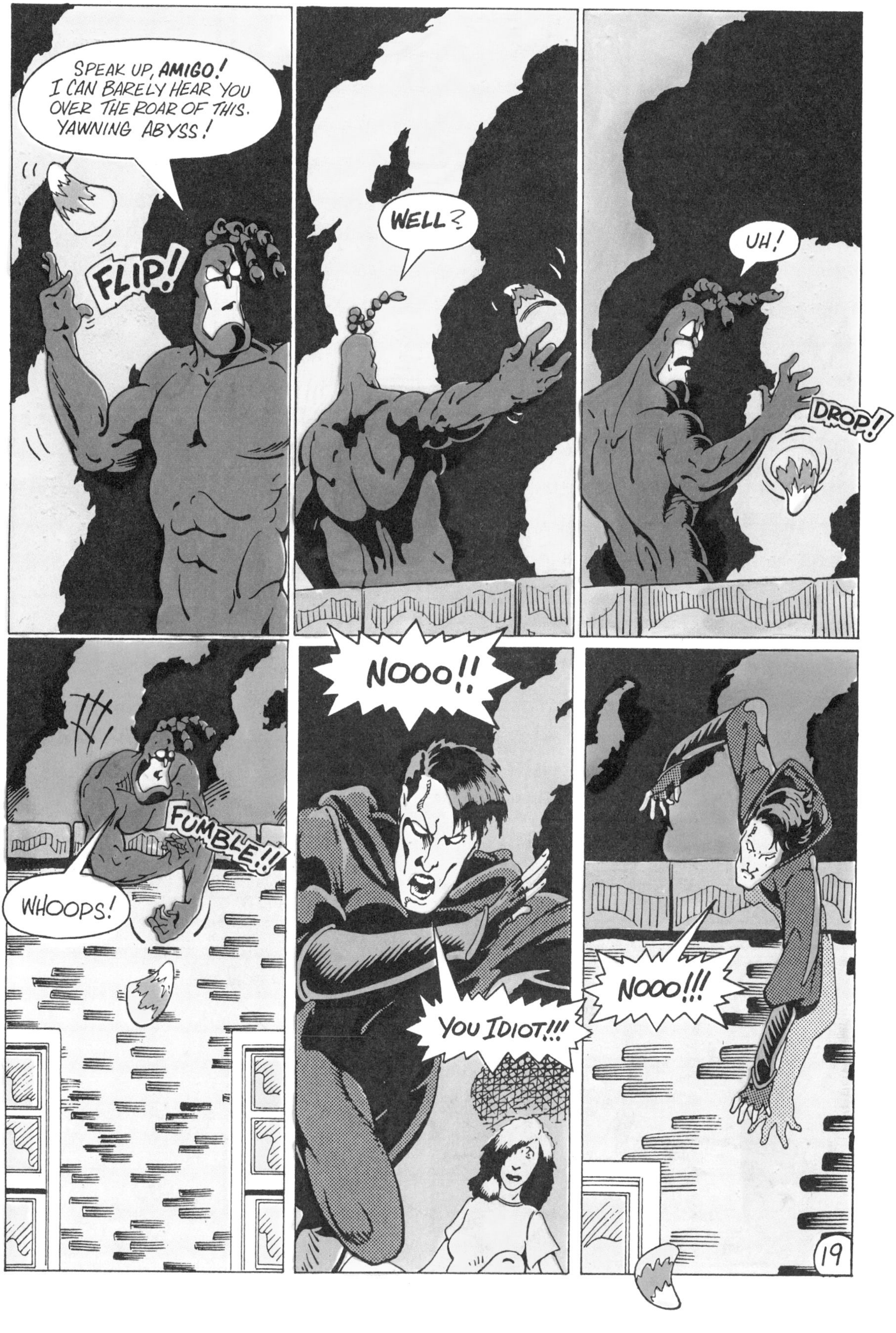

SPEAK UP, AMIGO! I CAN BARELY HEAR YOU OVER THE ROAR OF THIS. YAWNING ABYSS!
FLIP!
WELL?
UH!
DROP!
FUMBLE!!
WHOOPS!
NOOO!!
YOU IDIOT!!!
NOOO!!!

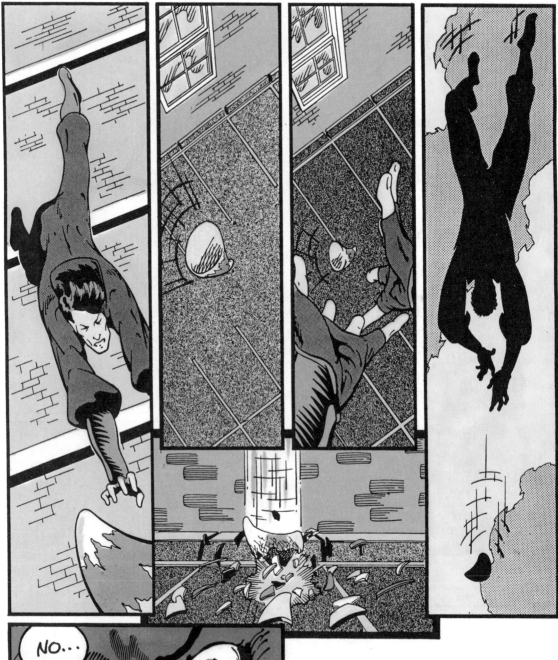

NO...

20

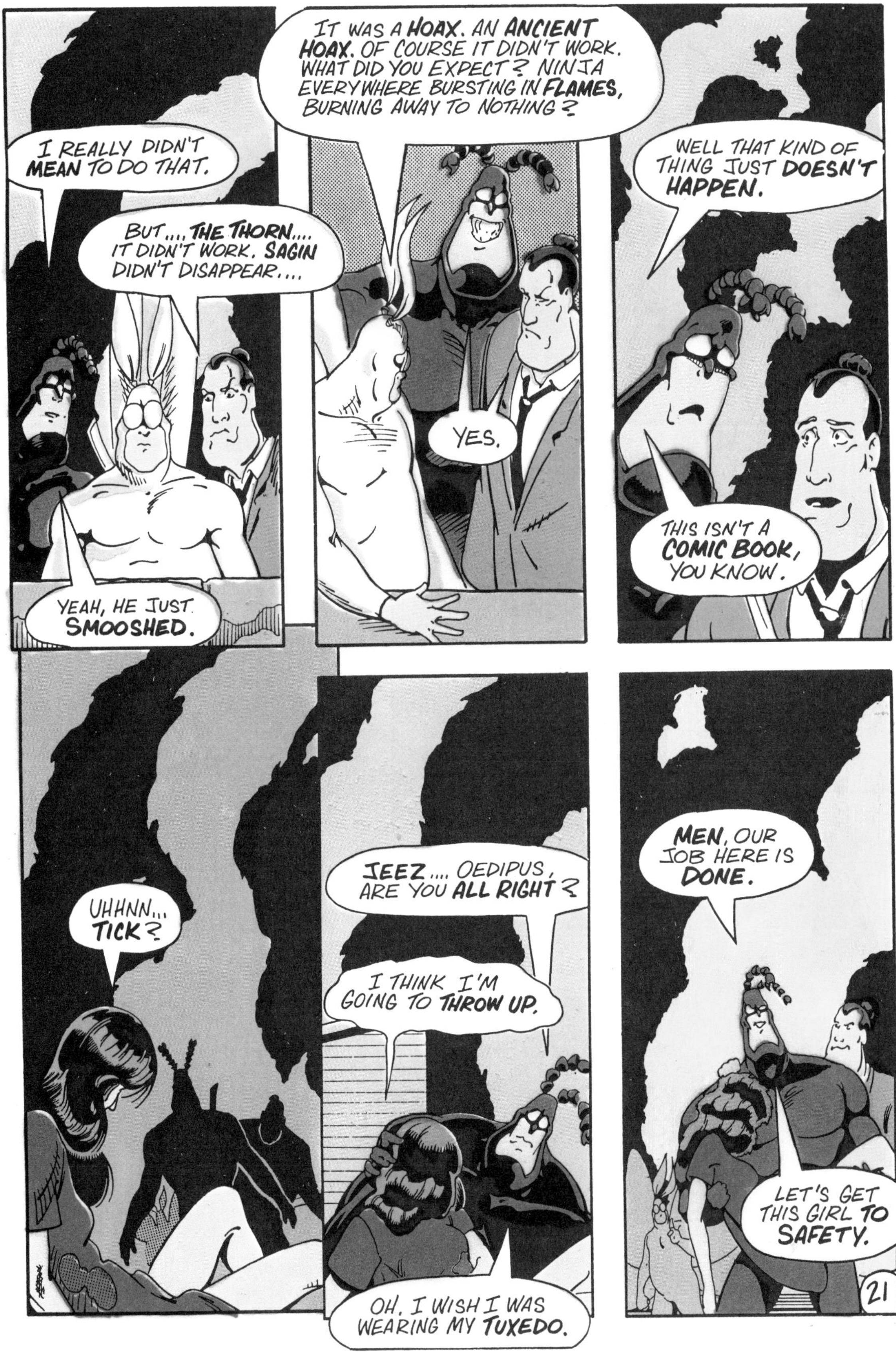

I REALLY DIDN'T MEAN TO DO THAT.
BUT.... THE THORN.... IT DIDN'T WORK. SAGIN DIDN'T DISAPPEAR....
YEAH, HE JUST SMOOSHED.
IT WAS A HOAX. AN ANCIENT HOAX. OF COURSE IT DIDN'T WORK. WHAT DID YOU EXPECT? NINJA EVERYWHERE BURSTING IN FLAMES, BURNING AWAY TO NOTHING?
YES.
WELL THAT KIND OF THING JUST DOESN'T HAPPEN.
THIS ISN'T A COMIC BOOK, YOU KNOW.
UHHNN... TICK?
JEEZ.... OEDIPUS, ARE YOU ALL RIGHT?
I THINK I'M GOING TO THROW UP.
OH, I WISH I WAS WEARING MY TUXEDO.
MEN, OUR JOB HERE IS DONE.
LET'S GET THIS GIRL TO SAFETY.

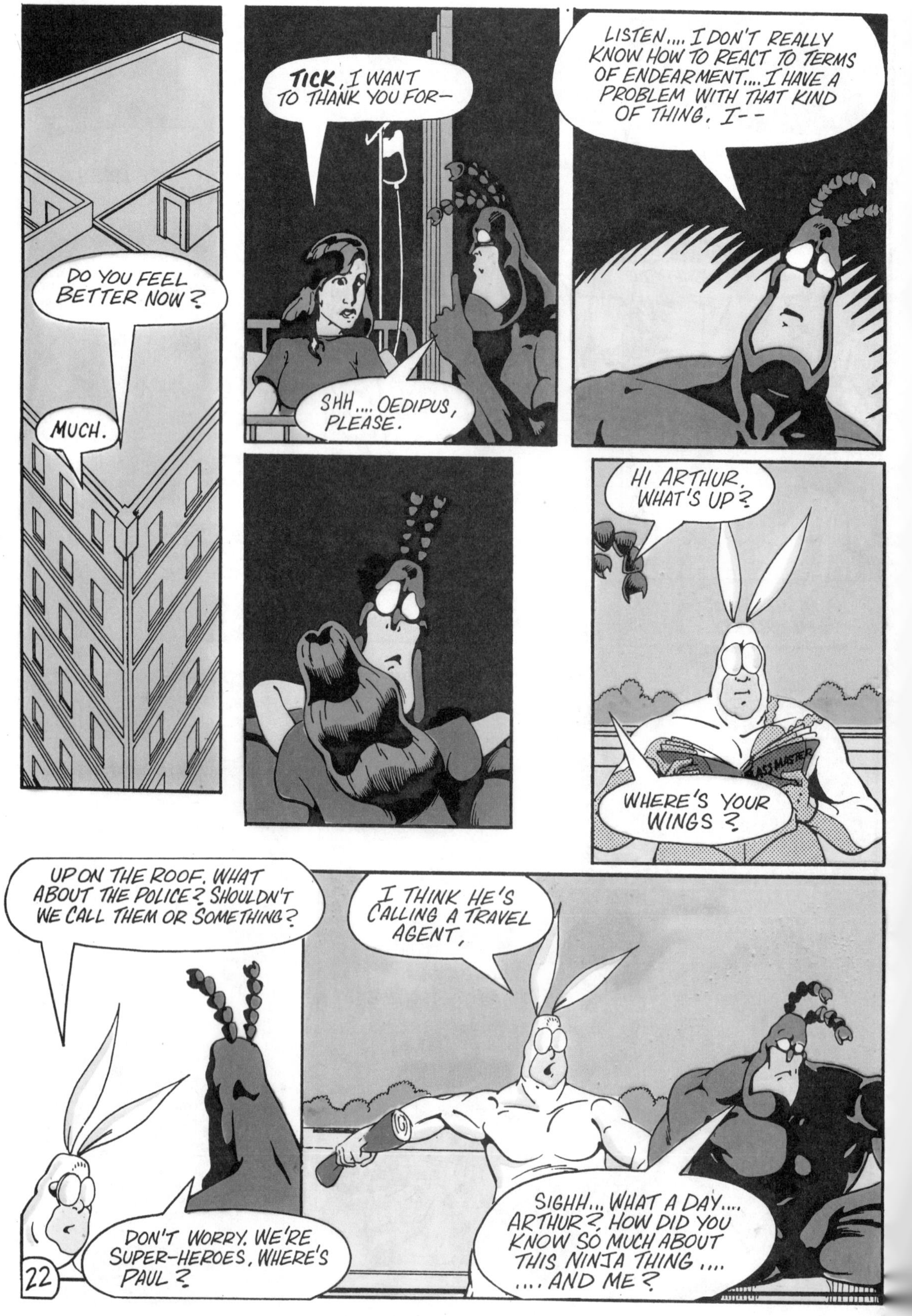
DO YOU FEEL BETTER NOW?
MUCH.
TICK, I WANT TO THANK YOU FOR—
SHH.... OEDIPUS, PLEASE.
LISTEN.... I DON'T REALLY KNOW HOW TO REACT TO TERMS OF ENDEARMENT.... I HAVE A PROBLEM WITH THAT KIND OF THING. I--
HI ARTHUR. WHAT'S UP?
WHERE'S YOUR WINGS?
UP ON THE ROOF. WHAT ABOUT THE POLICE? SHOULDN'T WE CALL THEM OR SOMETHING?
DON'T WORRY. WE'RE SUPER-HEROES. WHERE'S PAUL?
I THINK HE'S CALLING A TRAVEL AGENT.
SIGHH... WHAT A DAY.... ARTHUR? HOW DID YOU KNOW SO MUCH ABOUT THIS NINJA THING.... .... AND ME?

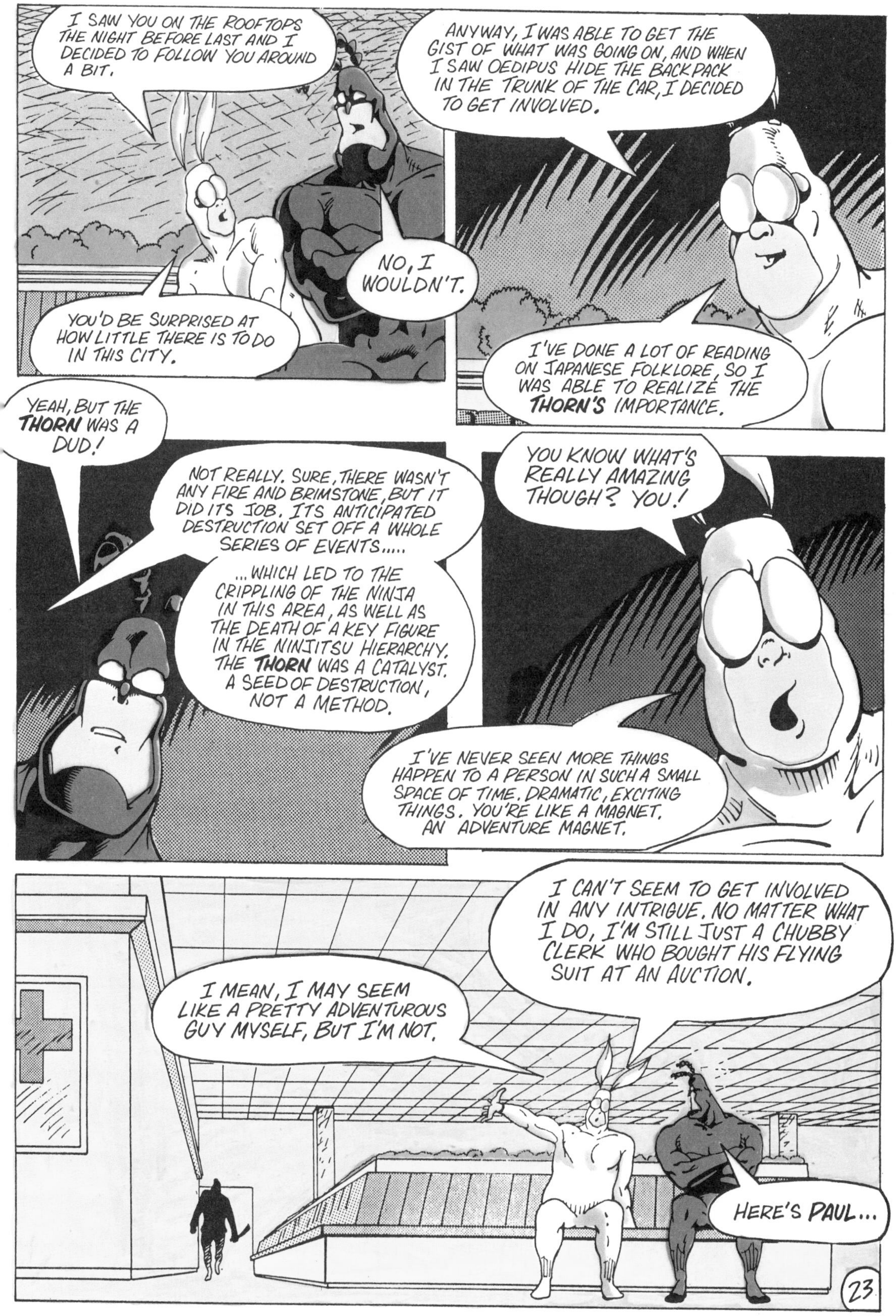
I SAW YOU ON THE ROOFTOPS THE NIGHT BEFORE LAST AND I DECIDED TO FOLLOW YOU AROUND A BIT.
YOU'D BE SURPRISED AT HOW LITTLE THERE IS TO DO IN THIS CITY.
NO, I WOULDN'T.
ANYWAY, I WAS ABLE TO GET THE GIST OF WHAT WAS GOING ON, AND WHEN I SAW OEDIPUS HIDE THE BACKPACK IN THE TRUNK OF THE CAR, I DECIDED TO GET INVOLVED.
I'VE DONE A LOT OF READING ON JAPANESE FOLKLORE, SO I WAS ABLE TO REALIZE THE THORN'S IMPORTANCE.
YEAH, BUT THE THORN WAS A DUD!
NOT REALLY. SURE, THERE WASN'T ANY FIRE AND BRIMSTONE, BUT IT DID ITS JOB. ITS ANTICIPATED DESTRUCTION SET OFF A WHOLE SERIES OF EVENTS.....
...WHICH LED TO THE CRIPPLING OF THE NINJA IN THIS AREA, AS WELL AS THE DEATH OF A KEY FIGURE IN THE NINJITSU HIERARCHY. THE THORN WAS A CATALYST. A SEED OF DESTRUCTION, NOT A METHOD.
YOU KNOW WHAT'S REALLY AMAZING THOUGH? YOU!
I'VE NEVER SEEN MORE THINGS HAPPEN TO A PERSON IN SUCH A SMALL SPACE OF TIME. DRAMATIC, EXCITING THINGS. YOU'RE LIKE A MAGNET. AN ADVENTURE MAGNET.
I MEAN, I MAY SEEM LIKE A PRETTY ADVENTUROUS GUY MYSELF, BUT I'M NOT.
I CAN'T SEEM TO GET INVOLVED IN ANY INTRIGUE. NO MATTER WHAT I DO, I'M STILL JUST A CHUBBY CLERK WHO BOUGHT HIS FLYING SUIT AT AN AUCTION.
HERE'S PAUL...
23

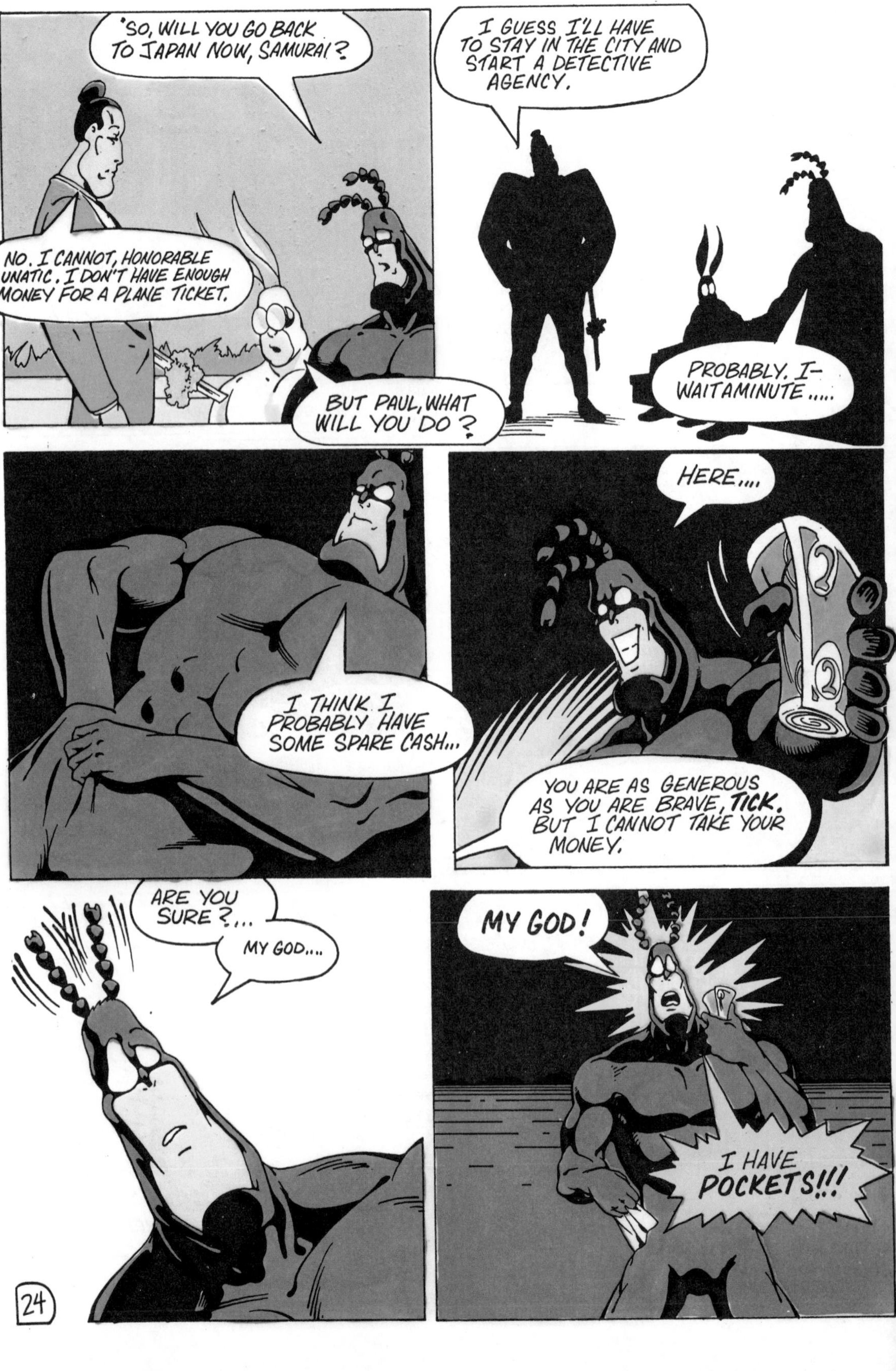

"SO, WILL YOU GO BACK TO JAPAN NOW, SAMURAI?
NO. I CANNOT, HONORABLE LUNATIC. I DON'T HAVE ENOUGH MONEY FOR A PLANE TICKET.
BUT PAUL, WHAT WILL YOU DO?
I GUESS I'LL HAVE TO STAY IN THE CITY AND START A DETECTIVE AGENCY.
PROBABLY. I- WAITAMINUTE.....
I THINK I PROBABLY HAVE SOME SPARE CASH...
HERE....
YOU ARE AS GENEROUS AS YOU ARE BRAVE, TICK. BUT I CANNOT TAKE YOUR MONEY.
ARE YOU SURE?...
MY GOD....
MY GOD!
I HAVE POCKETS!!!

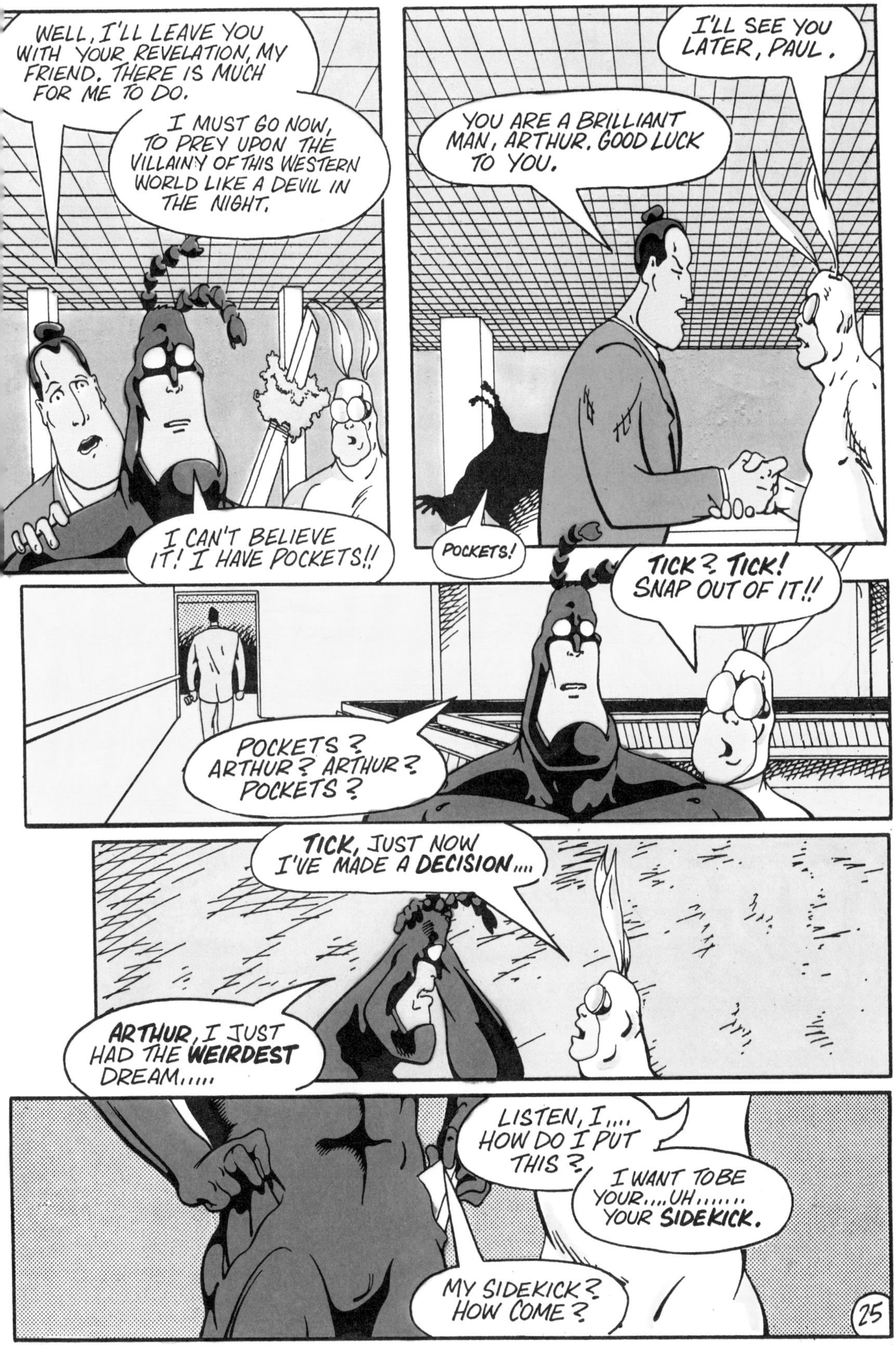
WELL, I'LL LEAVE YOU WITH YOUR REVELATION, MY FRIEND. THERE IS MUCH FOR ME TO DO.
I MUST GO NOW, TO PREY UPON THE VILLAINY OF THIS WESTERN WORLD LIKE A DEVIL IN THE NIGHT.
I CAN'T BELIEVE IT! I HAVE POCKETS!!
I'LL SEE YOU LATER, PAUL.
YOU ARE A BRILLIANT MAN, ARTHUR. GOOD LUCK TO YOU.
POCKETS!
TICK? TICK! SNAP OUT OF IT!!
POCKETS? ARTHUR? ARTHUR? POCKETS?
TICK, JUST NOW I'VE MADE A DECISION....
ARTHUR, I JUST HAD THE WEIRDEST DREAM.....
LISTEN, I.... HOW DO I PUT THIS?
I WANT TO BE YOUR....UH...... YOUR SIDEKICK.
MY SIDEKICK? HOW COME?

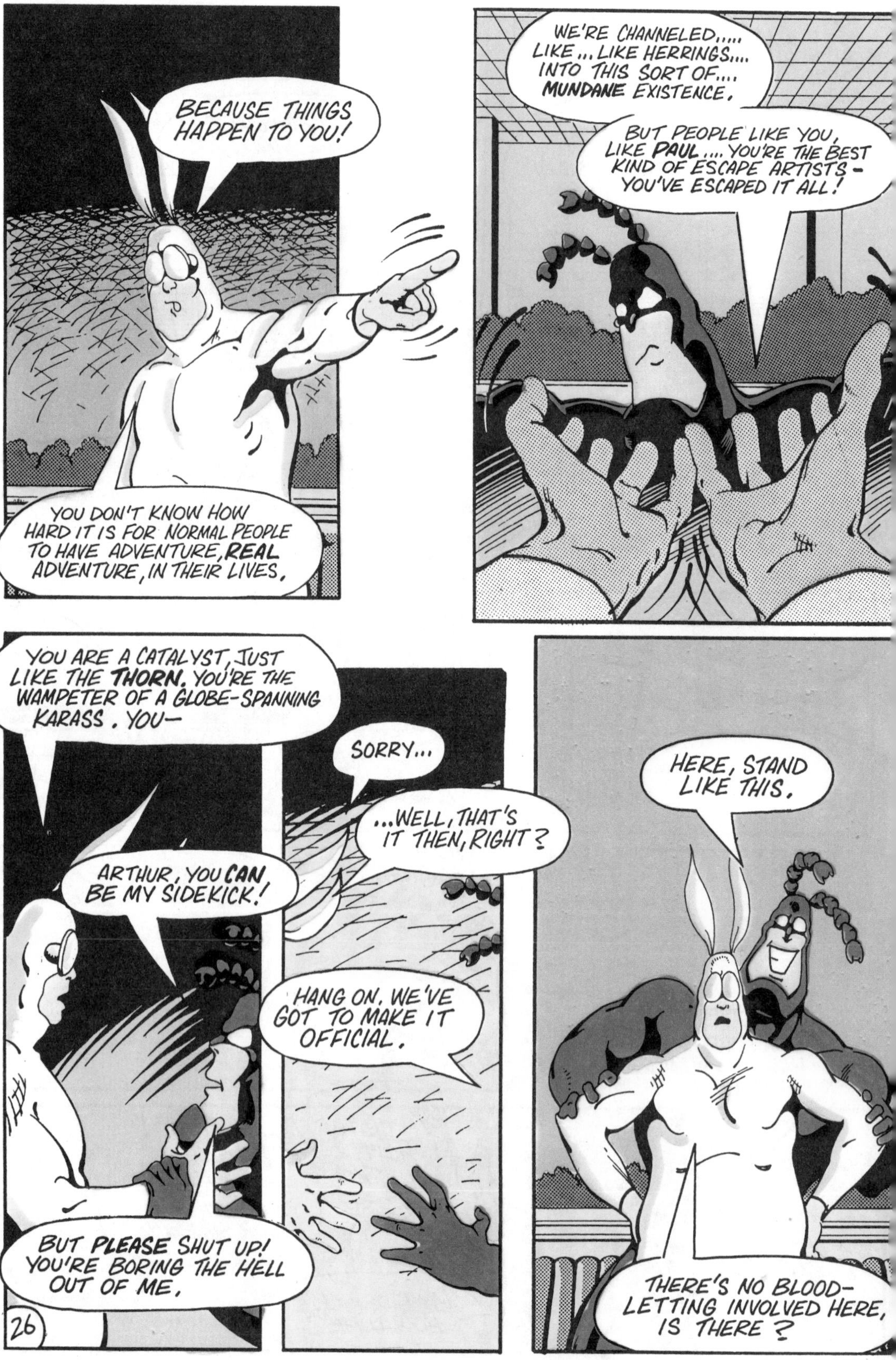
BECAUSE THINGS HAPPEN TO YOU!
YOU DON'T KNOW HOW HARD IT IS FOR NORMAL PEOPLE TO HAVE ADVENTURE, **REAL** ADVENTURE, IN THEIR LIVES.
WE'RE CHANNELED..... LIKE... LIKE HERRINGS.... INTO THIS SORT OF.... **MUNDANE** EXISTENCE.
BUT PEOPLE LIKE YOU, LIKE **PAUL**.... YOU'RE THE BEST KIND OF ESCAPE ARTISTS - YOU'VE ESCAPED IT ALL!
YOU ARE A CATALYST, JUST LIKE THE **THORN.** YOU'RE THE WAMPETER OF A GLOBE-SPANNING KARASS. YOU—
ARTHUR, YOU **CAN** BE MY SIDEKICK!
BUT **PLEASE** SHUT UP! YOU'RE BORING THE HELL OUT OF ME.
SORRY...
...WELL, THAT'S IT THEN, RIGHT?
HANG ON. WE'VE GOT TO MAKE IT OFFICIAL.
HERE, STAND LIKE THIS.
THERE'S NO BLOOD-LETTING INVOLVED HERE, IS THERE?

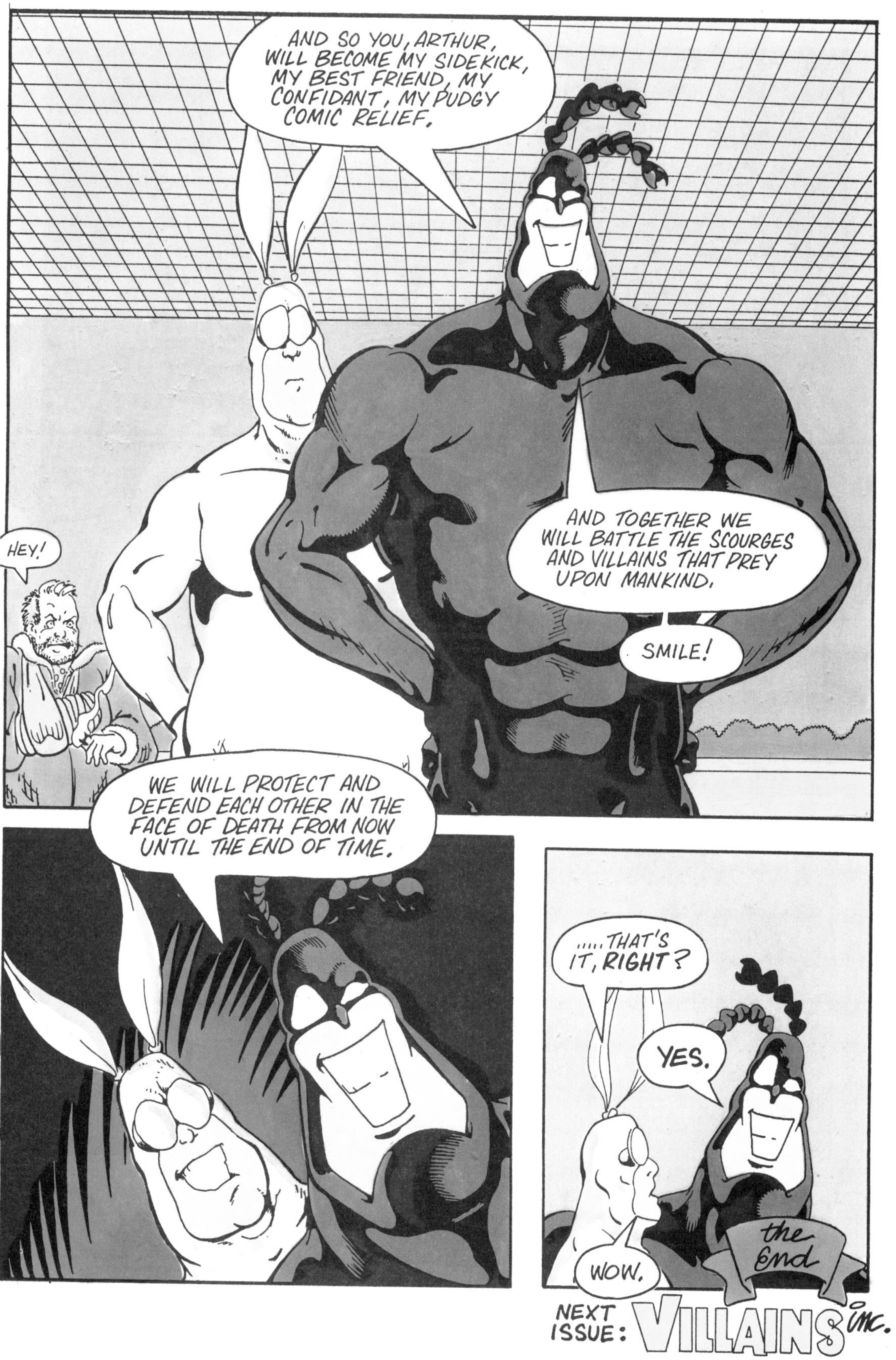
AND SO YOU, ARTHUR, WILL BECOME MY SIDEKICK, MY BEST FRIEND, MY CONFIDANT, MY PUDGY COMIC RELIEF.
AND TOGETHER WE WILL BATTLE THE SCOURGES AND VILLAINS THAT PREY UPON MANKIND.
SMILE!
HEY!
WE WILL PROTECT AND DEFEND EACH OTHER IN THE FACE OF DEATH FROM NOW UNTIL THE END OF TIME.
.....THAT'S IT, RIGHT?
YES.
WOW.
the end
NEXT ISSUE: VILLAINS inc.

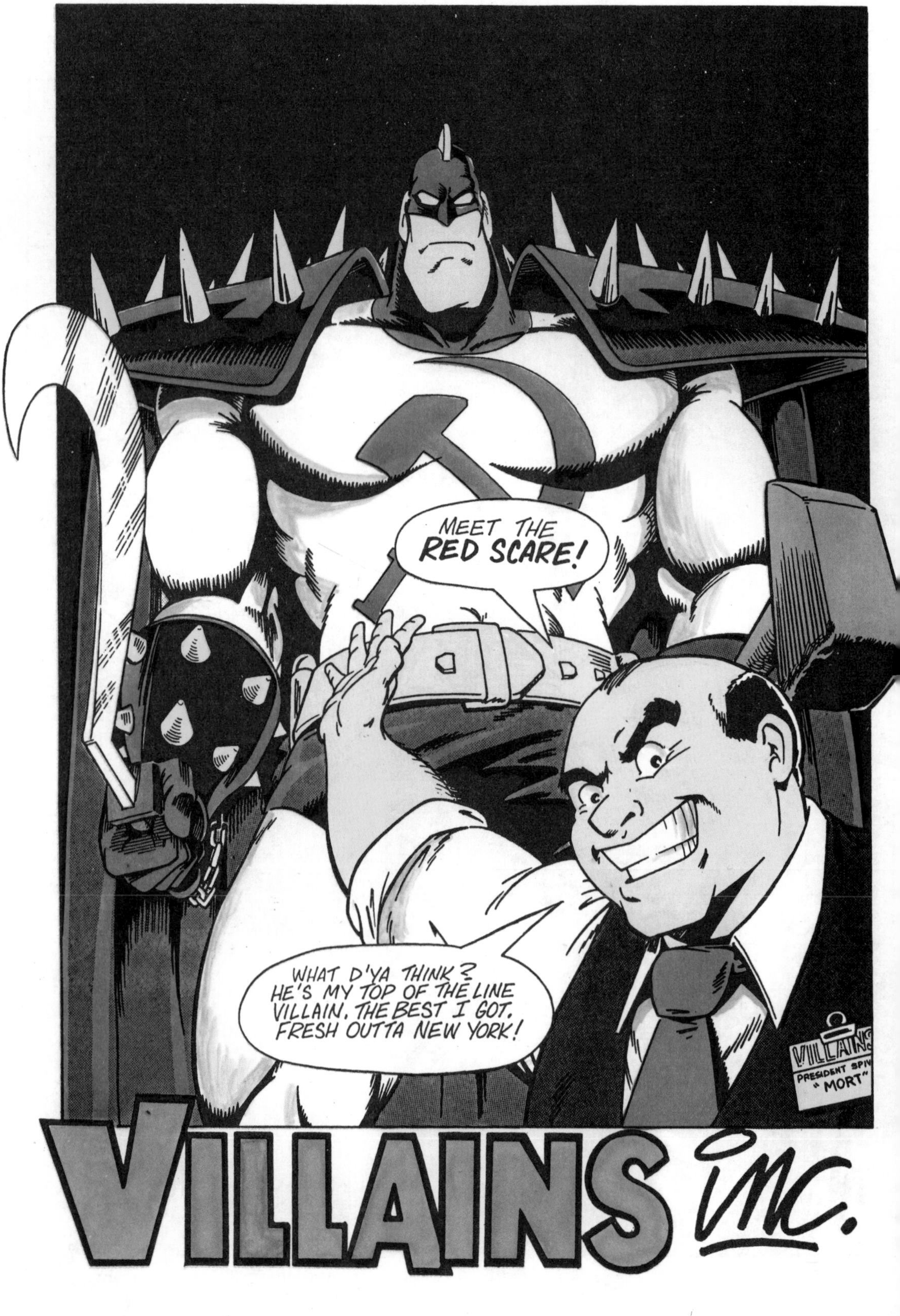
MEET THE RED SCARE!
WHAT D'YA THINK? HE'S MY TOP OF THE LINE VILLAIN, THE BEST I GOT, FRESH OUTTA NEW YORK!
VILLAINS
PRESIDENT SPIV
"MORT"
VILLAINS inc.

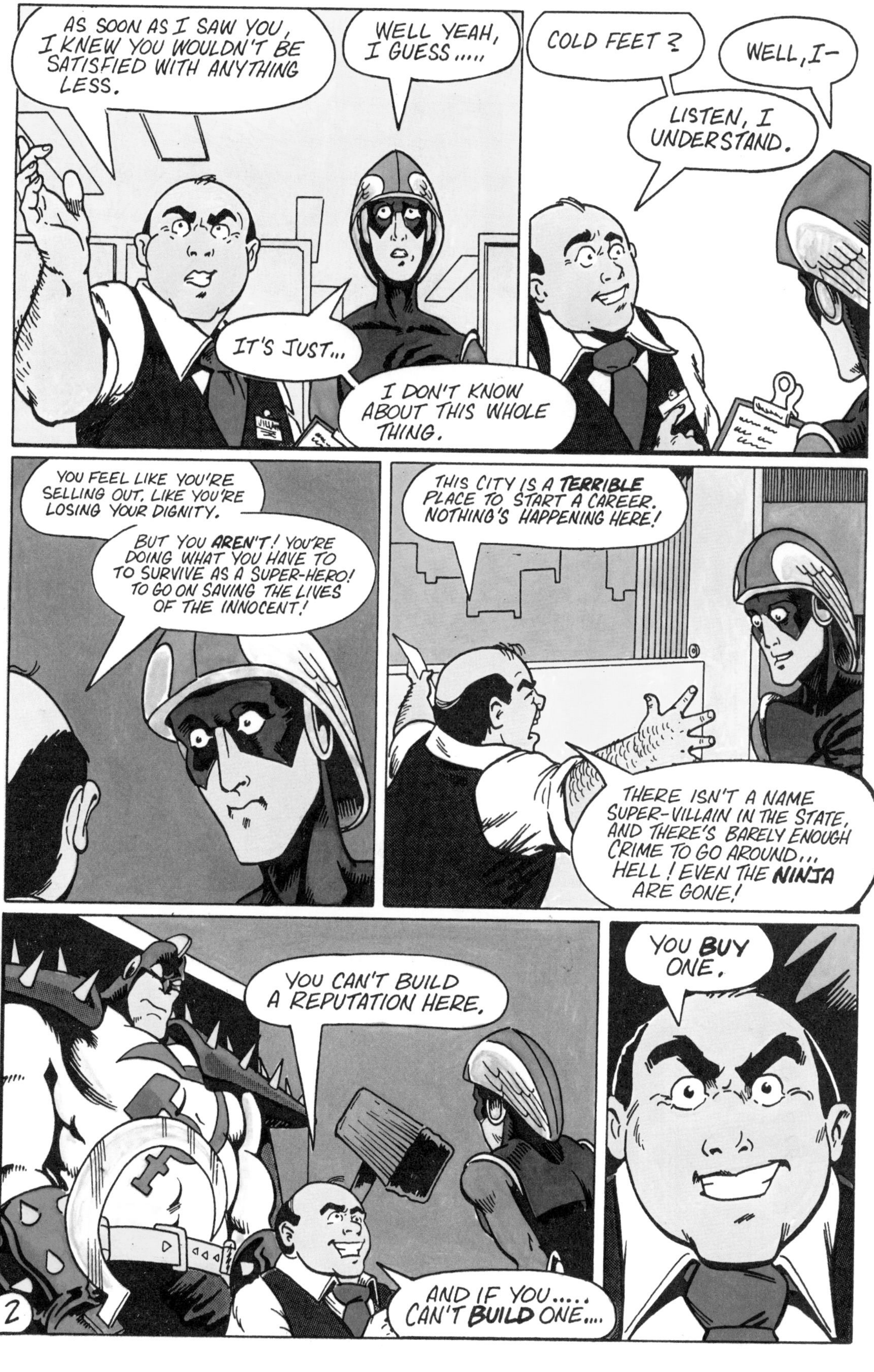
AS SOON AS I SAW YOU, I KNEW YOU WOULDN'T BE SATISFIED WITH ANYTHING LESS.
WELL YEAH, I GUESS.....
IT'S JUST...
I DON'T KNOW ABOUT THIS WHOLE THING.
COLD FEET?
WELL, I-
LISTEN, I UNDERSTAND.
YOU FEEL LIKE YOU'RE SELLING OUT, LIKE YOU'RE LOSING YOUR DIGNITY.
BUT YOU AREN'T! YOU'RE DOING WHAT YOU HAVE TO TO SURVIVE AS A SUPER-HERO! TO GO ON SAVING THE LIVES OF THE INNOCENT!
THIS CITY IS A TERRIBLE PLACE TO START A CAREER. NOTHING'S HAPPENING HERE!
THERE ISN'T A NAME SUPER-VILLAIN IN THE STATE, AND THERE'S BARELY ENOUGH CRIME TO GO AROUND... HELL! EVEN THE NINJA ARE GONE!
YOU CAN'T BUILD A REPUTATION HERE.
AND IF YOU..... CAN'T BUILD ONE....
YOU BUY ONE.
2

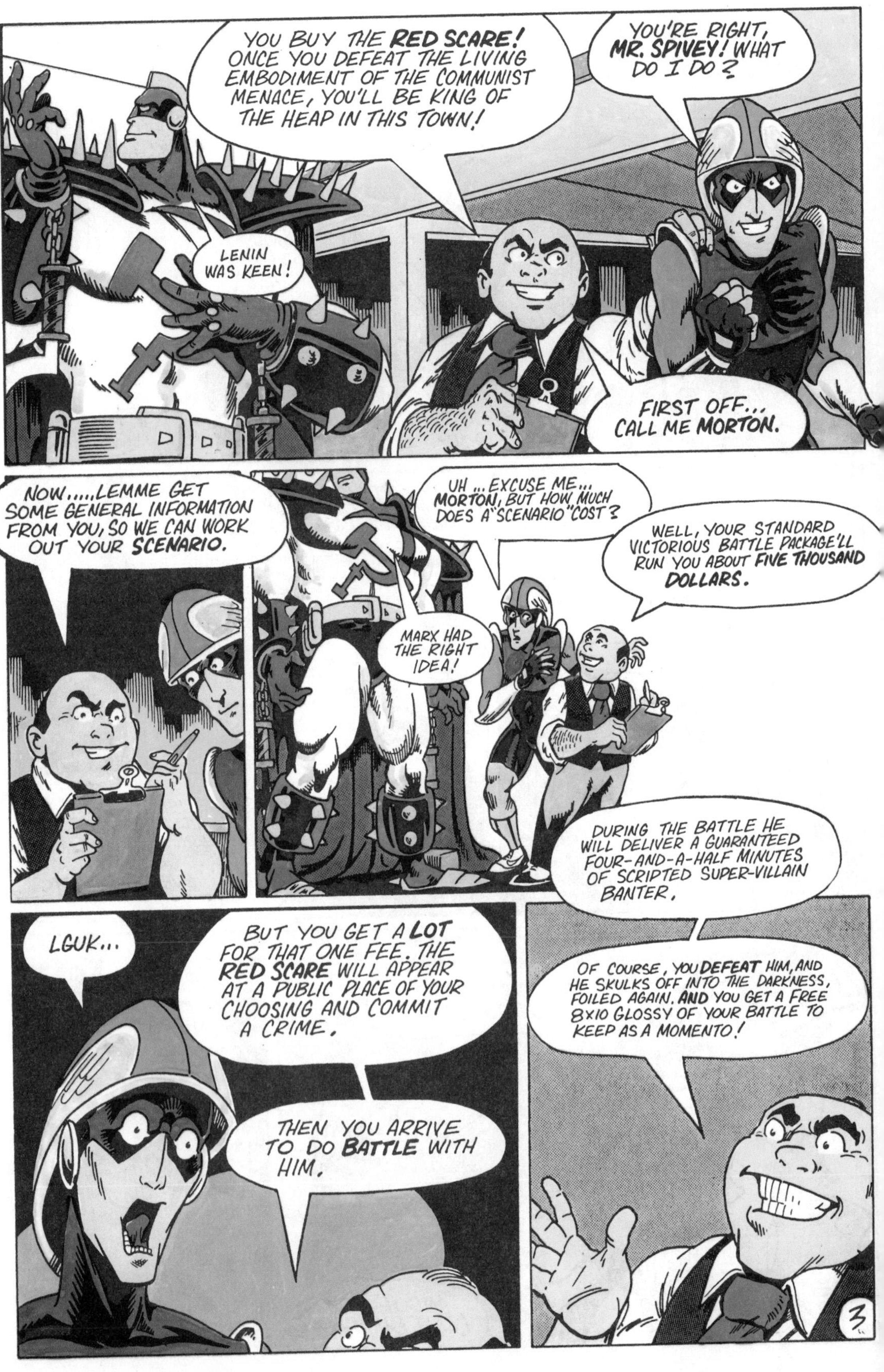
YOU BUY THE **RED SCARE!** ONCE YOU DEFEAT THE LIVING EMBODIMENT OF THE COMMUNIST MENACE, YOU'LL BE KING OF THE HEAP IN THIS TOWN!
YOU'RE RIGHT, **MR. SPIVEY!** WHAT DO I DO?
LENIN WAS KEEN!
FIRST OFF... CALL ME **MORTON.**
NOW.....LEMME GET SOME GENERAL INFORMATION FROM YOU, SO WE CAN WORK OUT YOUR **SCENARIO.**
UH ... EXCUSE ME... **MORTON**, BUT HOW MUCH DOES A "SCENARIO" COST?
WELL, YOUR STANDARD VICTORIOUS BATTLE PACKAGE'LL RUN YOU ABOUT **FIVE THOUSAND DOLLARS.**
MARX HAD THE RIGHT IDEA!
DURING THE BATTLE HE WILL DELIVER A GUARANTEED FOUR-AND-A-HALF MINUTES OF SCRIPTED SUPER-VILLAIN BANTER.
LGUK...
BUT YOU GET A **LOT** FOR THAT ONE FEE. THE **RED SCARE** WILL APPEAR AT A PUBLIC PLACE OF YOUR CHOOSING AND COMMIT A CRIME.
THEN YOU ARRIVE TO DO **BATTLE** WITH HIM.
OF COURSE, YOU **DEFEAT** HIM, AND HE SKULKS OFF INTO THE DARKNESS, FOILED AGAIN. **AND** YOU GET A FREE 8x10 GLOSSY OF YOUR BATTLE TO KEEP AS A MOMENTO!
3

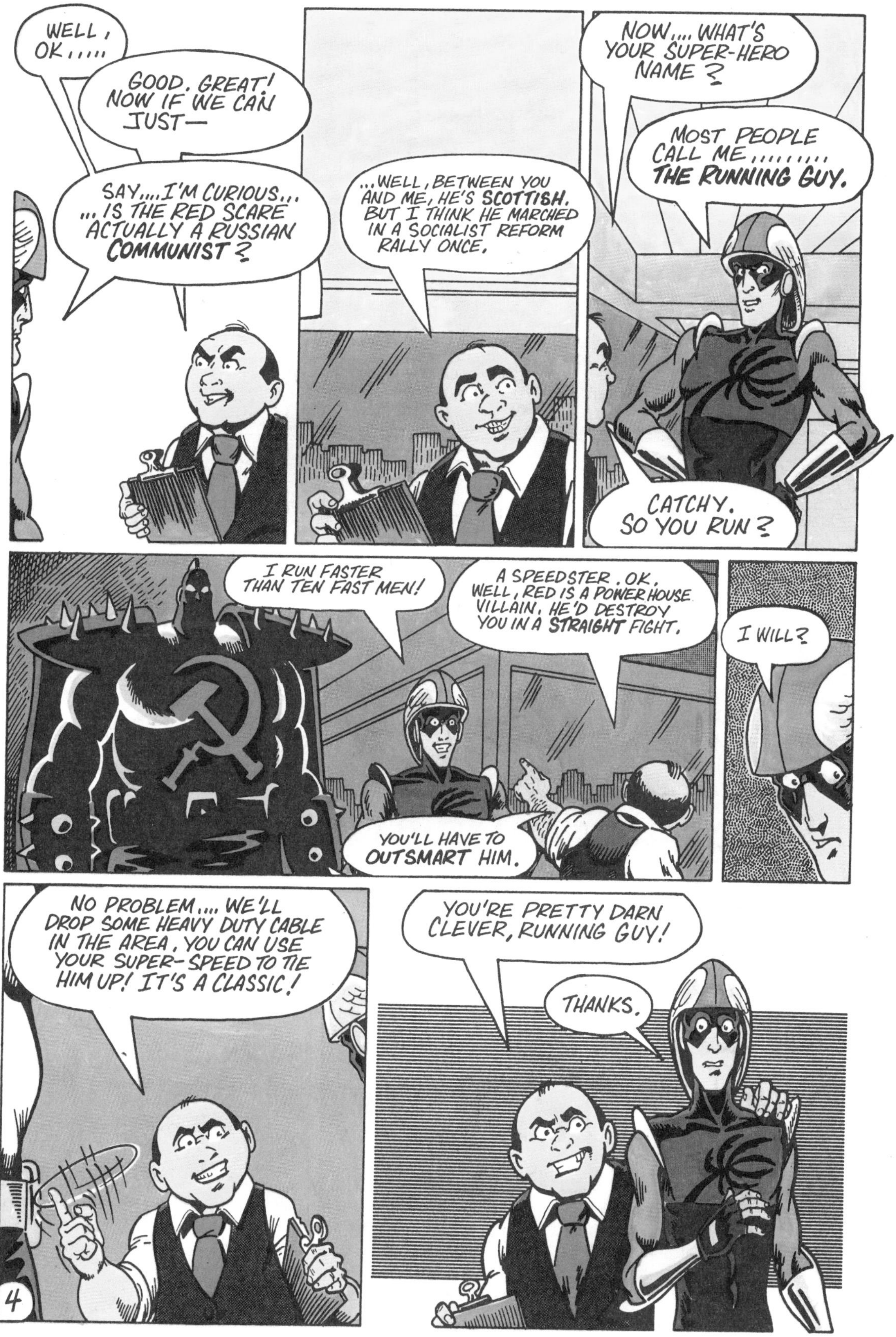
WELL, OK,....
GOOD. GREAT! NOW IF WE CAN JUST—
SAY,...I'M CURIOUS... ...IS THE RED SCARE ACTUALLY A RUSSIAN COMMUNIST?
...WELL, BETWEEN YOU AND ME, HE'S SCOTTISH. BUT I THINK HE MARCHED IN A SOCIALIST REFORM RALLY ONCE.
NOW,...WHAT'S YOUR SUPER-HERO NAME?
MOST PEOPLE CALL ME.......... THE RUNNING GUY.
CATCHY. SO YOU RUN?
I RUN FASTER THAN TEN FAST MEN!
A SPEEDSTER. OK. WELL, RED IS A POWERHOUSE VILLAIN. HE'D DESTROY YOU IN A STRAIGHT FIGHT.
YOU'LL HAVE TO OUTSMART HIM.
I WILL?
NO PROBLEM.... WE'LL DROP SOME HEAVY DUTY CABLE IN THE AREA, YOU CAN USE YOUR SUPER-SPEED TO TIE HIM UP! IT'S A CLASSIC!
YOU'RE PRETTY DARN CLEVER, RUNNING GUY!
THANKS.

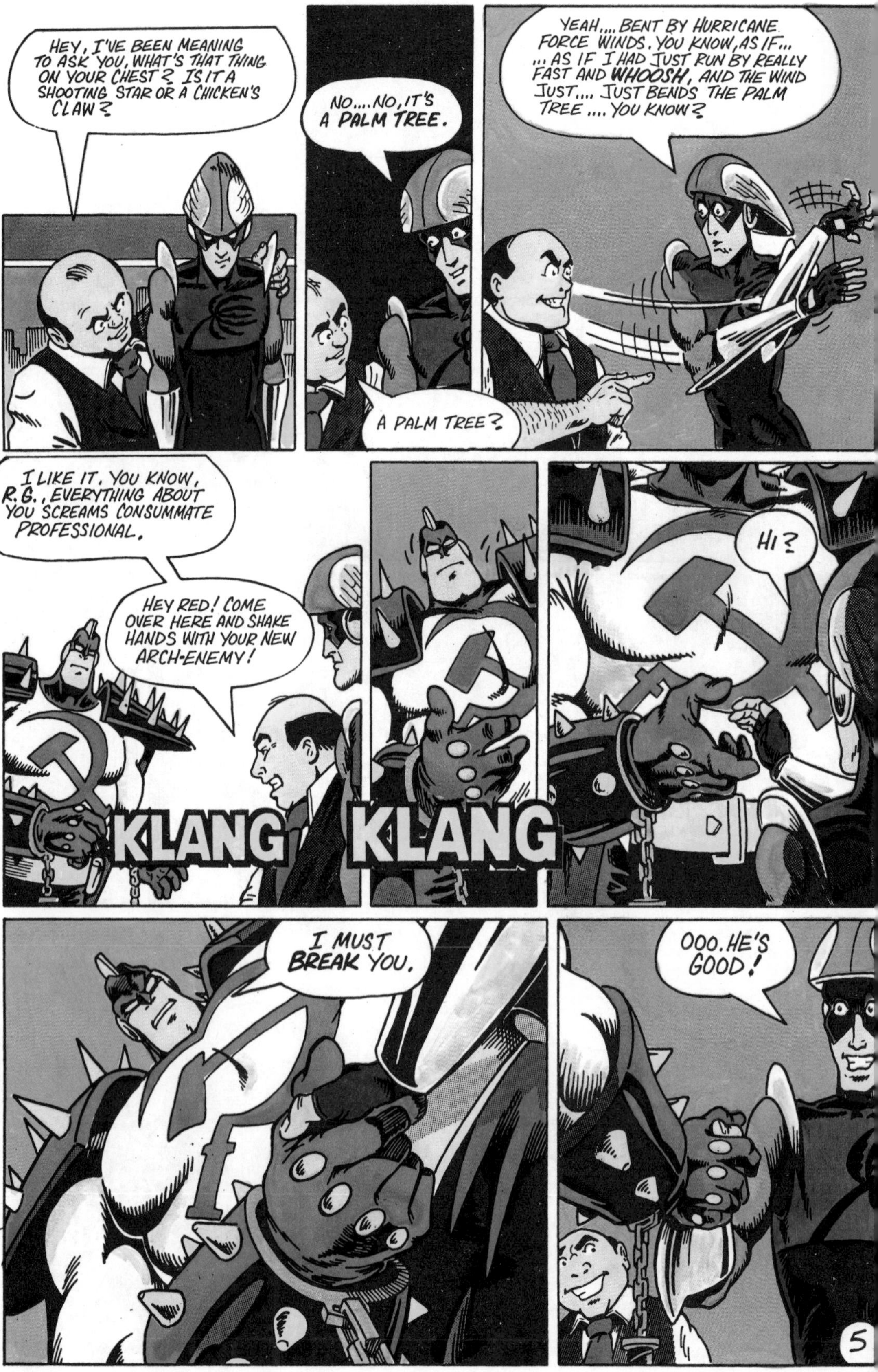

HEY, I'VE BEEN MEANING TO ASK YOU, WHAT'S THAT THING ON YOUR CHEST? IS IT A SHOOTING STAR OR A CHICKEN'S CLAW?
NO.... NO, IT'S A PALM TREE.
A PALM TREE?
YEAH,... BENT BY HURRICANE FORCE WINDS. YOU KNOW, AS IF... ...AS IF I HAD JUST RUN BY REALLY FAST AND WHOOSH, AND THE WIND JUST.... JUST BENDS THE PALM TREE .... YOU KNOW?
I LIKE IT. YOU KNOW, R.G., EVERYTHING ABOUT YOU SCREAMS CONSUMMATE PROFESSIONAL.
HEY RED! COME OVER HERE AND SHAKE HANDS WITH YOUR NEW ARCH-ENEMY!
KLANG
KLANG
HI?
I MUST BREAK YOU.
OOO. HE'S GOOD!

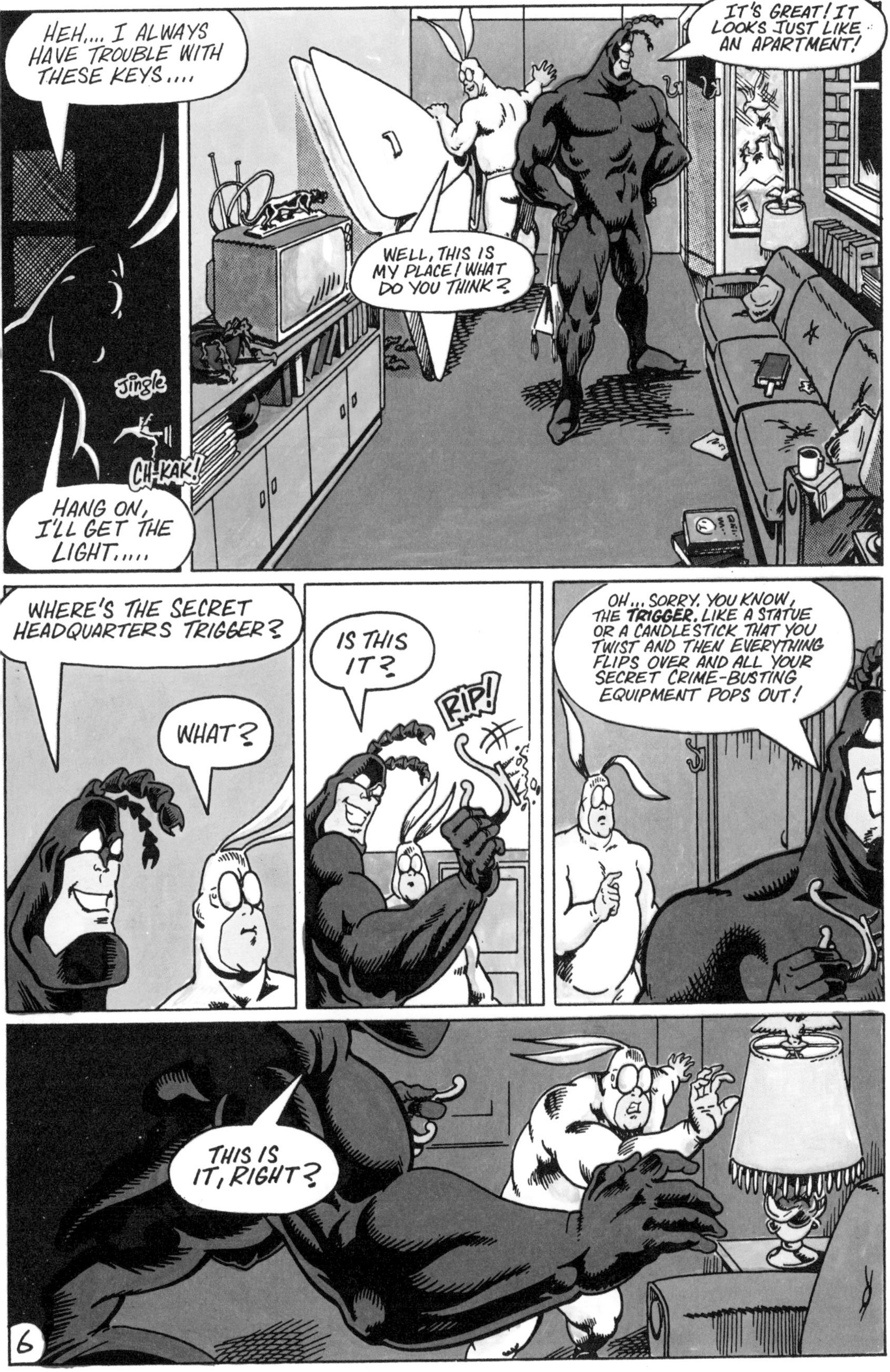

HEH,... I ALWAYS HAVE TROUBLE WITH THESE KEYS....
Jingle
CH-KAK!
HANG ON, I'LL GET THE LIGHT.....
WELL, THIS IS MY PLACE! WHAT DO YOU THINK?
IT'S GREAT! IT LOOKS JUST LIKE AN APARTMENT!
WHERE'S THE SECRET HEADQUARTERS TRIGGER?
WHAT?
IS THIS IT?
RIP!
OH... SORRY. YOU KNOW, THE TRIGGER. LIKE A STATUE OR A CANDLESTICK THAT YOU TWIST AND THEN EVERYTHING FLIPS OVER AND ALL YOUR SECRET CRIME-BUSTING EQUIPMENT POPS OUT!
THIS IS IT, RIGHT?

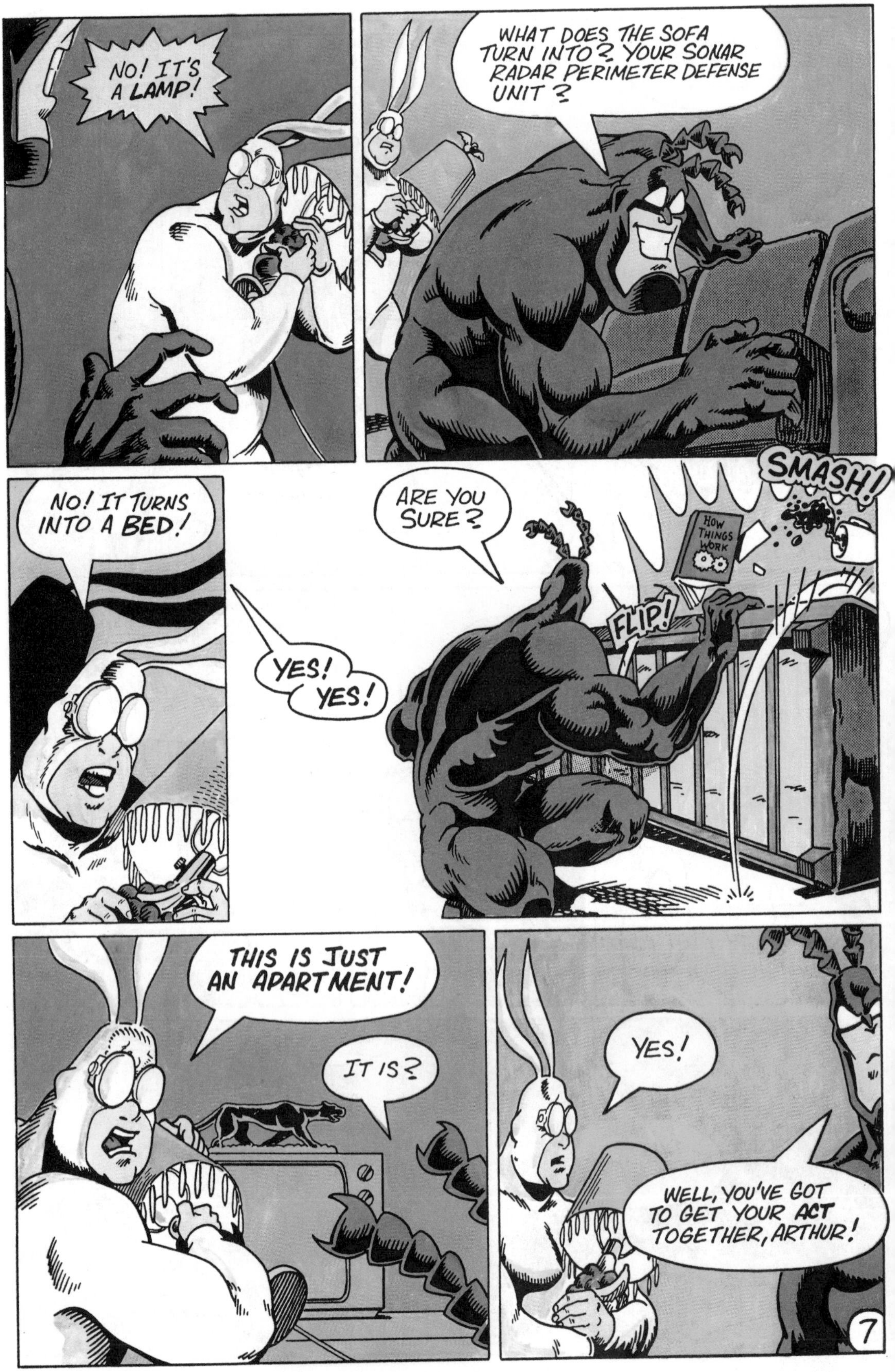
NO! IT'S A LAMP!
WHAT DOES THE SOFA TURN INTO? YOUR SONAR RADAR PERIMETER DEFENSE UNIT?
NO! IT TURNS INTO A BED!
ARE YOU SURE?
YES! YES!
SMASH!
HOW THINGS WORK
FLIP!
THIS IS JUST AN APARTMENT!
IT IS?
YES!
WELL, YOU'VE GOT TO GET YOUR ACT TOGETHER, ARTHUR!

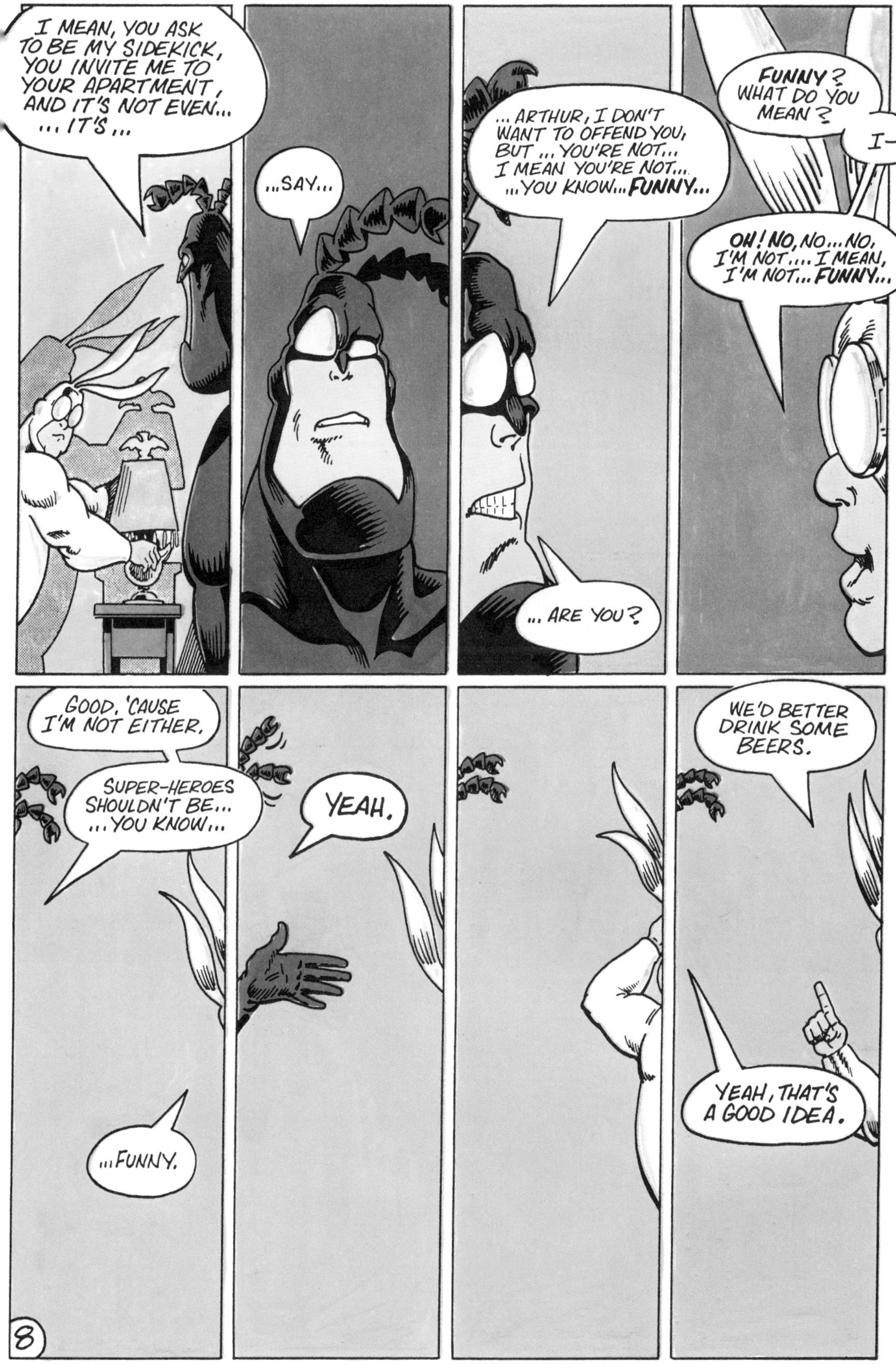

I MEAN, YOU ASK TO BE MY SIDEKICK, YOU INVITE ME TO YOUR APARTMENT, AND IT'S NOT EVEN... ...IT'S...
...SAY...
...ARTHUR, I DON'T WANT TO OFFEND YOU, BUT ... YOU'RE NOT... I MEAN YOU'RE NOT... ...YOU KNOW...FUNNY...
...ARE YOU?
FUNNY? WHAT DO YOU MEAN?
I–
OH! NO, NO...NO, I'M NOT.... I MEAN, I'M NOT...FUNNY...
GOOD, 'CAUSE I'M NOT EITHER.
SUPER-HEROES SHOULDN'T BE... ...YOU KNOW...
...FUNNY.
YEAH.
WE'D BETTER DRINK SOME BEERS.
YEAH, THAT'S A GOOD IDEA.

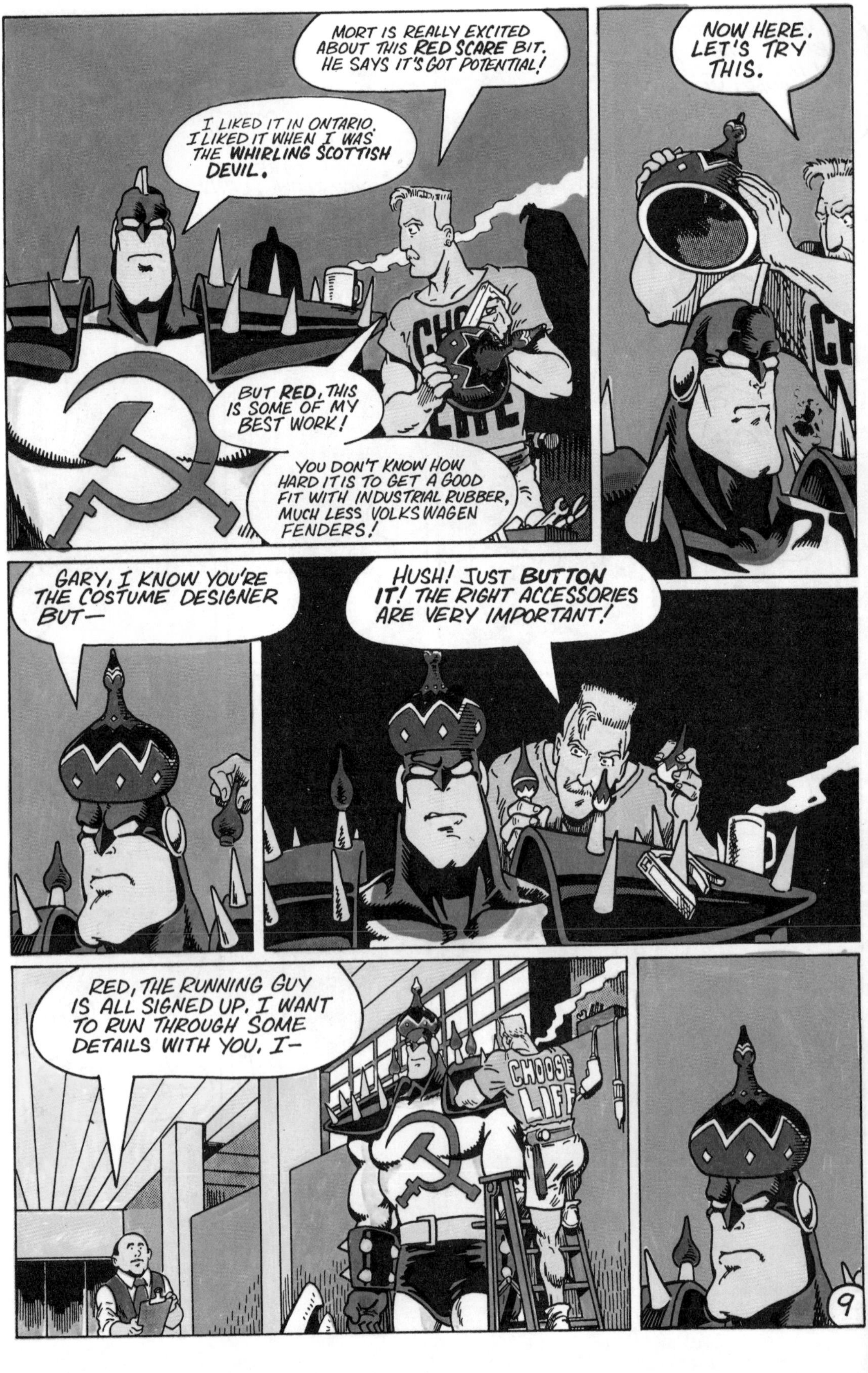
MORT IS REALLY EXCITED ABOUT THIS RED SCARE BIT. HE SAYS IT'S GOT POTENTIAL!
I LIKED IT IN ONTARIO. I LIKED IT WHEN I WAS THE WHIRLING SCOTTISH DEVIL.
BUT RED, THIS IS SOME OF MY BEST WORK!
YOU DON'T KNOW HOW HARD IT IS TO GET A GOOD FIT WITH INDUSTRIAL RUBBER, MUCH LESS VOLKSWAGEN FENDERS!
NOW HERE. LET'S TRY THIS.
GARY, I KNOW YOU'RE THE COSTUME DESIGNER BUT—
HUSH! JUST BUTTON IT! THE RIGHT ACCESSORIES ARE VERY IMPORTANT!
RED, THE RUNNING GUY IS ALL SIGNED UP. I WANT TO RUN THROUGH SOME DETAILS WITH YOU. I—
CHOOSE LIFE

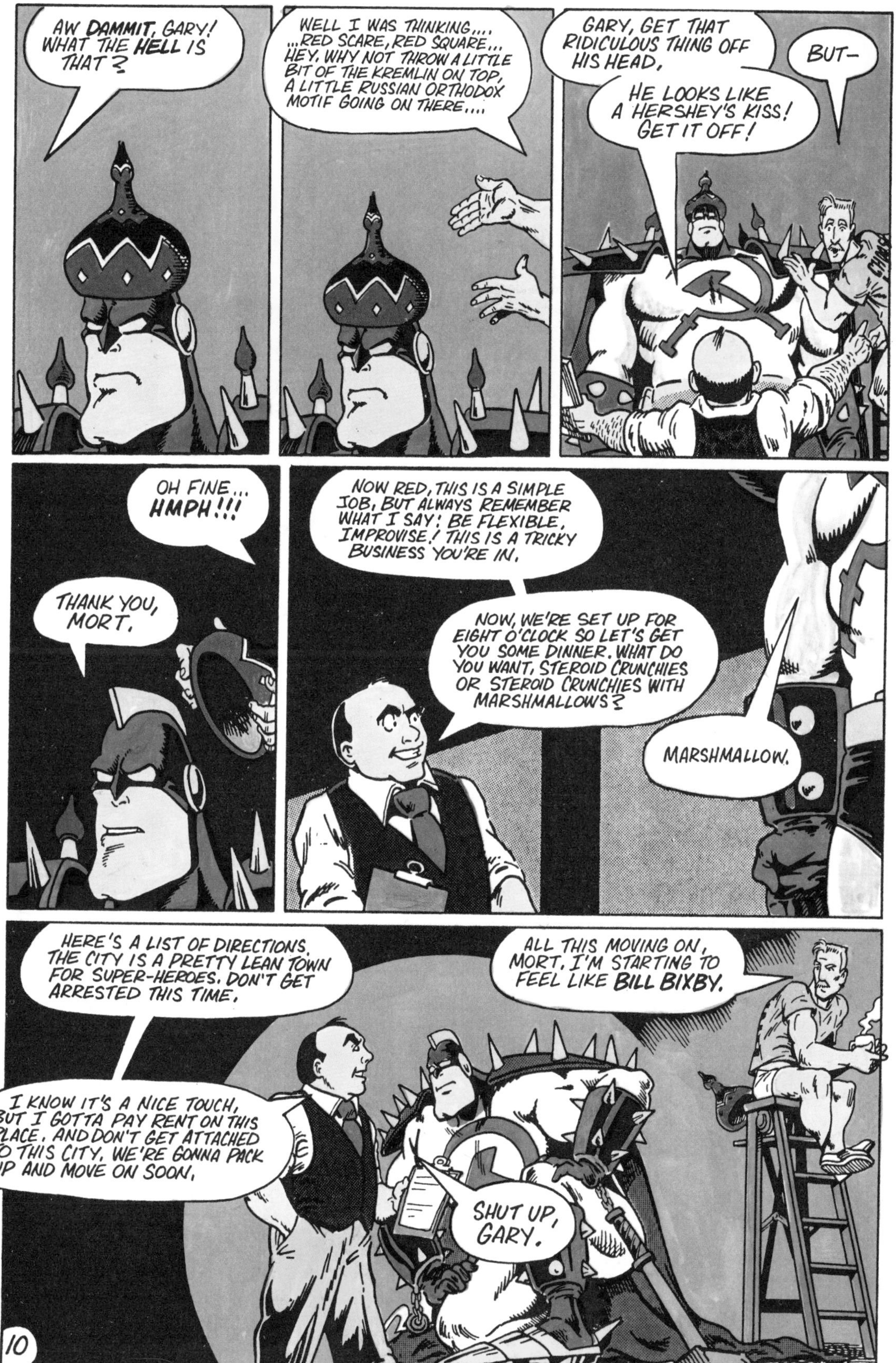
AW DAMMIT, GARY! WHAT THE HELL IS THAT?
WELL I WAS THINKING.... ...RED SCARE, RED SQUARE... HEY, WHY NOT THROW A LITTLE BIT OF THE KREMLIN ON TOP, A LITTLE RUSSIAN ORTHODOX MOTIF GOING ON THERE....
GARY, GET THAT RIDICULOUS THING OFF HIS HEAD.
HE LOOKS LIKE A HERSHEY'S KISS! GET IT OFF!
BUT-
OH FINE... HMPH!!!
THANK YOU, MORT.
NOW RED, THIS IS A SIMPLE JOB, BUT ALWAYS REMEMBER WHAT I SAY: BE FLEXIBLE, IMPROVISE! THIS IS A TRICKY BUSINESS YOU'RE IN.
NOW, WE'RE SET UP FOR EIGHT O'CLOCK SO LET'S GET YOU SOME DINNER. WHAT DO YOU WANT, STEROID CRUNCHIES OR STEROID CRUNCHIES WITH MARSHMALLOWS?
MARSHMALLOW.
HERE'S A LIST OF DIRECTIONS. THE CITY IS A PRETTY LEAN TOWN FOR SUPER-HEROES. DON'T GET ARRESTED THIS TIME.
I KNOW IT'S A NICE TOUCH, BUT I GOTTA PAY RENT ON THIS PLACE. AND DON'T GET ATTACHED TO THIS CITY. WE'RE GONNA PACK UP AND MOVE ON SOON.
ALL THIS MOVING ON, MORT, I'M STARTING TO FEEL LIKE BILL BIXBY.
SHUT UP, GARY.

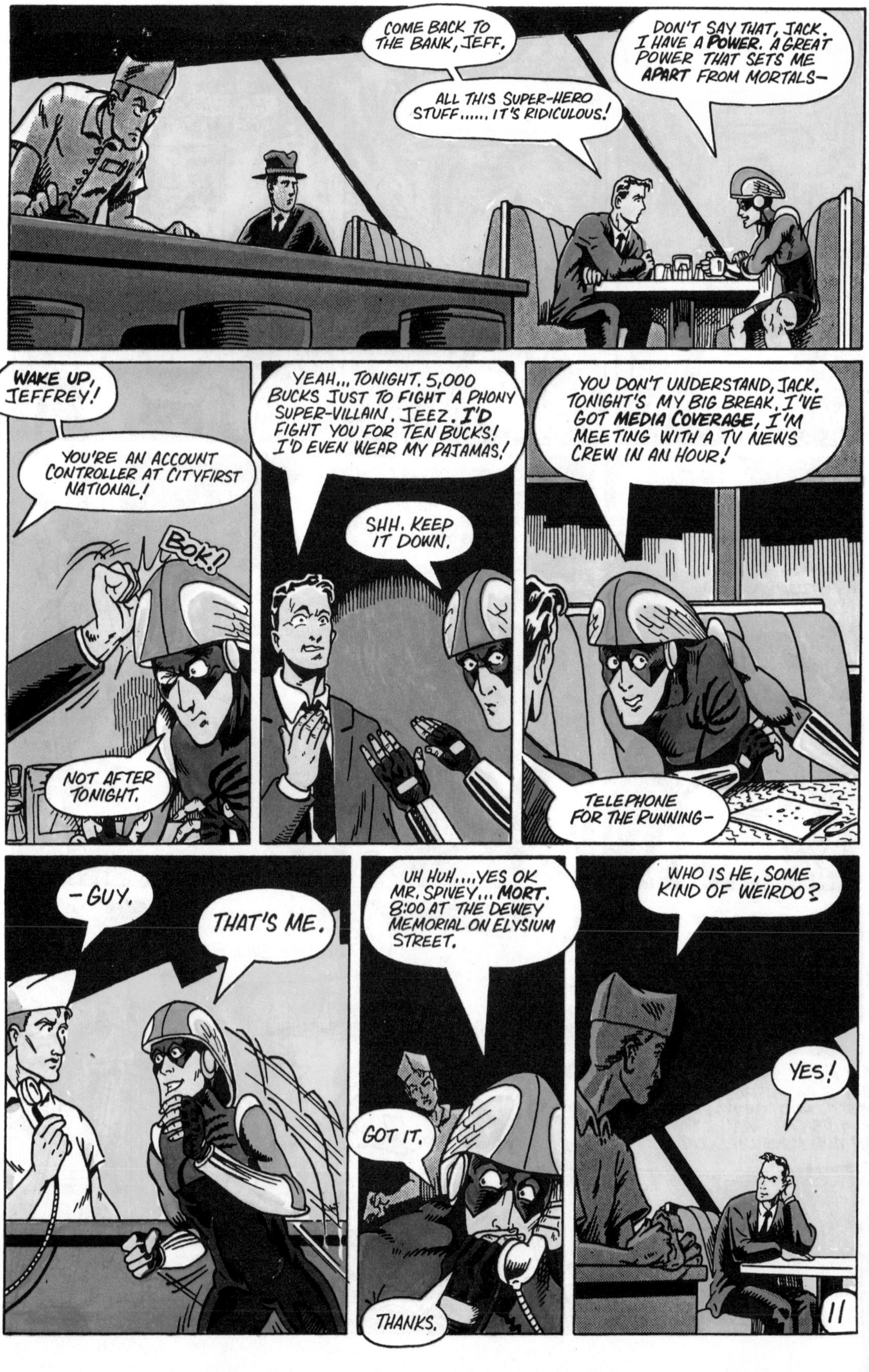
COME BACK TO THE BANK, JEFF.
ALL THIS SUPER-HERO STUFF...... IT'S RIDICULOUS!
DON'T SAY THAT, JACK. I HAVE A POWER. A GREAT POWER THAT SETS ME APART FROM MORTALS-
WAKE UP, JEFFREY!
YOU'RE AN ACCOUNT CONTROLLER AT CITYFIRST NATIONAL!
BOK!
NOT AFTER TONIGHT.
YEAH... TONIGHT. 5,000 BUCKS JUST TO FIGHT A PHONY SUPER-VILLAIN. JEEZ. I'D FIGHT YOU FOR TEN BUCKS! I'D EVEN WEAR MY PAJAMAS!
SHH. KEEP IT DOWN.
YOU DON'T UNDERSTAND, JACK. TONIGHT'S MY BIG BREAK. I'VE GOT MEDIA COVERAGE. I'M MEETING WITH A TV NEWS CREW IN AN HOUR!
TELEPHONE FOR THE RUNNING-
-GUY.
THAT'S ME.
UH HUH....YES OK MR. SPIVEY... MORT. 8:00 AT THE DEWEY MEMORIAL ON ELYSIUM STREET.
GOT IT.
THANKS.
WHO IS HE, SOME KIND OF WEIRDO?
YES!
11

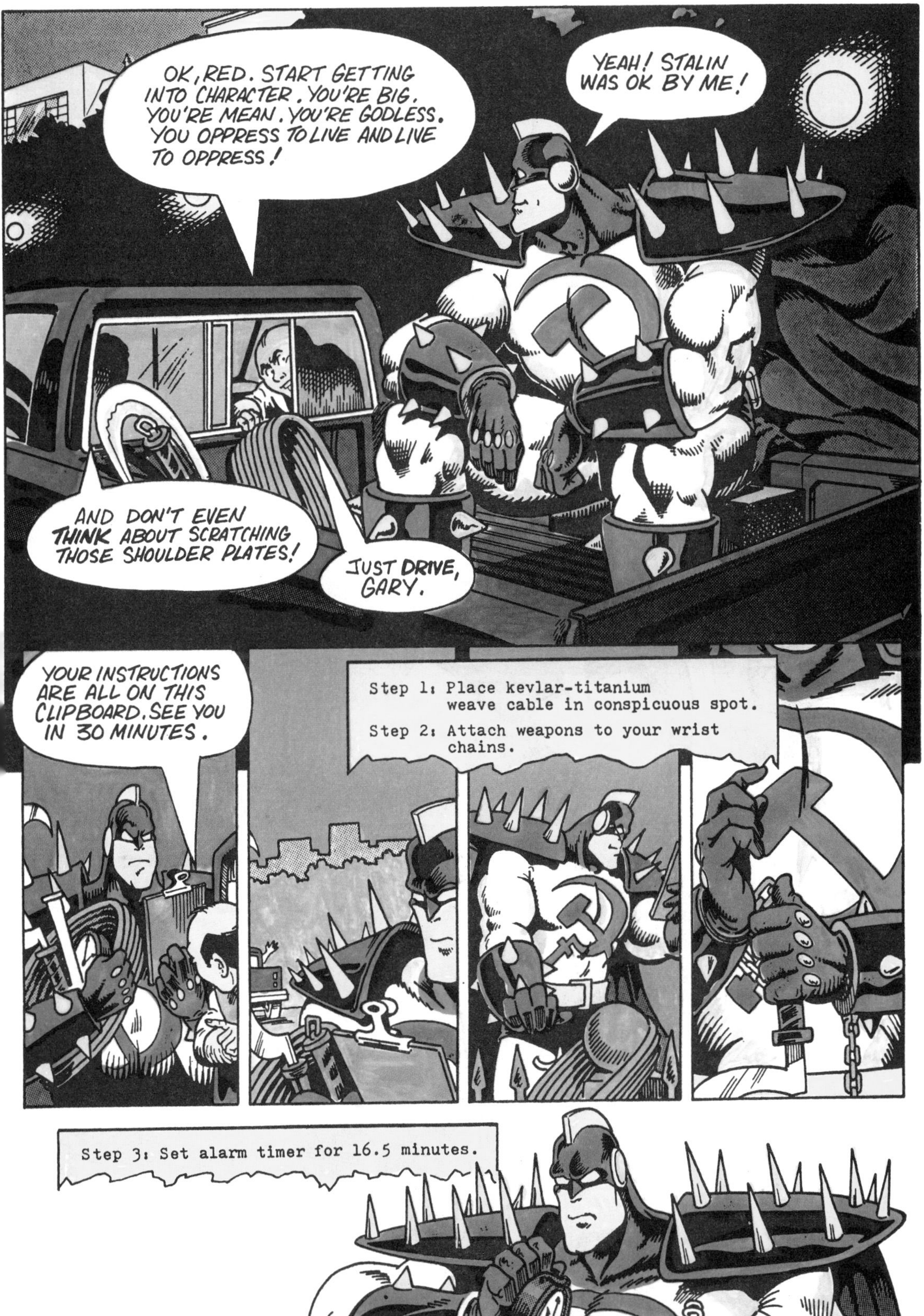
OK, RED. START GETTING INTO CHARACTER. YOU'RE BIG. YOU'RE MEAN. YOU'RE GODLESS. YOU OPPRESS TO LIVE AND LIVE TO OPPRESS!
YEAH! STALIN WAS OK BY ME!
AND DON'T EVEN THINK ABOUT SCRATCHING THOSE SHOULDER PLATES!
JUST DRIVE, GARY.
YOUR INSTRUCTIONS ARE ALL ON THIS CLIPBOARD. SEE YOU IN 30 MINUTES.
Step 1: Place kevlar-titanium weave cable in conspicuous spot.
Step 2: Attach weapons to your wrist chains.
Step 3: Set alarm timer for 16.5 minutes.

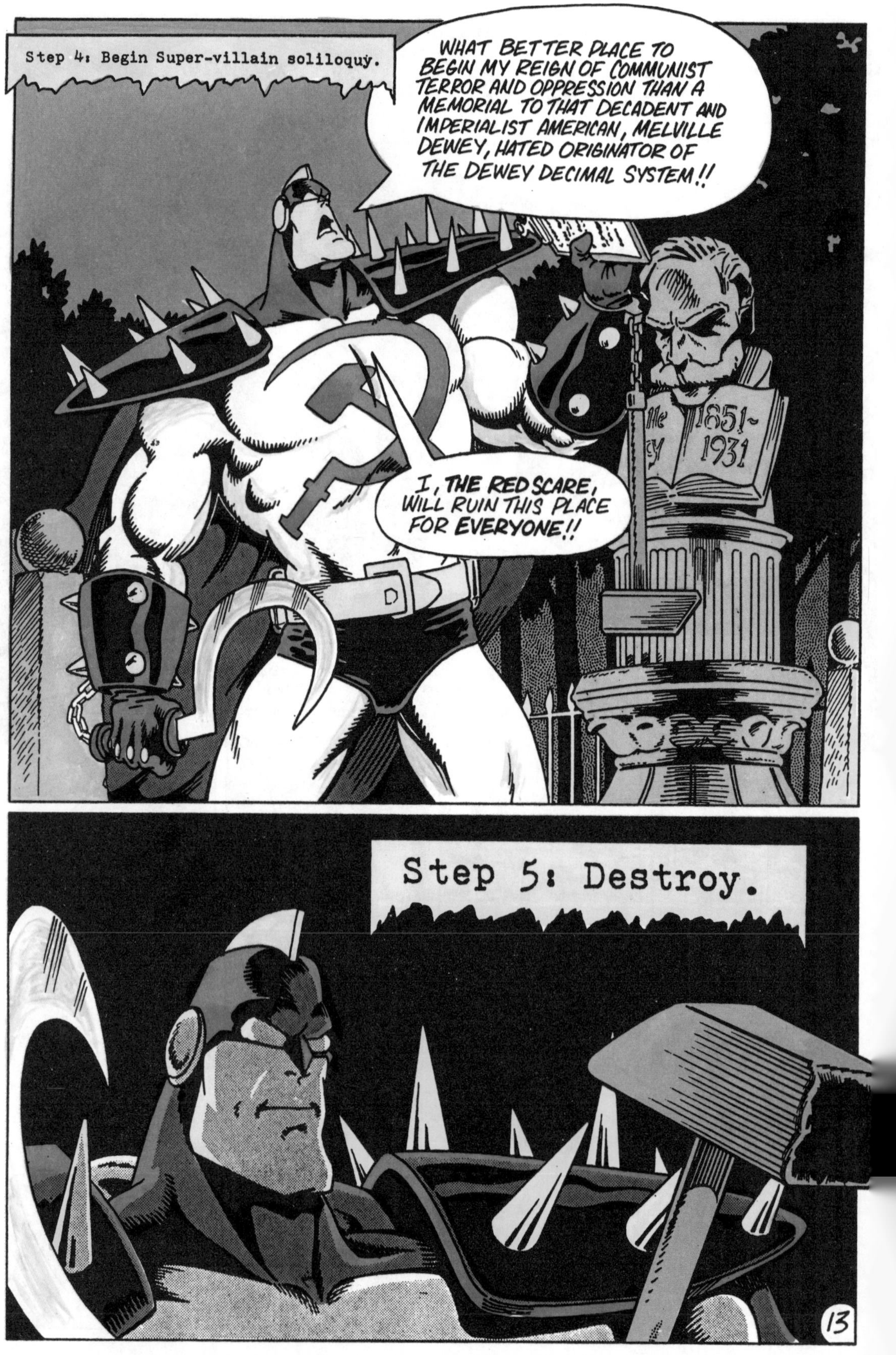
Step 4: Begin Super-villain soliloquy.
WHAT BETTER PLACE TO BEGIN MY REIGN OF COMMUNIST TERROR AND OPPRESSION THAN A MEMORIAL TO THAT DECADENT AND IMPERIALIST AMERICAN, MELVILLE DEWEY, HATED ORIGINATOR OF THE DEWEY DECIMAL SYSTEM!!
1851-1931
I, THE RED SCARE, WILL RUIN THIS PLACE FOR EVERYONE!!
Step 5: Destroy.

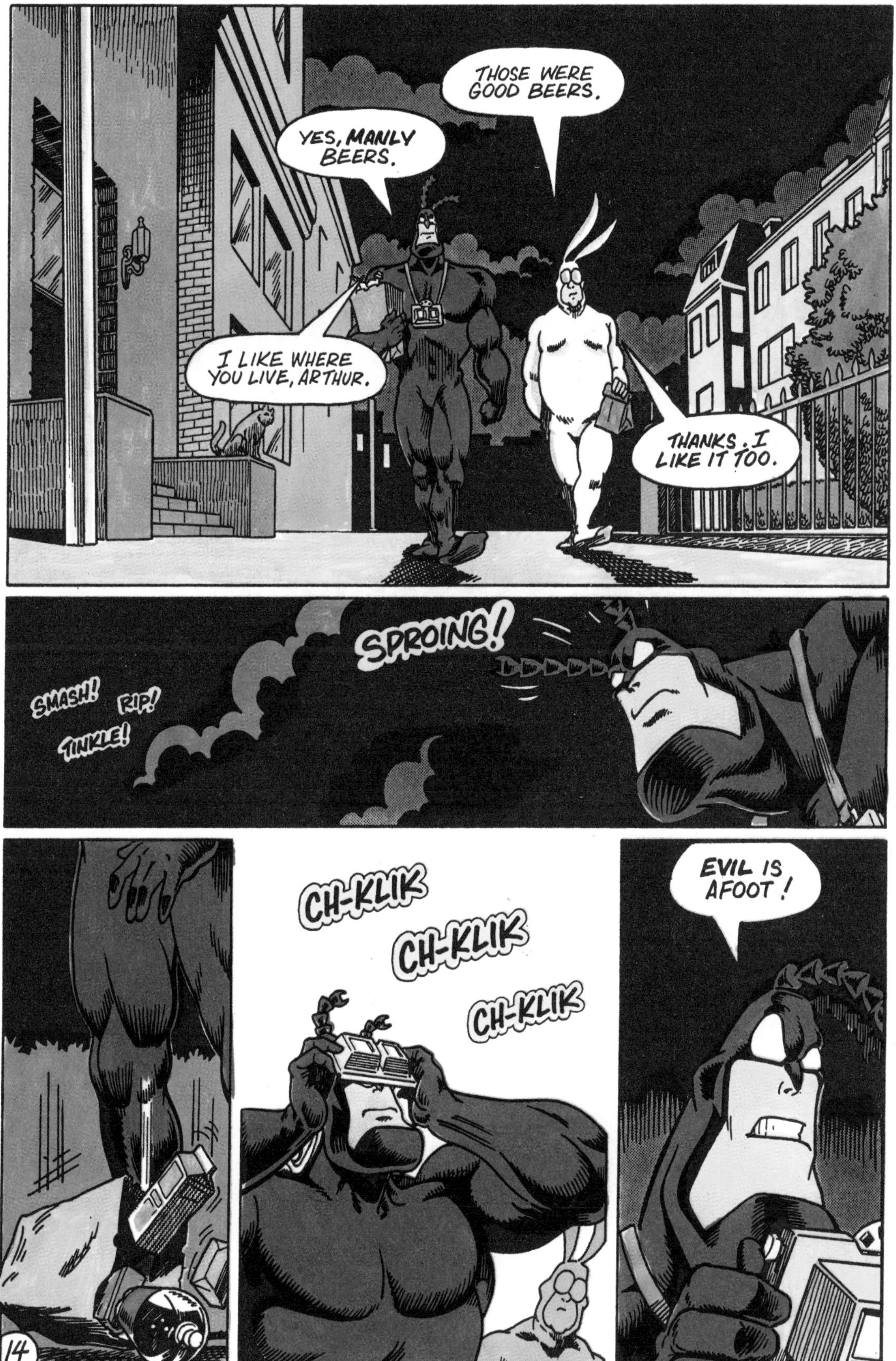
THOSE WERE GOOD BEERS.
YES, MANLY BEERS.
I LIKE WHERE YOU LIVE, ARTHUR.
THANKS. I LIKE IT TOO.
SPROING!
SMASH!
RIP!
TINKLE!
CH-KLIK
CH-KLIK
CH-KLIK
EVIL IS AFOOT!

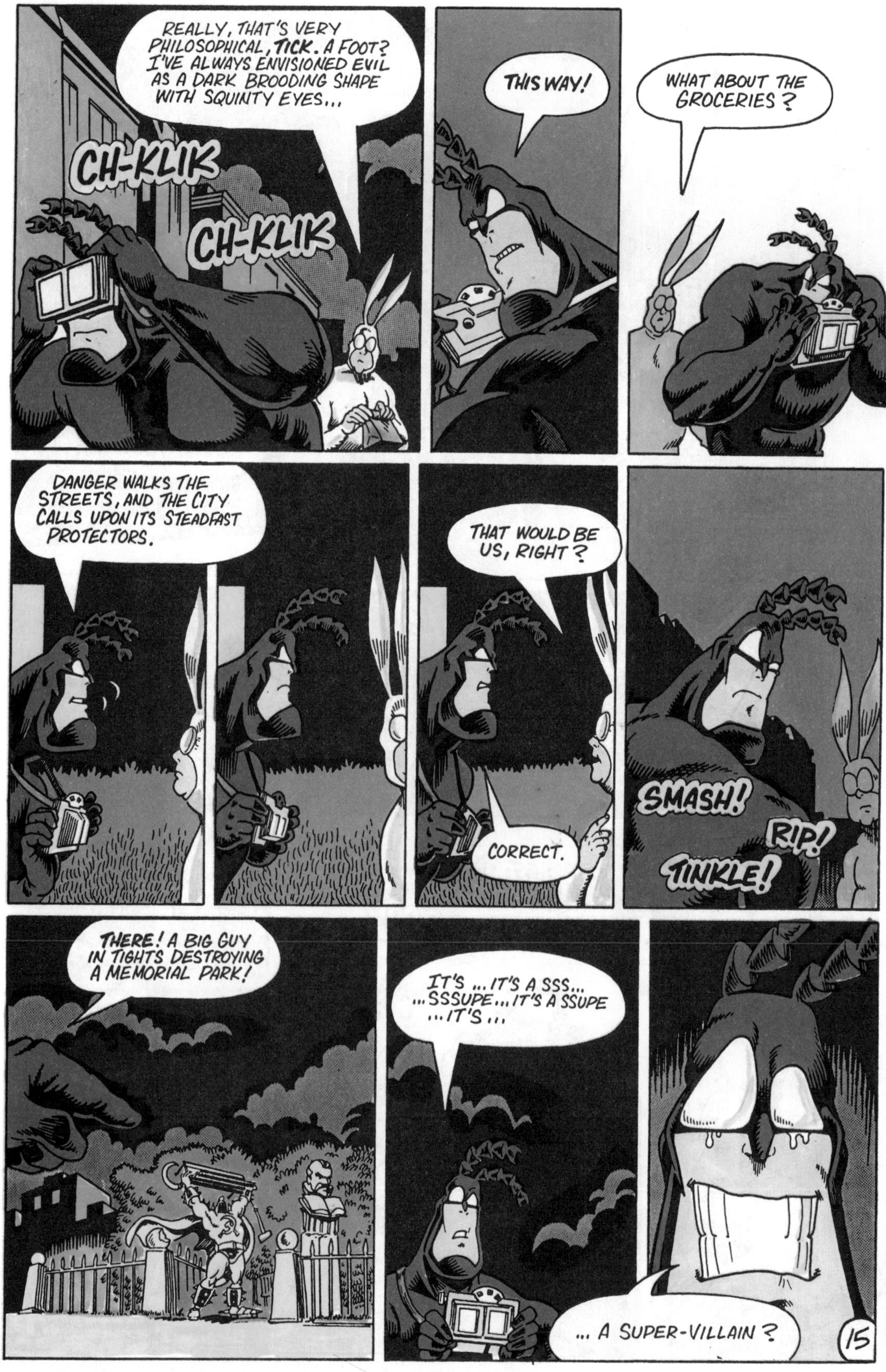
REALLY, THAT'S VERY PHILOSOPHICAL, TICK. A FOOT? I'VE ALWAYS ENVISIONED EVIL AS A DARK BROODING SHAPE WITH SQUINTY EYES...
CH-KLIK
CH-KLIK
THIS WAY!
WHAT ABOUT THE GROCERIES?
DANGER WALKS THE STREETS, AND THE CITY CALLS UPON ITS STEADFAST PROTECTORS.
THAT WOULD BE US, RIGHT?
CORRECT.
SMASH!
RIP!
TINKLE!
THERE! A BIG GUY IN TIGHTS DESTROYING A MEMORIAL PARK!
IT'S ... IT'S A SSS... ...SSSUPE... IT'S A SSUPE ...IT'S...
... A SUPER-VILLAIN?

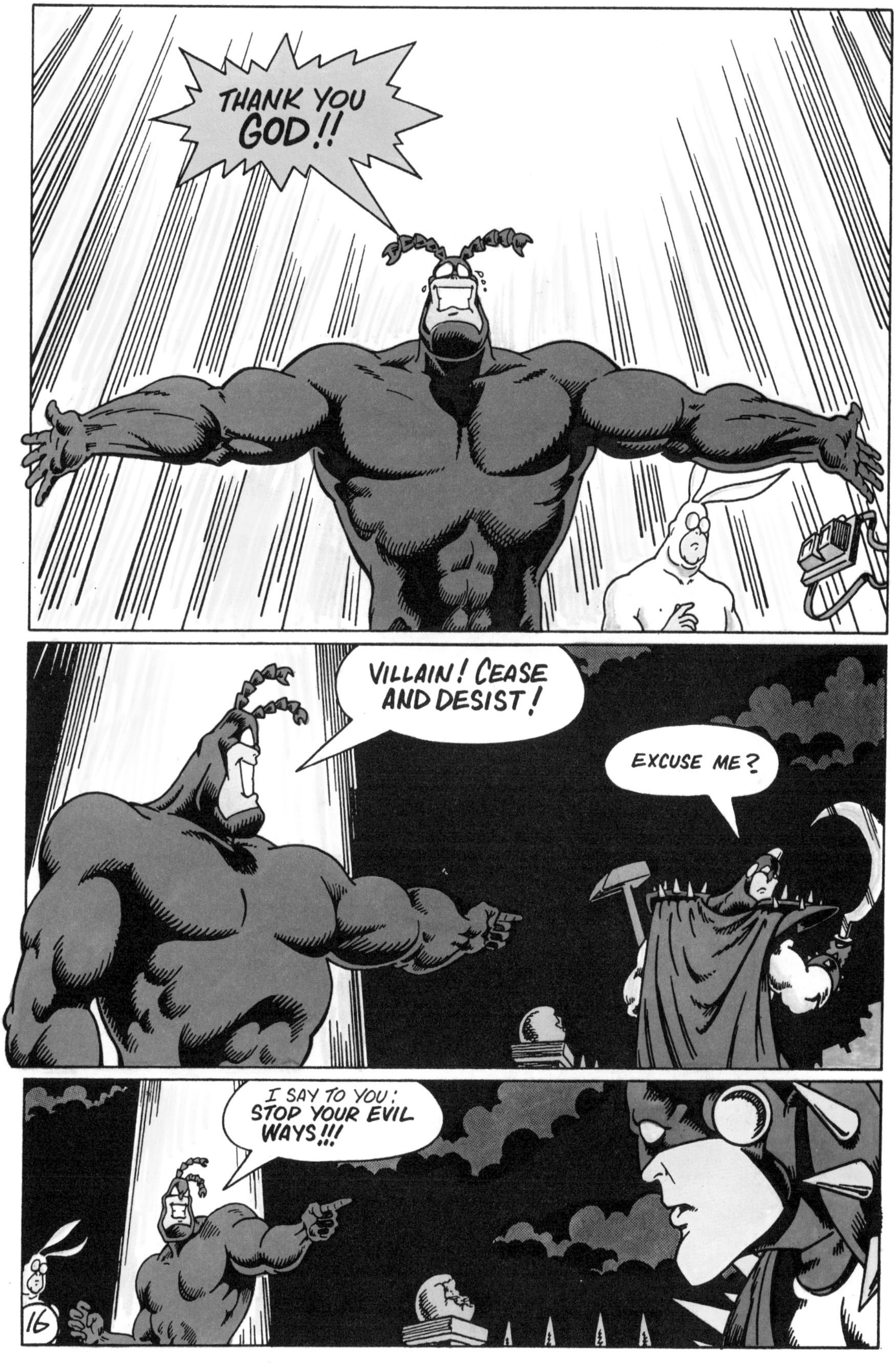
THANK YOU GOD!!
VILLAIN! CEASE AND DESIST!
EXCUSE ME?
I SAY TO YOU: STOP YOUR EVIL WAYS!!!

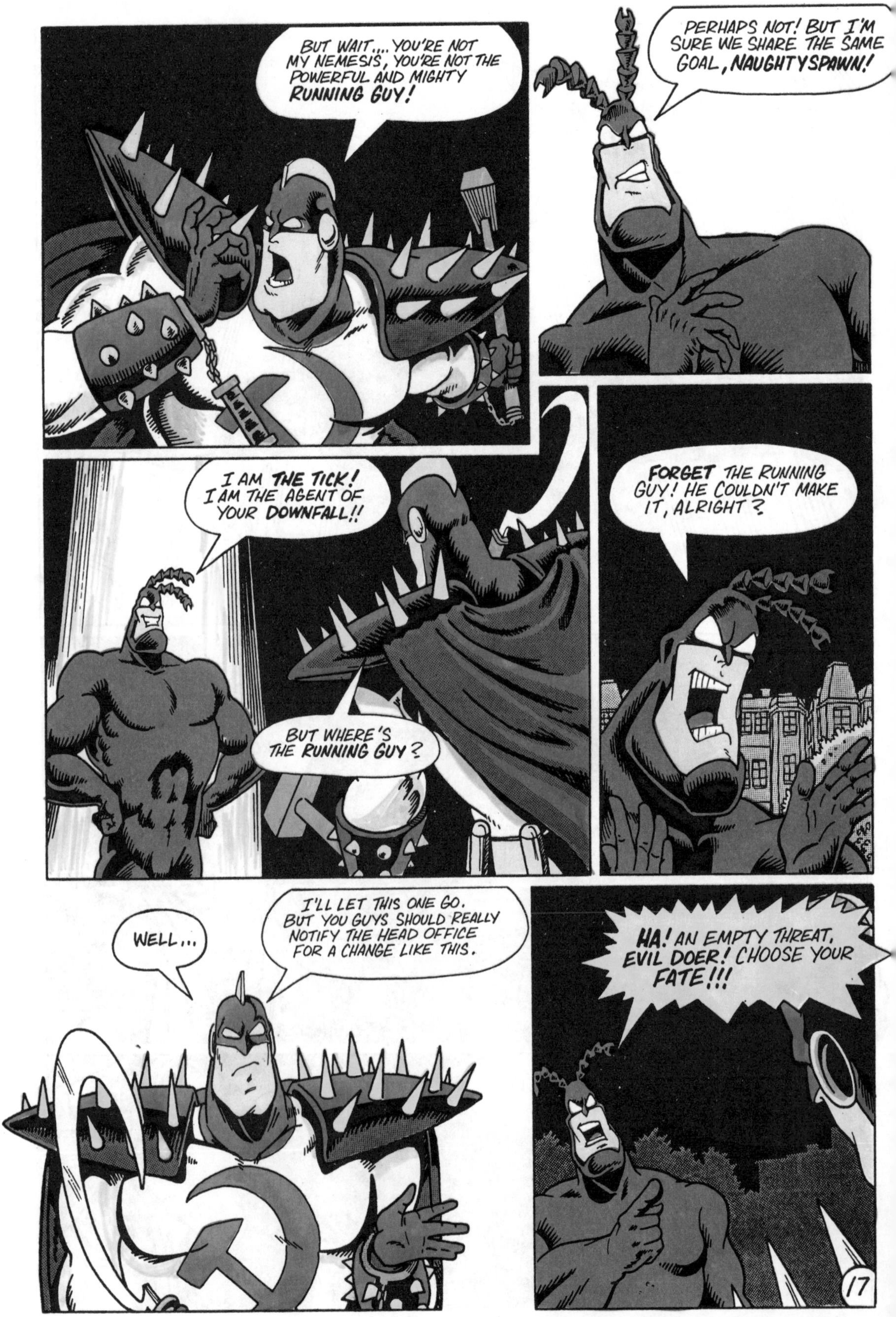
BUT WAIT.... YOU'RE NOT MY NEMESIS, YOU'RE NOT THE POWERFUL AND MIGHTY RUNNING GUY!
PERHAPS NOT! BUT I'M SURE WE SHARE THE SAME GOAL, NAUGHTYSPAWN!
I AM THE TICK! I AM THE AGENT OF YOUR DOWNFALL!!
BUT WHERE'S THE RUNNING GUY?
FORGET THE RUNNING GUY! HE COULDN'T MAKE IT, ALRIGHT?
WELL...
I'LL LET THIS ONE GO. BUT YOU GUYS SHOULD REALLY NOTIFY THE HEAD OFFICE FOR A CHANGE LIKE THIS.
HA! AN EMPTY THREAT, EVIL DOER! CHOOSE YOUR FATE!!!

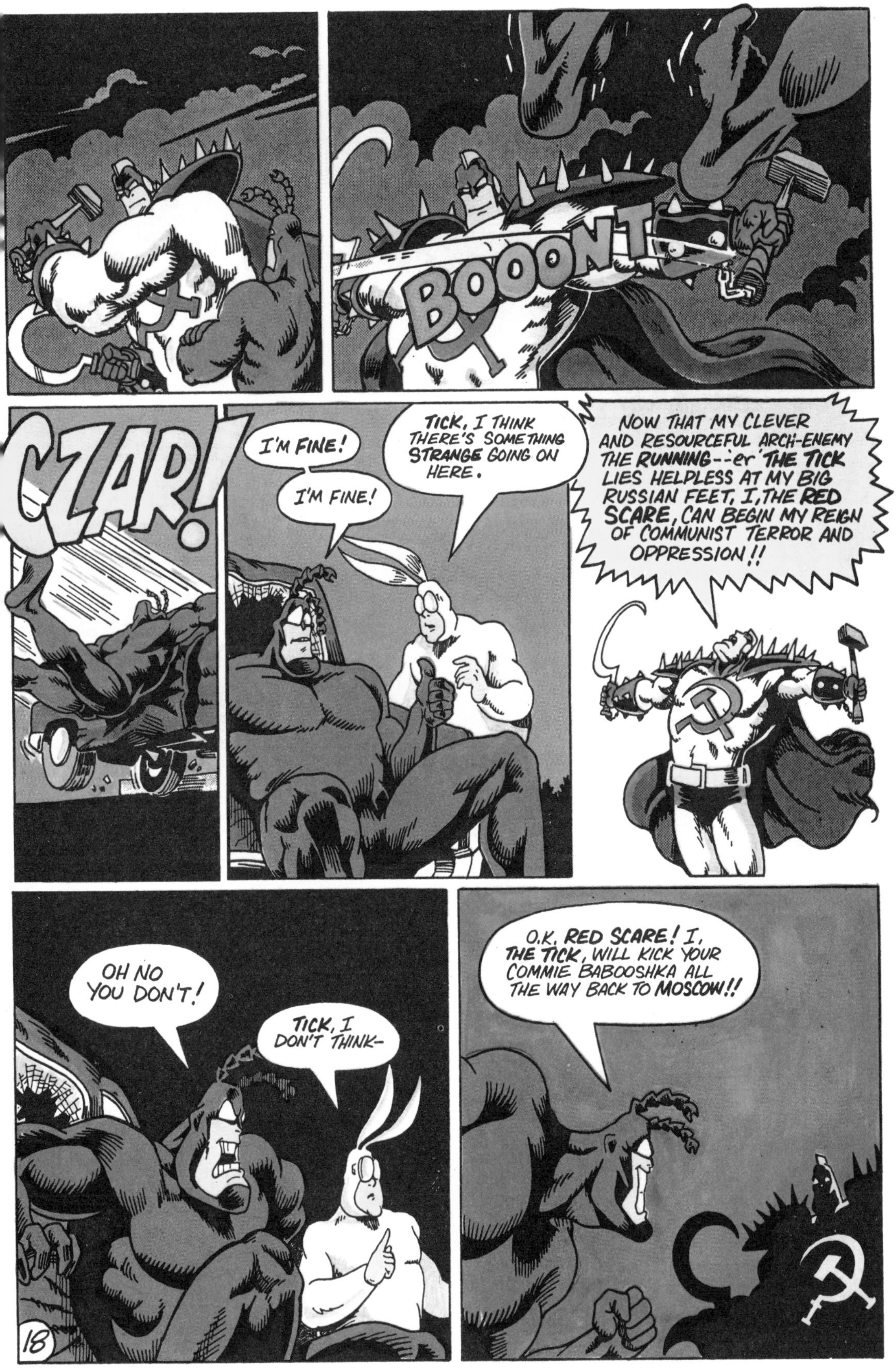
BOOOONT
CZAR!
I'M FINE!
I'M FINE!
TICK, I THINK THERE'S SOMETHING STRANGE GOING ON HERE.
NOW THAT MY CLEVER AND RESOURCEFUL ARCH-ENEMY THE RUNNING--er THE TICK LIES HELPLESS AT MY BIG RUSSIAN FEET, I, THE RED SCARE, CAN BEGIN MY REIGN OF COMMUNIST TERROR AND OPPRESSION!!
OH NO YOU DON'T!
TICK, I DON'T THINK-
O.K. RED SCARE! I, THE TICK, WILL KICK YOUR COMMIE BABOOSHKA ALL THE WAY BACK TO MOSCOW!!
18

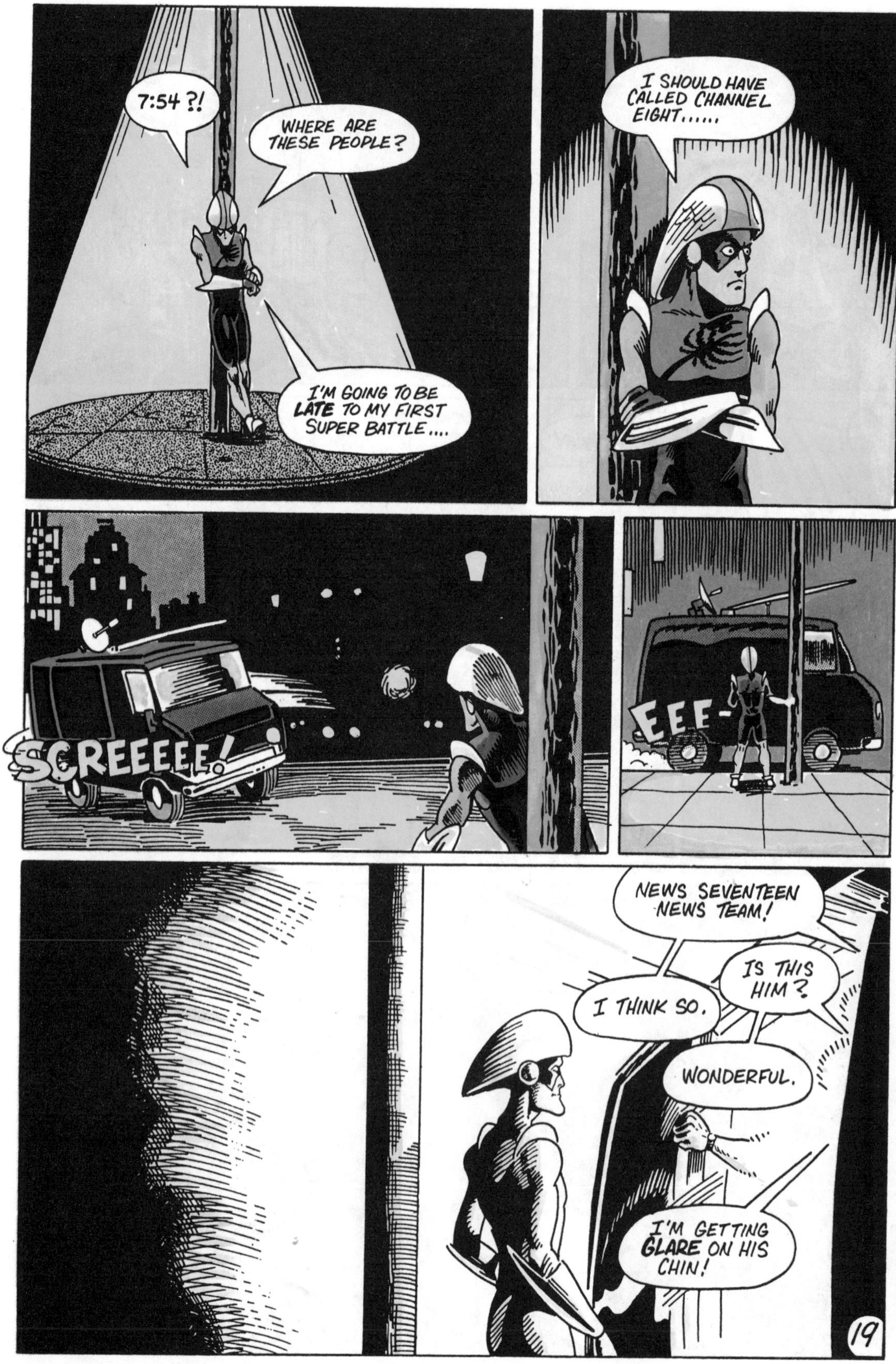
7:54 ?!
WHERE ARE THESE PEOPLE?
I'M GOING TO BE LATE TO MY FIRST SUPER BATTLE....
I SHOULD HAVE CALLED CHANNEL EIGHT......
SCREEEEEE!
EEE-
NEWS SEVENTEEN NEWS TEAM!
IS THIS HIM?
I THINK SO.
WONDERFUL.
I'M GETTING GLARE ON HIS CHIN!
19

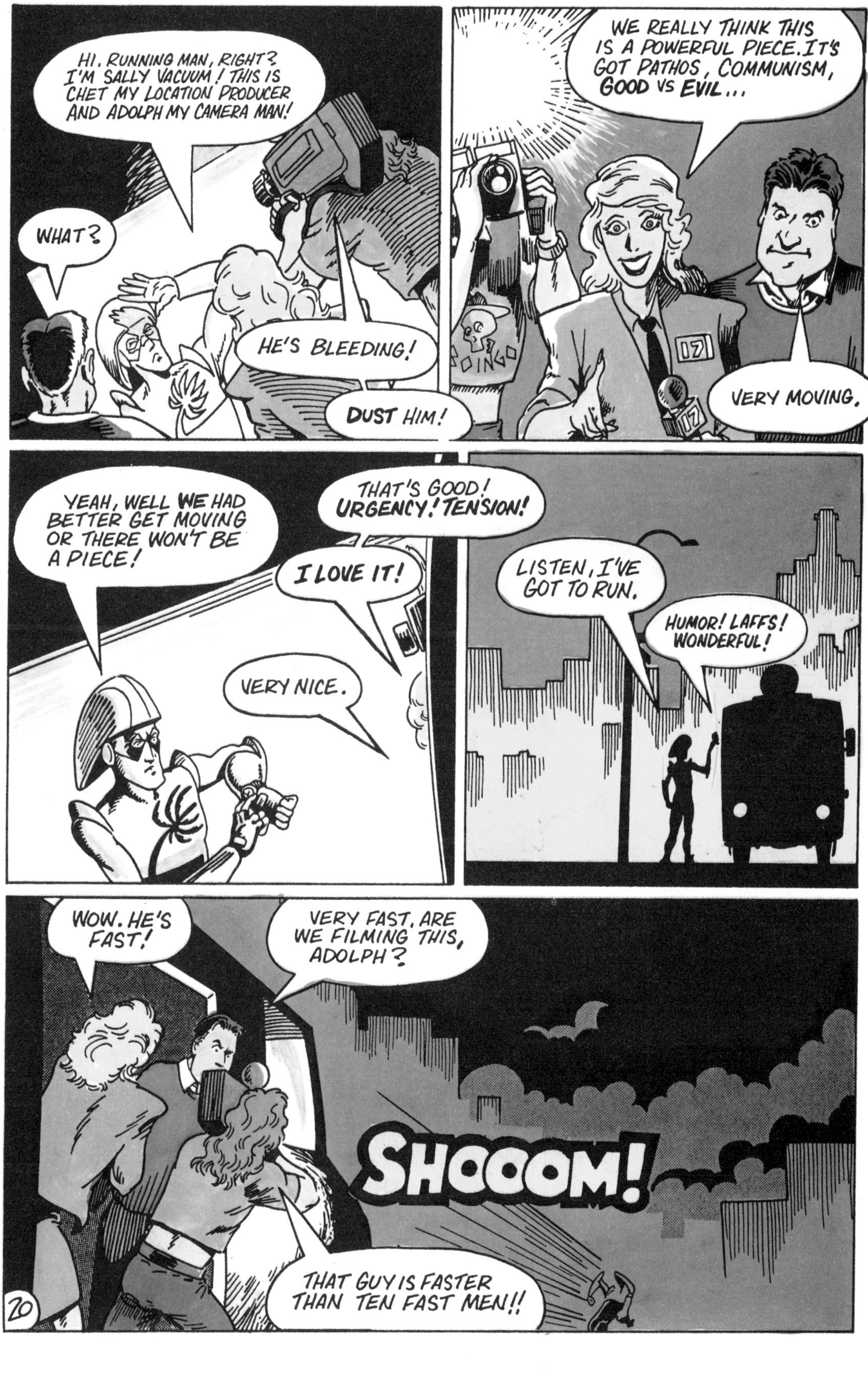
HI. RUNNING MAN, RIGHT? I'M SALLY VACUUM! THIS IS CHET MY LOCATION PRODUCER AND ADOLPH MY CAMERA MAN!
WHAT?
HE'S BLEEDING!
DUST HIM!
WE REALLY THINK THIS IS A POWERFUL PIECE. IT'S GOT PATHOS, COMMUNISM, GOOD VS EVIL...
VERY MOVING.
YEAH, WELL WE HAD BETTER GET MOVING OR THERE WON'T BE A PIECE!
THAT'S GOOD! URGENCY! TENSION!
I LOVE IT!
VERY NICE.
LISTEN, I'VE GOT TO RUN.
HUMOR! LAFFS! WONDERFUL!
WOW. HE'S FAST!
VERY FAST. ARE WE FILMING THIS, ADOLPH?
SHOOOM!
THAT GUY IS FASTER THAN TEN FAST MEN!!

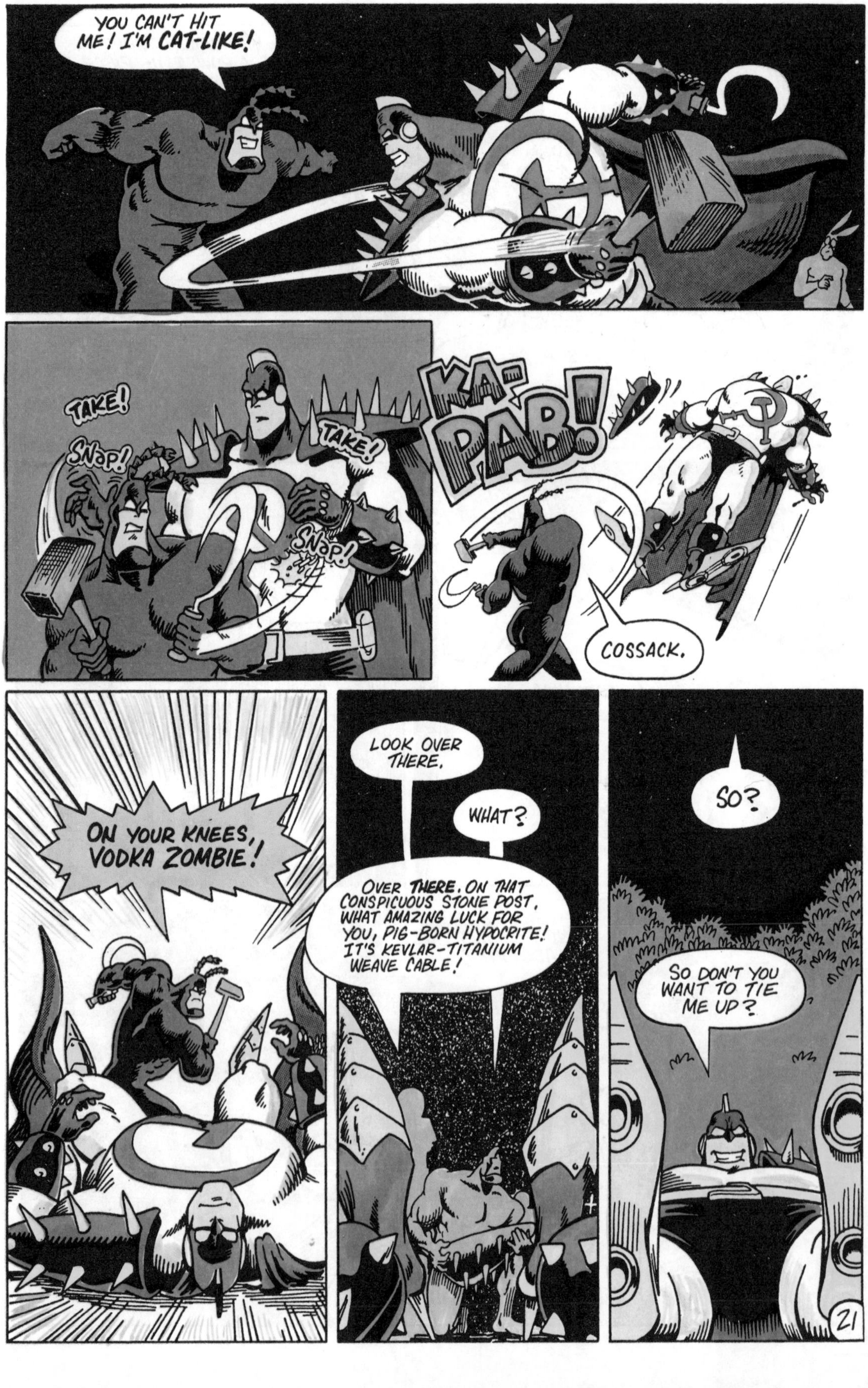
YOU CAN'T HIT ME! I'M CAT-LIKE!
TAKE!
SNAP!
TAKE!
SNAP!
KA-PAB!
COSSACK.
ON YOUR KNEES, VODKA ZOMBIE!
LOOK OVER THERE.
WHAT?
OVER THERE. ON THAT CONSPICUOUS STONE POST, WHAT AMAZING LUCK FOR YOU, PIG-BORN HYPOCRITE! IT'S KEVLAR-TITANIUM WEAVE CABLE!
SO?
SO DON'T YOU WANT TO TIE ME UP?

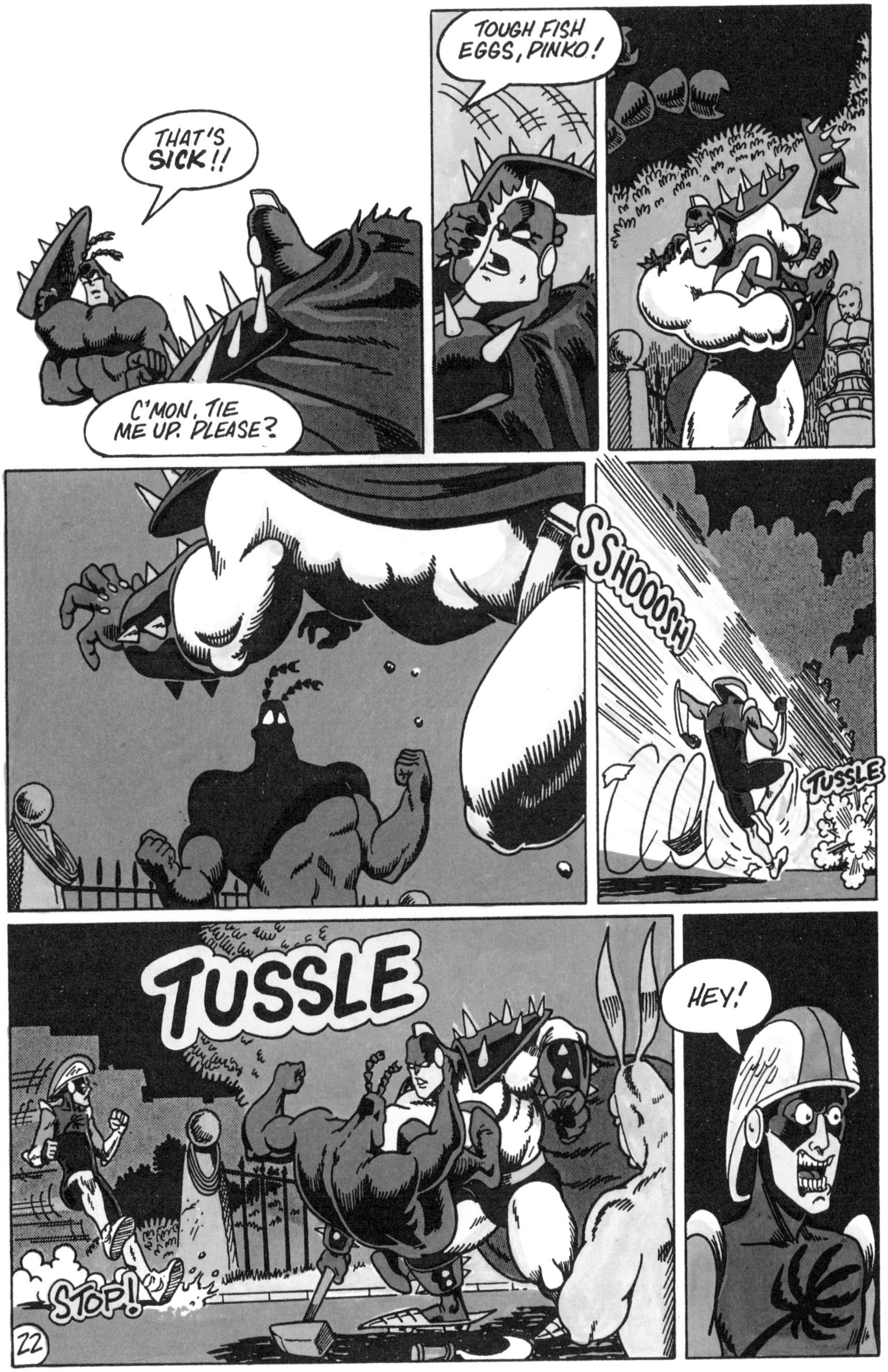
THAT'S SICK!!
C'MON, TIE ME UP. PLEASE?
TOUGH FISH EGGS, PINKO!
SSHOOOSH
TUSSLE
TUSSLE
STOP!
HEY!

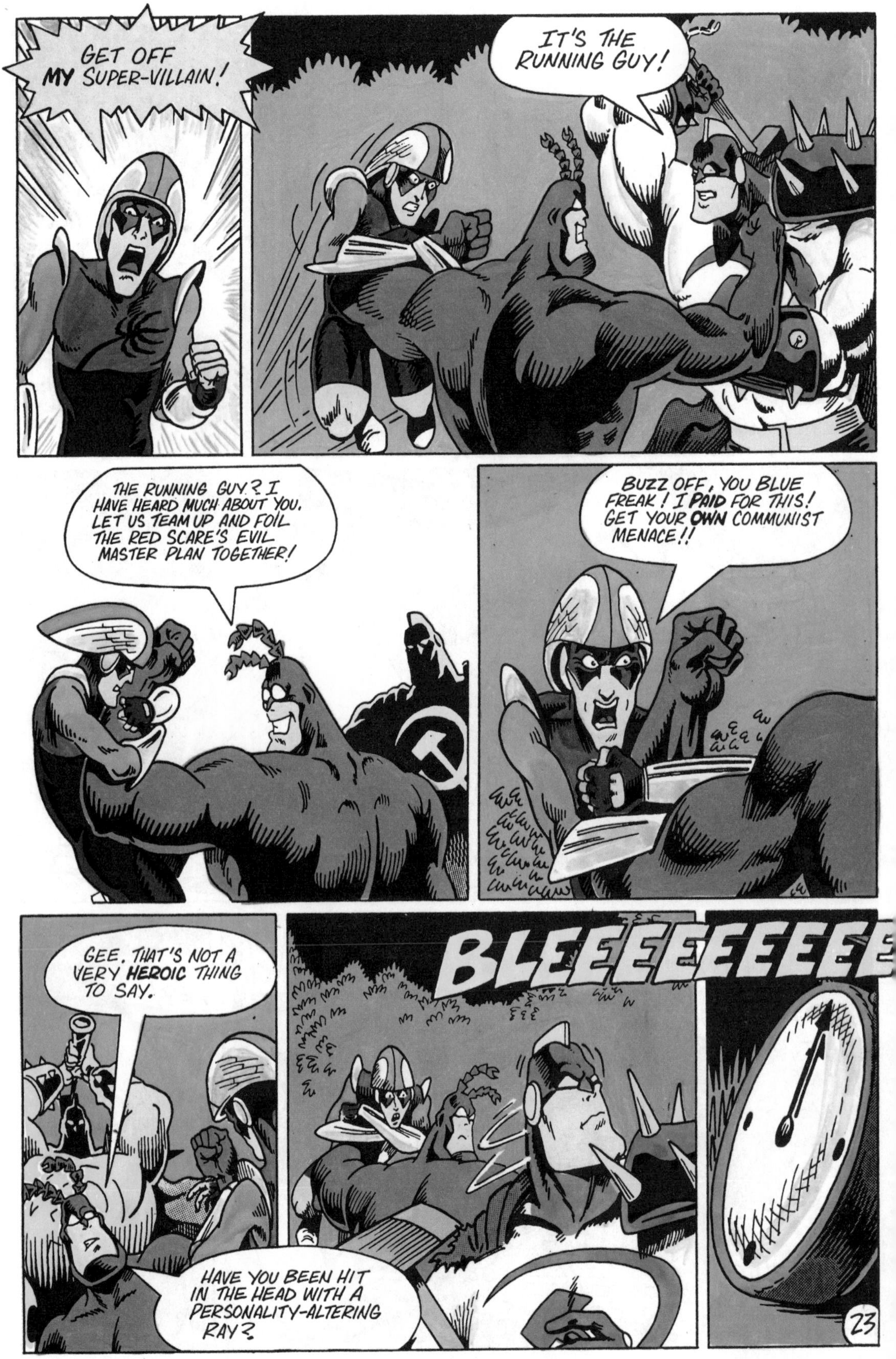
GET OFF MY SUPER-VILLAIN!
IT'S THE RUNNING GUY!
THE RUNNING GUY?! I HAVE HEARD MUCH ABOUT YOU. LET US TEAM UP AND FOIL THE RED SCARE'S EVIL MASTER PLAN TOGETHER!
BUZZ OFF, YOU BLUE FREAK! I PAID FOR THIS! GET YOUR OWN COMMUNIST MENACE!!
GEE. THAT'S NOT A VERY HEROIC THING TO SAY.
HAVE YOU BEEN HIT IN THE HEAD WITH A PERSONALITY-ALTERING RAY?
BLEEEEEEEEE
23

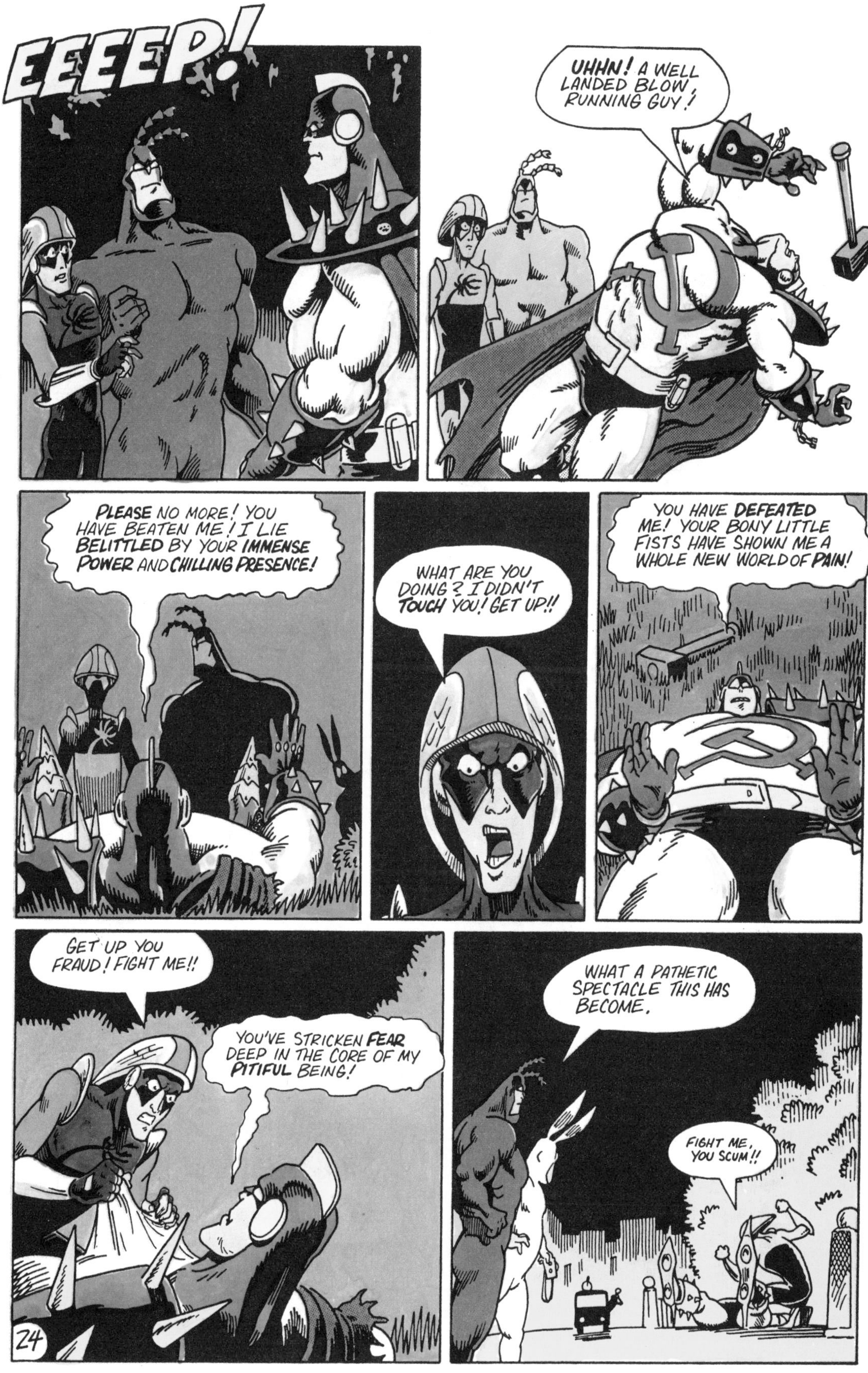
EEEEP!
UHHN! A WELL LANDED BLOW, RUNNING GUY!
PLEASE NO MORE! YOU HAVE BEATEN ME! I LIE BELITTLED BY YOUR IMMENSE POWER AND CHILLING PRESENCE!
WHAT ARE YOU DOING? I DIDN'T TOUCH YOU! GET UP!!
YOU HAVE DEFEATED ME! YOUR BONY LITTLE FISTS HAVE SHOWN ME A WHOLE NEW WORLD OF PAIN!
GET UP YOU FRAUD! FIGHT ME!!
YOU'VE STRICKEN FEAR DEEP IN THE CORE OF MY PITIFUL BEING!
WHAT A PATHETIC SPECTACLE THIS HAS BECOME.
FIGHT ME, YOU SCUM!!

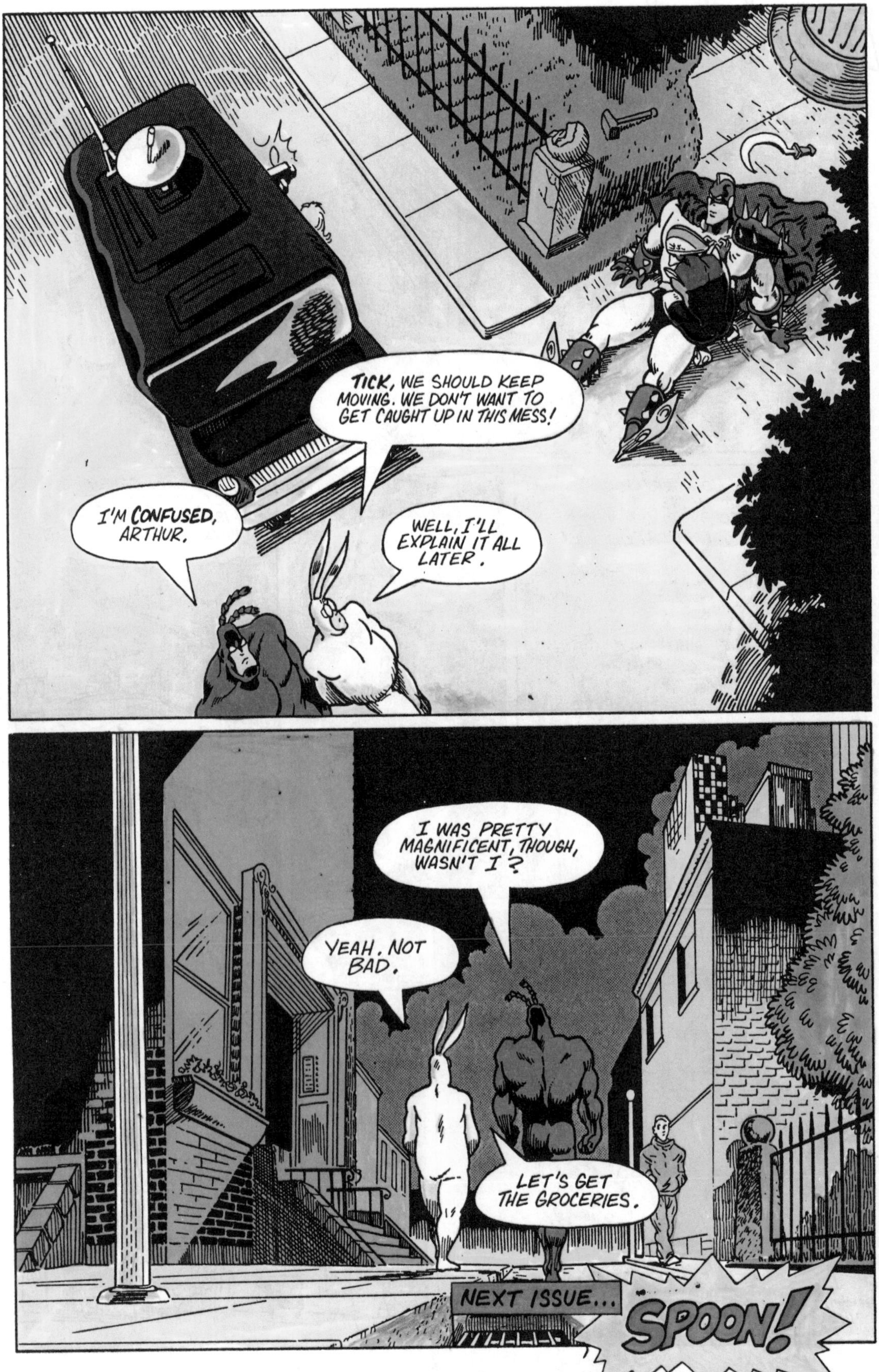
TICK, WE SHOULD KEEP MOVING. WE DON'T WANT TO GET CAUGHT UP IN THIS MESS!
I'M CONFUSED, ARTHUR.
WELL, I'LL EXPLAIN IT ALL LATER.
I WAS PRETTY MAGNIFICENT, THOUGH, WASN'T I?
YEAH. NOT BAD.
LET'S GET THE GROCERIES.
NEXT ISSUE...
SPOON!

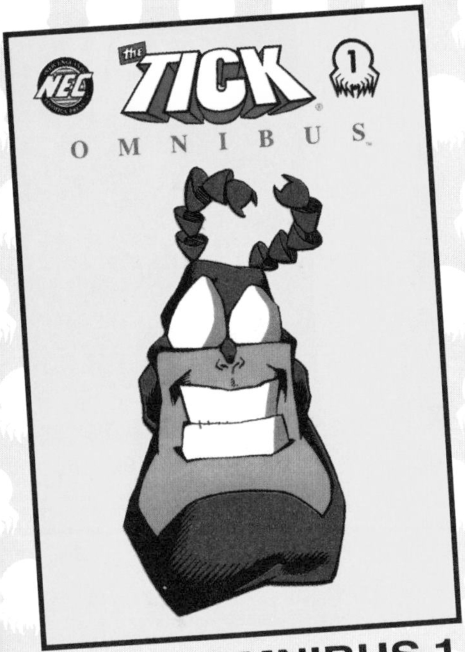
NEC
the TICK
1
OMNIBUS

TICK OMNIBUS 1

Presents issues of Ben Edlund's The Tick #1 through 6, plus a new short story and other cool features!

184 pages, only $15.95 (avail now)

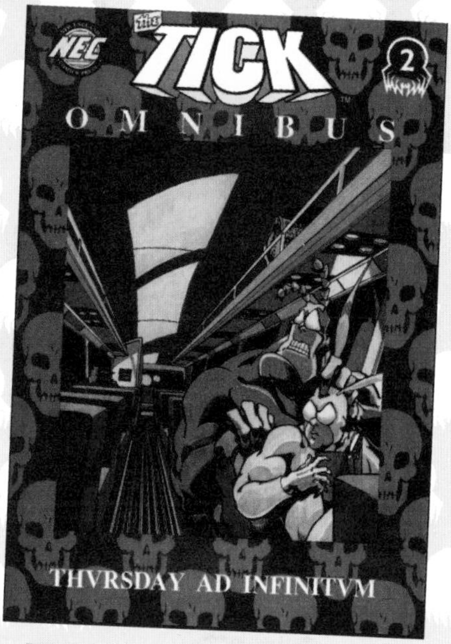
NEC
the TICK
2
OMNIBUS
THVRSDAY AD INFINITVM

TICK OMNIBUS 2

Presents issues of Ben Edlund's The Tick #7 through 10, plus additional features!

120 pages, only $10.95 (avail now)

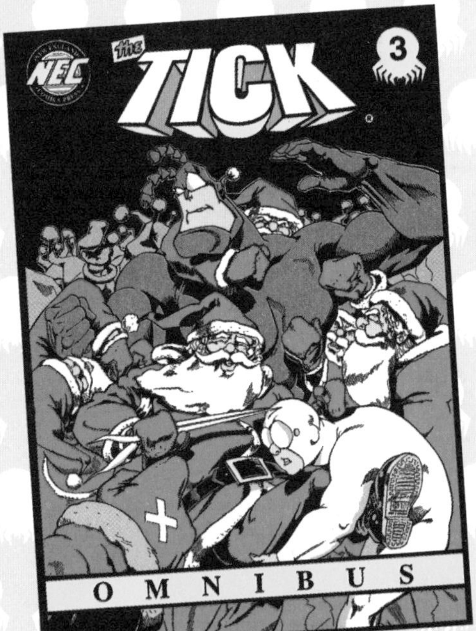
NEC
the TICK
3
OMNIBUS

TICK OMNIBUS 3

Presents issues of Ben Edlund's The Tick #11 and 12, plus many additional pages of unpublished art and background material!

88 pages, only $10.95 (avail April 1996)

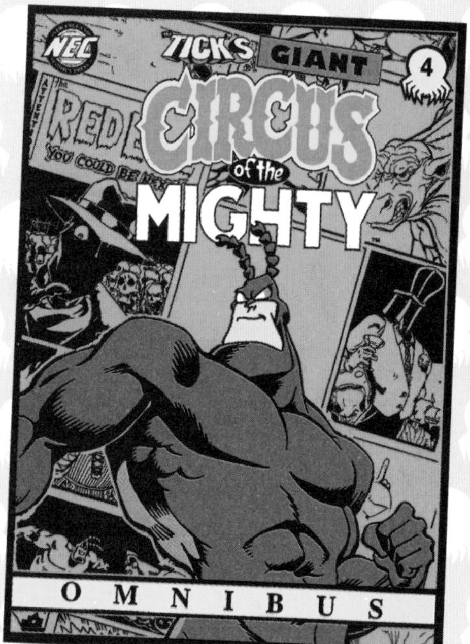
NEC
TICK'S GIANT
4
CIRCUS of the MIGHTY
OMNIBUS

TICK OMNIBUS 4

Presents all three issues of The Tick's Giant Circus of the Mighty, the awe-inspiring "encyclopedia" of The Tick Universe!

96 pages, only $10.95 (avail April 1996)

To order any of the above, see HOW TO ORDER on Tick Mart page.

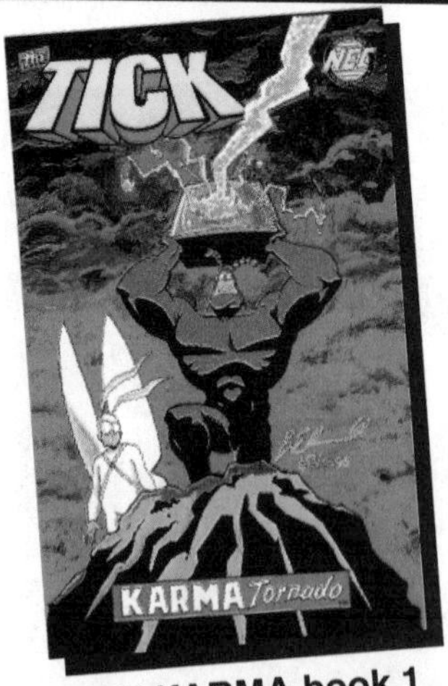
the TICK
NEC
KARMA Tornado

TICK KARMA book 1

Presents the first FIVE issues of The Tick: Karma Tornado, the sequel title to The Tick comic! Issues #2-5 are now out of print, so this is the only place to find these great stories!
128 pages, only $13.95 (avail now)

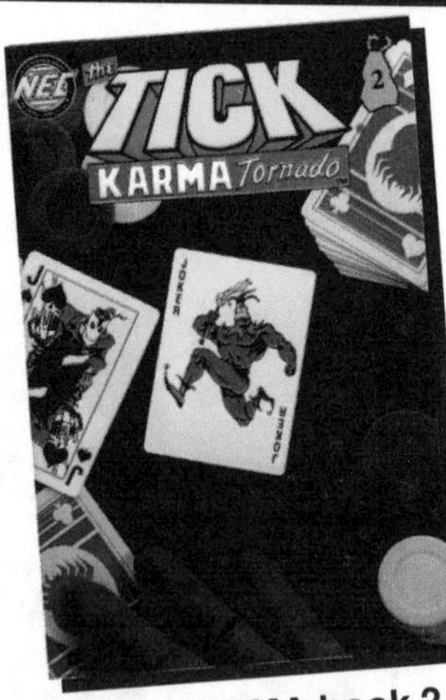
NEC
the TICK
2
KARMA Tornado
JOKER

TICK KARMA book 2

Presents issues 6 through 9 of The Tick: Karma Tornado, the sequel title to the original Tick comic! These are the latest Tick stories to appear in comics!
104 pages, only $11.95 (avail now)

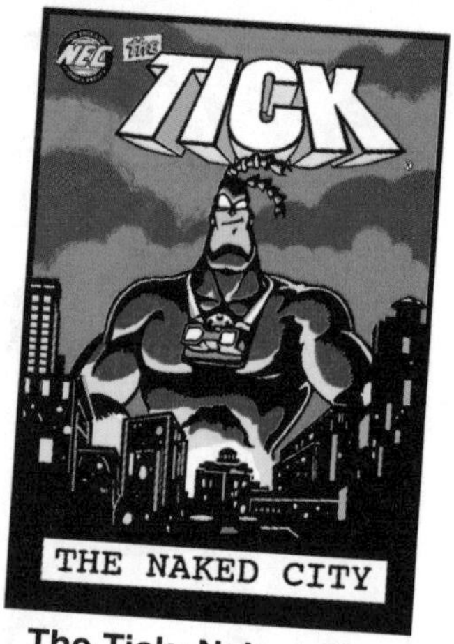
NEC
the TICK
THE NAKED CITY

The Tick: Naked City

Collects Chroma-Tick #1-6, the first six issues of The Tick, in full color!
176 pages, only $14.95 (avail June 1996)

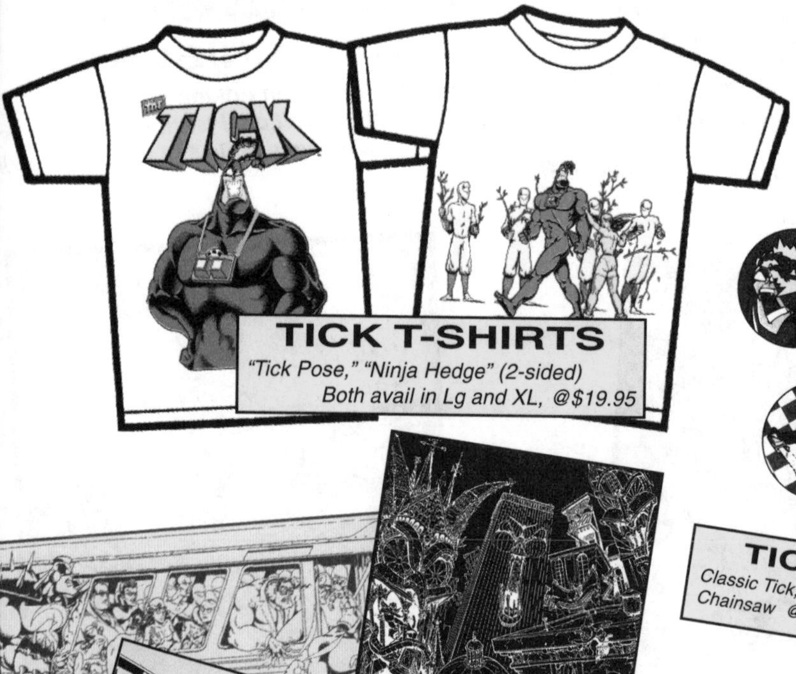
the TICK

TICK T-SHIRTS

"Tick Pose," "Ninja Hedge" (2-sided)
Both avail in Lg and XL, @$19.95

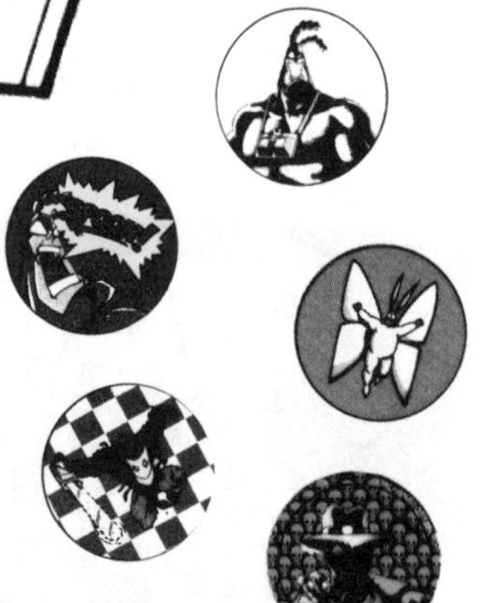

TICK BUTTONS

Classic Tick, Spoon!, Red Eye, Arthur, Chainsaw @$1.25, or set of 5 for only $4.95

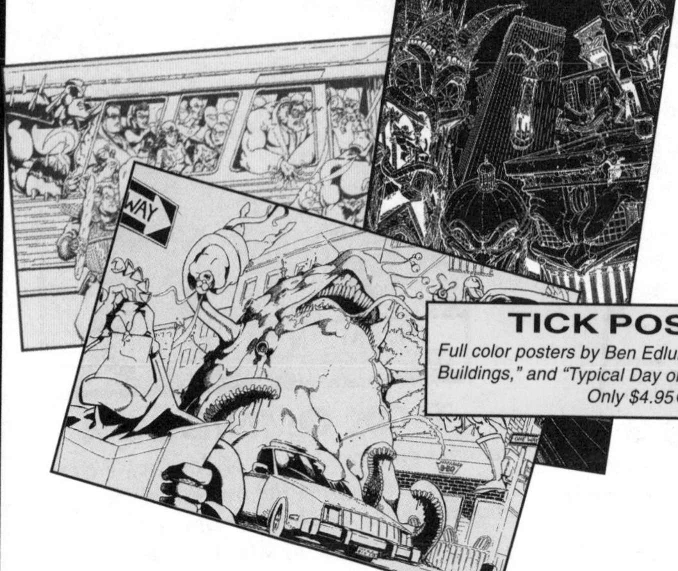
WAY

TICK POSTERS

Full color posters by Ben Edlund! "Bus," "Evil Buildings," and "Typical Day on the Lower East Side"
Only $4.95@ or all three for $7.49!

*To order any of these, see **HOW TO ORDER** on the Tick Mart page.*

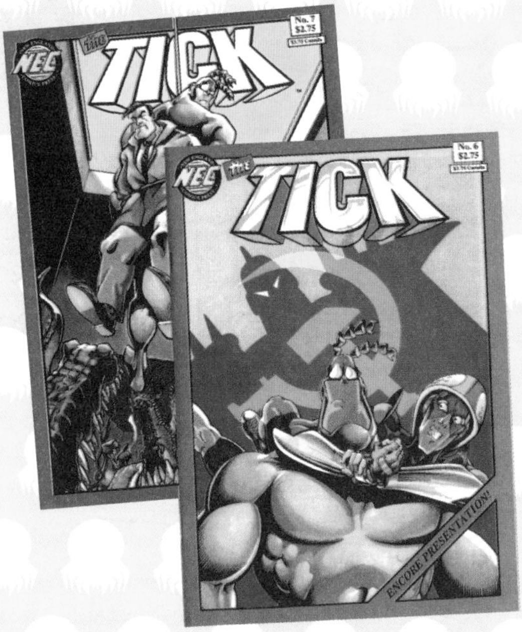
NEC
the TICK
No. 7
$2.75
No. 6
$2.75
ENCORE PRESENTATION!

THE TICK #1-12

Due to heavy demand from new readers, we keep all 12 issues of the original Tick comic (by Ben Edlund) in print all the time!
$2.75 per issue; or set of 12 for $30

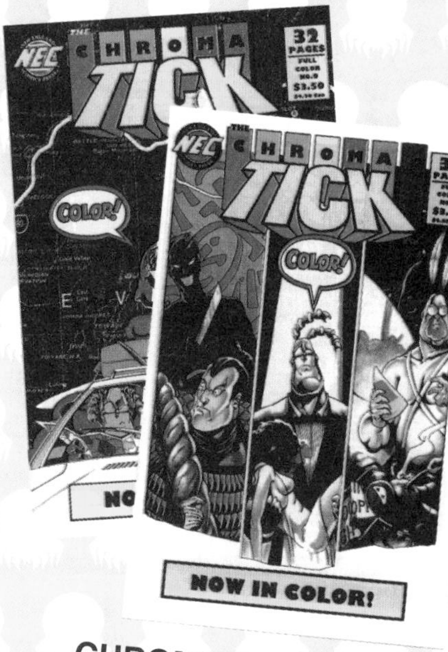
NEC
CHROMA TICK
32 PAGES
COLOR!
NOW IN COLOR!

CHROMA-TICK #1-9

Color edition of the Tick! Issues 1 and 2 are both "special" with posters, trading card inserts and a lengthy interview with Tick creator Ben Edlund!
#1, 2 @$3.95; #3-9, @$3.50; set of 9, $30

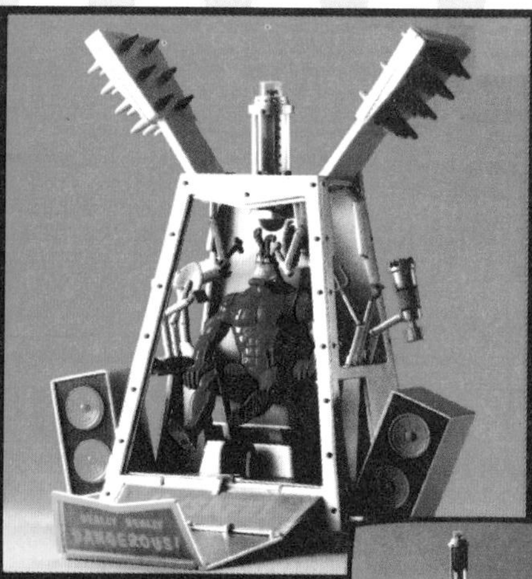
DEADLY DEADLY DANGEROUS!

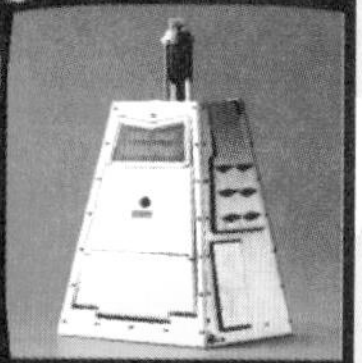

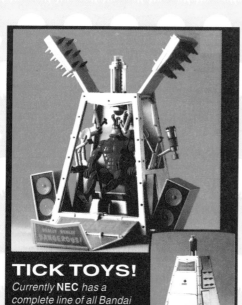

TICK TOYS!

Currently **NEC** *has a complete line of all Bandai Tick toys including the ultra-rare* ***Man-Eating Cow***, ***Die Fledermaus*** *Action Figures, and infamous* ***Steel Box*** *(shown above)! Write or call for complete list with current prices. See the Tick Mart ad page elsewhere in this publication for how to get prices and order instructions.*

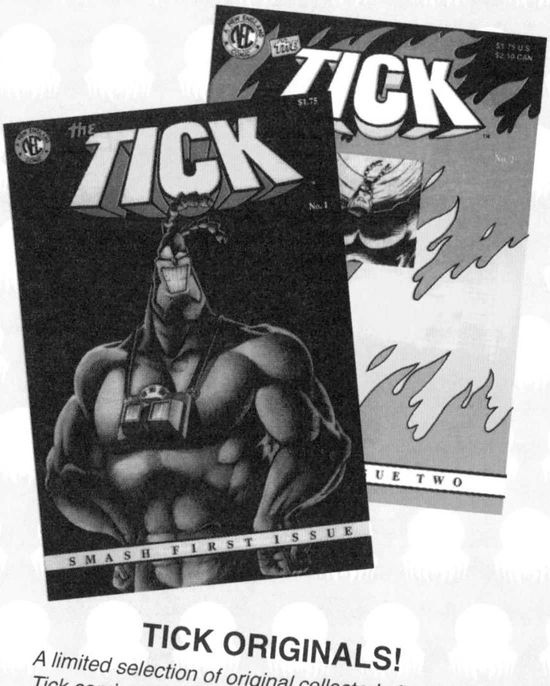
the TICK
the TICK
SMASH FIRST ISSUE
UE TWO

TICK ORIGINALS!

A limited selection of original collector's first print Tick comics is available. See ***HOW TO ORDER*** *on Tick Mart page, or Call/Write for full catalogue!*

To order any of the above, see ***HOW TO ORDER*** *on the Tick Mart page.*

the TICK MART!

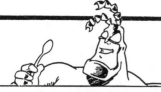

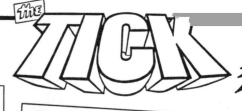

TICK COMICS!
(current prints)

Note: please check with your local comic retailer *first!* Many of these items may be obtained by him from his comics distributor. If he has trouble getting NEC Press back issues from his distributor, have him contact NEC Press *directly*. If you have no luck, *well...* we wanna make you *happy*, Tick fan!

Prices are PER issue, unless set price is noted.

THE TICK #1-12 (CURRENT PRINTS) . . @2.75
Complete set of #1-12. . . . . 30.00
THE CHROMA-TICK (color) #1,2. . . . . @3.95
THE CHROMA-TICK #3,4,6-9 . . . . @3.50
THE CHROMA-TICK #5 *(very scarce!)* . . . 12.50
THE TICK Circus of The Mighty #1-3 . . . @2.75
Tick Karma Tornado #1 $3.25 2,9 . . . . @2.75
KARMA 3-8 . . . . *(call for price)*
CHAINSAW VIGILANTE #1 $3.25 #2,3 . . @2.75
PAUL THE SAMURAI Limited series #1-3 @2.75
Reg series #1 $4.00 2,4. . . . . 3.00
Reg #3 *(scarce!)* $5.00 5-10. . . . . @2.75
MAN-EATING COW #1 (scarce!) 6.00
2-4 *(scarce!)* $4.00 5-10. . . . . @2.75

TICK 1st Prints

...and other special issues for the advanced collector. See the TICK COMICS box for current prints at cover prices.

1 Limited Edition (numbered to 5000) . 150.00
2 Limited Edition (numbered to 3000) . . 85.00
REGULAR EDITIONS:
1 FIRST PRINT 25.00
2 FIRST PRINT 15.00
2 VERY RARE *"UNCUT"* FIRST PRINT! 125.00
3 FIRST PRINT, 5 FIRST PRT ***(scarce)*** @15.00
4 FIRST PRINT, 7 FIRST PRINT . . . . . . @10.00
6,8 FIRST PRINT . . . . ***(call for price)***
8 SCARCE *"NO LOGO"* VARIANT. 10.00
9-12 FIRST PRINTS . . . . @9.00
UN-NUMBERED TICK *"PROMO"* COMIC:
SCARCE 2-COLOR "ASHCAN" edition . . 12.00
TALES TOO TERRIBLE TO TELL #1 (Has Tick story—***few left!***) Serially numbered . 10.00
2nd printing 3.50

CALL OR WRITE FOR FREE CATALOG! (INCLUDED WITH EVERY ORDER, OF COURSE!)

TICK BOOKS

Each book reprints several Tick comics in a handy, softcover paperback!

TICK OMNIBUS 1 (Reprints Tick #1-6) . . 15.95
TICK OMNIBUS 2 (Reprints Tick #7-10 . . 10.95
TICK OMNIBUS 3 (Reprints 11-12+more!) 10.95
TICK OMNIBUS 4 (Tick "Encyclopedia") . 10.95
TICK OMNIBUS 5 (4-issue crossover story with Tick, ME Cow, Paul and many others . . 11.95
TICK KARMA BOOK 1 (Karma 1-5) 13.95
TICK KARMA BOOK 2 (Karma 6-9) 11.95
THE TICK—THE NAKED CITY (July 1996) (Reprints Chroma-Tick #1-6) 1st Print . . 14.95
Man-Eating Cow Bonanza (issues 1-4) . . 4.95
Paul the Samurai Book (Ltd series 1-3) . . 8.95
Paul Bonanzai Book (reg series #1-4) . . . 4.95

TICK T-SHIRTS

Choose from two styles in Large or XL. These 100% cotton pre-shrunk shirts are in FULL color on white T-shirts!

CLASSIC TICK POSE. 19.95
NINJA HEDGE wraparound *(double-sided)* . 19.95

TICK STUFF!

NEW TICK POSTERS:
NIGHTMARE BUILDINGS 4.95
OMNIBUS BUS COVER. 4.95
"TYPICAL DAY ON LOWER EAST SIDE" . 4.95
ORDER ALL THREE FOR ONLY!. 7.49
NEW TICK BUTTONS:
THE CLASSIC TICK POSE 1.25
SPOON!, RED EYE, MOTH, CHAINSAW @1.25
SPECIAL! Order all 5 pins for 4.95
TICK VIDEO *has first two episodes*. 10.95

TICK TOYS!

*Currently NEC has a complete line of all Bandai Tick toys—including the ultra-rare **Man-Eating Cow and Die Fledermaus Action Figures!** Write or call for complete list with current prices (included with each catalog request.)*

6-27-96

HOW TO ORDER:

1. Mail to: **NECP, Box 310, Quincy, MA 02269.**
2. NO MINIMUM ORDER!
3. List what you want on a piece of paper.
4. Add for shipping: $3.00 USA; $4.00 Canada/Mexico; $7 Other Foreign.
5. Include payment for the total by check, money order, Visa, MC, Discover or Amex. *PAYMENT MUST BE IN US FUNDS.*
6. Orders may be held for personal checks.
7. Allow 4-6 weeks for delivery.
8. Mass. residents MUST add 5% sales tax on "TICK BOOKS" and "TICK STUFF".
9. We reserve the right to limit quantities and refuse orders.
10. Prices subject to change without notice. After **Oct. 31, 1996** we suggest you call or write for price updates and a free catalog.
11. Orders may be *PHONED* to **(617) 774-0140.**
12. Our 24-hour auto order line :**617) 774-0490.**
13. Orders may be *FAXED* to **(617) 774-1747.**

JOIN THE TICK SOCIETY
Mystic Order of Arachnid Vigilance

SPOON!
BUTTON
DECODER
PHOTO
VERY SECRET
Certificate of Oneness
CERTIFICATE
MEMBERSHIP CARD
OFFICIAL MOAV IMPLEMENT OF MENACE

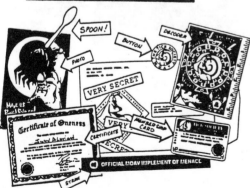

YES! I am enclosing $12.00. (Mass. residents must add 60¢ sales tax.) (Foreign, see below.*) Please *INITIATE* me into The Tick Society Mystic Order of Arachnid Vigilance! The world has too long suffered without our help! Print *clearly!* Send to: NEC Press Inc., PO Box 310, Quincy, MA 02269.

Name:____________________

Address:____________________

City:________________ State:________

Zip:________ Phone: (   )--________

The sooner you apply for membership, the lower your *Secret Agent number* will be! *YES*, this coupon may be photocopied!

*Europe, Asia and other far-away enchanting lands send $14.00!

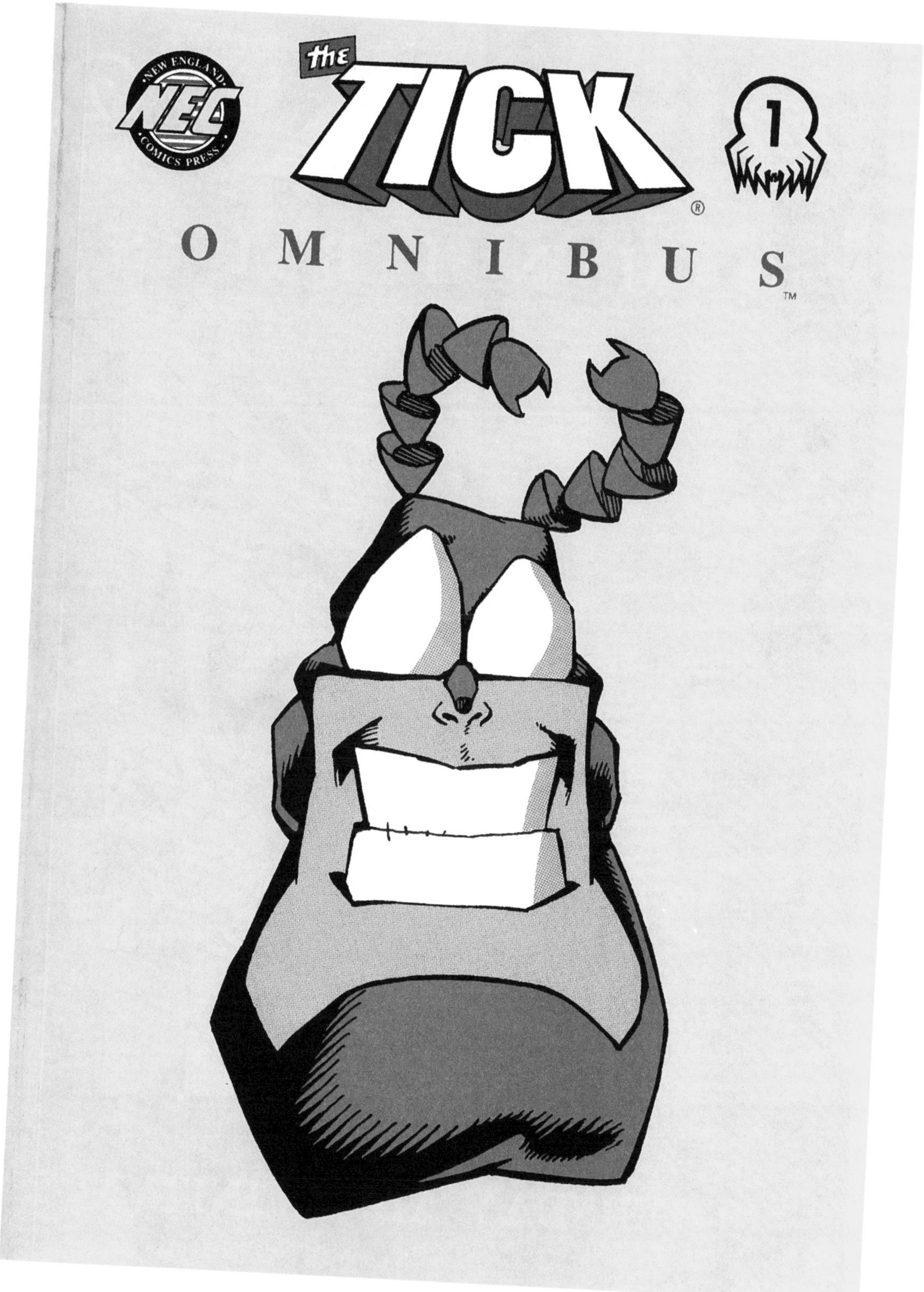
NEW ENGLAND
NEC
COMICS PRESS
the TICK®
OMNIBUS™
1

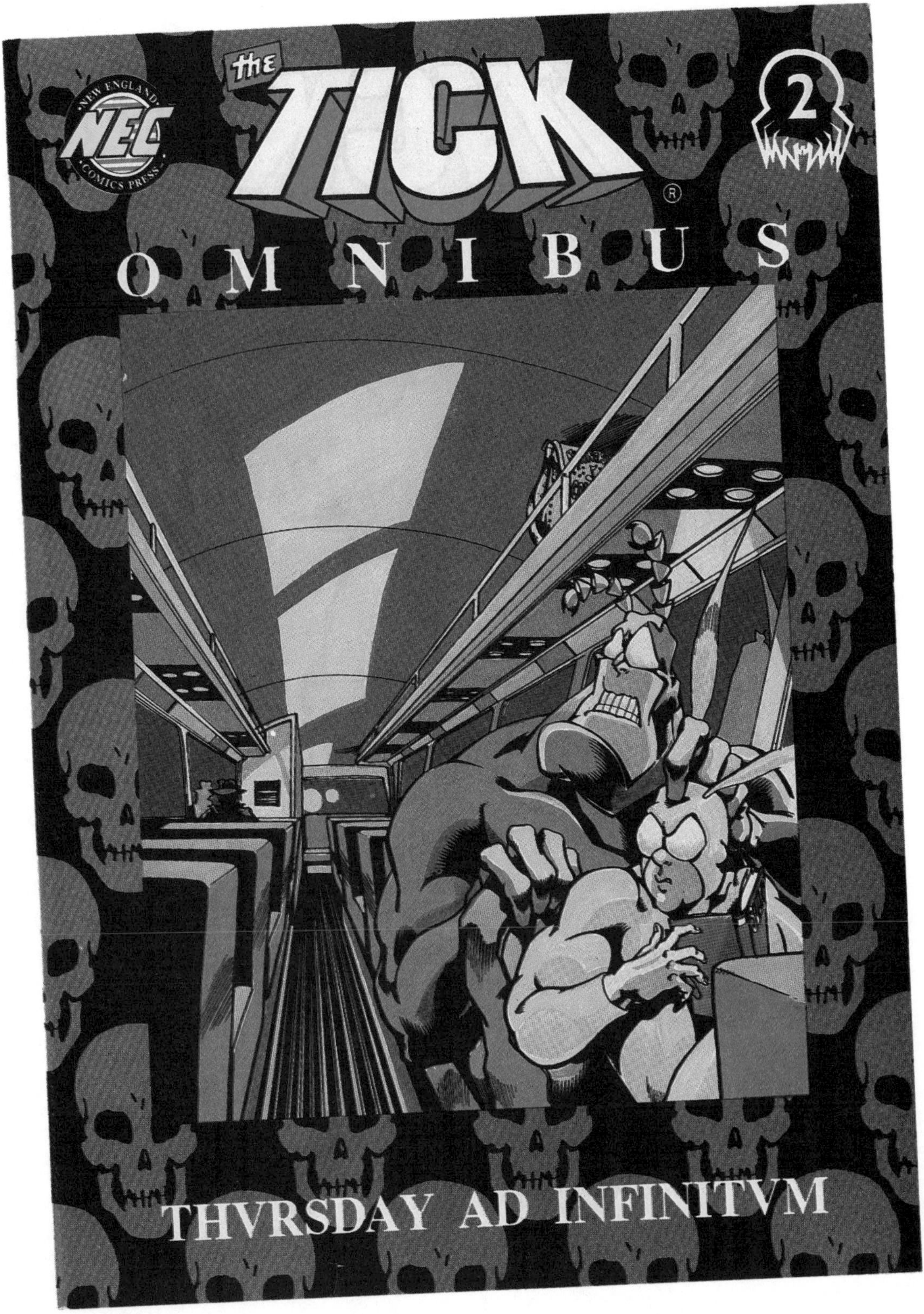

NEW ENGLAND
NEC
COMICS PRESS
the
TICK
2
OMNIBUS
THVRSDAY AD INFINITVM

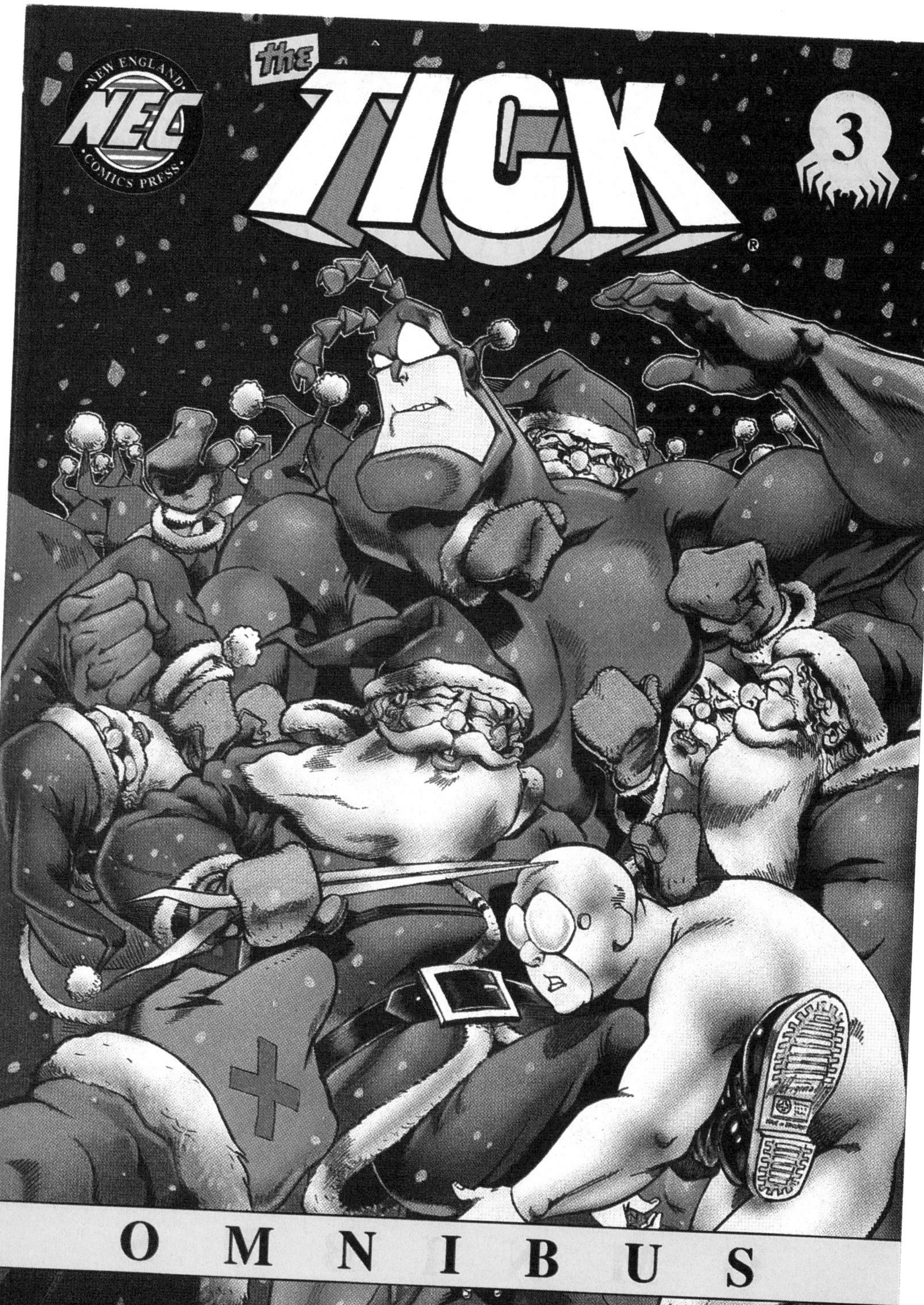
NEW ENGLAND
NEC
COMICS PRESS
the TICK
3
OMNIBUS

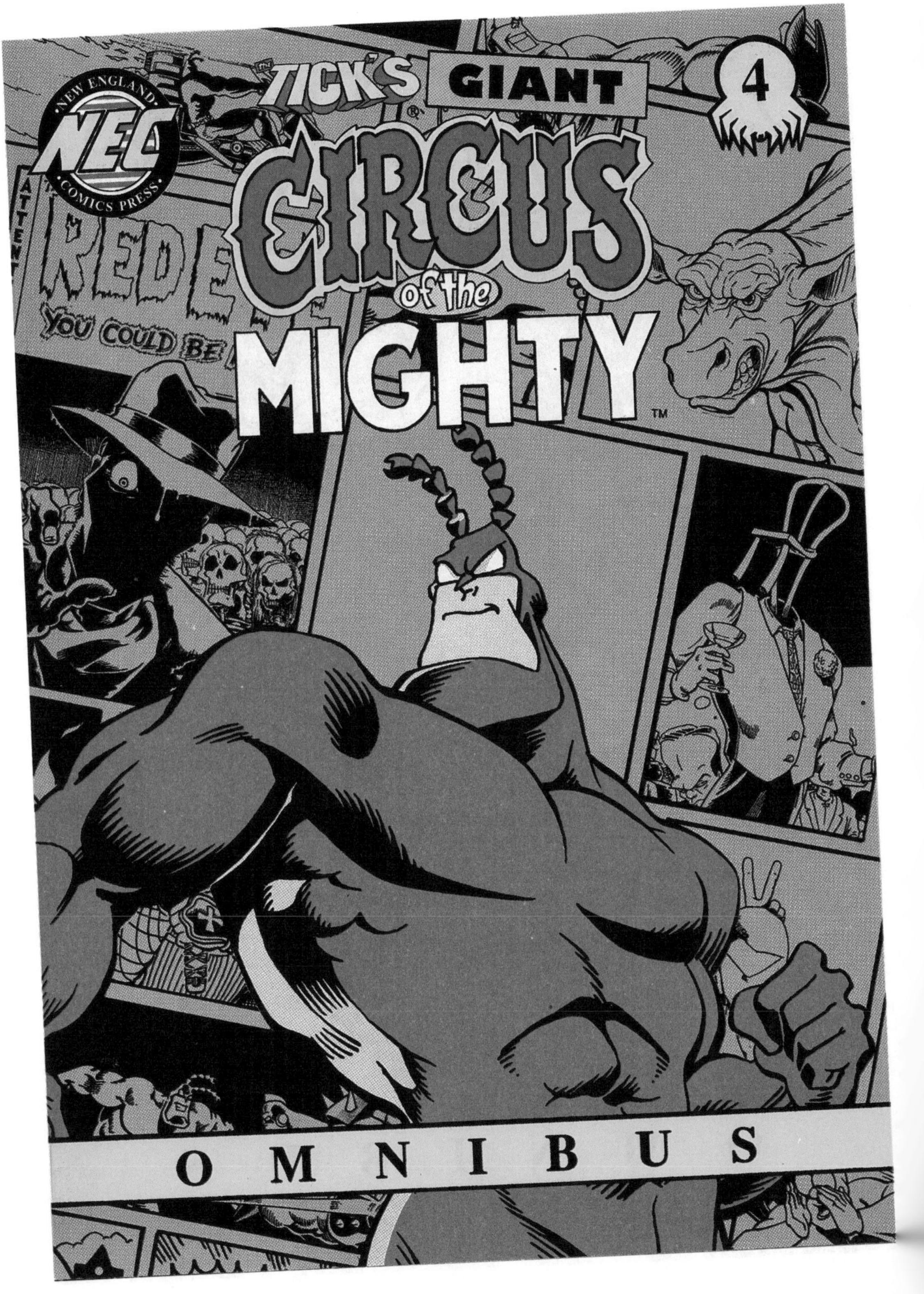
NEW ENGLAND
NEC
COMICS PRESS
TICK'S GIANT
CIRCUS of the MIGHTY
4
REDE
YOU COULD BE
OMNIBUS

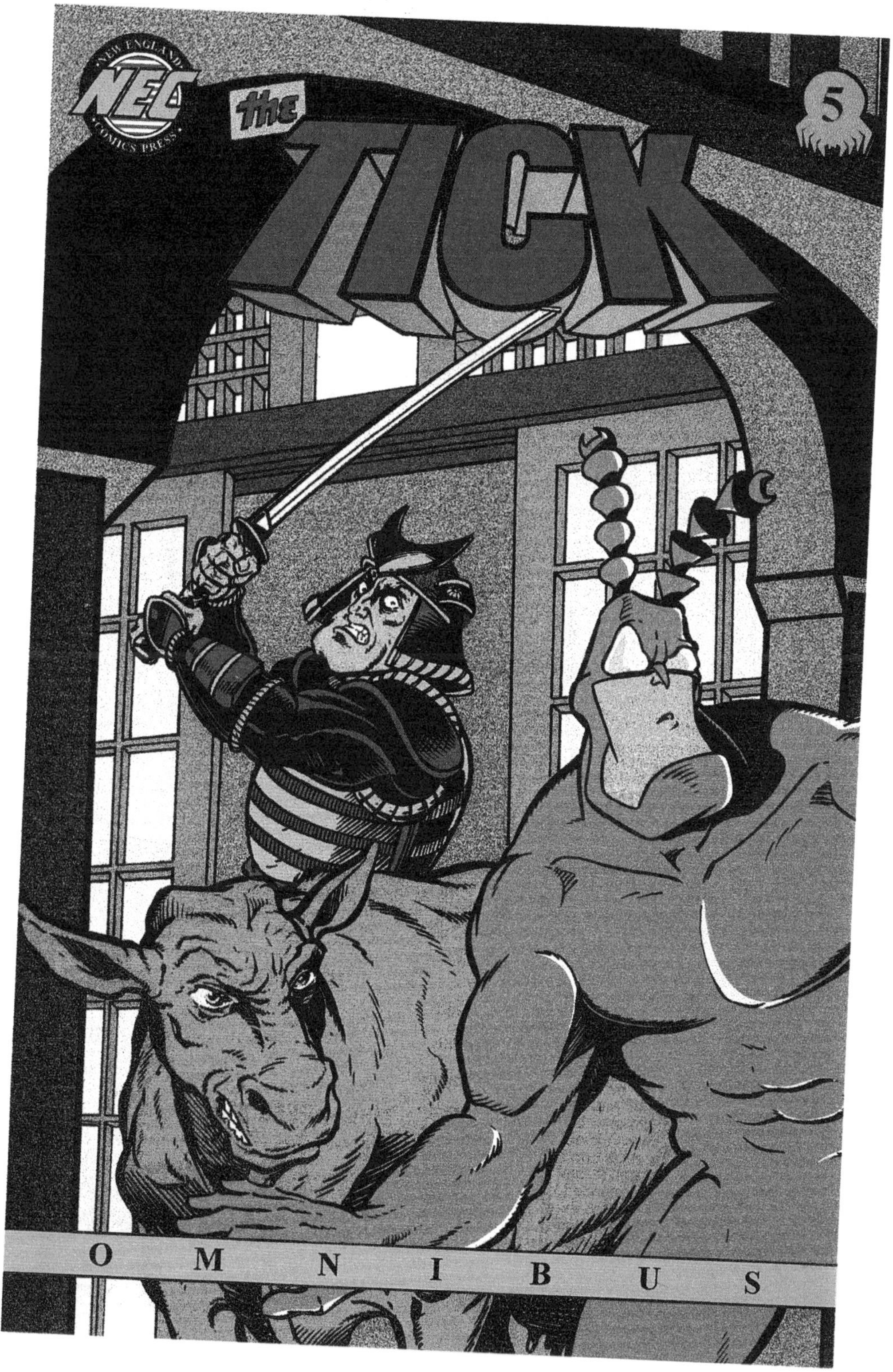
NEW ENGLAND NEC COMICS PRESS
the TICK
5
O M N I B U S

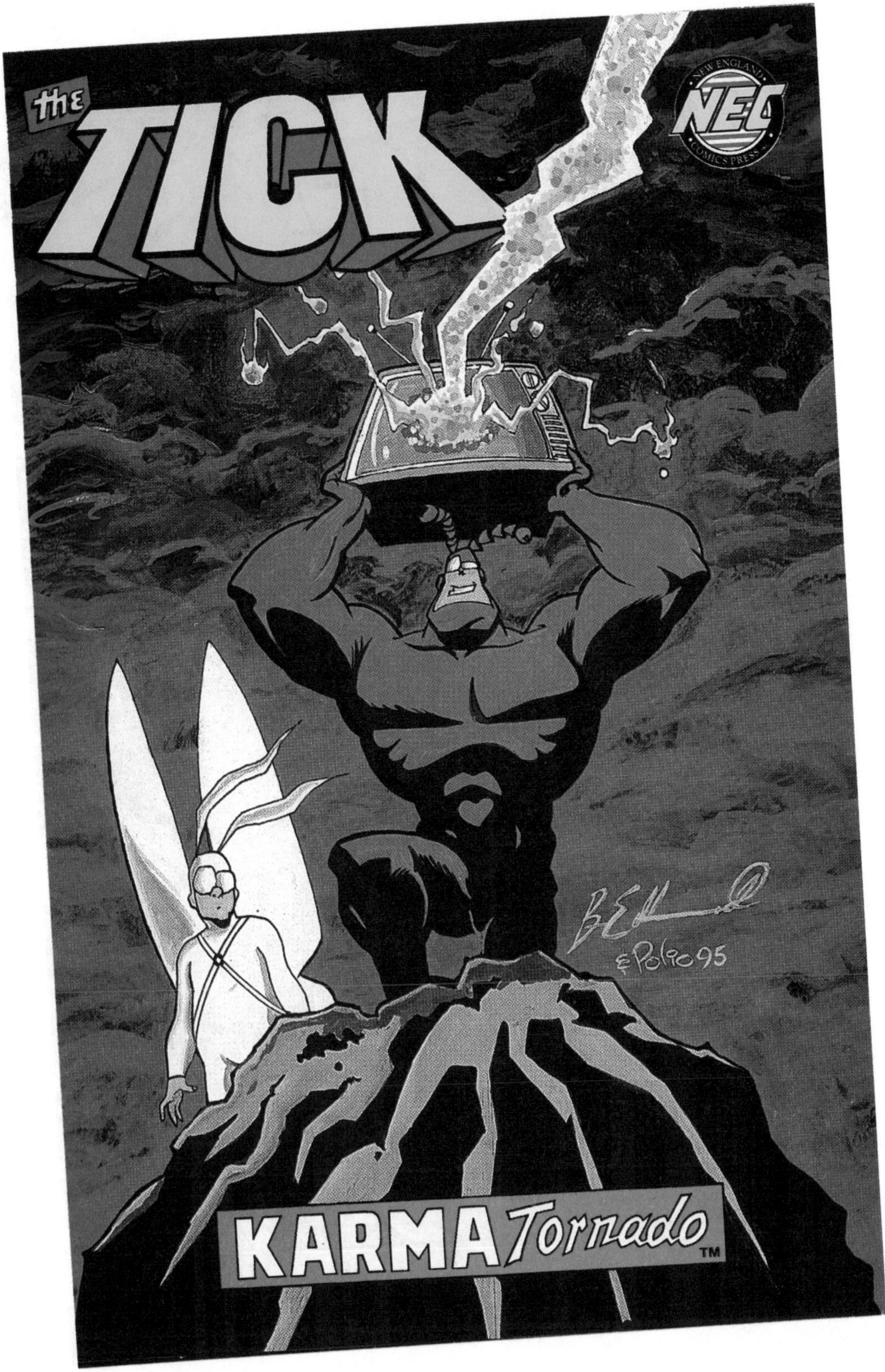

the TICK
NEW ENGLAND NEC COMICS PRESS
KARMA Tornado ™

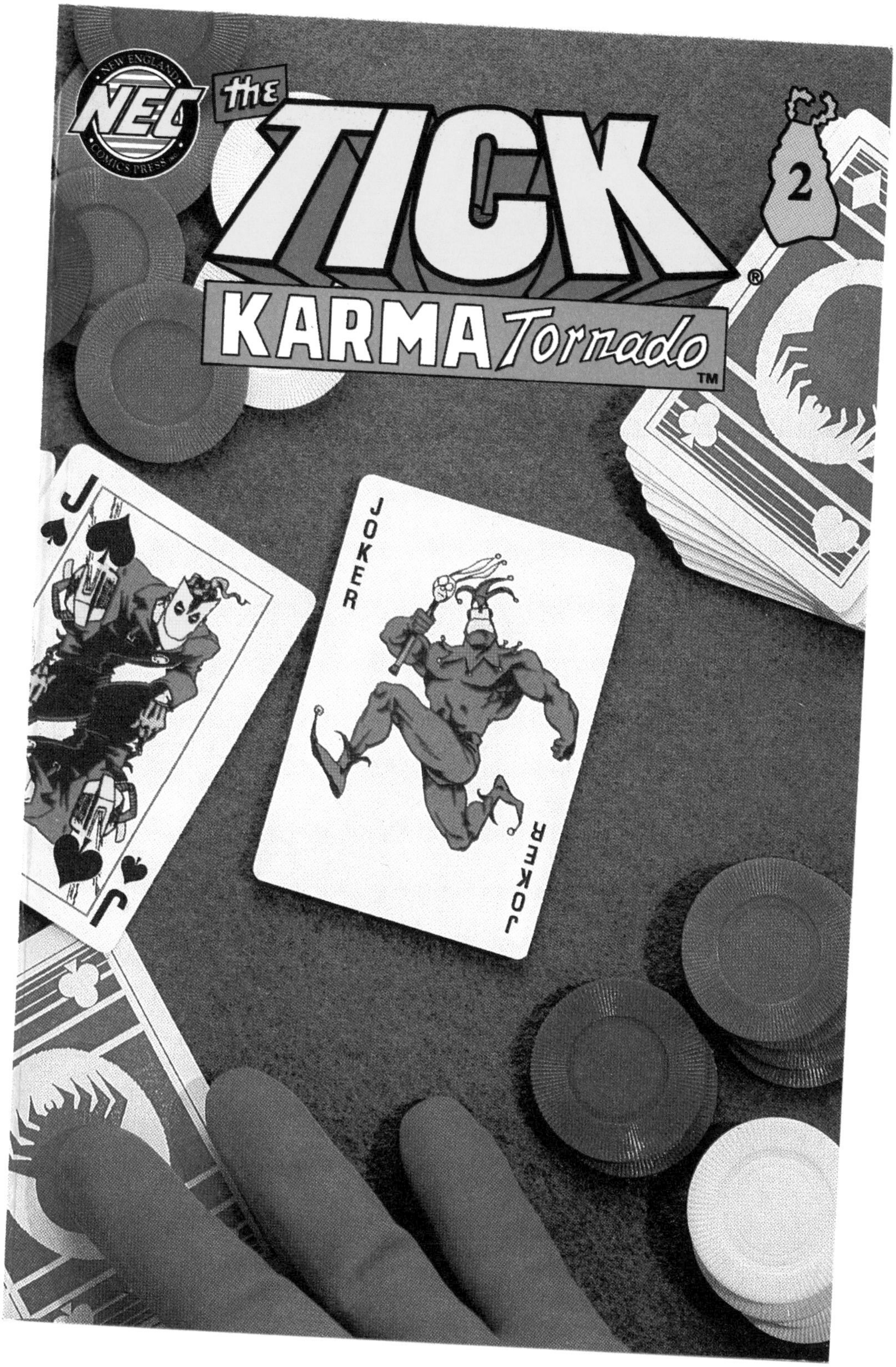

NEW ENGLAND NEC COMICS PRESS INC.
the TICK®
KARMA Tornado™
2
J
JOKER
JOKER
J

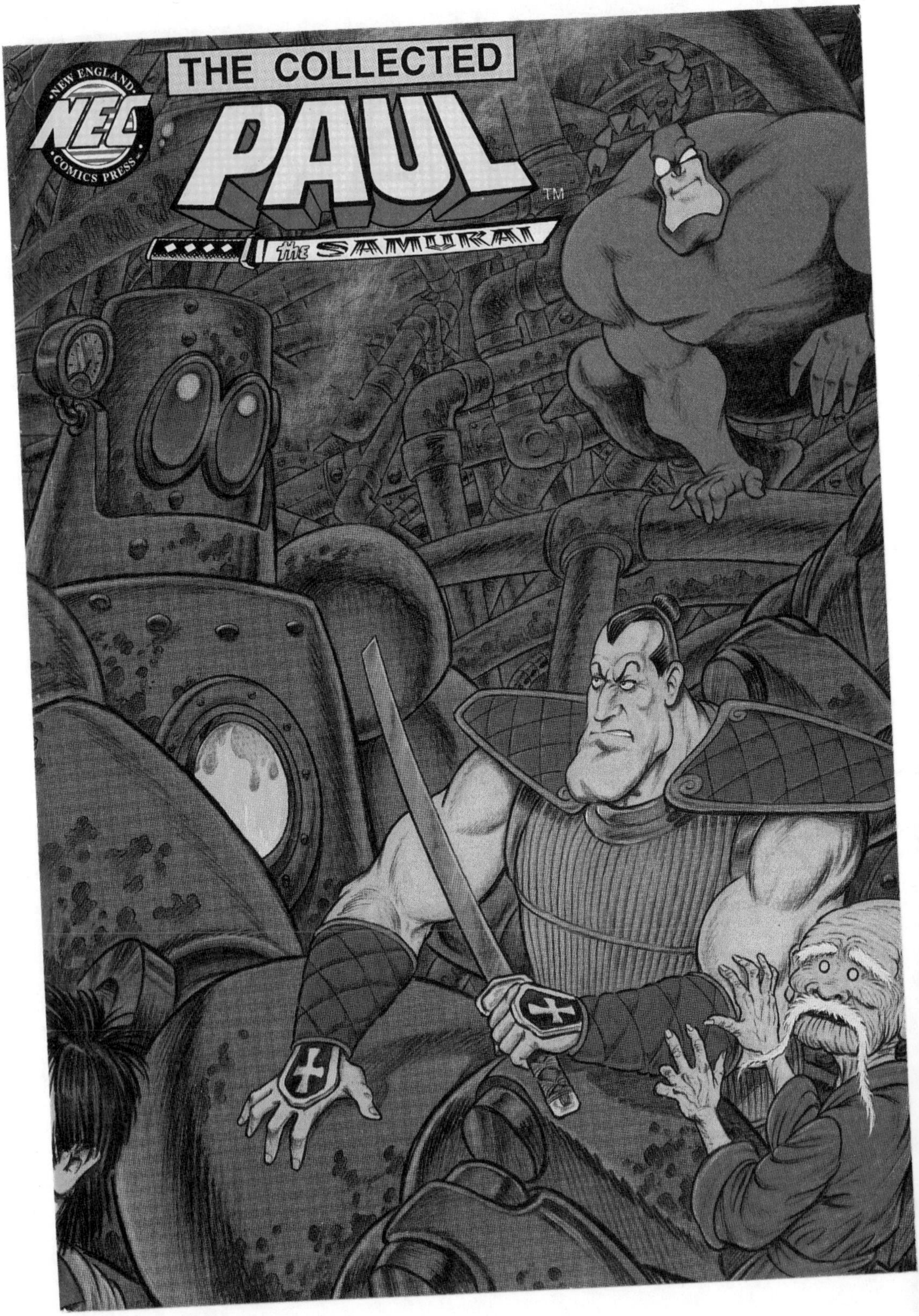
NEW ENGLAND
NEC
COMICS PRESS
THE COLLECTED
PAUL
TM
the SAMURAI